With this book, Fohle Lygunda has successfully responded to the global cry that all theological education, and especially missiology, should equip leaders to equip church members to be missional churches. The book is the result of the author's vision for missiology in the DRC and in other places to be transformed to successfully equip students to be agents of revitalization and transformation. *Transforming Missiology* will help seminaries, theological schools, and Bible schools to offer missiological education that will contribute to the church becoming the hands and the feet and the compassionate heart of Jesus Christ.

Fika J. van Rensburg, ThD
Professor of New Testament, and former Dean of
Faculty of Theology, North-West University
Rector, Potchefstroom Campus, North-West
University, Potchefstroom, South Africa

In colonial times missiology was created and established by Europeans and Americans. In postcolonial times Asians and Africans contributed to this academic discipline as well. It is great to witness how, through *Transforming Missiology*, Fohle Lygunda develops a global missiology from a sub-Saharan perspective, with special reference to Francophone Africa. His study is balanced because it fruitfully combines new African insights with a thorough recognition of the European and American scholarly tradition.

Jan A. B. Jongeneel, PhD
Professor Emeritus of Missiology, Utrecht University, The Netherlands
Author of *Missiological Encyclopedia*

Fohle Lygunda's alternative approach to missiological education deserves careful reading by mission administrators and theological educators everywhere. This is not the work of a mere theorist. This is the work of a well-informed, deeply committed, and experienced practitioner/educator whose familiarity with both the theory and practice of mission makes credible this innovative model of missiological education. Advocated and tested in the DRC, his model has significant ramifications and application wherever churches take seriously their divine mandate.

Jonathan Bonk, PhD
Director Emeritus, Overseas Ministries Study Center, New Haven, CT, USA
Editor of *Dictionary of African Christian Biography*
Author of *Mission and Money*

The vibrant churches of the Majority World hold great hope for the future vitality of the global Christian movement. Speaking from the challenging but vibrant context of Congo, Fohle's *Transforming Missiology* is a timely call to see God's mission as the defining hub for programs of theological education. Both the theory and practical advice given here hold genuine potential to see the church transformed by the divine call and agents of missional transformation in a needy world.

Perry Shaw, EdD
Professor of Education, Arab Baptist Theological Seminary, Beirut, Lebanon
Author of *Transforming Theological Education*

In *Transforming Missiology*, Fohle has provided a valuable, well-documented resource for envisioning a complete missiological program in academic settings. Most helpful is his recognition that missiology as a discipline cannot be isolated from the rest of theological education or from the goal of helping the local church fulfil its local and global mission.

Judith L. Hill, PhD
Missionary with SIM in Africa
Professor of New Testament, Faculté de Théologie
Evangélique de Bangui, Central African Republic

I wholeheartedly endorse this important book, *Transforming Missiology*, by Fohle Lygunda. It is both scholarly in nature and applicable to the desperate situation for the church in Africa to help fulfil the Great Commission of Jesus Christ. This book will transform readers' perspectives to spearhead change and expand God's kingdom throughout the world. As I read it, my thinking was challenged and I have incorporated a powerful principle into my life to help lead transformation in my ministry.

Michael Wicker, PhD
Director of Education and Communication,
International Leadership Foundation, Orlando, FL, USA
Professor of Educational Leadership, International Leadership Universities, Africa

Transforming Missiology is a thorough endeavour, a genuine call to always assess and adjust our missiological education to the purpose of God's mission in the world. Church leadership will also be transformed in the process, bringing a greater openness and broadening the horizons of ecumenism.

Symphorien Ntibagirirwa, PhD
Director, Institute of Development and Economic Ethics, Kigali, Rwanda
Senior Lecturer, Leadership Ethics and Social Responsibility

I have had the immense privilege of knowing Fohle Lygunda first as my student in Congo and now as a colleague in missions. Born of his own experience and praxis, he applies a vibrant personal insight and a rather intense understanding of missiology to the Congolese context, but applicable to other contexts as well. Not to be missed!

Bradley N. Hill, DMin
Former educational missionary in the DR Congo
Adjunct Faculty, Fuller Theological Seminary, Northwest, Seattle, WA
Adjunct Faculty, North Park Theological Seminary, North Park, Chicago, IL
Senior Pastor of Selah Covenant Church, Selah, WA, USA

In *Transforming Missiology*, Dr Lygunda calls for the expansion of missiological education to help Congolese Christians become mission-sending rather than mission-receiving churches. His perspective will be welcomed by all who care about mission education in Africa today.

Dana L. Robert, PhD
Truman Collins Professor of World Christianity and History of Mission,
Boston University School of Theology, Boston, MA, USA

I followed Fohle Lygunda's first steps in academic mission studies in Bangui and it is now a great pleasure to commend his *Transforming Missiology*. In the new context of the *missio Dei* paradigm, the shift of gravity in the worldwide church, and the contextualization of theological education, Fohle's work will surely contribute to a transformed and transforming missiology in Africa and elsewhere.

Göran Janzon, PhD
Former missionary in Central Africa
Lecturer in Mission Studies, Orebro School of Theology, Sweden
Visiting Professor of Missiology, Faculté de Théologie
Evangélique de Bangui, Central African Republic

While Fohle Lygunda details meticulously the integration of missiological education at the bachelor, master, and doctoral levels of tertiary education, he never loses sight of the goal that it must "lead to the practice of God's glocal mission." I pray this volume will contribute mightily to a nascent but growing passion for missiology in Francophone Africa – a vibrant missiology that not only stimulates missional engagement in the Central Africa region but also informs missional praxis globally.

Richard L. Starcher, PhD
Professor of Intercultural Education and Missiology, Cook School of Intercultural Studies, Biola University, La Mirada, CA, USA
Editor-in-Chief, *Missiology: An International Review*

Impressive! This book is primarily an African response to Northern missiology, rather than an African missiology in dialogue with African theologians who hold different positions. This is not a negative judgement, since the dialogue that is pursued is an important dimension of our task as African missiologists.

J. N. J. Kritzinger, ThD
Professor Emeritus of Missiology, University of South Africa (UNISA)

In its comprehensive grand design, this fascinating book demonstrates how "transforming" missiology is clarified and articulated. This book is a long-awaited and amazing work for those seeking to be engaged in God's mission and missiological education.

Masanori Kurasawa, DMiss
Former President, Tokyo Christian Univeristy, Japan
Executive Director, Faith and Culture Center

Transforming Missiology

An Alternative Approach to Missiological Education

Fohle Lygunda li-M

MONOGRAPHS

© 2018 Fohle Lygunda li-M

Published 2018 by Langham Monographs
An imprint of Langham Publishing
www.langhampublishing.org

Langham Publishing and its imprints are a ministry of Langham Partnership

Langham Partnership
PO Box 296, Carlisle, Cumbria, CA3 9WZ, UK
www.langham.org

ISBNs:
978-1-78368-364-2 Print
978-1-78368-002-3 ePub
978-1-78368-400-7 Mobi
978-1-78368-401-4 PDF

Fohle Lygunda li-M has asserted his right under the Copyright, Designs and Patents Act, 1988 to be identified as the Author of this work.

All rights reserved. No part of this publication may be reproduced, stored in a retrieval system or transmitted, in any form or by any means, electronic, mechanical, photocopying, recording or otherwise, without the prior written permission of the publisher or the Copyright Licensing Agency.

Scriptures taken from the Holy Bible, New International Version®, NIV®. Copyright © 1973, 1978, 1984, 2011 by Biblica, Inc.™ Used by permission of Zondervan. All rights reserved worldwide. www.zondervan.com. The "NIV" and "New International Version" are trademarks registered in the United States Patent and Trademark Office by Biblica, Inc.™

British Library Cataloguing-in-Publication Data
A catalogue record for this book is available from the British Library

ISBN: 978-1-78368-364-2

Cover & Book Design: projectluz.com

Langham Partnership actively supports theological dialogue and an author's right to publish but does not necessarily endorse the views and opinions set forth here or in works referenced within this publication, nor can we guarantee technical and grammatical correctness. Langham Partnership does not accept any responsibility or liability to persons or property as a consequence of the reading, use or interpretation of its published content.

Contents

List of Tables xiii

List of Figures xv

Foreword xvii

Preface xxi

Abbreviations xxvii

Part I: The Significance of the Research in Missiology and Missiological Education Today

Chapter 1 3
The Need for Research on Missiological Education
    1.1 Background: Motivation and Context 3
    1.2 Problem Statement and Substantiation 9
    1.3 Research Questions 20
    1.4 Aim and Objectives 22
    1.5 Central Theoretical Statement 22
    1.6 Methodology 23
        1.6.1 Literature Analysis 24
        1.6.2 Empirical Investigation 24
    1.7 Concepts Clarification 25
        1.7.1 Transformation 25
        1.7.2 Missionary-Sending Country 26
        1.7.3 Missiology 27
        1.7.4 Missiological Education 29
        1.7.5 Educational Approach 30
        1.7.6 *Missio Dei* 31
        1.7.7 Theology of Mission 32
    1.8 Organizational Structure of the Study 33

Part II: Exploring the Literature on Missiology and Missiological Education

Chapter 2 39
Trends in Missiology as a Scientific Reflection on Christian Mission
    2.1 Introduction 39
    2.2 Exploring Variant Trends in Missiological Literature 42

2.2.1 Towards a Comprehensive Understanding of Missiology 42
2.2.2 Missiology as Threefold Scientific Reflection on Mission 45
2.3 Emerging Trends in Missiology from Nineteenth to
Twenty-First Centuries 58
   2.3.1 Working Time Frame 59
   2.3.2 Craig Van Gelder's Framework 61
2.4 Missiology as a Threefold Scientific Reflection during the
Period of 1811–1910 65
   2.4.1 General Context 65
   2.4.2 Theory and Practice of Mission: A Missiology *for*
      Foreign Missions 67
   2.4.3 Study and Teaching of Mission: Preparing People *for*
      Foreign Missions 72
2.5 Missiology as a Threefold Scientific Reflection during the
Period of 1910–1950 74
   2.5.1 General Context 74
   2.5.2 Theory and Practice of Mission: A Missiology *of*
      Foreign Missions 77
   2.5.3 Study and Teaching of Mission: Preparing People *for*
      Foreign Missions 81
2.6 Missiology as a Threefold Scientific Reflection during the
Period of 1950–1975 81
   2.6.1 General Context 81
   2.6.2 Theory and Practice of Mission: A Missiology of
      Mission *versus* Missions 84
   2.6.3 Study and Teaching of Mission: Preparing People for
      Mission *in* Context 88
2.7 Missiology as a Threefold Scientific Reflection during the
Period of 1975–1995 88
   2.7.1 General Context 88
   2.7.2 Theory and Practice of Mission: A Missiology for
      Convergence *and* Divergence 91
   2.7.3 Study and Teaching of Mission: Preparing People for
      Mission *in* Context 93
2.8 Missiology as a Threefold Scientific Reflection during the
Period of 1995 to Present 94
   2.8.1 General Context 94
   2.8.2 Theory and Practice of Mission: A Missiology *for*
      Missional Ecclesiology 96

  2.8.3 Study and Teaching of Mission: Preparing People
    for Mission *in* Context 97
 2.9 Some Significant Conclusions 98
  2.9.1 Mission and Missiology: Beyond Mere Practical
    Perspective 98
  2.9.2 Mission: Its Purpose, Methods and Locus 99
  2.9.3 Ecumenical and Evangelical Differences 101
  2.9.4 Missiological Education as the Missing Link..................102

Chapter 3 .... **105**
Conceptual and Philosophical Considerations in Missiological Education
 3.1 Introduction 105
 3.2 The Concept of Missiological Education 105
  3.2.1 Understanding Missiological Education..........................106
  3.2.2 Missiological Education in Theological Curriculum........107
 3.3 Contemporary Models of Missiology in
  Theological Education 113
  3.3.1 Mission Studies...118
  3.3.2 Ecumenism, Mission, and Religious Studies 120
  3.3.3 School of World Missions 121
  3.3.4 Intercultural Studies..123
  3.3.5 World Christianity and Mission.......................................124
  3.3.6 Missiology 126
  3.3.7 Synthesis...127
 3.4 Missiological Education in the Light of Typologies of
  Theological Education 129
  3.4.1 From Athens Typology to Antioch Model 129
  3.4.2 Another Face of Theological Education in the
    African Context 134
 3.5 Missiological Education in the Light of Philosophies
  of Education..140
  3.5.1 Learning Theories of Adult Education 140
  3.5.2 Threefold Mandate of Higher Education 148
  3.5.3 The Transformative Purpose of Higher Education...........152
  3.5.4 The Bolognization of the Educational System 155
 3.6 Concluding Considerations 171
  3.6.1 Missiology in the Context of Theological Education.......172
  3.6.2 Missiology in the Context of Higher Education 173

Part III: Missiology and Missiological Education in the DR Congo

Chapter 4 177
   Mapping the Historical Roots of the Protestant Missiology and Missiological Education in the DR Congo
      4.1 Introduction 177
      4.2 Important Terminologies 180
      4.3 Discussion about Frameworks to Understand the Missionary Work in the DRC 181
          4.3.1 An Analysis of Existing Frameworks by Some Authors 181
          4.3.2 Toward a New Framework to Understand Missionary Work in the DRC 190
          4.3.3 Time Frame Referring to Missions and Global Mission Trends 192
      4.4 Protestant Missions, Mission and Missiological Education in the DRC (1878–1970) 195
          4.4.1 From One Mission to Several Missions: Revisiting *Their* History 195
          4.4.2 The Significance of the Congo Missions News and Other CPC Publications 198
          4.4.3 The Significance of the International Review of Mission(s) 200
          4.4.4 Educational Background of Missionaries 209
      4.5 Some Roots of Missiology and Missiological Education in the RDC 215
          4.5.1 Protestant Missiology in the DRC: Theory and Practice of Mission 215
          4.5.2 Protestant Missiology in the DRC: Training for Mission 223
      4.6 Protestant Church, Mission and Missiological Education in the DRC (1970–2016) 228
          4.6.1 Understanding the Legacy of Protestant Missions in the DRC 228
          4.6.2 From Several Churches to One Church: Revisiting *Our* History 232
      4.7 Concluding Remarks 233
          4.7.1 Problems to Expect in Reconstructing the Historical Facts and Events 235
          4.7.2 Profound Root Causes of the Current Status of Missiology 239

Chapter 5 249
   Missiology in Theological Education in the DR Congo: Empirical Investigation and Findings
      5.1 Introduction 249
      5.2 Research Design...250
         5.2.1 The Nature of This Research 250
         5.2.2 Understanding Descriptive Research Applied to
            This Study...253
         5.2.3 The Choice of Case Study...256
         5.2.4 Research Questions..259
         5.2.5 Research Instruments...261
         5.2.6 Population 265
         5.2.7 Variables 270
         5.2.8 Validity and Accuracy 271
      5.3 Data Analysis..272
      5.4 Ethical Considerations 274
      5.5 Findings Presentation and Interpretation 274
         5.5.1 Paradigms of Theology of Mission 275
         5.5.2 Theological Education and *Missio Dei*...............................280
         5.5.3 Educational and Conceptual Frameworks.........................283
         5.5.4 Missiological Education and Research...............................289
         5.5.5 Summary of the Findings...294

Part IV: An Alternative Approach to Missiology and Missiological Education

Chapter 6 299
   Towards a Transforming Missiology for a Fruitful Missiological Education
      6.1 Introduction 299
      6.2 Need for a Transforming Missiology 300
         6.2.1 The Need for a Well-Structured Missiological
            Program 301
         6.2.2 The Need for a Transforming Missiology 303
      6.3 Attributes of Missiology..304
         6.3.1 Missiology as a Scientific and an Applied Discipline 305
         6.3.2 Missiology as an Interdisciplinary Discipline....................307
         6.3.3 Missiology as an Intentional Discipline............................310
         6.3.4 Missiology as a Discipline of God's Glocal and
            Holistic Mission..312

    6.4 The Tripartite Concern of Missiology 316
        6.4.1 Concern for a Transforming Mission Theory 316
        6.4.2 Concern for a Transforming Mission Education 322
        6.4.3 Concern for a Transforming Mission Practice 329
    6.5 A Model of Missiological Higher Education Study Program 331
        6.5.1 Conditions for a Transforming Missiological
        Education 331
        6.5.2 A Three-Level Study Program: Undergraduate,
        Graduate and Postgraduate 337
        6.5.3 Evaluating Missiological Education 354
        6.5.4 Need for Applied Research Projects in Missiology 356
        6.5.5 Serving Meaningfully the Community 378
    6.6 Summary 379

Chapter 7 381
Conclusions, Implications and Recommendations
    7.1 Introduction 381
    7.2 Conclusions 382
    7.3 Implications 382
    7.4 Recommendations for Future Research 384

Bibliography 389

Appendix 413

Person Index 419

Subject Index 425

Scripture Reference Index 433

List of Tables

Table 1.1 Organizational Structure and Content of the Book 35

Table 2.1 Tripartite nature of missiology 48

Table 2.2 The Orientation of Doctoral Dissertations in Missiology from 1945 to 2011 52

Table 2.3 The Orientation of Some Selected Books in Missiology 54

Table 2.4 Key Features of Missiology Development 63

Table 2.5 Summary of the Debate on Mission Purpose and Methods 100

Table 3.1 Typologies of Theological Education 130

Table 3.2 Antioch Model of Missiological Education 133

Table 3.3 Teaching and Learning Continuum: Moving from Pedagogy to Heutagogy 145

Table 3.4 Ingalls's Seven Steps in Managing Adult Education 148

Table 3.5 DRC Educational System Compared to French Old System and the Bologna Process 159

Table 3.6 The Dublin Descriptors of Three Cycles 163

Table 3.7 Comparing Educational Paradigm – From Teaching to Learning ... 169

Table 4.1 Possible Time Frames to Understand Missionary Work in the DRC 190

Table 5.1 Strengths and Weaknesses of Case Study 258

Table 5.2 Schematic Presentation of the Research 260

Table 5.3 Tertiary Theological Education in the DRC 269

Table 5.4 General Perception on the Biblical Justification of the Existence of the Church 276

Table 5.5 Actions That the Church Is Supposed to Perform as Part of Its Mission 278

Table 5.6 Universities Offering Some Programs in Mission Studies as of December 2015 283

Table 5.7 Perception of Students on the Prevailing Educational Approach.....284

Table 5.8 Perception of Students on Possible Outcomes If Missiology Was Well-Promoted in the DRC 287

Table 6.1 Antioch Model of Missiological Education 332

Table 6.2 A Model of the Threefold Level of Missiological Higher Education Following the Bologna Process 338

Table 6.3 Purpose-Driven Missiological Higher Education 342

Table 6.4 Evaluation Plan for the Overall Study Program 355

Table 6.5 Biblical Foundation of Missiological Applied Research...........358

Table 6.6 Samples of the Outlines of a Research Proposal...........360

Table 6.7 Chapters Division of a Dissertation or a Thesis in Missiology 364

Table 6.8 Missiological Studies Applied to Mainline-Related Churches...........368

Table 6.9 Missiological Studies Applied to African Initiated Churches 370

Table 6.10 Missiological Studies Applied to African Immigrant (Diaspora) Churches 371

Table 6.11 Missiological Studies Applied to Contemporary Religions and Society...........373

Table 6.12 Missiological Studies Applied to Glocal and Intercultural Ministries...........374

Table 6.13 Missiological Studies Applied to Community Holistic Transformation 376

Table 6.14 Missiological Studies Applied to Higher Christian Education 377

Table 7.1 Implications and Recommendations for a Transforming Missiology...........383

Table 7.2 Perception of Professors of Theology on Typologies of Theological Education...........386

List of Figures

Figure 1.1 Conceptual Framework: Missiology at the Service of *Missio Dei* 23

Figure 1.2: Cyclical Process of Scientific Research in Missiology......................34

Figure 3.1: The Fifth Typology of Theological Education 132

Figure 4.1 Matching Protestant Mission Work with Global
Mission Trends...189

Figure 5.1 Some Key Protestant Universities in the DRC 268

Figure 5.2 Theological Education and Church Ministry 290

Figure 6.1 Interplay between Attributes, the Nature of Missiology
and Other Disciplines 302

Figure 6.2 Missiology and Its Interplay with Other Disciplines for
God's Glocal Mission 305

Figure 6.3 The Cycle of Teaching Process 334

Figure 6.4 How BTh Missiology Graduates Can Serve the Church
and Its Glocal Mission 347

Figure 6.5 How MTh Missiology Graduates Can Serve Theological
Institutions and the Church 350

Figure 6.6 How PhD Missiology Graduates Can Serve Theological
Institutions and the Church 353

Figure 6.7 Missiological Study Areas and Application Settings.......................367

Foreword

By Flip Buys and Richard Starcher

In 2010, the Cape Town Commitment of the international gathering of 4,000 people of the Lausanne Movement stated:

> The mission of the Church on earth is to serve the mission of God, and the mission of theological education is to strengthen and accompany the mission of the Church. Theological education serves first to train those who lead the Church as pastor-teachers, equipping them to teach the truth of God's Word with faithfulness, relevance and clarity; and second, to equip all God's people for the missional task of understanding and relevantly communicating God's truth in every cultural context. Theological education engages in spiritual warfare, as 'we demolish arguments and every pretension that sets itself up against the knowledge of God, and we take captive every thought to make it obedient to Christ.

Recently in June 2016, one of the largest ever consultations on Theological Education took place at the Global Proclamation Congress for Pastoral Trainers (GProCongress) in Bangkok, Thailand. More than 3,000 theological educators and missionaries from 120 nations attended the conference to connect, unite and strengthen pastoral trainers in order to better deliver training to the world's 2 million-plus untrained and undertrained pastors. The vision of the consultation was

> . . . to obey the global proclamation commission of the Lord Jesus – "that repentance and forgiveness of sins is to be proclaimed in His name to all nations" (Luke 24:47; cf. Acts 1:8).

The mission was to accelerate church health that will keep pace with church growth, especially in Asia, Africa, and Latin America. Everywhere, and especially where the Church is growing, people mourn the hollowness of the Christian message because of the shallowness of Christian obedience. When the health of the Church is nurtured (Eph 4:7–16), personal transformation affects marriages, families, vocations, and societies (Gal 6:10). The strategy was to improve pastoral health by providing ministry skills, tools, and relationships at every necessary level of pastoral training. Even pastoral training is not for the sake of pastoral training, but for the sake of Christ's final commission to "go and make disciples of all nations . . . teaching them to obey everything" that He has commanded us. (Matt 28:19–20)

It is clear that there is a global cry that all theological education and especially missiology should equip leaders to equip church members to be missional churches.

I had the privilege to work with Fohle for a few years in his doctoral research that has led to this publication. I have seen his sincere desire to see missiology in the DRC and in other places to be transformed to successfully equip students to be agents of revitalization and transformation of churches to be part of God's mission to usher in his kingdom.

My sincere prayer is that the Lord may use this publication to help seminaries, theological schools and Bible schools to offer missiological education that makes a significant contribution to the church really becoming the hands and the feet and the compassionate heart of Jesus Christ and obey the instruction of Jesus: "Let your light shine before men, that they may see your good deeds and praise your Father in heaven" (Matt 5:16).

Flip (P) Buys,
International Director, World Reformed Fellowship

In the mid-1980s I resigned from my pastorate in rural Nebraska with a vision to help disciple the burgeoning church in what was then Zaire (now the Democratic Republic of Congo). A year and half after arriving in Zaire with my wife and three young children, my mission organization sent me to teach in a small Bible College where I met Fohle Lygunda, one of the brightest students in the school. I taught Bible and Theology, but have no memory of any missiological courses in the curriculum. I encountered Fohle again when he pursued his Master of Theology degree at the Bangui Evangelical School of Theology (BEST) in Central African Republic, where I taught systematic theology. I do recall BEST having mission courses taught by an adjunct professor from Sweden, but like such courses at seminaries in the US, they did not appear central to the school's program-learning outcomes. By and large, missionaries of my generation, as well as the more visionary church leaders in my francophone circles, had just begun to apprehend God's call to African churches to be more than mere recipients of mission. We were about one hundred years late.

Fast-forwarding another thirty years, Christian universities and institutions of theological education, particularly in Francophone Africa, have yet to eradicate the colonial missionary legacy. Dr Fohle's *Transforming Missiology: An Alternative Approach to Missiological Education* not only sounds a loud and clear wakeup call to the Francophone African church, but also maps a way forward toward theologically and educationally sound missional engagement. I imagine many readers of this volume will have read David Bosch's landmark opus, *Transforming Mission*. As that important work focused on new paradigms in the theology of mission, Dr Fohle's *Transforming Missiology* focuses on new paradigms for missiological education. He insightfully observes that missiological education at the tertiary level tends toward bifurcation: either "as visionless professional study" or an "impractical scientific exercise" (p. 18). Missiological education must be rooted in world-class, indigenous African research that also bears fruit for relevant, global, missiological engagement. Put simply, it must be transformed into a scientific *and* applied discipline so that it can be genuinely transformational.

While it is true that, due in part to its interdisciplinary qualities, missiology is not universally recognized as a distinct academic/scientific discipline,[1] Dr Fohle argues convincingly that it is both academic and scientific, without losing its application to mission practice. Under the rubric, "Concern for a transforming mission education," he explores various models for providing missiological higher education but concludes, "Missiological education can be offered through a department of missiology, through a faculty of missiology or through a missiological research centre without accomplishing the [essential] threefold mission of providing quality teaching, promoting [intensive] research and serving meaningfully the community" (p. 329). Hence, while Dr Fohle details meticulously the integration of missiological education at the bachelor, master, and doctoral levels of tertiary education, he never loses sight of the goal that it must "lead to the practice of God's glocal mission" (p. 328).

I pray this volume will contribute mightily to a nascent but growing passion for missiology in Francophone Africa – a vibrant missiology that not only stimulates missional engagement in the Central Africa region but also informs missional praxis globally.

Richard L. Starcher
Professor of Intercultural Education & Missiology, Cook School of Intercultural Studies, Biola University, La Mirada, CA, USA
Editor-in-Chief, Missiology: An International Review

---

1. cf. Langmead, "What Is Missiology?"

Preface

This book is a revised version of a doctoral thesis submitted to North-West University (NWU), Potchefstroom, South Africa. When, in 2012, I was crafting the research proposal for my second doctorate, a google search couldn't find a single reference to the phrase "Transforming Missiology." In place, thousands of hints displayed only Bosch's magisterial *Transforming Mission*. It was in November 2015, while visiting the University of South Africa (UNISA) in Pretoria, that I met Professors Nico Botha and Reggie Nel. I held a copy of the completed draft of my thesis. Professor Botha was so excited to see the title "Transforming Missiology" on the thesis and said something like this to his colleague: "Wow! Look at what we have been talking about here at UNISA!" Being himself excited, Professor Nel couldn't hesitate to share with me some copies of *Missionalia*, a journal published by the Southern African Missiological Society. Both journal and society were initiated by the late Professor David Bosch. It was the celebratory issue of *Missionalia* published in 2011 on the twentieth anniversary of Bosch's *Transforming Mission* that contained two articles with the phrase "Transforming Missiology" authored by Botha and Nel. I got myself even more excited to see that the preoccupation I had for Francophone Africa was also a concern for my colleagues in South Africa. I couldn't wait to review and incorporate their articles in my thesis, highlighting the points of convergence and divergence. Having realized that I was not the first person to use the phrase "Transforming Missiology," I then went back to google search if there were more hints on the issue. I found out that only the abstract of Botha's article was posted on the website of UNISA in 2013. One can then see how, with this book, the concept of "Transforming Missiology" is becoming an emerging and provocative theme not only in missiological conversation, but also in discussion about theological education.

In my case, the concern about "Transforming missiology" emerged from an observation on the reality of the Democratic Republic of Congo (DRC) as being less "missionary-sending country" at the global level while housing several tertiary theological institutions and churches in full bloom. The assumption was that missiology and theological education in such a context needed to be revisited. If graduates had training which encompasses a personal and profound inner conviction for *missio Dei*, they would realize the power of *transforming* missiology. While being subject to change, their missiology would also be an activity susceptible to bring change to their life and churches. Therefore, the purpose of this concurrent mixed method study was to better understand how the prevailing missiological training programs in the DRC aligned with the preoccupation of providing missiological education for God's *glocal* and holistic mission.

The key question was: How does the prevailing missiological education in the DRC align with the purpose of *missio Dei*? Undertaken from an evangelical perspective through a study of selected Protestant universities, the study strived to relate educational and conceptual frameworks, didactics and pedagogics of missiology to God's *glocal* mission. Mission history, theology and education made the backbone of the study. Based on theoretical and empirical findings, some profound root causes of the current status of missiology and missiological education in the DRC were identified and discussed: historical legacies, theological convictions, educational realities, economic and political factors, and ecclesiastical structures. In the light of the findings, a proposition of transforming missiology for a fruitful missiological education was made. Although undertaken in the strict context of the DRC, the findings of this study can be generalized to other contexts, including the particular context of the Francophone Africa. Four parts make the overall content of this book:

> Part 1: **The significance of the research in missiology and missiological education today.** One introductory chapter substantiates the need for a research in missiology and missiological education in the general context of the world but with a special reference to Francophone Africa and the DR Congo.
>
> Part 2: **Exploring literature on missiology and missiological education.** Two chapters respectively

analyze and discuss literature based on theological, historical and philosophical considerations at the global level in order to set up a theoretical framework for the study.

Part 3: **Missiology and missiological education in the DR Congo**. Using the case study of the DR Congo, in the light of the aforementioned theoretical framework, two chapters respectively survey the historical roots of missiology and missiological education in the country, and their current status in theological institutions.

Part 4: **An alternative approach to missiology and missiological education**. Based on the findings of literature and empirical investigations, two chapters are devoted to the proposition of transforming missiology as an alternative approach to missiology and missiological education, not only in the DR Congo, but in any other context.

I would like to express my gratitude to so many people whose names cannot nearly all be mentioned here. To name a few, the following professors, friends, colleagues, students and family members have played a particular role toward the completion of this study. My gratitude is expressed to Almighty God for his protection during many travels I had to undertake for the purposes of this research, by foot, by car, by boat and by plane and for his direction to appropriate sources of information. It has been amazing to see how some inaccessible materials suddenly became accessible at the very moment that I felt that I had reached a dead end. The people named from here on were instruments of God whom he used to help me achieve the purpose of this study.

Dr Timothy Van Aarde, former missionary in Burundi and an alumnus of NWU, Professor Fika Janse van Rensburg, the Dean of the Faculty of Theology at NWU-Potchefstroom Campus that time, and Professor Henk Stoker, the manager of master and doctoral programs, were helpful in the process of selecting a university which could meet my expectations. Professor Flip Buys, my promoter, has been so kind and friendly. His worldwide exposure as international director of World Reformed Fellowship and practical insights prompted by his experience in theological education have stimulated me to search for appropriate theoretical frameworks. While working on the thesis project, I also served as the Academic Dean and Quality Assurance Director of International Leadership University (ILU) Burundi. Professor Bosela Eale, the Vice-Chancellor of ILU provided me with an opportunity to undertake this research with high morale. Mrs Hester Lombard, the librarian of the Faculty of Theology at North-West University, Potchefstroom Campus, rendered much needed services in finding appropriate literature. Professor N'Kwim Bibi of Université Protestante au Congo, Professor Muteho Kasongo of Université Libre des Pays de Grands Lacs Goma, Dr Robert Magoola of Uganda Christian University and Rev Canon Donald Werner of Bujumbura Christian University, Burundi, facilitated my access to the libraries of their respective institutions.

Empirical data collection was a challenging experience in a country where access to all geographical locations was not possible. Friends, colleagues and students facilitated the administration of the questionnaire to their respective universities: Professor Timothée Mushagalusa of Université Libre des Pays de Grands Lacs Bukavu, Professor Nyembo Imbanga of Université Evangélique de l'Afrique Bukavu, Professor Musolo Kamuha of Université Libre des Pays de Grands Lacs Goma, Professor Enosh Anguandia of Université Shalom de Bunia, Dr Matundu Zulu of Université de l'Alliance Chrétienne Boma, Dr Jean-Marie Nkonge of Université Méthodiste du Katanga, Professor Faustin Alipanazanga of Université Chrétienne de Kinshasa, pastors Joel Mananga and Clement Mputu, both missiology students under my supervision at International Leadership University, Burundi, and pastor Jean-Baptiste Mbongo of Centre Universitaire de Missiologie, Kinshasa.

Some internationally renowned missiologists and scholars whose personal contact and friendship have challenged me to add a voice from the Central African region to the ongoing conversation on the future of missiology deserve to be named: Professors Gerald H. Anderson, Jonathan Bonk, Tite Tienou, Göran Janzon, Jan A. B. Jongeneel, Dana Robert, Andrew Walls, Darrell Whiteman, Jean Paul Wiest, Richard Starcher, Christopher Wright, Todd Johnson, Randy Jessen, Kenneth Ross and Dela Adadevoh. Insights shared and discussed in this book echo what I could grasp some time back from the physical contact with them and through reading some of their works. Whereas Overseas Ministries Study Center (OMSC), New Haven, CT, was a good place to meet most of them and learn from their personal experiences and lectures, the Bangui Evangelical School of Theology in Central Africa, Boston University, Gordon Cromwell Seminary, Asbury Theological Seminary, and International Leadership University were *lieu-de-rendez-vous* for others.

Friends and students provided valuable input to improve the quality of this work. To name a few: Professor J. N. J. Kritzinger of the University of South Africa; Professor Mike Wicker of International Leadership Consortium; Dr Gabriel Basuzwa, adjunct faculty at International Leadership University, Burundi; Dr Bradley N. Hill, former missionary in the DRC; Professor Isaac Mbabazi of Université Shalom de Bunia, DRC; and pastor Emmanuel Nkuku, missiology student under my supervision at International Leadership University, Burundi. Their comments have stimulated my reflection. Administrative and academic staff at International Leadership University, Burundi, assisted me in many ways, either for trip arrangements or for typing or proofreading some manuscripts. Langham Partnership deserves a special word of appreciation for its willingness to publish this book. Clarina Vorster at NWU and the staff at Langham Partnership have done a great job in the language editing and publication process.

My ministry through the following churches and Christian ministries have fuelled my understanding of the opportunities and challenges of God's glocal mission in the African context: Communauté Evangélique de l'Ubangi-Mongala, DRC, where I served as pastor from 1989 to 2003; Evangelical Covenant Church, USA; Holy Tabernacle Church, USA; and Tokyo Christian University, Japan, through which I expanded my horizon about partnering for and in mission; Centre Missionnaire au Coeur d'Afrique (CEMICA) which I founded in 2003; and Eglise Evangélique en Afrique Centrale (EEAC), Bujumbura, where I served as missionary pastor in charge of French services.

My family, Mamie Butu and our children – Fohle Janvion, Fohle Emmanuel, Fohle Mikal, Fohle Lucie, Fohle Rachel, Fohle Dan-Lester and Fohle Betsy – supported me through prayer and encouragement, despite my recurrent absences.

To all named and unnamed ones, may this work be considered as the fruit of their legacy, joyfully shared with many other people in God's glocal mission.

Glory and praise be to the Lord!

Fohle Lygunda li-M

Abbreviations

AACC	All African Council of Churches
ABCFM	American Board of Commissioners for Foreign Mission
AEA	Association of Evangelicals in Africa
AIM	African Inland Mission
APM	Association of Professors of Mission
ASTHEOL	Association des Institutions Théologiques en Afrique Francophone
ATS	Association of Theological Seminaries
BMS	Baptist Missionary Society
CBM	Congo Balolo Mission
CCC	Church of Christ in Congo
CECU	Communauté Evangélique du Christ en Ubangi
CEUM	Communauté Evangélique de l'Ubangi-Mongala
CMN	Congo Mission News
CPC	Congo Protestant Council
CUM	Centre Universitaire de Missiologie
DCCM	Disciples of Christ Congo Mission
DRC	Democratic Republic of Congo
EAC	East African Community
ECTS	European Credit Transfer System
ECU	Eglise du Christ en Ubangi
IBMR	*International Bulletin of Mission(ary) Research*
ILU	International Leadership University
IMC	International Missionary Council
IRM	*International Review of Mission(s)*

IUCEA	Inter-University Council for East Africa
LIM	Livingston Inland Mission
LMS	Livingston Missionary Society
MEU	Mission Evangélique en Ubangi
OBE	Outcomes-Based Education
OCMS	Oxford Centre for Mission Studies
PBL	Problem-Based Learning
PUC	Protestant University in Congo
REMEAF	Réseau de Missiologues Evangéliques en Afrique Francophone
SIS	School of Intercultural Studies
TEF	Theological Education Fund
UCKIN	Université Chrétienne de Kinshasa
UNISA	University of South Africa
WCC	World Council of Churches
WEA	World Evangelical Alliance

Part I

The Significance of the Research in Missiology and Missiological Education Today

CHAPTER 1

The Need for Research on Missiological Education

1.1 Background: Motivation and Context

A recent global survey on theological education discovered that missiology was among the four areas which have been either ignored or side-lined in the prevailing theological curricula.[1] It is without surprise that when I went to establish the department of missiology in 2011 at International Leadership University, Burundi, which already had programs in leadership and governance, people wondered if *missiology* was synonymous to *criminology* or *musicology*. One could wholeheartedly agree with Esterline and his colleagues that these forgotten areas need to be strengthened in order to make theological education obedient to its calling. Eisner is correct in referring to "null curriculum," arguing that, of deep significance in the education system, is "what is taught through what is not taught."[2] Not having missiology in theological curriculum is a way to send out a strong message about the relevance or irrelevance of the prevailing theological education, or about the meaninglessness and uselessness of missiology.

When considering missiology as a scientific discipline which is concerned with mission theory, mission education and mission practice,[3] the observa-

---

1. Esterline et al., *Global Survey*. The three other areas are cross-cultural communication, spiritual formation, and practical skills related to ministry.

2. Eisner, *Educational Imagination,* as quoted in Shaw, *Transforming Theological Education*, 88.

3. This is actually the working definition of *missiology* in this study which is introduced later in this chapter, elaborated in chapter 2, and expanded in chapter 6.

tion is that research on mission education is not as popular as these other two components. As demonstrated further in this study (section 2.2.2), whereas literature on mission theory and mission practice flourishes, research on mission education at tertiary level has not been equally attractive. In preparation of its annual meeting scheduled for 19–20 June 2014 at Saint-Paul, Minnesota, USA, the Association of Professors of Mission (2014) released a call for papers on the theme "Transforming the teaching for mission: Educational theory and practice." Organizers wanted papers to focus on "how the teaching of missiology engages with educational theorists and teaching methods which include but also extend beyond missiology's cognate fields of history, biblical studies, anthropology, and theology." According to these organizers, this new interest in mission education arises after sixty years since the first gathering of the Association held in 1954 on the theme "teaching issues as missiologists." To fill the gap and to seriously engage in discussion about mission education, the 2014 call for papers then encouraged researchers and scholars to reflect more specifically on "educational theory for mission education," "theological and historical perspectives on mission education," "curricular and instructional innovations for mission education," "anthropological considerations for mission education" and other subjects. At the time the present study was completed, the proceedings of the above-mentioned conference were not yet published as to access, grasp and evaluate the findings of its various papers.

In his well-applauded book published two years earlier, Skreslet suggested that "education as an academic field might constitute another parallel worth considering, so long as that large-scale scholarly enterprise is understood to encompass the particular concerns, source materials, and methods of Christian education and theological education."[4] However, Skrestlet did not actually elaborate on how education could play such a role. One year after Skreslet released his book, the American Society of Missiology held its annual meeting under the theme "the future of the discipline of missiology." According to participants, one of the emerging themes in missiology today includes the "growing emphasis on experimentation, innovation, and

---

4. Skreslet, *Comprehending Mission*, 15.

participation in mission education."⁵ Nevertheless, several years earlier, while reflecting on the missiology's journey for acceptance in the educational world, though without providing in-depth elaboration of mission education, Steffen already asserted that "the goal for education, curricula and ministry would be to move from good to better."⁶ Therefore, mission education seems to call for researchers' attention.

Although the call is for all researchers, it is easily observable that such an endeavour is mostly undertaken by Western schools and scholars, and to some extent by Western-related scholars from the Global South (Latin America, Asia and Africa) whose reflections simply follow the Western agenda. While there is now global interest in mission education, because of its perceived importance in developing theory and instructional tools, there is much less clarity about how mission education relates to mission engagement of churches from the Global South to both local and global missions. Nowadays, the tendency is to speak of *missio Dei* while at the same time applauding these churches which focus only on local mission. For instance, in his recent reflection on the future of the discipline of missiology, Van Gelder says with excitement: "The majority church in the South is teaching us that every location is a mission location. Having been the recipients of mission, they are well attuned to understanding their own contexts as mission locations."⁷ One might wonder if mission education in perspective is promoted to maintain the majority churches' focus on their local contexts and on their surviving theologies (theology of liberation, identity theology, interfaith dialogue, etc.,) at the expense of God's entire *glocal* mission⁸

---

5. Feshman, "Group Discussion Conclusions," 82.

6. Steffen, "Missiology's Journey," 148.

7. Van Gelder, "Future of the Discipline of Missiology," 6. A good expression of Van Gelder's observation and which closely relates to the context of this study is the declaration from Bishop Bokeleale who served as the President of the CCC from its inception in 1970 to his retirement in 1998: "At the General Assembly of the former Congo Protestant Council in that year [1969], Zairian churchmen decided that after almost a century of missionary endeavour in their country, **missions** as institutions no longer had any reason to exist, and the Church in Zaire had to assume its responsibilities for *the true mission of the Church to evangelize the Zairian people*" (emphasis added) (Bokeleale, "From Missions to Mission," 433). According to Bokeleale, the true mission of the church in the DRC is the effort to do the work of evangelization within the country.

8. *Glocal* has become a popular and technical concept to designate how the world can be reached locally (Engelsviken, Lundeby, and Solheim, *Church Going Glocal*). From the

In Sub-Saharan Africa, except some historical training institutions in the English part of Africa (South Africa, Nigeria, Kenya, etc.,) the last two decades have witnessed the advent of schools which provide missiological tertiary education.[9] If this situation has had a long history in the English part of Africa, missiological education in Francophone Africa is still in its early stages and can only be traced after 1990.[10] According to Kasdorf, of the seventy-six theological schools in Africa, thirteen have created a chair or department of missiology.[11] Eleven of these schools are located in South Africa alone. Several years after Kasdorf's finding, this reality has not much changed. In a recent work, Amanze states that few associations in Africa promote missiology through theological education and the existing ones are mostly from English-speaking countries.[12] As consequence, lack of clear and in-depth educational theoretical frameworks, rarity of academic conferences and a shortage of scholarly publications in missiology by and for Francophone Africans are patent. Undoubtedly, missiological education in such a context deserves particular attention.

In the Democratic Republic of Congo (henceforth designated as the DRC)[13], the largest francophone country in Africa and one of the largest Christian countries in the continent, the situation is not different.

---

contraction of the first three letters of *global* and the last three letters of *local*, this neologism simply means that God's mission is altogether local and global, internal and external, domestic and foreign, and that without moving from one's own country someone can reach the world through migrants who live in the country. This understanding which has affected several areas of human and public life, political (Brenner, "Global Cities"), business (Maynard, "Global to Glocal"), public health (Ilona Kickbusch, "Global + Local"), education (Mehra and Papajohn "'Glocal' Patterns") poses a real hermeneutical problem when one applies the concept as such to Acts 1:8. In this study, glocal is used in dual meaning, having local situation on the one side and global realities on the other. God's mission is local and it is global (Van Engen, "Glocal Church," 157, Engelsviken, "Church," 67).

9. For instance Faculté de Théologie Évangélique de Bangui (Central African Republic), Faculté de Théologie Évangélique de l'Alliance (Ivory Coast), Université Protestant en Afrique Centrale (Cameroon), Faculté de Théologie Évangélique du Cameroun (Cameroon), Faculté de Théologie des Assemblées de Dieu (Togo), and those from the DRC, concerned in this study.

10. Lygunda, "Missiologie comme," 293–295.

11. Kasdorf, "Current State of Missiology," 64.

12. Amanze, "History and Major Goals," 346.

13. Since there are two "Congo" in Africa, the abbreviated form of the Democratic Republic of Congo (formerly Zaire) will be "DRC" whereas the Republic of Congo will go by "Congo."

Throughout the three waves of evangelization by Western missions to Africa in 15th, 19th and 20th centuries, the DRC has been a place of notable Christian presence.[14] Already in 1970, concluding his paper on the Protestant witness in Congo, Crawford stated: "The Congo contains the largest French-speaking Protestant community in the world; the future and God's will can bring it to a vital witness within its continent and the universal church."[15] Almost a decade later, in their book on the centenary of mission presence in the DRC (1878–1978), McGavran and Riddle observed that the country "has been most responsive to the gospel" before predicting that the same country would be "one of the substantially Christian nations of the twenty-first century."[16] *World Christian Trends*, edited by Barrett and Johnson, reported that the Church of Christ in Congo (CCC) was respectively the eighth and the fifth of the ten largest Protestant denominations in the world in 1970 and in 1995.[17] Recently, the *Atlas of Global Christianity*, edited by Ross and Johnson, has set the projection that the DRC will be the fifth of the top ten countries which will have the largest Christian population in 2050.[18]

While being depicted as a geographical space where the gospel is easily proclaimed and received, where strong churches (Western-based mainline churches and African initiated churches) are burgeoning, the DRC can also be portrayed as a space from where few nationals have been intentionally and formally sent out for world mission.[19] For example, in his recent and well-appraised book, *The Future of the Global Church*, Johnstone reports that out of the top twenty missionary-receiving countries in the twentieth century, the DRC was the eighth nation in 1900 receiving 300 missionaries, the fifth in 1960 with 2,258 missionaries, and the sixth in 1975 with 1,830 missionaries.[20] In 2000, the DRC was no longer on the list because

---

14. Stonelake, *Congo Past and Present;* Hastings, *Church in Africa;* Isichei, *History of Christianity.*

15. Crawford, "Protestant Missions," 22.

16. McGraven and Riddle, *Zaire,* 19.

17. Barrett and Johnson, "Global Top Ten Lists," 403. With respectively 4,628,000 and 9,260,000 members.

18. Ross and Johnson, *Atlas of Global Christianity,* 44.

19. Lygunda, "Understanding and Evaluating," 311–319.

20. Johnstone, *Future of the Global Church,* 232–233.

the number of missionaries from outside dropped to less than a thousand, undoubtedly due to the political unrest which characterized the country in the 1990s. On the opposite side, when reporting on the top twenty missionary-sending countries, figures became both different and remarkable. The report shows that the DRC has never been among the top twenty countries which sent more than 1,000 missionaries, be it in 1900, in 1960, in 2000 or in 2010, while names like Nigeria, South Africa and Ghana appear on the list. Mandryk, the editor of the well-known *Operation World*, has already reported a year earlier that only 445 missionaries were sent from the DRC by Protestant, independent and Anglican churches.[21] Mandryk provides a pathetic comment on mission engagement of churches in the DRC:

> Missionary involvement is reduced to a mere fraction of what it once was, due to war, instability and the breakdown of communications and government. Due to fruitful past ministry, most agencies are highly integrated into their daughter indigenous movements and churches. *But the staggering needs and the lack of workers mean that the DRC has openings for expatriate Christian ministers on a greater scale than any other African nation* – church planting, discipleship, development and holistic ministry, Bible and leadership training and specialized areas such as media, translation and medical work.[22]

The DRC is then in a paradoxical situation, where the Christian presence misses mission mindset, making the country more a "missionary-receiving" than "missionary-sending" nation. While some futurists might project a bright future for the church in the DRC, internal observers lament its state, pointing to the fact that the number of Protestant church members have dropped.[23] To address such a reality, the department of evangelism and mission of the CCC has designed a 2011–2020 strategic plan of doubling

---

21. Mandryk, *Operation World*, 269. Later I will debate these kinds of categorizations and statistics.

22. Ibid., 273 (emphasis added).

23. According to the 15th session of the National Synod of the Church of Christ in Congo, August 2010. In the DRC, since 1970, all Protestant denominations work under the umbrella of the Church of Christ in Congo. The 2013 statistics report 82 denominations. The present study refers mostly to them and their related theological institutions. Much will be said on the matter in chapters 4 and 5.

the number of local churches.²⁴ The strategic plan states that the idea was inspired by the Lausanne International Congress on World Evangelization held in 2010 in Cape Town, South Africa, which some participants attended. One has to question the feasibility of all the above projections if churches in the DRC continue to be mission-mindless communities and theological institutions are still unaware of such a strategic plan²⁵.

1.2 Problem Statement and Substantiation

While some literature exists on the above matters,²⁶ few, if any, purposefully focus on a critical examination of missiological education in the DRC and its impact on mission involvement of churches in God's glocal and holistic missions. The book, *Les vingt-cinq ans de la Faculté de Théologie Protestante au Zaire 1959–1984*,²⁷ authored by Munayi is worth mentioning due to the fact that it traces the historical development of the first graduate School of Theology in the DRC for a 25-year time frame.²⁸ However, missiology doesn't make the author's concern. Besides missiology not being mentioned, one needs to ask to what extent the whole curricula and pedagogics within this leading institution radiated mission mindedness? One could at least expect that the important colloquium held on the campus of the Protestant University in Congo, Kinshasa, 14–16 July 2012, could have made even a

---

24. According to the Département d'Evangélisation, Vie de l'Eglise et Mission, unpublished, 2011. These five strategies include: (1) Planting new churches in towns and villages through holistic evangelism, (2) Bring church members to become accomplished disciples and equipping pastors for a transformational leadership, (3) Reach out to children and youth aged 4–18 and street children, (4) Focus on the family as a center of evangelism, discipleship, and development, (5) Reach out to unreached, the poorly-reached, and the less-reached and the diaspora in the DRC and beyond.

25. During the national congress organized in Kinshasa, 2–9 August 2015, by the Church of Christ in Congo, I was asked to talk about "When theology ceases to be in the service of evangelization." For the organizers, my presentation had to help the whole Church of Christ in Congo and all theological institutions to address the felt need of getting the latter to the mission business of the former. Unfortunately, these theological institutions were not officially represented, and no one can tell if this strategic plan of the Church of Christ in Congo is really understood and cared of within these institutions.

26. Crawford, *Protestant Missions*; Braun, *Winning Zaïre*.

27. Twenty-five years of the Faculty of Protestant Theology in Zaire 1959–1984. Professor Munayi teaches church history in the Protestant University in Congo.

28. Most of current church leaders of Protestant denominations in the DRC are either alumni of that training institution, or they have been taught by alumni of the same institution.

casual reference of missiology. Speakers presented papers on the theme *Le rôle des universités [protestantes] face aux défis du développement en Afrique*.²⁹ Surprisingly enough, none of the eighteen papers have dealt with the issue related to either missiological education, or its implication for the church involvement in community transformation or theological education and God's mission, etc.³⁰

One year earlier, I published the book, *Missiologie: identité, formation et recherche dans le contexte Africain* [Missiology: Identity, Training and Research in African Context], and the same year of the above colloquium, I released a reflective paper entitled *Toward a Reconstructionist Philosophy of Missiological Education in Francophone Africa: Case of DR Congo*.³¹ The two works provide a generalized understanding of missiology in the academic setting without specifically developing crucial aspects and analyses proposed by this study. While the first publication was conceived as a textbook on general introduction to missiology, the second was a comparative reflection on some philosophies of education applied to missiology. Musolo focused a study on the "mission cycle" of three denominations in the Eastern part of the DRC, in which he complains that churches under study were "more devoted to working internally, rather than both internally and externally."³² Without specifically devoting the study to the examination of the missiological education, the author assumes that the maintenance-mindedness

---

29. Bakengela et al., "*Rôle des universités*." The role of universities in regard to the development challenges in Africa. The proceedings of this conference were published in 2014. This title is however incomplete. It should have included "Protestant" due to the fact that the focus was actually on Protestant universities. The colloquium was organized by the *Réseau des Universités Protestantes en Afrique* [the Network of Protestant Universities in Africa]. All speakers were from Protestant universities members of that network. The observation is that, for a colloquium organized by Protestant universities where all speakers were Protestant, either missiological education or the implication of theological education for mission engagement of the church were left aside.

30. The article by Sebastien Kalombo, a professor in the department of the Science of mission at the Protestant University in Congo, could be the unique paper to deal with such a preoccupation. The author however designed the content away from clear concern of the mission of the church and ethical considerations of educational system. While the title of the paper seems apparently to do with "mission of the church," the content actually has to do with something like "ethics" or "educational system" without direct connection with missiology and its corollaries such as theory of mission, practice of mission, mission education, etc.

31. This paper was part of an academic research in education at Atlantic International University, USA.

32. Musolo, *Towards a Mission Cycle*, 2.

of the three denominations resulted from a lack of mission mindedness in their theological schools. The same concern was expressed a long time ago by Brown in his critical examination of the Church in Congo, through an article entitled "The Church and Its Missionary Task in Congo." The author, who was on ground as a missionary, prioritized the link between the education of Congolese pastors and the engagement of their churches in mission: "The factors contributing to the failure of the Congo church to be missionary are many. First we may cite the fact of an untrained ministry. Very few Congo pastors have had more than nine years' schooling at the very most."[33] Though some readers of his time agreed with him, Brown's statement can be questioned today in a context of flourishing theological institutions in the DRC. I then share Musolo and Brown's assumptions and make them the main concern for this study.

Besides the aforementioned works, there are some unpublished master's dissertations and doctoral theses.[34] Few, if any, have actually addressed the specific issue of educational and conceptual frameworks for missiological education applied to God's global and holistic mission.[35] Moreover, even the recently published handbook of university training programmes in the DRC neither mentions missiology as a theological discipline nor contains any missiological training curriculum.[36] This official and massive document of more than 600 pages is the result of the ongoing process of educational

---

33. Brown, "Church and Its Missionary Task," 303.

34. Bahigwa, "Approche biblique"; Mpinga, "Towards Mission Spirituality"; Gibungola, "Vivre l'évangile"; Musolo, "Encountering the Mbuti Pygmies." Whereas in other settings (e.g. USA) *thesis* and *dissertation* are used respectively for master and doctoral final works, North-West University from where this study is undertaken goes other way around, preferring the terminology of master's *dissertation* and doctoral *thesis*. In the DRC, a *thesis* is the doctoral final work. At this stage, the study is not concerned about such a debate. It just conforms to the practice of the household, using *dissertation* for master, and *thesis* for doctoral work. Further in the study, in the process of sorting out the local production on missiology in the DRC, such a debate would certainly pump up due to the implication that these concepts have on the value of the academic production. The questions will be, "how does the educational system in the DRC value work done at bachelor, master and doctoral levels?" "Which works bear academic authority for a scientific decision?"

35. These works were produced by students in theological institutions on some specific topics as contextual theologies, reconciliation, Islam, ecumenism, mission strategies, interreligious dialogue, evangelism, urban mission, women and mission, contextualization, church growth, church history, etc.

36. *Programmes des cours* : *Réforme de la table ronde des universités du Congo* [Programme Handbook: The Roundtable Reform of Universities in Congo], (Kinshasa: CPE, 2010).

reform in the country which started in 2004. Missiology as usual seems out of the game. What Johannes Verkuyl reported about the struggles that missiology faced a long time ago, is still to some extent relevant in the DRC: "There was a day when missiology was accorded no place in the encyclopedia of theology. She was not even given standing room."[37]

For instance, while collecting data for this study, a friend who had just completed his PhD in Missiology abroad shared the story of his struggle to re-integrate his university in the DRC as professor of missiology and to establish a department of missiology. The scientific committee, which had the responsibility of accrediting professors, declined his request about the department of missiology and appointed him as one of the instructors in the department of practical theology. They then assigned a course on evangelization and mission with the recommendation to split these two aspects in two separate courses. The strong argument was articulated through some words like "There is no such thing as 'missiology' in the official and recognized disciplines of theology in the DRC. If you want to establish such a department here, you should first show us a legal document from the government. The handbook of universities' programs in the DRC does not contain such a thing as 'missiology' or 'department of missiology.' Please, be comfortable to serve under the department of practical theology." Missiology in such a context is still at the stage of "standing room" while not knowing when it will move to a "sitting room." Undoubtedly, such an experience cannot go without practical consequences.

One might raise the question about the above-mentioned discrepancy which exists in the DRC as being more "missionary-receiving country" than "missionary-sending country," when at the same time this country contains more theological training institutions than any other country in Central, West and East Africa.[38] Whereas some observers would find the answer to this contrast in the prevailing ministerial training in this country,[39] other scholars might find the reason elsewhere.[40] Quoting Barth and Scherer, Bosch

---

37. Verkuyl, *Contemporary Missiology*, 6

38. Gatwa, "Survey of Theological Education," 175–180; Dossou, "tour d'horizons," 193–217.

39. Musolo, *Towards a Mission Cycle*; Brown, "Church and Its Missionary Task."

40. Bosch, *Transforming Mission*.

contends that there are things missiology can and cannot do. He argues that theology, including missiology, is not the proclamation of the gospel, but a reflection on the message and on how it is proclaimed. He then adds, what I struggle to understand, that missiology "does not in itself mediate the missionary vision; it critically examines it (Barth). Missiology cannot, as such, issue in missionary involvement. In short, a missionary vision is caught, not taught (Scherer)."[41]

The apparent logic behind such a statement would simply be, "missiology doesn't have the responsibility of helping students and their churches engage in mission." This is actually what Bosch had already said in a previous occasion about church and theology: "It is, for instance, not the task of theology to arouse and stimulate missionary favour in the church . . . It is, nevertheless, outside the province of theology to motivate and activate the church to engage in mission."[42] While speaking specifically of missiology, Bosch adapted the same statement: "It is not the task of missiology to arouse and stimulate missionary fervor in the church. True, it does serve the church and can also help it attain greater clarity regarding missionary aims and motives . . . but it remains outside its province to motivate and activate the church to mission."[43] If that is the case, the present study would not have its *raison d'être*. Otherwise, Bosch's idea needs more convincing explanation because the historical account on the reason why Gustav Warneck and other *missiophiles*[44] (i.e. Abraham Kuyper, Olav Myklebust, Johannes Verkuyl, Emil Brunner, Alan Tippett, etc.,) promoted missiology was for the purpose of the propagation of the gospel throughout the world.[45] Verkuyl would even insist that "all good missiology should be able to be translated into action. If there is no action, you're missing something."[46]

---

41. Ibid., 498.
42. Bosch, *Witness to the World*, 23.
43. Bosch, "Mission in Theological Education," xxxvii.
44. I coined this "strange" word in a book published in 2011 (*Missiologie: Identité, formation et recherche dans le contexte africain*) as to stress the fact that mission (theory and practice) proceeds from love and passion for God's plan to save humankind. Those with this kind of passion are *missiophiles*, they have love of mission (as in *Theophile*).
45. Terry et al., *Missiology*, 1–3; Jongeneel, *Philosophy, Science and Theology*, vol. 1; Sundquist, *Understanding Christian Mission*.
46. Verkuyl, *Contemporary Missiology*, 3.

However, the truth is that, throughout years and geographical locations, mission studies have been provided for different reasons. In his article entitled "Globalization and the teaching of missions," Thomas identifies the following reasons. As per his findings, while some training institutions prepare their students for a local ministry, others train their students for a global context. While some others train their students for maintenance (here), others prepare their students for mission (from here to there). While some others train their students for clericalism, others prepare their students for universal sacerdotal ministry. While some others train their students as analysts, others prepare their students as catalysts. Therefore, the main question remains, for what reason should we promote missiology and missiological education today? Thomas's categories of paradigms represent two extremes of missiological education and the balanced point of view would be that of paradigm shift. Depending on the context, the ideal would be to fill in the void created by one or another of these extremes. There is a need of alternative paradigms or frameworks for missiology and missiological education. Den Hollander is right to observe that theological colleges and faculties play a major role in the process of mission interpretation, equipping, relating and sharing.[47] What Hollander has said about Western theological institutions is applicable anywhere, even in the context of the DRC.

Therefore, the title of this work is *Transforming Missiology: An Alternative Approach to Missiological Education*. It is undertaken with special reference to the Democratic Republic of Congo. Apart from what has been said above, a closer look at how missiological education at the tertiary level has been organized and provided in Francophone Africa in general, and in the DRC in particular, leads to the following critical questions: How does the prevailing theological education align with and contribute to the purpose of *missio Dei*, as evidenced by the degree of engagement of graduates and their churches in God's global and holistic mission? What would be a model of fruitful educational curriculum (including didactics and pedagogics) for a transforming missiology in the current context of both theological institutions and growing churches?

---

47. Den Hollander, "Some European Notes," 216.

As in Bosch's *Transforming Mission,* the assumption here is that missiology in "mission-mindless countries" can and need to be both *transformed* (e.g. subject to change, or to be transformed) and *transforming* (e.g. activity which can transform).[48] It is not evident that Bosch used specifically the phrase "transforming missiology" whether in his writings in general, or in his magisterial *Transforming Mission* in particular. However, in the celebratory issue of *Missionalia* (April/August 2011) focusing on the twentieth anniversary of Bosch's *Transforming Mission*, two articles authored by Bosch's successors at the UNISA, mention the concept "Transforming Missiology." Nico Botha and Reggie Nel use the term as a new way of doing missiology. While evaluating Bosch's missiology in the light of his reviewers, authors suggest that missiology should take new forms. For Botha, to transform missiology means to make it more relevant, more African, more contextual, more postmodern while using a children-based hermeneutic.[49] His specific proposition is that the new missiology should be characterized by "the new focus on children as agents in mission."[50] This children-based hermeneutic denotes how missiology can take a new form because "the negligence about children and the virtual absence of children" have characterized the existing missiology. For Nel, transforming missiology means a "shift on an epistemological level . . . which should relate to the emergence of the various expressions of liberation theologies"; it is a "quest for an appropriate methodology in the current age" calling for "a shift towards a liberation hermeneutic or praxis-based hermeneutic."[51] He contends that, in the context of postcolonial South Africa, the new approach of doing missiology should deal more with "theological methods" in order to enable students to *do* missiology rather than to merely *study* missiology, helping them to discern the situation for the purpose of action, transformation and liberation of their communities.

It is evident that both Botha and Nel are quite innovative in their use of the term "transforming missiology" (in comparison with their predecessor, David Bosch), mainly in the first sense of a need for missiology to be transformed. Although there are no clear procedures and outlines in these

---

48. Bosch, *Transforming Mission,* xv.
49. Botha, "Transforming Missiology," 28.
50. Ibid., 29.
51. Nel, "Mixing African Colours," 123–124.

two articles on how missiology should help students to be transformed, the authors insist on the necessity to transform missiology by enabling students to engage their communities. Without doubt, authors simply echo one of the tasks of their department of missiology at UNISA, to "design teaching in such a way that students have to engage with their communities" (see more details later in this book, section 3.3.6). However, the whole project of transforming missiology shouldn't be confined in children-based hermeneutic and in theological methods of liberation. Also, while being true that missiology should cause students to transform their communities, the point is that such an enterprise could be more bearing and contagious only after these students had been transformed themselves. In fact, *doing* missiology as fruit of missiological studies without *being* personally transformed would be just another way of merely *studying* missiology.

Unlike in other parts of the world or other scientific disciplines, higher education is the *locus* from which concepts and theories are conceived, developed, and disseminated, whether by faculty or students for application. For instance, it is reported that scholarly Bantu philosophy was developed in 1949 by Placide Tempels, a Belgian Franciscan priest who served as missionary in the DRC among the Luba.[52] It is the same with African theology which is reported to have its root in the University of Kinshasa, DRC, due to the debate between Tharcisse Tshibangu and his professor Vaneste in 1960.[53] Bosch recognizes that Tshibangu's *Théologie positive et théologie speculative* was among the first steps for the vigorous development of autochthons African theology.[54] Therefore, it would not be historically correct to assert with Botha that Amba Oduyoye, from Nigeria, and Kwame Bediako, from Ghana, are respectively the mother and the father of African theology.[55]

The Bologna Process, the European-based educational reform system which impacts many Francophone African nations today, urges higher education institutions to train students to solve societal problems.[56] In his insightful discourse on the urgency of transforming Christian higher education in

---

52. Schreiter, *Constructing Local Theologies*, 9.
53. Bujo and Muya, *Théologie africaine*, 183.
54. Bosch, *Transforming Mission*, 452.
55. Botha, "Transforming Missiology," 21.
56. European Communities, *ECTS Users' Guide*.

Africa, Van der Walt amply demonstrates that "Christian higher education is no longer a luxury, but essential for development and survival."[57] Implied to the present study, Van der Walt's statement sets an alarm for missiological education in the DRC whether it will pass such a test of being an essential tool for *missio Dei*, due to the fact that, based on their missionary nature,[58] churches should not exist only for their development and survival.

However, as far as missiological education at the tertiary level is concerned, one can discern two orientations: missiology studied as a practical professional training or as a scientific theoretical training. Taken from a dichotomist perspective, these two approaches can be described as one, striving for a teaching-learning experience which is immediately applicable, practicable and professionally to the point and another, wrestling with a strictly scientific teaching-learning experience with an essentially theoretical orientation. One has to agree with Van der Walt that the dichotomy between theory/science and practice/profession is a false dichotomy because it certainly results in a "visionless professional training" and an "impractical scientific training."[59] A third way is needed, which combines "both scholarly education and professional training."[60]

In a doctoral thesis submitted to the University of Nebraska (USA), entitled "Africans in pursuit of a theological doctorate: a grounded theory study of theological doctoral program design in a non-Western context," Starcher discerned the same tendencies in current missiological education in the world. Unlike Van der Walt, he advocates for a non-dichotomist program for Africa, a program which "facilitates Africa-relevant research and provides relevant preparation for the 'real' work awaiting African doctoral graduates."[61] Starcher, who has served as missionary in the DRC prior to moving to the Central African Republic and Kenya, concludes with the following thoughtful recommendations for future research: "I recommend exploring the experiences of Francophone Africans pursuing theological

---

57. Van de Walt, *Transformed*, 131.
58. Brunner, *Word and the World*, 108. Emil Bruner is known for having stated that "the church exists by mission, just as fire exists by burning."
59. Van der Walt, *Transformed*, 133.
60. Ibid.
61. Starcher, "Africans in Pursuit."

doctorates in francophone contexts. In addition, it would [be] helpful to have a clearer picture of the specific theological disciplines favoured by Africans in pursuit of a theological doctorate."[62] While concluding his book, Skreslet predicted that non-Western perspectives on the field of mission studies will become increasingly prominent as the integrative potential of missiology is not yet achieved.[63] The present study is an attempt to implement Starcher's recommendation and to verify Skreslet's prediction. Missiological education for Africa in general, and francophone Africa in particular, should not be undertaken, either as a visionless professional study or as an impractical scientific exercise. Attention will be directed to these different orientations as they would have occurred in the history of mission-related education in the DRC. For these different reasons, the conviction for this research is that higher education institutions are the indicated arena to initiate a dialogue on the urgent need of *transforming* missiology. This concept calls for two actions.

On the one side, as an educational discipline which involves human beings and which applies to different contexts, missiology should be transformed according to biblical revelation and the actual needs felt by people. The latter aspect is so important that one could notice how mission theologies in both ecumenical and evangelical fraternities have been shaped by the exigencies of secularization, nationalization and rapid social change.[64] Bassham observed: "Historical factors have created a radically different environment for mission, and generated new developments in mission theology, even as the internal life of churches has developed through theological reflection and response to changing historical circumstances."[65] Subsequently and notwithstanding constant references to the biblical revelation, some crucial aspects of mission theologies from both sides have undergone modification, re-examination, reconceptualization, reformulation and even abandonment. In this dynamic process, Stott, after having stood for a previous different point of view about mission, could later say: "Today, however, I would express myself differently . . . I now see more clearly that not only the

---

62. Ibid., 209.

63. Skreslet, *Comprehending Mission*, 197.

64. Glasser, "Conciliar Perspectives," 82–99; Utuk, "From Wheaton to Lausanne," 99–112.

65. Bassham, *Mission Theology*, 2.

consequences of the commission but the actual commission itself must be understood to include social as well as evangelistic responsibility, unless we are to be guilty of distorting the words of Jesus."[66] The felt needs have shaped Stott's understanding of biblical revelation about mission, moving from one aspect of mission theology to another. Bosch is right when he states that, "There is no such missiology, period. There is only missiology in draft."[67] He himself underwent the same experience when he said in 1982: "The major change in my theological thinking took place during the previous decade (the sixties), and not to the same extent during the seventies."[68] Much of Bosch's transformational experience in theology of mission is elaborated by his student and colleague, J. N. J. Kritzinger.[69] *Status quo* missiology should not make the agenda of missiological studies because these studies are provided in an ever-changing world with ever-changing expectations and understanding. Missiology should always be on the move, but without losing its essence.

On the other side, as a tool for God's ultimate purpose, missiology should lead to transformation. Missiology should not be a sterile academic exercise which releases unchanged and unchallenged graduates. The learning process should lead to the change of a learner's mindset. Similar to Paul's advice to Christians in Rome, the intended change is about to "be transformed by the renewing of mind" in order to "be able to test and approve what God's will is" (Rom 12:2). The ultimate expression of God's will is that "all people be saved and come to a knowledge of the truth" (1 Tim 2:4). In that way, the vision for God's mission is altogether taught and caught: "Whatever you have learned or received or heard from me, or seen in me, put it into practice. And the God of peace will be with you" (Phil 4:9). Jesus Christ couldn't send his disciples without training them. Matthew (10:5) makes it clear that Jesus sent his disciples after having given them instructions, undoubtedly as to transform their ministerial worldview, as long as their ministry purposed the transformation of people they were called to serve.

---

66. Stott, *Christian Mission*, 23.
67. Bosch, *Transforming Mission*, 498.
68. Quoted in Botha, "Transforming Missiology," 24.
69. Kritzinger, "Mission As," 32–43.

If graduates of theological education had such an aforesaid foundational insight, coupled with a well-mentored inner conviction, they would realize the power of a *transforming* missiology, evidenced by the degree of the engagement of their churches in God's global and holistic mission. There is need to connect theological education with God's mission with regard to both orthodoxy (theory) and orthopraxis (practice). Therefore, the purpose of this concurrent mixed method study was to better understand how the prevailing missiological training programs in the DRC aligned with such a preoccupation of providing missiological education for God's glocal mission. Attention is given to mission-related higher education programs. The study is specifically focused on missiological education rather than on generally well-known theological education. Missiology is understood as a scientific reflection on how mission is conceptualized, how it is executed and how it is taught, but within the context of existing theological institutions.

1.3 Research Questions

Some literature states that mission engagement in history has been the fruit of revival, rather than of formal theological education.[70] Other literature along with the assumption of the present study, however, recognizes the crucial role theological institutions might have in the process of mission articulation and engagement.[71] Forman therefore points to the inevitable relation which somehow exists between "mission practice" and "mission theory," either upstream or downstream of any mission statement: "Christian missions, though they are a very practical activity, involve inevitably a great deal of theory and theology. The methods they use, the goals they work for, the way they treat people, all are based on theories and theologies whether these are fully articulated or not."[72] Verkuyl perceives theological education as one way of equipping individuals for their pastoral and missionary work.[73] Drawing on his long experience as a mission student, mission practitioner

---

70. Beaver, "American Protestant," 65–80; Fiedler, *Story of Faith Missions*, 112–124; Smither, "Impact of Evangelical Revivals."

71. Thomas, "Globalization"; Hollander, "Some European Notes"; Cape Town 2010; Du Preez et al., "Missional Theological Curricula."

72. Forman, "History of Foreign Mission," 69.

73. Verkuyl, *Contemporary Missiology*, 207.

and mission professor, Jongeneel concluded an article in his previously published *Missiological Encyclopedia* with a statement that brings some light: "My deep conviction is that growing maturity in mission studies will stimulate the growth of maturity in mission."[74]

While engaging literature produced locally and internationally within the wider field of missiology, with a focus on mission history, theology and education, an effort is made to address, from an evangelical perspective, the following key question: How does the prevailing missiological education in the DRC align with the purpose of *missio Dei*? To fully address such a concern, the following sub-questions will be discussed:[75]

1. Through which paradigms of theology of mission and for which reasons has missiological education been provided in the DRC?
2. To what extent has a *missio Dei* vision or the lack of it in the whole of theological education influenced missiological education and mission practice?
3. Through which educational and conceptual frameworks has missiological education been offered in the DRC?
4. To what extent is missiological education and research really serving the churches in the DRC for its glocal mission?

---

74. Jongeneel, "Philosophy, Science, and Theology," 29.

75. In February 2005, International Baptist Theological Seminary in Prague initiated a meeting focused on the real need of local churches and mission agencies during which a group of scholars with experience in missions, theological education and the church explored whether contemporary theological education is relevant to the current context. The following questions framed their discussion (Bailey, "From the Editor," 8). These questions can apply to any context where the preoccupation is to relate theological education to *missio Dei*.
 1. What is the mission of the church?
 2. What is the historical and cultural context within which a given church exists?
 3. How does this impact the church's mission and engagement with society?
 4. How does the way people reason vary across cultures, and how should that affect teaching?
 5. How do people learn, and therefore how should the learning experiences be structured?
 6. What would a theological curriculum look like if it truly took into account the mission of God in the world?
 7. How does encountering the work through mission shape the church's theology?
 8. What are the implications of the unity of the church for shape and focus of theological education?

1.4 Aim and Objectives

The main aim of this study is to conduct a missiological evaluation of the missiological education provided by Protestant universities in the DRC, as to determine to what extent they contribute to mission engagement of graduates and their churches. This research attempts to attain the following objectives:

1. To determine the key paradigms of theology of mission and those of educational and conceptual frameworks through which missiological education has been offered in the DRC.
2. To determine the extent to which a *missio Dei* vision or the lack of it in the whole of theological education has influenced missiological education and mission practice, and how missiological education and research really serve the churches in the DRC for its glocal mission.

1.5 Central Theoretical Statement

The specific concern here is to relate educational and conceptual frameworks, didactics and pedagogics of missiological education to *missio Dei* and to *missio praxis*. Francophone Africa in general, and the DRC in particular, desperately needs this kind of research. As stated earlier, the assumption is that if graduates in missiological education had such a well-oriented training program which encompasses a personal and profound inner conviction, they would realize the power of *transforming* missiology. While being an object of transformation, their missiology will also be a transformational activity.

The evaluation of missiological education is done in light of current reflections on the theory of mission, practice of mission and training for mission, taking into account the threefold mission of a given university and to what extent missiological education contributes to God's global and holistic mission (fig. 1.1). Therefore, the epistemological investigation includes the following key elements of literature:

1. Scientific reflection on how mission is conceptualized (mission theory)
2. Scientific reflection on how mission is executed (mission practice)
3. Scientific reflection on how mission is taught (mission education)

The Need for Research on Missiological Education 23

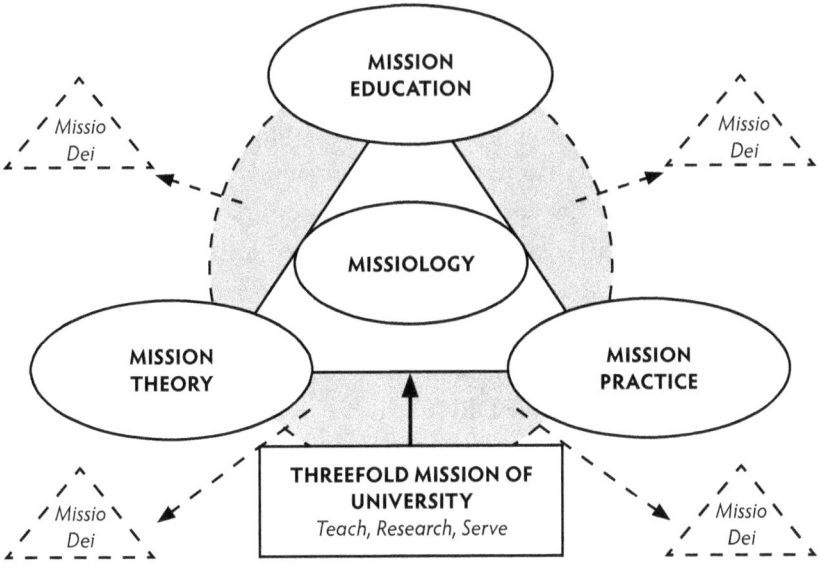

Figure 1.1 Conceptual Framework: Missiology at the Service of *Missio Dei*

1.6 Methodology

Though primarily qualitative in nature, this study also draws on some aspects of quantitative data as the work focuses on both literature analysis and empirical investigation. The main preoccupation of this study is not to discuss how research is to be done in missiology,[76] but to discern through relevant literature and empirical research how mission studies (missiological education) have been and are conceptualized and provided with reference to God's mission (*missio Dei*) in the DRC. Being a descriptive and interdisciplinary research (drawing from theology of mission, history of mission and higher education), this study focuses on exploration, description and critical analysis. Chapter 5 provides detailed explanation of the research design. Meanwhile, the following sections sketch the major two approaches used in data collection.

---

76. Elliston, *Introduction*.

1.6.1 Literature Analysis

The approach combined two methods, namely a *chronological study*, focusing particularly on important missionary conferences and documents and a *comparative study*, using available theoretical models promoted through some contemporary theories (Confession, Declaration, Covenant, Affirmation and Manifesto). The literature comprised printed and electronic materials (books, articles, papers, and reports) and included historical and doctrinal aspects. The historical account helped reconstruct and trace the evolution of missiological education in the DRC, whereas the doctrinal aspect wrestled with the issue of theology of mission promoted within both these particular geographical locations of the DRC and other contexts. Libraries – physical and virtual – represented potential sources of information. The literature allowed to depict the educational and conceptual frameworks of missiological education which are set up and promoted in the DRC and in other parts of the world. Mission and church records, documents, publications and minutes of mission and church councils, school handbooks and reports, theses and dissertations were explored. Theoretical and applied approaches to mission guided the exploration in order to make a synopsis of key elements of both theologies of mission and conceptual frameworks in their convergence, divergence and complementarity.

1.6.2 Empirical Investigation

The empirical research concentrated on evaluating the impact of missiological education with regard to God's global and holistic mission, as experienced and lived out by graduates and their respective churches. Participant observation, questionnaires, conferences followed by focus groups and some informal interviews helped generate the real information from grassroots. Thus, the empirical part of the study allowed me to understand and assess the prevailing educational and conceptual frameworks of missiological education within the context of the DRC.

The data derived from literature analysis and empirical investigation was synthetically presented in the form of a critical analysis, either through historical descriptive or missiological perspective.

1.7 Concepts Clarification

I will use some key terms and concepts which need to be briefly defined: (1) Transformation, (2) Missionary-Sending Country, (3) Missiology, (4) Missiological Education, (5) Educational Approach (Learning Process) (6) *Missio Dei*, and (7) Theology of Mission.

1.7.1 Transformation

Though previously mentioned, it is important at this point to clarify the understanding of this crucial concept in any mission-related study today. In their collective book entitled *Mission as Transformation*, edited by Samuel and Sugden, a dozen of authors have deployed their energy to describe how mission should be understood as transformation.[77]

As already stated earlier, the word *transforming* derives from *transformation* and is understood in correlation with *missiology*. Acting as both verb and adjective, *transforming* simply means that the call is for God's people to assess *their* missiology to match it with the purpose of *missio Dei*. Missiology can be transformed (or changed) by either empowering some of its aspects, or modifying some of its irrelevant categories, or replacing some of its non-applicable categories. For instance, the content, the methods and the delivery systems can be transformed through empowering, modifying or replacing. This study is an attempt to make readers aware of the possibility of transforming missiology and missiological education if they happen to no longer serve the cause of God's global and holistic mission.

Transforming also implies that missiology should bring change to the life of stakeholders who are instructors, students, their churches and the community. As stated elsewhere, to be of any sense, missiological education should help students "transform their churches into either mission-minded congregations or in-mission communities."[78] Therefore, the urgent task here is to call for a *transforming* missiology which strives to equip students as future graduates with the passion of making their respective churches not only mission-minded congregations but also communities in mission.

---

77. Samuel and Sugden, *Mission as Transformation*.
78. Lygunda, "Toward a Reconstructionist Philosophy," 19.

The suggestion submitted by Aina, while talking of the politics of higher education transformation in Africa, characterizes the process of discussion in this study:

> Transformation implies practical and epistemological ruptures with previous ways of doing things and a reconstruction of structures, relations, cultures, and institutions. In the case of African higher education, transformation entails going beyond reform; it involves a re-examination of inherited institutions and how we think about and live within them, and a reconstructing of these institutions as durable, sustainable structures geared to meet Africa's needs.[79]

Effort is made to revisit and assess the conceptual and epistemological features of missiology and missiological education.

1.7.2 Missionary-Sending Country

Drawn on Patrick Johnstone's work, the concepts of "missionary-sending country" and "missionary-receiving country" have their sense of existence in this study only when understood in a dualistic way.[80] One country can be described as a "missionary-sending country" if it maintains its momentum in sending out more and more missionaries. Consequently, a "missionary-receiving country" would simply be identified as a country that keeps receiving missionaries from outside more than it sends out its own sons and daughters. The earlier section on the problem statement already highlighted the fact that the DRC gives the impression of not being a "missionary-sending country." Such an assumption should not be understood in terms of the number of missionaries in comparison to other countries, but in terms of the ratio of sent missionaries as compared with the number of church members. For instance, according to the *Atlas of Global Christianity*,[81] of a Christian population of 65,803,000, only 1,200 were sent out as missionaries from the DRC. There is no doubt that such a ratio of 0,001 percent does

---

79. Aina, "Beyond Reforms," 33.
80. Johnstone, *Future of the Global Church*.
81. Ross and Johnson, *Atlas of Global Christianity*, 271.

not qualify the DRC to be a "missionary-sending country." This study will probably draw the real picture.

Using the same approach as the editors of *Atlas of Global Christianity*,[82] I use "sent missionaries" to designate church members who are sent from the DRC to other countries within Africa or outside of the continent. Though theologically the missionaries are sent by God, there still is no doubt that, practically, missionaries are commissioned by local bodies of Christians (cf. Acts 13:1–3). They are sent out for the mission of God to bring about redemption of the world.[83] This study explores and evaluates the ongoing debate in the DRC on these different mission-related concepts as a way to better understand the problem under consideration in the present study.

1.7.3 Missiology

In 1987, Scherer published a well-applauded article entitled "Missiology as a Discipline and What It Includes" in which he reported on the struggle scholars had to define missiology. At a time, the author observed that there was no agreed definition of missiology and that its understanding remained elusive.[84] Scherer's article was actually published when missiology underwent an identity crisis during the period of 1973–1988.[85] Even today, in the light of the ongoing discussion about the future of the discipline of missiology, the struggle continues as there is not a firmly agreed word-after-word definition.[86] In general, according to a recent work by Skreslet, missiology is referred to either in terms of "theology of mission" or in the perspective of "curricular objectives."[87] In the midst of this uncertainty, there is hope due to the consensual recognition that missiology is an interdisciplinary study of God's mission. To designate this interdisciplinary study, some universities use "missiology," others "science of mission," still others "intercultural studies" or "world Christianity." Much is said about this diversity further in chapter 3 (section 3.3).

---

82. Ibid., 260.
83. Sundquist, *Understanding Christian Mission*, 7.
84. Scherer, "Missiology," 509.
85. Robert, "Forty Years," 6.
86. Feshman, "Group Discussion Conclusions," 80–86; Langmead, "What Is Missiology?" 67–79.
87. Skreslet, *Comprehending Mission*, 2–8.

Walls prudently contends that missiology is "the systematic study of all aspects of mission."[88] By using the expression "all aspects of mission," Walls is certainly aware of the discussion whether *mission* is about either God's mission or merely church (human) mission. Moreau et al. define missiology with some details as "the academic study of missions, mission, and *missio Dei*" with three concerns about the nature, the goal and the method of mission.[89] Despite the struggle that scholars have to use these concepts interchangeably, the shared conviction among the majority of missiologists is that the church is *an* agent of God's mission. This is the reason for Steffen to describe missiology as "a constant conscience and challenge to the church, reminding her of God's unfinished agenda to establish his universal reign critically and contextually. [It] researches the positive and negative effects of the global Christian movement expressed through the planting, development, and multiplication of holistic communities of faith."[90] Steffen assigns to missiology the unique *scientific* role of a watchdog for the mission undertaken by the church. This definition is reminiscent of the dichotomy generally perceived in mission studies.

Missiology is therefore understood here as *a scientific and applied study based on the word of God and on other disciplines of social sciences in order to understand and orient the conceptualization, the teaching and the practice of God's global and holistic mission entrusted to the church*. This definition does not underline only the three components of missiological discourse (mission theory, mission education and mission practice), but also four compelling assumptions of its scientific duty. First, the fact that as an academic discipline, missiology is a "scientific and applied study." It has clear objects and methods, taking into account how mission is taught and practiced. Second, missiology is grounded in "the word of God" while also using "disciplines of social sciences." It gets light from both God's revelation and human ingenuity. Third, missiology is purposefully undertaken "to understand and orient" the mission. Missiology does not only identify problems and opportunities of thinking and doing mission, it also provides answer. Fourth, missiology is not about any kind of mission. It is concerned about "God's

---

88. Walls, "Missiology."
89. Moreau et al., *Introducing World Missions*, 19.
90. Steffen, "Missiology's Journey," 137.

global and holistic mission entrusted to the church regardless its context." Missiology sheds the light locally and globally while treating a human being as a whole entity.

1.7.4 Missiological Education

The Latin *educare* conveys the idea of impacting and acquiring knowledge through teaching and learning.[91] Education denotes the process of both putting new knowledge into the learners and helping them come out of themselves. In higher education, this process can be done either as a training for "a specific profession," through practical professional training or as a "scientific training," through scientific apprenticeship.[92] As stated earlier, this research doesn't conceive missiological education in a dualistic perspective of theory/science versus practice/profession. The conviction is that, if undertaken to achieve well-oriented and thoughtful actions, missiological education for Africa should not be undertaken, neither as visionless professional studies nor as an impractical scientific exercise.

Suffice it to say that this study has to do with higher education. It's about post-high school teaching-learning experience, done in the context of colleges and universities. In the DRC, higher education includes any training program offered after secondary school through the *Institut Supérieur* and *Université* which confers different kinds of bachelor, master or doctoral degrees.[93] Hence, missiological higher education relates to mission studies undertaken at bachelor, master or doctoral level. Though missiological education can also apply to those with a lower educational level, for the strict purpose of this study, it is the process by which the church, through its training institutions, prepares God's people to accomplish God's glocal and

---

91. Microsoft Encarta, *Encyclopedia*.
92. Van der Walt, *Transformed*, 131–133.
93. The educational system in the DRC can be correlated with the "Bachelor-Master-Doctorate" pattern of most the English-speaking system which disposes respectively 3/4 years, 2 years and 3/4 years. The scheme in the DRC comprises *Graduate* (3 years with mini-dissertation), *Licence* (2 years with mini-dissertation), and *Doctorat* (which includes 2 years of *DEA* in-depth seminars culminated in a major mini-dissertation, and 3 years of the final thesis). Therefore, while *Graduate* and *Licence* can be correlated with bachelor (5 years instead of 3 or 4 in the English system), *DEA* would correspond to master, and *doctorate* to PhD. However, only *Graduate*, *Licence* and *Doctorate* are recognized as degrees, *DEA* being a transitional step to *Doctorat*. See more details on page 159. For these reasons, the present study will mostly focus on formal education provided at bachelor, master and doctorate levels.

holistic mission at the tertiary educational level. Throughout the Bible, God has entrusted his mission to humankind, either through a relational training (Adam, Abraham, Moses and prophets) or through a hands-on training (Jesus's disciples). Regardless its nature (formal, non-formal or informal), training has been core of God's mission and, depending on the context, the period and the felt needs, such a training would involve different ever-changing factors and schemes.

As Skreslet recognizes it: "Education as an academic field might constitute another parallel worth considering, so long as that large-scale scholarly enterprise is understood to encompass the particular concerns, source materials, and methods of Christian education and theological education."[94] Skrestlet doesn't actually elaborate on how education could play such a role. Meanwhile, instead of using "might," as Skreslet states, I prefer to use "should," to say "education *should* constitute one of perspectives of approaching missiology." In 2013, The American Society of Missiology held its annual meeting under the theme "the future of the discipline of missiology." According to participants, one of the emerging themes in missiology today includes the "growing emphasis on experimentation, innovation, and participation in mission education."[95] Ten years earlier, Steffen already asserted that "the goal for education, curricula, and ministry would be to move from good to better."[96] I intend to explore means of making missional education a parallel worth considering for missiology.

The research also draws insights from general education (e.g. secular education), Christian education (e.g. as opposed to secular education) and theological education. The duty included instructive dialogue with these other educational systems. One of the main concerns was to understand what makes a training-learning process fruitful.

1.7.5 Educational Approach

Some theorists of education differentiate three approaches to education,[97] namely teacher-dependent learning, self-dependent learning and

---

94. Skreslet, *Comprehending Mission*, 15.
95. Feshman, "Group Discussion Conclusions," 82.
96. Steffen, "Missiology's Journey," 148.
97. Moulton and Bake, *Synergogy;* Lyons, "Cooperative Learning," "Cooperative and Workplace Learning"; Blair, "Understanding Adult Learners"; Gangel, "Delivering

interdependent learning. Educational approach is to be understood as the way education is provided. It is about the teaching and learning process. It entails different educational philosophies, learning styles and delivery systems. As Christine E Blair points out, the learning process takes on many forms and causes learners to acquire, retain, retrieve and apply knowledge, understanding or wisdom.[98] Each of the above-mentioned three levels of learning is described by many educators as more complex and profound than the former.[99] I discuss the taxonomy of learning with reference to a fruitful missiological education. The point is, what kind of educational approach has been promoted in the context of missiological education in the DRC and what alternatives can be explored and considered? Cole's survey conducted on the landscape of theological education in Africa[100] and Kirkpatrick's book[101] on evaluating training programs are outstanding works to be used as to explore and evaluate the curriculum of missiological education in the DRC.

1.7.6 *Missio Dei*

Since its official use, following the Willingen conference of the International Missionary Council in 1952, the concept of *missio Dei* has become a *passepartout* idea to the point that some scholars finally describe it as "a nearly ubiquitous concept,"[102] an "ambiguous phrase,"[103] but as "a popular place to begin an enquiry into mission."[104] Kirk actually echoes Lesslie Newbigin who is known as one of the most important pioneers of Trinitarian framework of missiology, when he stated that the Trinity is the starting point for the understanding of missions.[105] In his recent book on missiology, Tennent followed Newbigin's and Kirk's advice by structuring his material around *missio Dei*. He contends that "[T]he idea of understanding mission through the leans of the *missio Dei* is fundamentally sound, . . . the problem with

---

Theological Education."
   98. Blair, "Understanding Adult Learners," 12.
   99. Ibid.
   100. Cole, "Landscape," a, b.
   101. Kirkpatrick and Kirkpatrick, *Evaluating Training Programs*.
   102. Skreslet, *Comprehending Mission*.
   103. Engelsviken, "Missio Dei," 482.
   104. Kirk, *What Is Mission?* 25.
   105. Tennent, *Introduction*, 66.

the twentieth-century ecumenical notion of *missio Dei* was not so much in the concept itself as in the application of the concept."[106] Hence, *missio Dei* doesn't mean the same thing to all scholars, though the work of triune God in mission constitutes the common ground for both ecumenicals and evangelicals, academicians and practitioners. The two strains become easier to identify: creation focus and redemption focus.[107] Whereas radical ecumenicals would emphasize the God-World-Church theory, evangelicals retain an emphasis on the church as being the primary agent in the *missio Dei* concept, that is, God-Church-World.[108]

While recognizing the existence of different meanings attached to *missio Dei*, I describe it as God's glocal and holistic mission to save humankind in Christ through the sent church. In fact, though the mission doesn't proceed from any ecclesiastical and human initiative, God's mission has always been carried out by the obedient church (cf. Acts 13:1–4). The emphasis put on mission as God's initiative simply means that the salvation is perceived as a complete process that concerns the whole human being. It also denotes the fact that the salvation act belongs to triune God through the particular actions of the Father's love, the Son's sacrifice and the power of the Holy Spirit. It further points to the geographically unlimited space for God's mission, the whole earth (*oikoumene*) and all nations (*ethne*). The research seeks to determine the extent to what a training program would have facilitated the involvement of the trainees and their churches in God's mission which is both *global* (for all human beings) and *holistic* (for the whole human being).

1.7.7 Theology of Mission

Much has been said and written on theology of mission to the point that, without clairvoyance, the reader might get confused. Waiting for the discussion to be undertaken in a further chapter, suffice it to understand theology of mission as the justification of mission work. In their monumental book entitled *Contemporary Theologies of Mission*, Glasser and McGavran discover that theologies of mission have gradually become biblical justification of the varied works done by church constituents, whether within or outside

---

106. Ibid., 55.
107. Van Gelder and Zscheile, *Missional Church*, 30.
108. Whitworth, "Missio Dei," 29.

of their own context.[109] Even within one group of Christians (evangelical, ecumenical or Catholic), there are particular *theologies* of mission.

Therefore, for some, there should not be a single theology of mission, but several and not necessarily complementary. For others, while admitting the existence of different theologies of mission, there should be at least one compelling theology of mission. The discussion on theology of mission can be either on its content or on its function. Instead of following Yoder by retaining one (function) and putting aside the other (content),[110] or Skreslet who seems to undermine the role of theology of mission to approach the field of missiology,[111] I consider both aspects (function and content) to form a conceptual framework through which missiological education can be conceived, understood and done. Theology of mission has the function of providing direction to actions and its content provides detailed explanation to that direction. As Ott contends, theology of mission has the task of "providing biblical direction for the church's fulfilment of its missionary mandate."[112]

For the purpose of this study, theology of mission can be defined as the biblical and theological justification of mission work. While recognizing the existence of different theologies of mission, I align with evangelical theologies of mission to explain why it is important for the church to engage in God's global and holistic mission even today, and how to go about in it. I will picture and evaluate the existing theologies of mission promoted in the context of missiological education in the DRC.

1.8 Organizational Structure of the Study

I follow the steps used in a typical scientific process through which the researcher raises a question, collects new data, analyses the data, interprets and reports findings.[113] Being a missiological research, steps of this study follow the structure provided by Elliston, whereby chapters are known as addressing

---

109. Glasser and McGraven, *Contemporary Theologies*, 17.
110. Yoder, *Theology of Mission*, 42.
111. Skreslet, *Comprehending Mission*, 9.
112. Ott et al., *Encountering Theology*, xii.
113. Lodico et al., *Methods Educational Research*, 4; Bui, *How to Write*; Sampson, "A Guide."

the following important functions (see fig. 1): (1) Introduction where the missiological problem is amply described and substantiated, (2) Literature review where the researcher explores and evaluates the existing body of literature addressing the similar or related issues, (3) Research design where the researcher selects and describes in details how data were collected and analyzed, (4) Result where the researcher presents and interprets the findings, and (5) Discussion or Conclusion where the researcher discusses the result and proposes recommendations.

Nevertheless, depending on the scope of each research, these steps can bear different names (titles). They can be labelled as "chapters," each having several sections, or as "parts," each having several chapters (table 1.1). Therefore, irrespective of the numbers of chapters or parts, the thesis should undergo a cyclical process of problem, literature, methodology, findings, and discussion.[114] (fig. 1.2).

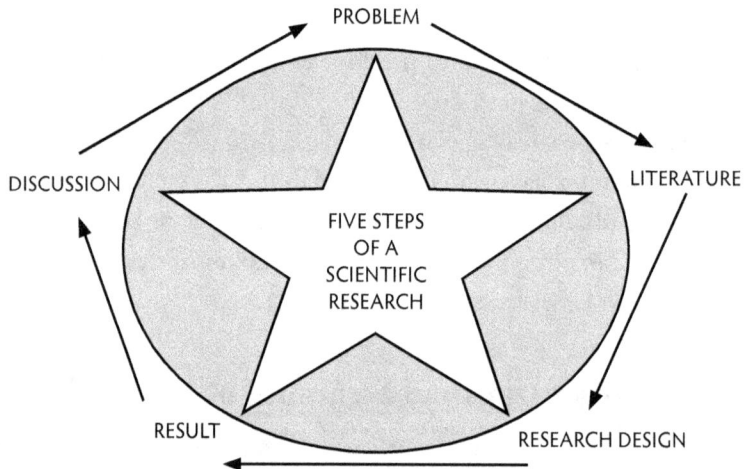

Figure 1.2: Cyclical Process of Scientific Research in Missiology

Based on the above requirements, the following overview of the present study provides a clear perspective on its organizational structure and content (table 1.1).

---

114. Bui, *How to Write*; Elliston, *Introduction*; Sampson, "A Guide"; Leedy and Ormrod, *Practical Research*.

Table 1.1 Organizational Structure and Content of the Book

Scientific Research Steps	Corresponding Chapters of the Book	Chapter Titles	Related Areas in Missiology (Research Concentrations)
Problem	Chapter 1	The need for a research on missiological education	Missiological research (related to theology, education and history)
Literature Review	Chapter 2	Trends in missiology as a scientific reflection on Christian mission	Theology of mission (evangelical & ecumenical), history of mission
	Chapter 3	Conceptual and philosophical considerations in missiological education	Philosophies of education and of theological education, educational administration
	Chapter 4	Mapping the historical roots of the Protestant missiology and missiological education in the DRC	History of Protestant missions in the DRC, and history of church in the DRC
Research Design / Result	Chapter 5	Missiology in theological education in the DRC: empirical investigation and findings	Applied missiological research (in theological education, in missiological education, and in missional leadership development)
Discussion	Chapter 6	Towards a transforming missiology for a fruitful missiological education	Missiology (with reference to the DRC and Francophone Africa at large)
	Chapter 7	Conclusions, implications and recommendations	Missiology (mission theory, education, and practice)

The first chapter has substantiated the need for conducting a research on missiological education in the context of the DRC. The second chapter surveys trends that characterized the conception, the training and the practice of mission as aspects of missiology in history focusing on nineteenth, twentieth and twenty-first centuries. Chapter 3 explores the conceptual and philosophical considerations applied to missiological education. The fourth chapter traces the historical roots of Protestant missiology and missiological education in the strict context of the DRC. Chapter 5 describes the research design for the empirical investigation of the current situation of missiology and missiological education in the DRC and it also displays, interprets and analyses the findings. The sixth chapter discusses the findings related to missiology and missiological education in the context of the DRC and proposes a model of missiological education at undergraduate (bachelor), graduate (master) and postgraduate (doctorate) levels. The seventh and final chapter draws conclusions and implications for the study in order to solve the raised problems, and provides recommendations to set path for future research.

Part II

Exploring the Literature on Missiology and Missiological Education

CHAPTER 2

Trends in Missiology as a Scientific Reflection on Christian Mission

2.1 Introduction

Chapter 1 provided the rationale of a research on missiological education in both the general context of Francophone Africa and more specifically about the situation in the Democratic Republic of Congo (DRC). The central question and its related sub-questions were formulated and substantiated. This chapter reviews both historical and theoretical literature on missiology and its related issues that were briefly defined in the first chapter, with the purpose of gathering general theoretical insights on the following two sub-questions:

- Through which paradigms of the theology of mission and for which reasons has missiological education been provided?
- To what extent has a vision of *missio Dei,* or the lack of it, in the whole of theological education influenced missiological education and mission practice?

Linked to these questions is the most fundamental concern of what missiology really is. Attending to these preoccupations will serve to construct the framework for addressing the specific case of the DRC in further chapters. In three forthcoming chapters, the remaining two sub-questions will be addressed as well.[1]

---

1. These sub-questions are stated in section 1.3 of the first chapter: To what extent has a *missio Dei* vision or the lack of it in the whole of theological education influenced missiological education and mission practice? Through which educational and conceptual frameworks

It was succinctly stated in chapter 1 that dozens of definitions of missiology exist and that the consensus depends on the tradition through which each definition is formulated. In general, four major missiological traditions have punctuated the history of this discipline, namely Evangelical, Ecumenical, Roman Catholic, and Orthodox.[2] Phillips and Coote omit Orthodox in their list of "Christian families in mission" replacing it by Pentecostal and Charismatic family. Scherer and Bevans do not mention Pentecostal and Charismatic as a separate family with a clear statement on mission and evangelization. In describing his paradigms shift, though recognizing the existence of Orthodox and charismatic streams, D. Bosch constructs his framework around Roman Catholic, ecumenical Protestant, and evangelical Protestant. Following the same spirit of the unity in the Protestant body in the DRC, this study does not exclude Pentecostal and Charismatic from what Scherer and Bevans label as "evangelical Protestant."[3] The CCC includes many of "Pentecostal and Charismatic" denominations, and in the real life of the churches in the DRC, even non-Pentecostal denominations such as Baptists, Presbyterians, Mennonites, Methodists and others have a strong "Pentecostal and Charismatic" expression of liturgy and worship to God.

Although undertaken from an evangelical perspective, the study in this chapter also considers some critical points of view contended by other bodies through the history of missiology in the last and present centuries, all have collaborated and still collaborate. Professional associations,[4] publishing

---

missiological education has been offered? To what extent is missiological education and research really serving the churches?

2. Scherer and Bevans, *New Directions*, vol. 1 & 2; Phillips and Coote, *Toward the 21st Century*.

3. Bosch, *Transforming Mission*. For a simple but comprehensive exposé of Pentecostal contribution to Christian mission, see Grant McClung ("Missiology"). By the time this paper was released, Dr Grant McClung served as President of Missions Resource Group (www.MissionsResourceGroup.org) and Missiological Advisor to the World Missions Commission of the Pentecostal World Fellowship.

4. International Association for Mission Studies (IAMS), Association of Professors of Mission (APM), American Society of Missiology (AMS). For more details, see Anderson ("Professional Academic Associations").

houses,[5] scholarly journals,[6] and books,[7] have often featured the particularities of each missiological mainstream. Though not without suspicion, it is easy to observe professors from one mainstream render teaching services to a school connected to another missiological tradition. Mission centers have been often an encountering crossroad for practitioners, scholars and researchers from different missiological traditions.[8] Missiological resources have even since become countless.

Amidst this cloud of resources, the task of reviewing literature becomes even more challenging than it was some generations back. Overwhelmed by the massive literature due in part to the progress that the discipline of missiology has achieved, David J. Hesselgrave has this to say: "A generation ago mission professors were hard put to find suitable materials even for the relatively few courses offered in most schools. Today the major problem is not to find materials but to sort them out. Bibliographies for most courses fill many pages."[9] Hesselgrave's observation is relevant to this study. Hundreds of books and scholarly articles have been released from different perspectives. Even within one perspective, be it evangelical or ecumenical, voices have been even more discordant. The approach in this chapter is to primarily consider the evangelical perspective in the light of other perspectives since, as it is observed in chapters 4 and 5, the Protestant missiology in the DRC is still hard to categorize as being strictly either "evangelical" or "ecumenical." To lay down the foundation for further discussion, the

---

5. Baker Book House (USA), Eerdmans (USA), Zondervan (USA), Orbis Books (USA), Brill (The Netherlands).

6. The case of some leading journals like *Ecumenical Review* (published by WCC); *Evangelical Mission Quarterly* (published by Evangelicals); *International Bulletin of Missionary Research* (Ecumenical, Evangelical, Roman Catholic) published by OMSC; *International Review of Mission* (published by the Division of World Mission and Evangelism DWME/WCC, World Council of Churches); *Mission Studies* (published by the International Association of Mission Studies); *Missiology: An International Review* ((Ecumenical, Evangelical, Roman Catholic); *Missionalia* (South Africa, especially useful for its abstracts); *Mission Frontiers* (US Center for World Mission).

7. Some books have been published with contributions from Evangelical, Ecumenical, and Catholic missiologists.

8. The case of Overseas Ministries Study Center (USA), Oxford Centre for Mission Studies (England).

9. Hesselgrave, *Today's Choices*, 138.

theoretical framework which conducts the discussion finds its starting point from the understanding of missiology.

2.2 Exploring Variant Trends in Missiological Literature

2.2.1 Towards a Comprehensive Understanding of Missiology

Along with the bourgeoning output on mission-related matters, one might also find it confusing to observe the divergence, though with some similarities, which characterizes the available literature on missiology. While some scholars would even hesitate to adopt such a hybrid word of "missiology,"[10] others would simply prefer to replace it with other concepts, not always without creating new problems, like science of religion, intercultural studies or world Christianity etc.[11] Raoul Allier[12] strongly rebuked the use of *missiologie* in his review of the book, *L'âme des peuples à évangéliser: compte-rendu de la Sixième Semaine de Missiologie de Louvain (1928)*: "I cannot approve of the word 'missiologie,' which, being half Latin and half Greek, has a barbarous appearance. Its structure is as bad as that of 'sociologie,' and has the same defects. This unnatural marriage of Latin and Greek hurts one's ears."

Such a reaction was common among Protestants. According to Justice Anderson,[13] two reasons made this concept take time to gain the Protestant adhesion. The first reason relates to the fact that it was a Catholic innovation, coined by Ludwig J. van Rijckevorsel in 1915 and promoted within Catholic milieu.[14] The second reason, similar to Allier's above reaction, is its monstrosity of being "barbarous appearance" and "hybrid." Consequently, for Scottish and German Protestants, being a serious matter, mission couldn't be linguistically misused through slang and neologism. Despite

---

10. Due to its monstrosity of being a blended word from Latin (*missio*) and Greek (*logia*), some protestants couldn't easily accept it in their academic jargon.

11. Case of several American and European schools and their overseas-related institutions in Africa and Asia who have changed the name of their school from missiology.

12. Allier, "Review," 282. Raoul Allier was the Dean of the Faculty of Theology at Paris University.

13. Justice Anderson in Terry et al., *Missiology*, 1.

14. Jongeneel, *Philosophy*, vol. 1, 63.

these wording gesticulations, the term was finally adopted by all groups as technical jargon for the study of mission after World War II.

But the acceptance of the term "missiology" did not terminate the struggle to define the concept. John Roxborogh is right when he observes that "clarity about the definition of the concept and content of mission continues to be problematic."[15] While some definitions tend to be too simplistic (i.e. "missiology is the study of mission,"[16] "missiology is applied theology,"[17] or "missiology is the science of the Christian world mission"),[18] other scholars would first prefer to spend several hours coming up with an academically articulated, but also complicated, definition. Some authors perceive missiology as "a theological reflection and study on God's mission and God's command and calling of the church to participate in that mission by witnessing to the coming of God's kingdom."[19] Far from solving the problem, such a perception of missiology creates double misunderstanding. First, this definition ambiguously limits missiology to a reflection on everything God does and commands, therefore, the frontier between missiology and theology becomes either confused or inexistent. Second, the structure of this definition tends to mean that missiology calls the church to witness to the fact that kingdom of God is coming, confining the kingdom only to the future ("not yet") while Jesus also insisted on the present ("already").

Even Fuller Seminary's initial definition of missiology as "the study of man being brought to God in history"[20] or Andrew Walls's prudent definition of missiology as being "the systematic study of all aspects of mission"[21] do not solve the problem. The ambiguity of the first definition doesn't allow the reader to grasp the essence of missiology as a scientific discipline which is concerned with a wider sphere than the sole aspect of bringing human beings to God. In the second case, though the generic expression "all aspects of mission" leaves the reader with indefinite understanding, Walls's

---

15. Roxborogh, "Missiology after Missions," 1.
16. Wright, *Mission of God*, 25.
17. Pratt, Sills, and Walters, *Introduction*, 67.
18. Hesselgrave, *Today's Choices*, 134.
19. Mashau, "A Reformed Perspective," 2.
20. Martin, *Means of World Evangelization*, 3.
21. Walls, "Missiology."

definition implies that missiology is a complex task because it deals with a complex mission which entails several and divergent aspects. Similar to Walls, Roxborogh's definition of missiology as being "the study of Christian mission and the issues that arise through commitment to it" points to the complexity of the task.[22] Mission that missiology studies is not just the fact of crossing geographical boundaries with the gospel, or mere philanthropic services to disadvantaged people. The various existing definitions, however, represent different variants of the above two distinct theological positions. Whereas one definition attempts to pull human beings from a sinful world and to direct them to the local church, the other stresses the need for social transformation as a Christian response to world misery. While the former emphasizes individual salvation through a personal relationship with Christ, the latter contends that the witness to the kingdom of God includes an engagement for the economic, political and social transformation of the systems and structures. If these are the two main orientations of understanding "mission," what will be the implication for the "study of mission" or "missiology"?

The understanding of missiology correlates with these two major mainstreams with direct implication on the field of study that it generates. To designate this complex discipline, due to reasons discussed later in this chapter, some universities use "missiology," others "science of mission," still others "intercultural studies," or "world Christianity."[23]

In a recently applauded book entitled *Comprehending Mission: The Questions, Methods, Themes, Problems, and Prospects of Missiology*, Skreslet discusses different ways through which missiology has been understood.[24] From his observation, literature produced on missiology since 1960s has taken two streams. While one stream considers missiology in curricular nature (teaching of missiology), the other conceives missiology in a form of theological reflection (theology of mission).[25] As one goes through Skreslet's book, another stream of the practice of mission emerges without attracting

---

22. Roxborogh, "Missiology after Missions."
23. See discussion in chapter 3 (section 3.3).
24. Skreslet, *Comprehending Mission*, 2–15.
25. In the light of table 2.1, Skreslet's statement that literature on teaching of missiology has been often produced could be relativized.

the author's attention. He believes however that missiology "properly encompasses every kind of scholarly inquiry performed on the subject of mission without necessarily subordinating any group of studies to any other."[26] Without elaborating how education could play such a strategic role in missiology, Skreslet concludes the section with this suggestion: "Education as an academic field might constitute another parallel worth considering, so long as that large-scale scholarly enterprise is understood to encompass the particular concerns, source materials, and methods of Christian education and theological education."[27]

One could be confused by Skreslet who, throughout the development of his material, gives the impression that one of the streams, the curricular nature of missiology, was not valid as a way to understand missiology. While recognizing education as an academic field for missiology, Skreslet joins the ongoing movement of capturing missiology through the educational lens. In 2013, the American Society of Missiology held its annual meeting under the theme "the future of the discipline of missiology." According to participants, one of the emerging themes in missiology today includes the "growing emphasis on experimentation, innovation, and participation in mission education."[28] Ten years earlier, Steffen already asserted that "the goal for education, curricula, and ministry would be to move from good to better."[29] As already said earlier in the chapter 1, this study will explore the means of making education a parallel worth considering for missiology, arguing that as an academic study, missiology is concerned about theory, training and practice of mission.

2.2.2 Missiology as Threefold Scientific Reflection on Mission

Definitions of missiology respectively by Alan Tippett and Samuel Escobar sound descriptive and more explanatory and deserve attention in the context

---

26. Skreslet, *Comprehending Mission,* 15.
27. Ibid.
28. Feshman, "Group Discussion Conclusions," 82.
29. Steffen, "Missiology's Journey," 148.

of this study.³⁰ Alan R. Tippett has defined "missiology" as the academic discipline or science:

> . . . which researches, records and applies data relating to the biblical origin, the history (including the use of documentary materials), the anthropological principles and techniques and the theological base of the Christian mission. The theory, methodology and data bank are particularly directed towards: (1) the processes by which the Christian message is communicated, (2) the encounters brought about by its proclamation to non-Christians, (3) the planting of the Church and organization of congregations, the incorporation of converts into those congregations, and the growth and relevance of their structures and fellowship, internally to maturity, externally in outreach as the body of Christ in local situations and beyond, in a variety of culture patterns.³¹

Thereafter, Samuel Escobar has defined missiology as:

> . . . an interdisciplinary approach to understand missionary action. It looks at missionary facts from the perspectives of the biblical sciences, theology, history, and the social sciences. It aims to be systematic and critical, but it starts from a positive stance towards the legitimacy of the Christian missionary task as part of the fundamental reason for the church's "being." A missiological approach gives the observer a comprehensive frame of reference in order to look at reality in a critical way. Missiology is a critical reflection on praxis, in light of God's Word.³²

Johannes Verkuyl had already provided an insightful, but disputable definition of missiology as:

> . . . the study of the salvation activities of the Father, Son, and Holy Spirit, throughout the world geared toward bringing the kingdom of God into existence . . . its task in every age is to

---

30. Tippett, *Introduction*; Escobar, "Evangelical Missiology."
31. Tippett, *Introduction*, xiii.
32. Escobar, "Evangelical Missiology," 101.

investigate scientifically and critically the presupposition, motives, structures, methods, patterns of cooperation, and leadership which the churches bring to their mandate. In addition missiology must examine every other type of human activity which combats the various evils to see if it fits the criteria and goals of God's kingdom which has both already come and is yet coming.[33]

Though these definitions of missiology as an academic discipline would gain preference due to their elaborated features on its nature, object of study, and method, they are still missing some important aspects to provide a whole picture of the discipline. As one can observe, it is obvious that these definitions emphasize "missionary action" (Tippett), "missionary praxis" (Escobar) or "mission reflection and examination" (Verkuyl) leaving behind other aspects of missiological studies. Also, to be an objective scientific discipline, missiology shouldn't only start from "a positive stance" (Escobar) ignoring the negative one. The same observation can be made against the following Catholic-based definition from Karl Muller when he perceives missiology as "the systematic study of the evangelizing activity of the church and of the ways in which it is carried out; the scientific study of the missionary reality of the church in which scientific discipline and missionary charism enrich each other."[34]

Therefore, coming back to the working definition provided in the first chapter, missiology is then understood in this study as *a scientific and applied study based on the word of God and on other disciplines of social sciences in order to understand and orient how God's glocal and holistic mission entrusted to the church is and should be conceptualized, executed, and taught.* This definition underlines four compelling assumptions to be stressed here. First, the fact that as an academic discipline, missiology is a "scientific and applied study." It has clear object and methods, taking into account how mission is conceptualized, taught and practiced in various contexts. Second, missiology is grounded in "the word of God" while also using "disciplines of social sciences." It gets light from both God's revelation and human ingenuity.

---

33. Verkuyl, *Contemporary Missiology,* 5.
34. Muller, "Missiology," 26.

Third, missiology is purposefully undertaken "to understand and orient" the mission. Missiology doesn't only identify problems and opportunities of thinking and doing mission; it also provides answer, how mission should be conceptualized, taught and executed. Fourth, missiology is not about any kind of mission; it is concerned about "God's glocal (global and local) and holistic mission entrusted to the church regardless its context." Missiology sheds the light for the work to be done both locally and globally while treating human being as a whole entity.[35]

The related trilogy of *orthodoxy* (theory), *orthopraxis* (practice), and *didache* (teaching) facilitates the formulation of the theoretical framework of understanding missiology. Put together, each of these three key words deals with a given central question, while being summarized in one main subject, using a particular source of reasoning, etc. Table 2.1 below makes the point clear:

Table 2.1 Tripartite nature of missiology

Threefold lines / Related features	A THEORY	B TRAINING	C PRACTICE
	Missiology as a systematic reflection on the theory of God's mission	Missiology as a systematic reflection on the training for God's mission	Missiology as a systematic reflection on the practice of God's mission
Key Question	How mission has been, is and should be conceived?	How mission has been, is and should be taught?	How mission has been, is and should be executed?
Objective	Setting the direction for mission and evaluating theories of mission	Preparing people for mission and evaluating the training programs	Describing and Evaluating the implementation of missionary work

While surveying literature on mission and missiology, it becomes easy to categorize the existing publications in one or another of these three lines.

---

35. This definition is lengthy elaborated and discussed in chapter 6 (sections 6.4 and 6.5).

While some works focus on "theory of mission," others align with the "practice of mission" and still others put emphasis on "training for mission." Some other literature would even embrace two of the three at once. The question then arises from such a reality in dealing with missiology: Is missiology the study of the theory of mission only, or the study of the training for mission, or the practice of mission? A careful examination of the works produced by several missiologists culminates in the conclusions that the tendency is to consider missiology as only the study of one of these three aspects, ignoring other important components of this scientific discipline. For instance, while struggling with the issue of "missiology as an interested discipline and where it is happening," Dwight Baker describes missiology as a discipline which does more than simply record missionary practice.[36] For him, missiology "seeks to reform or reshape missionary practice, missionary theory, even missionary strategy, and to refine missionary self-understanding in ways that will enhance missionary effectiveness." As one keenly observes Baker's reasoning, the gap becomes even clearer, concerning the mission education – that is how mission is studied or taught. This reality demonstrates the relevance of the framework used in this study.

One of the best ways to capture the relevance of our framework is to consider different orientations undertaken by students for their mission-related doctoral theses.[37] Important for this study is to find out which parts of the missiological curriculum may have attracted the most attention of missiological researchers: the theory of mission, the training for mission, or the practice of mission? The *International Bulletin of Missionary Research* (*IBMR*)[38] is known as the leading journal which commissions and publishes the review of English-language doctoral dissertations on mission submitted

---

36. Baker, "Missiology," 17.

37. In other contexts like North America, "dissertation" is used for a doctoral final report and "thesis" for master's work. At North-West University, South Africa, through which this research is done, dissertation and thesis are produced for master and doctoral qualifications respectively.

38. This journal has, since January 2016, changed its name from "missionary research" to "mission research" (*IBMR* 40, no. 1 [Jan 2016]). According to the editor, the change "reflects the global shift in world Christianity, with the recognition that, for some readers, "missionary" can too easily bring to mind previous centuries of cross-cultural ministries in the context of colonialism. In contrast, the term "mission" is both ancient and contemporary, particularly as we focus on God's mission in the world."

within a decade time frame. Because the review does not include works produced in languages other than English, it is important that speakers of other languages follow the steps of *IBMR*. Since 1983 four reviews have been provided respectively by E. Theodore Bachmann, William A. Smalley, Stanley H. Skreslet, and Robert J. Priest and Robert DeGeorge.[39] The particularity of the first two reviews in the series is that they only include dissertations produced from North American institutions. The difference between them resides in the fact that the first covers a longer time frame than ten years (1945–1981). The following two reviews didn't undergo the geographical restriction and feature of doctoral dissertations produced even outside of North America within a strict time frame of ten years each.

Authors of these reviews deserve applause due to their meticulous ingenuity in the interpretation and the categorization of the different fields of research or departments within the broad spectrum of mission studies, or missiology. The general feature for all reviews is the summary of the findings which not only shows how missiology has been understood, but also how it is undertaken as a scientific discipline. While in a certain period the accent is stressed on one or another field of research or department, things change in other periods. Not only that these changes demonstrate likewise the change in world church and mission movements, but they also shed light on the inclination and orientation of missiological thinking of each generation. Smalley recognizes, however, that the subjective decision of the authors of these reviews might also play an important role in the selection of dissertation titles to be included in the report. Though the figures do not convey the whole picture,[40] still these reviews provide an overall image of how missiology has been understood and undertaken during the period under consideration.

Bachmann reveals that from 1945 to 1981, the accent was mostly on theory of mission and practice of mission (table 2.2). Smalley has discovered that during the period from 1982 to 1991, most dissertations focused on theory of mission and practice of mission (table 2.2). One of the innovations

---

39. Bachmann, "North American Doctoral Dissertations"; Smalley, "Doctoral Dissertations"; Skreslet, "Doctoral Dissertations"; Priest and DeGeorge, "Doctoral Dissertations."

40. Skreslet, "Doctoral Dissertations."

of Skreslet's review is the provision of information per continent.[41] Out of 925 dissertations produced from 1992 to 2001, 181 came from the entire continent of Africa distributed as follows: 74 from East Africa, 10 from Middle [Central] Africa, 9 from North Africa, 26 from Southern Africa, 47 from West Africa, and 15 from other Africa. One would be interested to know how many doctoral dissertations in missiology would have been produced by scholars from the DRC which is the concern of this study. Skrestlet reports that the inclination for the years from 1992 to 2001 was towards theory of mission and practice of mission including few aspects of training for mission (table 2.2). Priest and DeGeorge have found that most dissertations produced from 2002 to 2011 put emphasis on theory of mission and practice of mission including some aspects of training for mission (table 2.2).

From these findings, and using our framework, it becomes clear that mission-related dissertations can be categorized in three main concerns. Table 2.2 submits that researchers focus either on how mission is and should be conceived (theory of mission), on how mission is and should be executed (practice of mission), or on how mission is and should be taught (training for mission).

---

41. Ibid.

Table 2.2 The Orientation of Doctoral Dissertations in Missiology from 1945 to 2011

Threefold lines / Related features	A THEORY	B TRAINING	C PRACTICE
	Missiology as a systematic reflection on the theory of God's mission	Missiology as a systematic reflection on the training for God's mission	Missiology as a systematic reflection on the practice of God's mission
Key Question	How mission has been, is and should be conceived?	How mission has been, is and should be taught?	How mission has been, is and should be executed?
Objective	Setting the direction for mission and evaluating theories of mission	Preparing people for mission and evaluating the training programs	Describing and evaluating the missionary work
Bachmann (1945–1981) 34 years	-Theology of mission -Theology of religions -Biblical studies -Liberation theology -Christian social ethics -Baptists; Southern Baptists -Catholic church and missions		-Geographical areas (Brazil, China, Japan, India, Korea, Mexico, Nigeria, the Philippines) and people groups (American Indians) -Christian education

Smalley (1982–1991) 10 years	-Non-traditional theologies (Liberation theology, Asian, African, black, and feminist theologies) with little if any missiological content, dominated by abstract theology! - Mission-sending agencies (less attention)		-Treatment of countries (Japan, Korea, etc.) -Cultural issues (indigenization and contextualization)
Skreslet (1992–2001) 10 years	-Bible and mission -Theology, culture, and mission -Theology of religions	-Study of mission as a discipline	-Historical studies -Forms of witness and service -Missionary vocation
Priest & DeGeorge (2002–2011) 10 years	-Mission studies/ world mission/ missiology -Theology/theological studies -Religion/religious studies	-Intercultural studies -History/historical studies -Mission studies/ world mission/ missiology -Theology/theological studies -Education/educational studies Religion/religious studies Psychology	-Intercultural studies -History/historical studies -Anthropology -Psychology -Sociology -English

As is displayed above, the missiological discourse might be directed towards establishment of theories, strategies or training for mission. However, attention on training for mission became a part of doctoral research by the 1990s (table 2.2). Using the same framework, works produced by some famous missiologists since the 1990s can also be categorized as follows:

Table 2.3 The Orientation of Some Selected Books in Missiology

Threefold lines / Related features	A THEORY	B TRAINING	C PRACTICE
	Missiology as a systematic reflection on the theory of God's mission	**Missiology as a systematic reflection on the training for God's mission**	**Missiology as a systematic reflection on the practice of God's mission**
Key Question	How mission has been, is and should be conceptualized?	How mission has been, is and should be taught?	How mission has been, is and should be executed?
Objective	Setting the direction for mission and evaluating theories of mission	Preparing people for mission and evaluating the training programmes	Describing and evaluating the missionary work

1990–2000	*Transforming Mission*, by D. Bosch 2) *New Directions in Mission and Evangelization 1*, by J. Scherer et al., 39 chs. 3) *Toward the 21st Century in Christian Mission*, by J. Phillips et al., about 7 chs. out of 29 4) *New Directions in Mission and Evangelization 2*, by J. Scherer et al., 12 chs. out of 16 5) *The Story of Faith Mission*, by K. Fiedler 6) *What Is Mission?* By A. Kirk, parts 1 and 2	1) *Transforming Mission*, by D. Bosch 2) *Toward the 21st Century in Christian Mission*, by J. Phillips et al., about 7 chs. out of 29 3) *New Directions in Mission and Evangelization 2*, by J. Scherer et al., 12 chs. out of 16	1) *Transforming Mission*, by D. Bosch 2) *New Directions in Mission and Evangelization 1*, by J. Scherer et al., 39 chs. 3) *Toward the 21st Century in Christian Mission*, by J. Phillips et al., about 7 chs. out of 29 4) *New Directions in Mission and Evangelization 2*, by J. Scherer et al., 12 chs. out of 16 5) *The Story of Faith Mission*, by K. Fiedler 6) *Global Mission Handbook: A Guide for Cross-Cultural Service*, by S. Hoke et al. 7) *What Is Mission?* By A. Kirk, part 3

2001–2011	7) *Announcing the Kingdom*, by A. Glasser, 23 chs. 8) *Introduction to World Missions*, by A. Moreau et al., parts 1, 2, 3, and 4 9) *Invitation to World Missions*, by T. Tennent, 15 chs. 10) *Encountering Theology of Mission*, by C. Ott et al., parts 1 & 2 11) *The Mission of God's People*, by C. Wright, 15 chapters	4) *Introduction to World Missions*, by A. Moreau et al., ch. 10 out of 19 5) *Interpreting Contemporary Christianity*, by O. Kalu, chs. 7 & 8 out of 14	8) *Introduction to World Missions*, by A. Moreau et al., part 5 9) *Interpreting Contemporary Christianity*, by O. Kalu 10) *Encountering Theology of Mission*, by C. Ott et al., part 3
2012–2014	12) *Comprehending Mission*, by S. Skreslet, chs. 2 and 4 13) *Understanding Christian Mission*, by S. Sunquist, parts 1 and 2 14) *Theology of Mission*, J. Yoder, 21 chs. out of 23	6) *Comprehending Mission*, by S. Skreslet, chs. 1 and 6	11) *Comprehending Mission*, by S. Skreslet, chs. 3, 4, 6, and 7 12) *Understanding Christian Mission*, by S. Sunquist, part 3 13) *Theology of Mission*, J. Yoder, 2 chs. out of 23

Table 2.3 is revelatory.[42] For a sample of fourteen books at our disposal, all of them deal in one or another way with the "theory of mission." Almost

---

42. The same exercise could also be done about the orientation of articles published in scholarly journals. In that case, one could survey a given journal at a time and use our framework as a template to determine how authors focus on the three aspects of missiological reflection within a defined time frame. As far as missiology is concerned, the following journals can be of particular interest due to their role of being among leading missiological journals in the world: *International Bulletin of Mission(ary) Research, Missiology: An International Review, Mission Studies, International Review of Mission, Missionalia, Exchange,* etc. For more information, see a comprehensive list in Jonathan Bonk et al. ("Missiological Journals," 42–49).

the same fourteen books deal also with the "practice of mission" while only some chapters within six books briefly mention the issue of the "training for mission." It is however worth mentioning that even if some books can be located in all three columns, the treatment of three lines is not equal. For example, as Kritzinger points out, Bosch's magisterial *Transforming Mission* mentions "mission practice" only incidentally.[43] The same could be said about "mission education" in Bosch's book. One of the implications is that missiological education might not be as popular subject in missiology treatment as are other two aspects of "theory" and "practice."

Authors tend to focus on how mission is and should be conceptualized and executed while paying little attention to how mission is and should be taught. Theories are conceived but the question about how to teach them is not attractive enough. Similar to the previous observation, authors seem to be also attracted by the question about the practice of mission without making sure that the practice should be done as a result of the training about mission. How do we make sure that theories are appropriately conceptualized if these theoreticians are not well-taught about mission practice? How the mission will be strategically appropriate if those reflecting on and implementing the practice of mission are not well-taught?

Without doubt, that is the reason for scholars like Gustav Warneck and others to battle for the promotion of missiology as an academic discipline.[44] As such, missiology could not bypass its educational aspect of "training for mission." Jongeneel suggests that "Missionaries and missiologists need to widen their horizon and to deepen . . . their formal mission studies (concentration upon the form [and the content] of mission studies as an academic discipline)."[45] Therefore, while recognizing the importance of the other two aspects of missiology (theory and practice), the investigation conducted in the present and the following chapters will pay particular attention on literature pertaining to how mission has been, is and should be taught.

The threefold line of understanding missiology, creates the structure of the following literature exploration, starting with keen observation on how the issue under consideration is perceived within the ecumenical and

---

43. Kritzinger, "Mission as," 38.
44. See Myklebust, *Study of Missions*, Vol. 1 & 2.
45. Jongeneel, "Philosophy, Science, and Theology," 29.

evangelical wings. Such a procedure is not unimportant for this study which strives to trace and locate the prevailing Protestant missiology and missiological education in the context of the DRC where both wings used to have, and still have, a direct influence on the life of churches and their educational institutions. Thereafter, key emerging concepts related to the study are explored in order to determine both their relevance and scope for the present research.

2.3 Emerging Trends in Missiology from Nineteenth to Twenty-First Centuries

As mentioned earlier, to different extents, authors from various theological traditions and through different missiological perspectives have produced scientific discourses (missio-*logia*) on how mission has been, is, and should be conceived, practiced and taught. The task of selecting literature becomes even harder, not only due to the massive number of works and the theological tradition through which the matter under consideration has been discussed, but also in light of the specific purpose, scope and context of the research. It is important that the present study is done from an evangelical perspective in order to explore, describe and evaluate the Protestant missiology and missiological education in the context of the DRC during the missionary and post-missionary eras (1878 to present). Therefore, while recognizing the validity of some outstanding publications of the past centuries[46] the effort is deployed to use the frameworks suggested by authors of the present century.[47]

---

46. Due to their actuality, exception is made for Viany Samuel and Chris Sugden's *Mission as Transformation*; Jan A. B Jongeneel's *Philosophy, Science and Theology of Mission in the 19th and 20th Centuries*; David Bosch's *Transforming Mission*; Arthur F. Glasser and Donald A. McGavran's *Contemporary Theologies of Mission*; John Stott's *Christian Mission in the Modern World*.

47. One may quickly refer to Andrew Kirk, *What Is Mission?*; James E. Engel and William A. Dyrness, *Changing the Mind*; Scott Moreau, *Evangelical Dictionary*; Andreas J. Kostenberger and Peter T. O'Brien, *Salvation*; Samuel Escobar, *New Global Mission*; Arthur F. Glasser, *Announcing the Kingdom*; Michael Pocock, Gailynn Van Rheenen, and Douglas McConnell, *Changing Face*; Christopher Wright, *Mission of God*; John Corrie (*Dictionary*), Terry Muck and Frances S. Adeney, *Christianity*; Craig Ott, Stephen J. Strauss and Timothy C. Tennent, *Encountering Theology*; Robert Coleman, *Heart of the Gospel*; Stanley H. Skreslet, *Comprehending Mission*; and Scott W. Sundquist, *Understanding Christian Mission*, to name a few.

It is however evident that these productions, though apparently recent as far as their years of publication are considered, there is no doubt that they are fruit of the past centuries. If not due to their authors' education completed or started in the twentieth century, at least due to the fact that their bibliographical sources comprise works produced in the past centuries. Therefore, while reviewing the account on how mission was, is, and should be conceived, taught and executed, reference will be made to either the above selected literature or to any other scholar from the previous centuries if the necessity imposes.

2.3.1 Working Time Frame

Throughout the history, mission theologies have taken various formulations, much of it due to fluctuations in both church and world struggles. From one focus to another, the church of Christ has been entrusted a particular task to address human struggles and expectations. Sometimes, and depending on the context, the answer to these struggles and expectations proved either productive or limitative. In some other stances, church's response ended up by complicating the situation. Reference can be made to the coincidence of mission enterprise and the colonial expansion. Such a historical reality served as an evidence for some people to categorize missionary work of the nineteenth and twentieth centuries as instrument of imperialism.[48] Christian mission found itself in the firing line, being attacked from inside the church as well as outside. Consequently, as authors observe, the church needed a new vision toward a different kind of missionary involvement while keeping the continuity with the best of what mission has been in the past decades and centuries.[49] Thus, there has always been a need for the reconceptualization of Christian mission from one period to another, and from one perspective to another.

Authors have a suggested time frame to depict the developments and changes in theologies of mission. In this century, works listed in the previous section provide some practical schemes of undertaking such a task. The difficulty arises when authors fail to distinguish between existing missiological

---

48. See for instance the change in the name IBMR (from "missionary research" to "mission research") on page 49, note 38.

49. Van Gelder, "Missiology," 19; Bosch, *Transforming Mission,* 1.x

wings (i.e. ecumenical vs evangelical), taking it for granted that a given prominent theology of mission in a period would certainly apply to all missionary contexts. *Assumption* in depicting theologies of mission can be a pitfall of which some researchers become victims. For instance, as one goes through the authors' description of what theology of mission is, the general impression is that theologies of mission crafted concerning one or another part of the Protestantism is assumed to be applicable to all settings.[50]

Another difficulty occurs when authors consciously or unconsciously omit to justify the reasons of the choice of a time frame used to determine the beginning and the end of each period. *Generalization* in depicting theologies of mission can be a pitfall of which some researchers become victims. For instance, authors may set a time frame such as early developments, Protestant beginnings, nineteenth and early twentieth centuries, late twentieth century, and entering the third millennium. However, it might happen that as one goes through the description of these periods, the general impression is that theologies of mission crafted as regards one or another part of the Protestantism become applicable to all settings.[51]

Still there is another difficulty pertaining to the way authors allocate a paradigm only to a given period of time. *Compartmentalization* in depicting theologies of mission can be a pitfall of which some researchers become victims. For instance, in his groundbreaking *Transforming Mission*, David Bosch identifies six paradigms of mission from the New Testament to the last decade of the twentieth century: New Testament, Eastern Orthodox, Roman Catholic, Protestant part 1 and Protestant part 2, and the emerging ecumenical paradigm. Bosch's paradigm models exceed the scope of this study which intends to be a brief survey of mid-nineteenth century to present, corresponding to his fifth paradigm about Protestant part 2 (1800–2000). Unfortunately, while describing this period of Enlightenment and modern era, Bosch doesn't exactly tell how the development of mission theologies has been progressively achieved.

To avoid the aforementioned difficulties of assumption, generalization, and compartmentalization, one would rather find in Craig Van Gelder's

---

50. The case of M. Pocock, Gailynn Van Rheenen, and D. McConnell, *Changing Face*.
51. The case of C. Ott, S. J. Strauss and T. C. Tennent, *Encountering Theology*, xxiv–xxx.

account a clear description of such development.⁵² Other authors have provided an overview of theories and models of Christian mission in the twentieth century from 1910 to 1990.⁵³ Van Gelder's account convers a wider period than these authors.

2.3.2 Craig Van Gelder's Framework

Craig Van Gelder has chaired the Association of Professors of Missions (USA) as its president in 2013. Prior to that, he taught for ten years at Calvin Theological Seminary, USA, before serving as professor of congregational mission at Luther Seminary, St Paul, Minnesota, by 1998. Van Gelder holds a PhD in mission from Southwestern Baptist Theological Seminary, and a PhD in administration in urban affairs from the University of Texas in Arlington, United States. His other books include *Confident Witness – Changing World* (Eerdmans), *The Essence of the Church: A Community Created by the Spirit*, *The Evangelizing Church: A Lutheran Contribution*, *The Ministry of the Missional Church: A Community Led by the Spirit*, *The Missional Church in Context: Helping Congregations Develop Contextual Ministry*, and one of the most recent books he has co-authored with D. Zscheile entitled *The Missional Church in Perspective: Mapping Trends and Shaping the Conversation*. Writing from a Lutheran context, he is among key proponents of the Missional Church Movement. Alan J. Roxborogh describes Van Gelder as one of leading people within the missional church movement who have made available "well-developed tools, processes and resources for innovating and cultivating missional church" so that the movement stays alive.⁵⁴

While discussing the place of missional church conversation in the corpus of missiological development, Craig Van Gelder sketches his account through a five-period scheme starting with the nineteenth century, the so-called great century of missionary enterprise.⁵⁵ He states, from one period to another, while demarcating it from the previous, how key missiological concepts have come to the existence as various ways to determine the nature of the theology of mission across centuries. The first phase (1811–1910)

---

52. Van Gelder, "Missiology."
53. Yates, *Christian Mission*; Snyder, "MI 750 Theories"; Skreslet, "Missiology."
54. Roxborogh, "Missional Church."
55. Van Gelder, "Missiology," 12–26.

focused on "missions" and promoted a missiology for foreign missions. The second phase (1910–1950) tended to emphasize "church and missions" leading to a missiology of foreign missions. The third phase (1950–1975) was marked by the emphasis on "church and mission" as a missiology of mission versus missions was developed. The fourth phase (1975–1995) witnessed both "convergence and divergence" between ecumenicals and evangelicals, and this period was marked by a quest for mission theologies to match the reconception of the world church. The final and ongoing phase (1995 to present) inaugurates the conversation on "missional church," a way to reconnect missiology and ecclesiology.

Though Van Gelder's time frame seems more justifiable for our research, the difficulty one could face while going through his description relates to the reason for the choice of the beginning and the end of each period, and which specific events may have triggered such delimitation. As far as this study is concerned, such a gap needs to be filled. In the process, effort is made to get involved other scholars and integrate key insights of these mission theologies.

As one can easily observe, that while the schematic table 2.4 sheds some light on the understanding of historical developments of theologies of mission across decades and centuries, still more details need to be provided as to clarify the components of a theology of mission. Van Gelder's work doesn't provide much details for each phase and for each wings (ecumenical or evangelical) on "What, Who, Where and How"[56] or "How, Wherefore, Whence, Whiter, Why, What."[57]

---

56. Kritzinger et al., *On Being Witnesses*. Through these questions authors discuss the goal and content of mission (*what*), the church and the missionary (*who*), the context of mission (*where*), and strategies and models (*how*).

57. Anderson, *Theology*.

Table 2.4 Key Features of Missiology Development

Phase	Period	World and missions context / events	Nature of the theology of mission	Personalia (year of publication)
1	1811–1910	**Missions** -Colonial expansion and great century of missions -Previous ecumenical conferences for foreign missions (1860, 1888, 1900)	**A missiology *for* foreign missions** -Geographical location of missions -Focus: Winning converts to the faith -Matthew 28:18–20 -Three-selves	-F. D. S. Schleiermacher, 1811 -G. Warneck, 1896 -H. Venn -R. Anderson -J. Nevius -R. Allen -J. R. Mott, 1910
2	1910–1950	**Church and Missions** -Edinburgh 1910 conference -World War I & II -Toward dismantling of colonial system -Impact of IMC '25 -Birth of WCC '48	**A missiology *of* foreign missions** -Focus: Still winning converts to the faith, but missiology focused on church planting, leadership development, anthropology, local cultures -Call for "Partnership in obedience" between *older* and *younger* churches (Whitby '47)	-J. R. Mott, 1910 -*IRM* 1912 -R. Allen -Mission programs/professorships in US seminaries -W. E. Hocking's book 1932 -H. Kraemer's book 1938

3	1950–1975	**Church and Mission** -Post-World War II -Colonial system began to be dismantled -APM '50 in USA -*Missio Dei* at Willingen '52 -Merge of IMC–WCC -Church Growth Movement. -Uppsala '68 and Bangkok '72–73 -Evangelicals' reaction at Berlin '66 and Lausanne '74	**A missiology of mission *versus* missions** -Trinitarian conception of mission connected to kingdom of God *but somehow to* church -Contextualized (and even revolutionary) theologies mostly from Third World and Western secularized/cultural theologies -Mission everywhere *but* social! -Mission *euthanisia* -Ending of mission programs in many denominational seminaries or changing from "mission" to "ecumenism" or "world religions" (*shalom*, humanization)	-R. P. Beaver's APM 1950 -K. Hartenstein -G. F. Vicedom -Radical sense of *missio Dei* '60s to early '70s (*Shalom*) -L. Newbigin's '61 influence on IMC–WCC merge -J. Verkuyl -J. C. Hoekendijk -TEF '58, '72 -J. R. W. Stott -R. Winter
4	1975–1995	**Convergence and divergence** -Call for moratorium -Growing distance between ecumenicals and evangelicals -*Missio Dei* used in both sides -Mission everywhere	**A missiology in search of appropriate mission theologies** and the reconceptualization of the world church -Clear distinction of theologies of mission between ecumenicals and evangelicals (exclusivism, inclusivism, pluralism)	-Lausanne Movement -WCC–CWME affirmation '82 -Millennial Manifesto of AD 2000 in '90s -F. A. Schaeffer -J. A. Scherer '87 -D. Bosch '91
5	1995–present	**Missional church (or missional ecclesiology)** -Missional church conversation -West as mission locus	**Reconnecting missiology and ecclesiology** (*missio Dei*, kingdom of God, and church) -Local congregation "missionary per nature" being the "very context of mission"	-Iguassu 1999 and *missio Dei* -J. Matthey 2001 of CWME and *2 missio Dei* -C. Wright '06 -Cape Town '10

Source: Developed from Craig Van Gelder's "Missiology and the Missional Church in Context."[58]

---

58. Van Gelder, "Missiology," 12–27.

In fact, if theology of mission can be understood simply as "a theological reflection on the *nature* and the *task* of mission,"[59] or as we already defined it in the first chapter (see section 1.7.7) as the biblical and theological justification of mission work, one would expect more than what Van Gelder has briefly sketched. He doesn't clearly elaborate on different aspects that a theology of mission might encompass in terms of *source* and *goal* of mission along with other questions raised by Kritzinger et al. and Gerald Anderson (see above). Nevertheless, while adopting Van Gelder's time frame, the following sections undertake to fill in the gap by explicitly elaborating more on the difference between ecumenical and evangelical conceptions of mission during each phase, if applicable. Along the way, key *personalia*, events or institutions that may have influenced the developments of missiology will be highlighted (see the last column of table 2.4).

2.4 Missiology as a Threefold Scientific Reflection during the Period of 1811–1910

2.4.1 General Context

The modern missionary movement took place in the early years of the nineteenth century,[60] a period described as a great century of missions (K. S. Latourette).[61] This movement reached its peak in the middle of the century. In most cases, missionaries were deployed by organizations outside the denominations. Nevertheless, it is important to observe that these movements were the continuity of prior mission initiatives wholeheartedly undertaken by committed people like William Carey and Hudson Taylor, to name a few. Another well-recognized factor was colonial expansion which, in some areas, paved the road to missionaries, while in others, like the DRC, the

---

59. Ott, Strauss, and Tennett, *Encountering Theology*, xix.

60. Sunquist, Understanding Christian Mission, 86.

61. Kenneth S. Latourette, *History of Christianity*, vii, 1063, observed that during the period between 1815 and 1914 the church responded with vibrant expansion every time modernism attacked its growth. People in the churches were convinced that the gospel was not a treasure to be kept by established churches but a message to be shared with all people and nations. That was the reason he called that period "the great century."

mission enterprise reached the country before colonialism.[62] It was during this century that some lasting theories on mission were formulated by influent mission statesmen like Henry Venn, Rufus Anderson, John Nevius, and Roland Allen. These eminent mission thinkers coined the three-self formula (self-governing, self-supporting, and self-propagating) which is still challenging the church even today. By formulating such a theory, they sought to organize new congregations differently, as to avoid the problem of Western domination over mission fields.[63] So far as the development of a formal discipline of missiology is concerned, the role of the German Friedrich Schleiermacher (1768–1834) can be highlighted. Being influenced by the Moravians,[64] Schleiermacher inserted mission studies as a discipline in the theological curriculum of his University of Berlin in 1811, but within practical theology.

Therefore, it is meaningful to consider 1811 as a starting point when someone plans to trace the historical roots of the development of our discipline.[65] Only thereafter other names will be added into the account. One can mention Charles Breckenridge who was appointed as the professor of "Practical Theology and Missionary Instruction" at Princeton Seminary in the United States in 1836. In Europe, the chair of "Evangelistic Theology" was established in 1867 at Edinburgh University and was assigned to Alexander Duff. At the University of Halle, in Germany, Gustave Warneck was appointed professor of the chair of "Missionary Science" in 1896. The next sections discuss how mission studies were conceived and provided.

It becomes important to observe that Protestant missionary work started in the DRC during this period, in February 1878 through Livingstone

---

62. It was on his way back after meeting the British missionary, David Livingstone, at the Lake Tanganyika (1871) that Henry M. Stanley explored the Congo River from Stanleyville to the mouth of the Congo River at the Atlantic Ocean and spread out news about the richness of the country. This news captured the attention of mission societies. While the first missionaries of Livingstone Inland Mission reached the DRC from Britain in February 1878 followed by those from Baptist Missionary Society in June 1878, King Leopold II hired Stanley from August 1879 to 1884 to build rail road as an important step to land occupation. It is then clear that in the situation of Congo, mission preceded colonialization. For more details see chapter 4 (section 4.4).

63. Van Gelder, "Missiology," 17.

64. Jongeneel, "Philosophy, Science, and Theology," 27.

65. Myklebust, *Study of Missions*; Scherer, "Missiology."

Inland Mission. Not too long after, over twenty other mission societies, coming from England, Sweden and United States followed. They worked when Congo was first a private property of King Leopold II (1879–1885) and when, under international pressure, it became a Belgian colony (1885–1908). Except some details that a further chapter (sections 4.1 to 4.5) will provide on the specific case study of Protestant missionary work in the DRC, the following account on theory, practice, study and teaching of mission paves the way to the understanding of these mission concerns in both global context of mission enterprise and particular situation of Protestant missionary work in the DRC.

2.4.2 Theory and Practice of Mission: A Missiology *for* Foreign Missions

As Van Gelder observes, the focus during this period was on foreign missions.[66] Missionaries ought to cross geographical boundaries far from their home countries. They were sent with a clear mandate of winning converts to the Christian faith. They had to announce the gospel to all nations (cf. Mark 16:15) in order to make disciples to these lost nations (cf. Matt 28:18–20). Through numerous mission agencies, called "home mission boards," hundreds of missionaries were strategically deployed and millions of funds from Britain, North America, France and Germany were poured to support the cause.[67] The general observation is that, even when referring back to the previous century of William Carey, mission movement flowed out of spiritual revival; institutions came after renewal.[68] However, during the late nineteenth century, classic mission theories emerged and were developed on the necessity of planting and establishing indigenous churches which could self-govern, self-support and self-propagate. Such a theory of mission could simply lead to a corresponding practice of mission which emphasizes preaching and church planting. It is then important to observe that social preoccupations didn't formally make the agenda of much of mission activities.

The key phrase one would use to describe the missionary climate in the beginning of this period is *spirit of unity*. As Sundquist records, "Protestant

---

66. Van Gelder, "Missiology," 17.
67. Sundquist, *Understanding Christian Mission*, 86.
68. Sundquist, *Understanding Christian Mission*.

missionary ideas were grounded in cooperation and unity"[69] since the first missionary societies, English Baptist Missionary (1792), the Missionary Society (1795), and the Netherlands Missionary Society (1797). William Carey wanted even to convey a meeting of all missionaries in South Africa in 1810 and 1812. Sundquist observes that until mid-1830s cooperation and unity were part of missionary life before disappearing when denominational mission societies began to multiply.[70] The search for denominational identity became an obstacle to missionary unity which, fortunately, was not definitively eradicated. However, the preoccupation for unity was not totally eradicated. The General Conference of Foreign Missions held in Liverpool, England, in March 1860 and was attended by mission boards and supporters, church leaders and missionaries. The account of this gathering is more expressive than any comment:

> The meetings of the Conference occupied four days; a great amount and variety of information were contributed by men who had been labouring in all parts of the world; the discussions on the various plans adopted and experiences detailed were frank and free; and the spirit of brotherly regard and mutual cooperation exhibited on every side was very striking. The deliberations of the Conference were purely consultative. The object aimed at was to gather information and to compare experience. No attempt was made to judge the methods of societies or individuals; or to press the acceptance of common conclusions. Every missionary and every society was left perfectly free to use in their own way the facts and conclusions presented by their brethren. The subjects discussed ranged over the entire field of missionary labour. It was observed, with special interest, that there was a wonderful similarity in the plans carried out, in the methods by which agencies were adapted to their different spheres of effort, and in the results which all these societies were gathering in. It was seen that with "differences of administration" there was the one Spirit; and that the same

---

69. Ibid., 114.
70. Ibid., 115.

Lord over all had been rich in blessing all His faithful servants. The record of these deliberations was heartily welcomed on all sides, and was extensively circulated.[71]

Another ecumenical meeting held in London in October 1878 and consigned the following insightful and conveying items in its agenda:

> Questions which are pressed to the front by the present condition of the various foreign missions, and a complete understanding of which would tend to make those missions more efficient. A careful review (for instance) of the position which has been attained, of the agencies now employed, of the resources available, and of the direction in which plans and results are moving – would furnish an excellent starting point for these new deliberations. The number, character, and growth of the Native churches already gathered, the number, training, and strength of the Native Pastors and Missionaries available; and the degree to which, with a moderate amount of guidance from English Missionaries, these new Christian communities may be expected to run alone, and so Christianity be firmly planted in foreign lands with a prospect of continuance, would furnish other topics of useful discussion. It might be well, also, more or less to review the position and needs of general Education, of Christian Literature, and Bible translation, with other details of work, as well as the home methods of raising funds and securing economical administration.[72]

Both conferences held in Liverpool (1860) and London (1878) where ecumenical in the sense that they brought together mission boards, church representatives, and missionaries from different organizations and denominations. The shared concern was the need of exchanging experiences and information on how to better carry on the work of mission among non-Christians. In the process, they were also concerned about the quality of missionaries, mission activities to incorporate in their mainly role of preaching the gospel for the salvation of people of all nations, and the future of

---

71. Proceedings of General Conference, 1–2.
72. Ibid., 2–4.

churches planted on the mission field. It is also worth noting that there were no uniformed methods and strategies, but that at the surprise of participants, some similar methods and strategies were noticed.

It was during one of the sessions of the London meeting held on 22 October 1878, while speaking of "Discovery and Christian Missions in South Africa," that Thomas Fowell Baxton announced the following news about Congo as a new mission field under exploration:

> We cannot regard our recent discoveries in Central Africa without comparing the knowledge to which they have advanced us, with the state of knowledge which prevailed at the beginning of the century . . . Again, we must not forget that another attempt is being made to reach the interior from the West Coast. The Baptist Missionary Society has chosen the Congo as their route towards the interior, and have already taken steps towards obtaining the best information.[73]

On 9–19 June 1888, the Centenary Conference on Protestant Missions of the World was held in London and participants coined the concept of *comity*. The aim of comity was to facilitate cooperation among denominations, being a "gentleman's agreement whereby one mission agreed not to intrude in the territory or interfere in the work of another mission in the same country."[74] To maintain the spirit of the conference, a World Missionary Committee was installed. Therefore, with the adoption of comity agreement, the practice of sharing major urban areas, but dividing up the work in more rural areas, became a standard way of operating among mission societies.[75] It was the same in the DR Congo.

Early in the beginning of the twentieth century, another missionary gathering, Ecumenical Conference on Foreign Missions took place in New York, from 21 April to 1 May 1900. The conference set the objective of "providing a forum for missionaries to discuss topics including geographical surveys of missionary work, medicine, education, evangelism, literature, and women's

---

73. Ibid., 38.
74. Kane, *Understanding Christian Missions*, 156.
75. Sundquist, *Understanding Christian Mission*, 115.

work."[76] The following statement of the historical background of the conference demonstrated the problems that churches and mission boards faced:

> The Conference developed out of a growing sense that the responsibility for grappling with the problems related to *the world's evangelization should not be placed wholly upon administrative boards and missionaries but on the Church as a whole.* Thus, the Conference sought to amass the "united thought of Christendom" by convening thoughtful Christian men and women from all over the world who had been engaged in the study of such problems, so that they might relate their findings to the worldwide missionary movement.[77]

From the above records, few challenges to mission at a time can be featured: mission used to be affair of the mission board and missionaries; the church (local congregation) as a whole was not really involved; the situation had become a research preoccupation for some interested people, or scholars; the need for unity and cooperation in work and information was expressed. Regardless these challenges, the state of Protestant missionary work was fruitful. The appendix to the London Conference of 1878 comprised an overall report entitled "The Wide Work and Great Claims of Modern Protestant Missions: Prepared at the Suggestion of the Conference." The very first sentence of the report demonstrates the importance of that document: "Rarely has there been presented to the Church of Christ an opportunity of learning the progress and extent of Christian work in the world."[78] This 7-page report provides a thorough account of the missionary activities, experiences and results, which include the ministry of preaching the gospel to non-Christians as the priority of priorities, literary work and education of both men and women, Bible translation with a long list of versions of either Old Testament or New Testament being available in several local languages, humanitarian services rendered to natives in terms of fight against slavery, medical work, etc. It has been also pointed out that not all

---

76. MRL 12.
77. Ibid, emphasis added.
78. Proceedings of General Conference, 407.

these activities made the core of the missionary work at the same level as the supreme cause of eternal salvation of natives.

2.4.3 Study and Teaching of Mission: Preparing People *for* Foreign Missions

What is not much talked about in these above-referenced minutes is how studies on mission were provided for missionary purpose. However, in such a context as the one described in the precedent section, the training for mission would likely focus on how to make better preachers of the gospel and brave church planters who will endure the realities of mission enterprise in foreign and non-Christian territories. R. Pearce Beaver points out the fact that missionaries in the eighteen century, even in the first part of the nineteenth century, came to their vocation by way of revivals rather than by way of instruction about missions.[79] It is interesting to note that in the United States, for instance, this revival movement caused some college students at Princeton Seminary to initiate the Society of Inquiry on the Subject of Missions in 1813. In Beaver's account, the society assigned itself the objective of "inquiring into the state of the Heathen, the duty and importance of missionary labors, the best manner of conducting missions, and the most eligible places for their establishment."[80] One can already see in this statement of purpose a missiological curriculum for that time. Beaver contends that these societies of inquiry were found in several locations and then became "the backbone of the [missionary] movement and the resources for those in the undergraduate colleges."[81] That reality certainly paved the way to the appointment of Charles Breckenridge as the first professor of "Practical Theology and Missionary Instruction" in the country based at Princeton Seminary in 1836.

Not all seminary professors were excited for missions. Breckenridge's professorship would last only three years and no successor was provided. The subject disappeared from the curriculum in 1855 and did not return until 1914.[82] Beaver reports of an appeal document which was brought

---

79. Beaver, "American Protestant," 65.
80. Ibid., 67.
81. Ibid.
82. Conn, "Missionary Task."

from Hawaii and published in 1836 contending that twenty out of the twenty-eight missionaries of the mission society which issued the appeal affirmed that sixty-eight seminary professors, college presidents and minister had tried to discourage them from becoming missionaries.[83] The appeal even exhorted seminary professors to all resign their posts and go out as missionaries if they were really serious about the importance of missions.

The teaching of missions in universities or seminaries was not part of the theological corpus. As said earlier, the idea came to be thought of in 1811 when Schleiermacher proposed that mission studies be part of practical theology. As Mark Laing points out, throughout centuries missiology has existed as an appendix which could simply be ignored or dropped anytime from the curriculum if it proved troublesome.[84] Unfortunately Schleiermacher's Western design for theological education was ratified when churches in the West became introverted. The theological curriculum was then exported to the Majority World by missionaries to serve as the required model in theological education and seminaries. As a consequence, ministers most often could go out of theological institutions or seminaries with an introverted vision of the church and its mission.

Myklebust gives the account on different possibilities of the integration of the study of missions (missiology) into the theological corpus through the establishment of courses and professorship in both Europe and the United States. The year 1811 was also significant, not only due to Schleiermacher's curriculum proposal or due to the fact that it was when some college students at Princeton Seminary started to gather around the idea of initiating a Society of Inquiry on the Subject of Missions. According to Myklebust, it was in 1811 that Princeton University set a plan for a Theological Seminary to be "a nursery for missionaries to the heathen."[85] Therefore, the seminary had the responsibility of training and qualifying youth for missionary work. As far as the North American situation is concerned, the Bible School Movement which started in 1880s became the real locus for the training of missionaries, emphasizing home and foreign missions as well as evangelism and Bible.[86]

---

83. Beaver, "American Protestant," 68.
84. Laing, "Missio Dei," 94.
85. Myklebust, *Study of Missions*, vol. 1, 146.
86. Kane, *Understanding Christian Missions*, 160.

Where mission courses were provided and chairs for mission studies were established, lectureships and professorships were usually occupied by former directors of mission societies.[87]

2.5 Missiology as a Threefold Scientific Reflection during the Period of 1910–1950

2.5.1 General Context

Sundquist notes that the relationship of Christian unity and Christian missionary activity constituted one of the theological themes which punctuated the context of missionary enterprise during this period.[88] The turn of the century marked the eve of a new era in mission theory, from the focus on *missions* (full stop) and *church and missions*. As stated in the previous section, the nineteenth century was a great century for mission – missionaries' presence was noticeable in several places in the world, the gospel had been preached and accepted by many, and local congregations were established. Now, two groups have come to coexistence, a missionary group on one side and converted natives on another. On the global non-church side, the world started to be shaken through the process of dismantlement of the colonial system, the crash of international conflicts with two world wars as a result, the rise of communism and secularization, and also the revitalization of the non-Christian religions in the non-Western world.[89]

The Ecumenical Missionary Conference (EMC) which was held in Edinburgh, Scotland, on 14–23 June 1910 inaugurated the transition between the two eras. The quality of participants upgraded the significance of the conference. Its 1,200 delegates were officials who really represented their churches and about 160 mission societies. As Sundquist carefully points out, Edinburgh was the only conference that both modern-day ecumenical

---

87. Ott, Strauss, and Tennent, *Encountering Theology*, xxvi.

88. Sundquist, *Understanding Christian Mission*, 114. Though Sundquist's time frame (1840s–1910) is different from ours (1910–1950), one can see, as demonstrated in the previous section (2.3.2) that what happened during our time frame was actually the continuity of what had begun some decades before.

89. Jongeneel, "Philosophy, Science, and Theology," 29.

and evangelical leaders claim as being their heritage.[90] Also, some of the major themes of mission theories that fuel our mission thinking today derive from that conference. The Student Volunteer Movement is highly associated with this event through its leaders, John R. Mott, and his colleagues whose conviction was to contemplate the evangelization of the world in their generation. This first part of the twentieth century is also marked by the organization of several worldwide mission gatherings as the direct outcome of the Edinburgh Conference. The need for unity, expressed several times and in various manners, came to its realization through Edinburgh. Leaders of the ecumenical movement of the twentieth century came out of the Student Volunteer Movement of the preceding century.[91]

Given the fact that the main concern of the EMC Edinburgh 1910 was the evangelistic mandate of the church, one of the realities that the conveners of Edinburgh faced was whether or not the doctrinal aspects were a necessity and important to be addressed. This reality was so evident that the status of Catholic Latin America being considered as a "mission field" was not an agreed consensus.[92] To accommodate some Anglican participants to the conference, some sensitive matters related to doctrine were simply removed from the agenda. Such a position couldn't but create the disagreement and division between Protestant missions on the concept of "un-reached people." In his non-diplomatic assessment of Edinburgh entitled, "Will we correct the Edinburgh error? Future mission in historical perspective," David Hesselgrave argues that the difficulty that the theory of mission has encountered since the conference is due to the mistake made of not convening it based on common doctrinal agreement. This was a general point of view of many evangelicals.[93]

Three outcomes of the conference deserve our attention for the sake of the present research. The first to be mentioned is the establishment of a Continuation Committee whose role was to ensure the continuity and the

---

90. Sundquist, *Understanding Christian Mission*, 117; see also Rowdon, "Edinburgh 1910," 60.

91. Sundquist, *Understanding Christian Mission*, 116.

92. Ibid., 118.

93. Hesselgrave, "Will We Correct," 125–126; see also Rowdon, "Edinburgh 1910," 66–67.

ongoing influence of the conference. Two main components made the after-conference organization: (1) a *church*-related component (through Life and Work and Faith and Order) and (2) a *missions*-related component (through International Missionary Council). Unlike the previous phase (1811–1910) where everything revolved around *missions*, this second phase (1910–1950) was characterized by the presence of two entities, *church* and *missions*. The problem was raised when the World Council of Church (WCC) came to merge with International Missionary Conference (IMC) in 1961.[94]

Another result of the conference was the foundation of a quarterly journal, *International Review of Missions* (IRM) under the editorship of J. H. Oldham, secretary of the Edinburgh Continuation Committee. The first issue was released in 1912. This journal has been, and is still being, a channel through which debates on the discipline of missiology are discussed. The problem arose when, in 1969, the decision was made to rename the journal by simply removing "s" from "mission(s)" due to the fact that the concept of "mission" had taken another understanding.[95] The third important outcome of the conference was the creation of IMC in 1921 to replace the continuation committee which could not even meet before 1928 due to World War I. As already said, the situation exploded when IMC was transformed into the Division of World Evangelization Commission of WCC in 1961. The problem was more than that of daughter (WCC or church) becoming mother; and mother (IMC or missions) becoming daughter.[96] The real problem was felt through its implication on the mission field. As in the case of the DRC,

---

94. Evangelicals would prefer the verb "affiliate" rather than "merge." Harold H. Rowdon, "Edinburgh 1910," 58, demonstrates that IMC grew indirectly out of Edinburgh Conference. Therefore, the incident of 1961 was that IMC affiliated into WCC, but it didn't merge with WCC which was another institution established later in 1948. Also David J. Hesselgrave, "Will We Correct." Some authors (i.e. Max Warren, "Fusion of IMC"; Sundquist, *Understanding Christian Mission*) use "integrate" which still shows that IMC was a separate entity. He says, ". . . [B]ut not until 1961 was the International Missionary Council fully integrated into the larger ecumenical movement of the WCC" (*Understanding Christian Mission*, 122). See also the reaction and personal reflection of Lesslie Newbigin, "Missionary Dimension," 240–255, who served as director of both IMC and CWM.

95. The rationale of the decision of deleting "s" from "missions" on the title of the journal was provided in the editorial page of *International Review of Mission* 58, no. 230 (April 1969): 141. The key reason was to accommodate and comfort Third World readers from Asia, Africa, and Latin America who were frustrated by some negative aspects of the mission enterprise.

96. Van Gelder, "Missiology," 21.

this situation produced a dichotomy between the missions belonging to the missionaries and the church which was designed by missionaries for nationals who inherited the church that they didn't really understand.[97]

Therefore, the relatedness between the above-described general context and the Protestant missionary work in the DRC during this period becomes obvious. Alfred Stonelake who served in the DRC as a missionary with the Baptist Missionary Society in 1900 states: "In 1911 a local Continuation Committee was formed, in order that Congo might linked up with the World Missionary Conference, Edinburgh 1910."[98] Several years later, Herbert Smith, another missionary but with Disciples of Christ Missions, recalled Stonelake's remark on the common feeling among missionaries: "In 1911 Bolenge was host to the General Conference of Protestant Missionaries. The Congo Continuation Committee was then formed, the first field continuation committee to be organized anywhere on the pattern set by the 1910 Edinburgh Conference and its World Continuation Committee."[99] By the end of 1948, thirty National Christian Councils were members of the IMC. Only the DRC and South Africa were from Africa (see list in *IRM*, January 1949). J. R. Mott had already visited Congo in 1934 where he attended a series of missionary conferences. Stonelake reports that Mott's observations and recommendations caused missionaries to revise their theories and strategies of mission.[100] Except specific details that a further chapter (see sections 4.2 to 4.5) will provide on the Protestant missionary work in the DRC, the following account on theory, practice, study and teaching of mission may certainly pave the way of capturing the particular situation of the discipline of missiology in the DRC.

2.5.2 Theory and Practice of Mission: A Missiology *of* Foreign Missions

So far as the theory of mission is concerned, the proclamation of the gospel to save souls was at the core of the conviction. It was actually a continuation of the spirit of the previous century, "a culmination of what was its success in

---

97. Molo, "Quest," 109.
98. Stonelake, "Missionary Situation," 326.
99. Smith, *Fifty Years in Congo,* 30.
100. Stonelake, *Congo Past and Present,* 66.

foreign missions enterprise."[101] However, as the world situation underwent changes, and with the reality of having church (local congregation on mission field) on one side and missions on the other, the way of thinking and doing mission was equally affected. If in the previous phase the missiology was *for* foreign missions, now it becomes a missiology *of* foreign missions.[102] Though one couldn't easily seize the nuance between "for" and "of" in Van Gelder's own wordings, it becomes apparent that the reality of mission is no longer that of thinking about foreign missions as activities to be undertaken while crossing geographical frontiers. In addition, the presence of a local native church presumes that nationals become responsible of the destiny of their faith and local identity.

During this period, several gatherings took place as the continuity of Edinburgh Conference, either through IMC (1928 in Jerusalem, 1938 in Madras, Tambaram, 1947 in Whitby) or through other two commissions (Life and Work, and Faith and Order) which merged in 1948 to form WCC. The meetings of IMC served as a platform of evaluating existing concepts and practices about missions. They also served as a laboratory to elaborate and promote new concepts and practices about missions. The change in the world context brought the change in the missiological articulations. Van Gelder notes that the nationalism movements within many countries, and the eventual decolonization of these countries, increased attention on indigenous churches.[103] The new jargon includes *older* churches to designate the churches in the West, and *younger* churches to describe churches on the mission field. At IMC conference held at Whitby, Canada, in 1947, the common phrase was "Partnership in Obedience" demonstrating how two entities *church* and *missions* should now cohabitate and relate.

The constitution of WCC in 1948 came to reinforce the institutionalization of national churches and the empowerment of local leadership. Each country was encouraged to set up a National Christian Council, a kind of federation of churches whose leadership had to be entrusted to nationals. In many places, this new situation inaugurated an era of suspicion, and in worst cases, of confrontation. At stake was actually the new comprehension

---

101. Van Gelder, "Missiology," 18.
102. Ibid., 19.
103. Ibid.

of "church" and "mission." Ecclesiology and missiology had to be redefined. It is important to note that the situation in the DRC preceded this general consensus. The Constitution of the Congo Protestant Council contained already the mention "Native National Church" and "Church of Christ in Congo" before 1948.[104]

The focus of the newly emerging discipline of missiology was articulated around special themes such as church planting, leadership development, anthropology, and local cultures.[105] Regardless the particular position held by various streams of thinkers, missiology [as a reflection on missionary work] continued to focus primarily on foreign missions. In strictly academic setting, the term "missiology" begun to lose attention of many scholars and academic institutions to the expenses of "ecumenism" or "world religions."[106] This situation was also polluted by a report produced under the editorship of Harvard philosophy professor William Ernest Hocking in 1932 entitled *Rethinking Missions: A Laymen's Inquiry after One Hundred Years*.[107] The recommendations of the report brought a new perspective and orientation of mission – the missionary should "be willing to give largely without any preaching, to cooperate wholeheartedly with non-Christian agencies for social improvement."[108]

The basis for Hocking's report was that there is continuity between the Christian faith and other faiths. Simply put, non-Christian faiths share the same values with the Christian faith, both being enlightened by the same Creator. This continuity revokes any attempt to convince people of

---

104. Due to the visit and recommendation of Dr John R. Mott in 1934 conferences of the Congo Protestant Council (CPC), the phrase "Native Christian Church" became officially "Church of Christ in Congo" in 1942. When an amendment was made to the constitution of the CPC to change the article 2, the amendment statement was: "The words, Church of Christ in Congo without quotation marks be substituted for the words Native Christian Church." Although the name "Church of Christ in Congo" was introduced in 1934, the year 1942 is when this new name was officially inserted into the constitution, the year 1942 being its official birthday (see the Preamble to the Constitution of the Church of Christ in Congo of 1979).

105. Sundquist, *Understanding Christian Mission*, 19.

106. Ibid.

107. This report was initiated by seven North American mission boards and financed by John D. Rockefeller, but focused only on missionary work done in India, Burma, China, and Japan.

108. Hocking, *Rethinking Missions*, 326.

other faiths to join the Christian faith. Christian mission has to be done without preaching the gospel, a sign of proselytism. Instead, it should be done as means of promoting human well-being through free social actions. Therefore, the missionary "will look forward, not to the destruction of these [non-Christian] religions, but to their continued coexistence with Christianity, each stimulating the other in growth toward the ultimate goal, unity in the completest religious truth."[109] Two more books were published during this period, holding similar points of view.[110] While Baker suggested a culture-centered approach with the cross-fertilization of cultures as the objective of the missionary enterprise, White submitted that the service of man is the regulative aim of Christian missions, but done through witness and friendship.

This new missiology was a challenge for IMC. In preparation of the IMC meeting scheduled for 1938 in Tambaram, India, the Dutch theologian Hendrik Kraemer, former missionary in India, was commissioned to conduct a study on *The Christian Message in a Non-Christian World*. Kraemer's work based the reasoning on biblical realism, stating that "God is God and that if he is God, his Will is the Ground of all that is."[111] For him, all non-Christian religions, philosophies, and worldviews are the various limited efforts of man to apprehend the totality of existence, whereas the Christian revelation remains hidden except to the eyes of faith.[112] As the outcome of Kraemer's research, the IMC meeting issued a statement on "the faith by which the church lives" in non-compromising way: "We believe that Christ is the way for all, that he alone is adequate for the world's need . . . We are bold enough to call men out from them [other religions] to the feet of Christ. We do so because we believe that in him alone is the full salvation which man needs."[113]

By the end of this period, the unity promoted by Edinburgh 1910 found itself broken. Bipolarization of missiological discourse became evident between ecumenicals and evangelicals. One could even speak of

---

109. Ibid., 44.
110. Baker, *Christian Missions*; White, *Theology*.
111. Kraemer, *Christian Message*, 68.
112. Ibid., 113.
113. The Authority of Faith, 200.

multi-polarization due to the fact that even within each of these two streams, there were various sub-streams. This eventuality became evident during the next phase since 1950.[114]

2.5.3 Study and Teaching of Mission: Preparing People *for* Foreign Missions

Though in the late twentieth century many changes occurred, as already said previously, the discipline of missiology prospered. Surprisingly enough, as Van Gelder notes, "the theological academy was just beginning to expand courses [in mission studies], as well as the number of teaching positions for the newly emerging discipline of missiology."[115] The majority of theological schools offered at least some courses in missions and many of them created at least one chair in the field of missions related to the teaching of these course. However, this golden period was hindered and shorten by the "demise of colonialism, the tragedy of World War II, the rise of global communism, and forces of secularization."[116] This discussion is expanded in the next chapter (see 3.5).

2.6 Missiology as a Threefold Scientific Reflection during the Period of 1950–1975

2.6.1 General Context

The end of the previous phase concluded with sadness, not only for the discipline of missiology per se, but in regard to the entire global environment with consequences on Christian approach, attitude and placement vis-à-vis the non-Christian world. Following World War II colonial systems began

---

114. Jacques Matthey ("Missiology," 429–430) recognizes that there are at least two understandings of the conception of *missio Dei* within the WCC. Arthur P. Johnston (*Battle for World Evangelism*, 18, 302–303) criticizes John Stott (who is known as evangelical) for having accepted social engagement as one aspect of Christian mission. Peter Beyerhaus (evangelical himself, cited in Bosch, *Scope of Mission*, 30) identifies six distinguishable evangelical groupings: (1) New Evangelicals, the largest (Billy Graham), (2) Separatist fundamentalists (International Council of Christian Churches), (3) Confessional Evangelicals (Peter Beyerhaus), (4) Pentecostal and Charismatic Movements, (5) Radical Evangelicals (emerged from Lausanne Congress on World Evangelization in 1974, Samuel Escobar, René Padilla, Orlando Costas, Mennonites), (6) Ecumenical Evangelicals (Festo Kivengere).

115. Van Gelder, "Missiology," 18.
116. Ott, Strauss, and Tennent, *Encountering Theology*, xxvi.

to collapse and many countries gained political independence. In Africa, at least thirty-two countries became independent in 1960s. If there was good or bad news of independence (depending on one person or another), actual sad news of the assassination of the president of the United States, John F. Kennedy, followed by that of Malcolm X and Martin Luther King Jr., came to worsen the polluted world environment. The Vietnam War and the Cold War joined the list. Sundquist is right to observe that if "the 1950s was the lull before the storm; the 1960s was the storm."[117] Speaking in 1972, about "the emergence of a missionary-minded church in Nigeria," Ian M. Hay who had served there for thirteen years alerted his generation: "The old colonial days are long gone; those "winds of change" of 1960 have reached hurricane velocity now! . . . Disaster awaits those missions and individual missionaries who either will not or cannot adapt."[118]

This lull, storm and hurricane which occurred in the world strongly affected not only the future of the discipline of missiology, but also that of the work of foreign missions. In North America, for instance, the initiative of R. Pierce Beaver to form the Association of Professors of Missions (APM) in 1950 inaugurated a new era for our academic discipline. The newly installed association had to address the changes which emerged in the landscape of both world mission engagement and theological discourses. On one side, the question was whether or not the mission engagement should still be described in terms of "foreign missions" with the priority of converting souls. On the other side, the preoccupation was whether or not the study of mission was still relevant to be promoted in academia.

Due to their contribution to the overall missiological environment, influential figures emerged during this period. Karl Hartenstein is known for being the first person to relate the new concept of *missio Dei* to what was discussed at Willingen in 1952 as a Trinitarian understanding of mission. As Engelsviken demonstrates, none of the conference documents contained the term *missio Dei* as such until when Hartenstein presented his report of Willingen meeting.[119] Another figure is Lesslie Newbigin who served as the secretary of IMC (1959–1961) when it became a part of WCC in 1961.

---

117. Sundquist, *Understanding Christian Mission*, 132.
118. Hay, "Emergence," 195.
119. Engelsviken, "Missio Dei," 482.

He also served as director of the newly Division of World Mission and Evangelism from 1961 to 1965.[120] The incident paved the way to the bipolarization of world mission theories, opposing evangelicals against ecumenicals or vice versa. His writings on mission being of the essence of the church drawn from his discovery of a new cultural post-Christian environment of West influenced the theological reflection about the church and its mission. With their Church Growth Movement, the American, Donald McGavran, and his colleagues and disciples, brought hope to the evangelical perspective of mission. Peter Beyerhaus and John Stott are among important figures in this period due to their evangelical voices against ecumenical theories of mission. Given their published works and theological reflections, many other influential scholars can be added to the list, Johannes Verkuyl, Johannes C. Hoekendijk, and Ralph Winter, to name a few. Thanks to the Theological Education Fund initiated by IMC in 1958 to raise the level of theological education in the Third World, some figures from the Global South enjoyed advanced education which allowed them to raise their voices, either through contextualized theologies or through quest for moratorium.[121] These figures include John Gatu who pleaded for moratorium on missionaries[122] and Byang Kato who can be seen as the promoter of African evangelicalism.

As far as the DRC is concerned, one could see the immediate connection of how the global trends influenced the life of Protestant missions and church in the country.[123] Besides the political independence acquired in 1960 with the direct implication of expulsion of missionaries and the transfer of authority to nationals, this period witnessed the establishment of the first theological institution at tertiary level. It was during this period that the first president of the CCC, made the following strong and revelatory statement which was published in *IRM*:

---

120. Fey, *History*, xiv.
121. Hesselgrave, "Will We Correct," 126.
122. Robert Reese ("John Gatu," 245) recognizes that John Gatu's moratorium on foreign missionaries and funds in 1971 provoked a debate about mission that continues to have incidence on mission theory and practice even today.
123. It is however interesting to note with J. R. Mott that "the missionary program in Congo has seemingly failed to produce and adequate native leadership and worldwide renown men" (Stonelake, *Congo Past and Present*, 79).

It is quite some time now since the *International Review of Missions* became the *International Review of Mission*. The change in thinking revealed in this change in name characterizes also some of the thinking of the Church of Christ in Zaire (Protestant church), for since 1969 Protestant **missions** have ceased to exist in Zaire. At the General Assembly of the former Congo Protestant Council in that year, Zairian churchmen decided that after almost a century of missionary endeavour in their country, missions as institutions no longer had any reason to exist, and the Church in Zaire had to assume its responsibilities for the true **mission** of the Church to evangelize the Zairian people.[124]

Therefore the account below at the global level on the theory, practice and teaching of mission will undoubtedly shed light on forthcoming discussion about the development of missiology and missiological education in the DRC.

2.6.2 Theory and Practice of Mission: A Missiology of Mission *versus* Missions

Amidst the climate of uncertainty described above, the meeting of IMC at Willingen in 1952 was determinant. It is important to remember that IMC was constituted of members who finally underwent separation in 1961 due to its merger with, or integration to, WCC. Thus far, in 1952, both "ecumenicals" and "evangelicals" were part of IMC. This meeting was an enlarged conference which was attended even by Pentecostal leaders.

After the disaster caused by World War II and the dismantlement of the colonial system, the church had to provide a clear definition of its nature and mission in the world. The meeting of IMC in 1952 was critical and determinant for such an expectation. The conception of a Trinitarian understanding of mission was the major outcome of the meeting of the IMC at Willingen. As Van Gelder observes, this new understanding of mission provided a framework for reconceiving the nature of Christian mission with direct implication to the study of mission (missiology).[125] It also inaugurated

---

124. Bokeleale, "From Missions to Mission," 433.
125. Van Gelder, "Missiology," 21.

a shift from traditional Christ-centered mission (foreign missions) to a triune God-centered mission (mission everywhere). This movement from Christology to triune God doesn't go without consequences. While the first emphasizes the urgency of participating in the fulfilment of the Great Commission, the second perceives a Trinitarian God involved in mission in the world. While the first understanding of mission puts the church on a pedestal as an institution which conceives, plans, organizes and executes missionary works, the second contends that mission is God's mission – he is involved in mission in the world in which the church is invited to participate.

Although the word *missio Dei* was not directly used during the Willingen meeting in 1952 as Tormod Engelsviken ably points out, it actually became an official theological term to describe the new understanding of mission in both ecumenical and evangelical streams.[126] Nevertheless, as the existing massive literature from both sides reveal[127] the implications of using *missio Dei* are not the same in both streams as far as mission theory, practice and teaching are concerned. There are two ways of understanding *missio Dei*. The first is creation focused, a generalized way of understanding God's work in the world. It contends that *missio Dei* is the broader agency of God in relation to all creation and God's continuing care of that creation, using any organization, including secular ones, to provide *shalom* and humanization. The second is redemption focused, a specialized way of understanding God's work in the world. It states that *missio Dei* is God's work of redemption with the church being the primary channel through which God works in the world.[128] While the majority of Willingen participants supported the redemption point of view, the emerging post-Willingen was mostly creation focus. J. C. Hoekendijk is known as the spokesman of such a new focus. For him, the church needed to give up its life for the sake of the world.[129] Ecclesiology was no longer connected to missiology of *missio Dei*.

Subsequently, on the WCC side, the concept of *missio Dei* underwent an evolution to the point of becoming a revolution. From the Augustine perspective of the triune God lately echoed by Karl Barth, the new resurgence

---

126. Engelsviken, "Missio Dei," 482.
127. For instance, Matthey, "God's Mission Today," 581; Laing, "Missio Dei," 95–97.
128. Van Gelder and Zscheile, *Missional Church*.
129. Hoekendijk, *Church Inside Out*.

of the term in the realm of Willingen meeting resulted in radicalization. The concept suggests that the mission "is not just the conversion of the individual, nor just obedience to the word of the Lord, nor just the obligation to gather the church; it is the taking part in the sending of the Son, the *missio Dei*, with the holistic aim of establishing Christ's rule over all redeemed creation." The radicalization came when at Bangkok in 1972–1973, the concept on *missio Dei* turned to a strong position against the church.

On the evangelical side, four conferences served as platforms of discussion: The Wheaton Congress on the Church's World-Wide Mission (1966), the Berlin World Congress of Evangelism (1966), Green Lake (1971), and Lausanne (1974). While the first two conferences stressed evangelism and world mission, there was lack of sound theological rationale on the role of local church in missions.[130] At the Green Lake convention in 1971 the issue of the relationship between missions and local (home) churches in the United States, and between missions and national (receiving) churches on the mission field, were essential to the agenda. According to J. F. Shepherd, the attention was primarily on "the form of the mission organization or society in its relationship to sending and receiving churches."[131] Participants bitterly recalled that through history, churches produced missions and missions have produced churches, but unfortunately their success produced tensions.[132] They then discussed the role of church and came up with the equation "mission-church-mission" stressing the importance of the church. However, even there, the issue was more addressed through a functional perspective than through sound theological reflection.[133]

Harvie Conn observes that even at Green Lake 1971, "the activism of evangelical mission thinking continued to present the picture of 'church without theology' and a 'mission without theology.'"[134] In 1974, the World Evangelical Alliance (WEA) created six commissions including

---

130. Henry and Mooneyham, *One Race*; Lindsell, *Church's Worldwide Mission*.

131. Shepherd, "Is the Church Really Necessary?," 20–21.

132. Gerber, *Missions*, 9.

133. Though the gathering stressed on the importance of church, the definition of church was more functional than theological. At Green Lake, participants identified nine different ways in which the word church is commonly used (Shepherd, "Is the Church Really Necessary?" 20–21).

134. Conn quoted in Camp, "A Survey," 227.

the "Theological Commission" with the function of reflecting on issues of evangelical theology, and the important issues concerning the churches and society in the world. The "Missions Commission" had the function of coordinating activities of evangelism and Christian humanitarianism.[135] One wonders whether Conn's critics couldn't be relativized because evangelicals through WEA were present in world missions for more than a century. Could missions be undertaken without a related theology? Did evangelicals lack a "theology of mission" or a "biblical theology of mission"? This is where one probably needs to clarify the difference between "theology of mission" and "biblical theology of mission." One could rather agree with Forman that the methods mission societies used, the goals they worked for, and the way they treated people, are based on theories and theologies whether fully articulated or not.[136]

With the bell which was rung from WCC side, evangelicals became more attentive to the alert. The new concept of *missio Dei* was not denied, but was now strictly linked with *church* as the tool for God's mission. Also the social implications of *missio Dei* as conceived by WCC circles were yet to be addressed and defined by evangelicals. Thus came the Lausanne International Congress on World Evangelism held in 1974 in Lausanne. It was at this meeting, through the influence of John R. W. Stott, that evangelicals came up with a more structured theology of mission which could also include the social responsibility of the church. They articulated a mission theology which seeks a balance between pure proclamation of the gospel and social engagement of the church. However, in the evangelical perspective, the traditional understanding of foreign missions, reaching out to the world with the saving gospel, remains the priority. *Missio Dei* is understood as a salvation-based concept, and this salvation takes place through the church and its mission. Though being positive expressions of human responsibility, secular activities do not replace mission which is understood as the sole responsibility of

---

135. Leyden, "Unity and Mission," 10. Founded in 1856, the World Evangelical Alliance stressed the full authority of the Bible, the incarnation, the atonement, salvation by faith, and the work of the Holy Spirit, while also putting emphasis on missionary cooperation throughout the world. WEA is said to be a significant precedent for Edinburgh 1910 (Leyden, "Unity and Mission," 10).

136. Forman, "History of Foreign Mission," 69.

the church.[137] This new aspect in evangelicalism is that the proclamation of the gospel must be done from everywhere to everywhere. Mission is not just people from the West bringing the gospel to non-Western territories.

2.6.3 Study and Teaching of Mission: Preparing People for Mission *in* Context

Van Gelder observes that during this period "there was a need to reconceive the discipline [of missiology] beyond preparing persons to participate in foreign missions."[138] One can already see the shift which was about to occur while speaking of mission studies. The implication is that prior to 1950, mission studies aimed at preparing people for foreign missions; only those with a passion for missions to reach out to non-Christians were possible candidates for mission studies. It is even important to mention here that, as already mentioned previously (see section 2.2.1), though being in existence since 1915 in the Catholic milieu, the word *missiology* was not accepted by the majority of Protestant constituents before World War II. The common jargon was either "study of missions" or "school of world missions." Even if the word *missiology* was finally accepted, it was not enough to solve the burning preoccupation about the nature of this discipline. As Sundquist points out, "there was a need to develop a more substantive theological foundation for the discipline."[139] One would wonder if such a project was undertaken, and if so, what the outcomes were. This discussion is expanded in the next chapter (see 3.3).

2.7 Missiology as a Threefold Scientific Reflection during the Period of 1975–1995

2.7.1 General Context

Though not similar in its accent on the dualism between mission and missions that is described above, this phase constitutes a new step in the development of missiological discourse on mission. While the cleavage between "ecumenicals" and "evangelicals" continued to radically grow, it was surprising

---

137. Douglas, *Let the Earth Hear*, 3–9.
138. Van Gelder, "Missiology," 20.
139. Sundquist, *Understanding Christian Mission*, 20.

to see that there was a certain convergence in the general understanding of mission around the dividing concept of *missio Dei* and kingdom.[140] One can find the reason of this convergence in the formation of the American Society of Missiology few years earlier in 1973, which was made up of members from ecumenical, evangelical, and Roman Catholic traditions. The leadership of the association was alternatively assigned to people representing each group. They published together, each author reflecting from their theological perspective, and works were released by both ecumenical-related and either evangelical-related publishers.[141] Scientific journals were also good platforms for this kind of encounter and mutual exchange of ideas.[142] It is noteworthy that, to the best of my knowledge, there is no scholarly journal in missiology or mission studies in the whole Francophone Africa. Some individual university-based journals are mostly interdisciplinary in general without an external peer-review process.

One important note must be made on the contribution of Donald McGavran whose Church Growth Movement served as the key theological and methodological framework on the side of evangelicals. Fuller Theological Seminary, founded in 1947, and its School of World Mission established in 1965, formed the bedrock of this movement. Both proponents and detractors of this movement give the account on it.[143] The movement was generated in the 1960s by Donald McGavran as a philosophy of foreign missions, popularized in the United States by Peter Wagner through his

---

140. Van Gelder, "Missiology," 25.

141. Some books have been published by Orbis Books, a Roman Catholic-related publishing house based in Maryknoll, New York. The recent Edinburgh Series of 28 volumes authored by scholars of all theological strands in the context of Edinburgh 2010 and published by Regnum is an illuminative example. I enjoy a great privilege of hosting 23 volumes in his own electronic library.

142. Case of *Missiology: International Review* published by the American Society of Missiology; *International Bulletin of Missionary* [now *Mission*] *Research* published by Overseas Ministries Study Center; *International Review of Mission*, an outcome of Edinburgh 1910 conference and published by the International Missionary Council (today the Division of World Mission and Evangelism of WCC), *Mission Studies* published by the International Association for Mission Studies, etc. In Africa, only *Missionalia* published by the Southern African Missiological Society is known as an internationally accredited journal of missiology. The *African Evangelical Journal of Theology* (AEJET) published in Kenya by the Scott Theological Seminary also includes some missiological articles.

143. Shenk, *Challenge of Church Growth*; Parsons, "History and Impact."

work at Fuller Seminary in the 1970s, and exploded through the evangelical enthusiasm in the 1980s.

Bosch, who was involved in both ecumenical and evangelical global meetings, and due to his *Transforming Mission* which has become a classic work in the study of theology of mission, deserves to be mentioned here. Though conceived through Western patterns of doing theology and thinking mission, Bosch's book has contributed to the understanding of the development of mission theories and practices from the early beginning of the church to 1990s. As any human work, the book has also faced critiques of different natures,[144] from the fact that not much about African scholarship and authorship was seriously discussed, to the difficulty of applying his Enlightenment-based framework to the reality of world Christianity during the post-Enlightenment period of the twentieth and twenty-first centuries. These critiques are summarized in Nussbaum and Nico Botha.[145] They relate to the book as a whole, to particular topics, and to the need of expanding or supplementing Bosch. One could also question Bosch about his missiological identity, whether his personal perspective was ecumenical or evangelical. Such critiques and many more have caused one of his students, Stan Nussbaum, to publish *A Reader's Guide to Transforming Mission: A Concise, Accessible Companion to David Bosch's Classic Book*. The author discloses the motivation of his book: "That book [Bosch's *Transforming Mission*] has become the most widely used mission textbook in the world, but many readers who never had the privilege of his personal teaching do not find his book as clear and easy to follow as I do."[146] He even concludes his book with seven critiques against his mentor.[147]

As one revisits the history of Christianity during this period, it would not be an exaggeration to observe that the climate of polarization between ecumenicals and evangelicals which started since IMC integrated WCC in 1961 affected the whole Christian body in the world, even in small details. In Africa, the cleavage between ecumenical and evangelical was tangibly felt through the All African Churches Council (AACC) and the Association of

---

144. Thomas, *Classic Texts*; Saayman and Kritzinger, *Mission in Bold Humility*.
145. Nussbaum, *A Reader's Guide*, 140–145; Botha, "Transforming Missiology," 18–31.
146. Nusbaum, *A Reader's Guide*, xv.
147. Ibid., 145–155.

Evangelicals of Africa, (AEA) representing the World Council of Churches (WCC) and the World Evangelical Alliance (WEA) respectively, both holding their continental related headquarters in the same city of Nairobi, Kenya. However, not all people supported the atmosphere of separation because they could find value in both sides. While some would not identify themselves as "ecumenicals" or "evangelicals," others could see themselves as "ecumenical evangelicals" or "evangelical ecumenicals."[148] In the DRC, the same division and tension were felt to the point that the unity of the Congo Protestant Council (CPC), formed in 1902 several years before Edinburgh Conference, was shaken even before or after 1970 when the leadership of the CCC was entrusted to nationals.[149] However, according to the constitution of the CCC, whereas individual denominations have the possibility to adhere to one or another of these associations (WCC/AACC or WEA/AEA), the CCC itself claims to be neutral. In practical, such a neutrality can be questionable due to the real influence of WCC on the CCC as seen throughout the history.

2.7.2 Theory and Practice of Mission: A Missiology for Convergence *and* Divergence

Bosch's view of mission can be used here to depict the theory of mission of this period.[150] Two main points of view have punctuated the debate: universalism (that mission concerns the entire world, not only Israel) and particularism (that mission concerns only Israel). While the universalistic

---

148. Bosch, *Witness to the World*, 29; Van Gelder, "Missiology," 25; Pruitt, "Ecumenism and Theological Convergence," 22. Without identifying himself to which stream he belongs, Bosch (*Witness to the World*, 29) makes an interesting but non-exhaustive list of ecumenicals (Burgess Carr, J. D. Davies, Johannes Hoekendijk, Ludwig Rutti, Richard Shaull, M. M. Thomas, Thomas Wieser, etc.); evangelicals (Peter Beyerhaus, Arthur Johnson, Herbert Kane, Byang Kato, Donald McGavran, Arthur Glasser, Ralph Winter, etc.), and the category of those who would probably refuse to be categorized (Stephen Neill, Lesslie Newbigin, Johannes Verkuyl, Gerhard Rosenkranz, Hans-Werner Gensichen, Gerald Anderson, Bengt Sundkler, Eric Sharpe, Mortimer Arias, John Mbiti, Olav Myklebust, etc.). I would describe myself as "evangelical-ecumenical" (Lygunda, *Missiologie*), holding first the evangelical confession of faith while being opened to learn from ecumenical insights.

149. Molo, "Quest," 144–189; Stenstrom, *Brussels Archives*, 289–292. According to the minutes of Congo Protestant Council of 1963, same factors which hindered a true unity included doctrinal differences, ecclesiastical structures, discipline, ministries, and personal interests.

150. Bosch, *Witness to the World*.

point of view states that the Old Testament perceives the whole world as the mission locus, the particularistic point of view sees mission in the Old Testament as an activity relative to Israel. While the former point of view identifies Jesus's mission with both Israel and Gentiles (cf. Matt 24:14; 26:13; 28:18–20), the latter confines it within the Jewish context (cf. Matt 10:5–6; 15:24–26). Bosch is right to submit that particularism and universalism should not be mutually exclusive.[151] They should rather be inclusive.

Another aspect relates to whether the mission should be centripetal or centrifugal. According to Nussbaum, Bosch was convicted that whereas "Israel's mission was centripetal, attracting other nations to God by modelling life as a society under God's rule, the church's mission is centrifugal, commanding Christians to go out among the nations and spread God's good news and grace everywhere."[152] This point of view, however, would result from a partial approach to the understanding of the whole piece of a coin, and poses the problem of polarizing mission being whether "attracting only" (centripetal mission) or "penetrating only" (centrifugal mission). Now, if one feels that the church's mission is the continuation of Israel's mission, the direct implication would be that foreign missions runs against God's will. The opposite is problematic as well. If the church's mission is seen to not have any relatedness with Israel's mission in the Old Testament, then the mission of being the light of the world and salt of the earth (Matt 5:14–16) departs from the real life of the church in mission. Therefore, one finds Bosch's reasoning reminiscent of both ecumenical and evangelical teachings. As his student attests, Bosch was influenced by both theological streams, being involved in global ecumenical and evangelical meetings.[153]

As usual, conferences held by both streams served as platforms to discuss and articulate the theories of mission and to propose orientations for mission practice. Van Gelder describes this period as a time of "convergence and divergence" during which missiology is in search of appropriate mission theologies.[154] Besides the call for a moratorium on missionary presence and the growing distance between ecumenicals and evangelicals, some common

---

151. Ibid., 66.
152. Nussbaum, *A Reader's Guide*, 5.
153. Ibid., 4.
154. Van Gelder, "Missiology."

words and concepts make the missiological discourse of both sides. *Missio Dei* is used in both sides, though with specific orientations as already discussed (see 2.6.2). The idea of "mission everywhere" is promoted on both sides, again, with some differentiation. For ecumenicals, "everywhere" would apply where mission is the responsibility of any church in any context, but it is not about churches from the West sending missionaries to the non-Western areas. For evangelicals, it implies that any church from any context should deploy missionaries throughout the world. From such a debate come other concepts such as exclusivism, inclusivism and pluralism. While some would argue that Christ alone is the way for salvation (exclusivism), others would contend that God's salvation can be offered through Christ and other means (inclusivism), and still others would insist that God's eternal favours go beyond one religious ideology (pluralism).

2.7.3 Study and Teaching of Mission: Preparing People for Mission *in* Context

The above debate has certainly influenced the study and teaching of mission as each context makes the mission locus. The implication for missiological education becomes clear. For some (exclusivists), the approach will be Christo-centric, focusing on the proclamation of the gospel to people of other faiths in order to convert them to Christian faith. For others (inclusivists), missiological education would provide opportunity to learners to grasp new insights and values from other religions which could lead to God's eternal favours. Still for others (pluralists), missiological education offers to learners an opportunity of gaining knowledge for peaceful cohabitation without attempting to undermine the freedom of others as a way to promote one's own religion or ideology. These orientations can be easily detected through the survey of some contemporary models of missiology in theological education (see the next chapter, section 3.3).

2.8 Missiology as a Threefold Scientific Reflection during the Period of 1995 to Present

2.8.1 General Context

Before describing this phase, it is of utmost importance to observe that Van Gelder's work from which the time frame for this section derives was published in 2007. In 1995, a three-year research project started, undertaken by The Gospel and Our Culture Network from which the first book on missional church, edited by Darrell Guder, was published. The ongoing conversation about missional church then started. Authors drew mostly on the works of Lesslie Newbigin about culture change and how the West needed to be considered as the context for mission.[155] Therefore, "present" in the context of Van Gelder's publication served to designate 2007 or some years later. The problem is, if Van Gelder considers 1995 to 2007 or so as being the period which is characterized by the conversation on missional church, what would that indefinite period mean to us today where our "present" in the context of this study is 2017? Does the conversation on missional church remain the unique preoccupation about the development of the discipline of missiology nowadays? One could also ask, between 1995 and 2007, was the missional church the unique preoccupation? The same question could be raised even for other previous phases. Writing during the same period, C. Neal Johnson observes that "much missiological reflection today [2003] centers around the concept of contextualization."[156] What is the relevance of Van Gelder's categories for us today, nine or ten years after they were published and more than twenty years after the debate was initiated? Is the conversation on missional church which was conceived in and for the particular Western context relevant to us in Africa?

Objectively speaking, the legitimacy of the time frame adopted in this section depends on the response to these pertinent preoccupations. More questions could even be added. For instance, how is the consensus on major missiological events determined? Is it through a given conference or just through a publication? Lesslie Newbigin's concerns, including that of those

---

155. Ibid., 24–25.
156. Johnson, "Toward a Marketplace Missiology" (electronic copy).

who used his work to initiate a conversation on missional church, were specifically in connection with the West (Europe and North America). The main concern was that the West had become the context of mission. One of the direct implications was that the nature and task of local congregations in the West had shifted from being foreign missions-oriented churches to local mission-oriented communities. Therefore, local congregations in the West must see themselves as "missional" churches or congregations. They are missionaries by nature, but their mission is done within their own immediate context of the West where the majority of citizens happen to be post-Christians and where God has sent people from all over the world through migration. If yesterday mission entailed sending out missionaries from the West to foreign and non-Christian countries, today, the mission is the whole local congregation reaching out to their immediate communities. That is being "missional."

If Africans identify themselves with this kind of reasoning, they join the missional church conversation using the same concepts through these aforementioned Western-based assumptions, and they literally apply them to the African context, then the result is clear – churches in Africa should be "missional" congregations which find the locus for mission already here at home without thinking of mission in terms of foreign or global missions. Our Jerusalem – regardless of the existence of Judea, Samaria and the ends of earth – becomes our unique mission locus and we should mobilize our local congregations to concentrate on that mission field. Such a blind-kindness reasoning and attitude of copying and pasting ideas from others cannot be anything but questionable. If churches in the West were engaged in foreign or global missions in the past, and they agree to change their paradigm by focusing on home mission, what have African churches done yesterday in foreign or global missions which causes them today to resign from their God-given global mission? What should "missional" mean for African churches? Is it being missionary by nature for local or global mission? The good news for this kind of debate is that brothers and sisters from the West don't prevent us from conceiving mission in accordance with our realities and biblically based convictions.

These comments suffice to submit that while adopting Van Gelder's time frame, this study doesn't adhere to that specifically Western-based meaning of missional church. However, since one of the major trends in missiological debates includes *missio Dei* and its newly coined adjective *missional* as to continue the debate on the relevance of church in mission, let's consider for now the term "present" as *chronos* (linear period) instead of *kairos* (set time).[157] It is not about 2007, but about the period which started from 1995 to 2007 onwards until today in 2017. Thus, this study considers "present" as the period comprising 2007 when Van Gelder published his work up to until when this study is published (2018). As the research continues, more clarification will emerge. However, instead of "missional church" as used by Van Gelder while categorizing this phase, the concept "missional ecclesiology" is preferable because it encompasses both "theology of Christian church" and "theology of Christian mission." Such a theological formulation which includes these categories aligns with those described in Van Gelder's four previous phases. The concept of "missional church" is a parcel within the whole theological reflection and discourse about missional ecclesiology.

2.8.2 Theory and Practice of Mission: A Missiology *for* Missional Ecclesiology

The question about the theory and the practice of mission during this period has derived from the legacy of Lesslie Newbigin. Much of his contribution resulted from his seminal work entitled *Foolishness to Greeks* (1986) where he raised the question, "Can the West be converted?" Newbigin contended that the West had gathered all the characteristics of the post-Christian situation which prevailed in the pre-Christian non-Western settings. For him, such a new situation required a clear missionary engagement similar to that which prompted Western missionaries who went to non-Western countries. He then argued that the West needed to be perceived as mission locus. In another book, *The Open Secret: An Introduction to the Theology of Mission*, Newbigin provides a thorough discourse on the understanding of mission which emphasizes key concepts such as the mission of the triune God, *missio Dei*, kingdom of God and church. For him, mission is "the proclaiming of

---

157. This researcher adopts Wright's (*Mission of God*, 24) definition of the adjective *missional* as "something that is related to or characterized by mission, or has the qualities, attributes or dynamics of mission." The adjective *missionary* would have double sense of "being entrusted a task or mission, and being sent for a task or mission." In this sense, the mission can be *here* (attracting the world) or *there* (penetrating the world).

the kingdom of the Father, and it concerns the rule of God over all that is and the church is actually the agent of such a mission."[158]

As Van Gelder observes, the ongoing conversation that started in 1995 around the concept of "missional church" makes a clear connection between missiology and ecclesiology.[159] Such a connection was put aside when some influential proponents of *missio Dei* provoked the divorce between mission and church in late 1960s (see 2.6.2). Now, with this reconnection, the local congregation is perceived as missionary per nature being the very context of mission. If in the past the discussion was framed around "church and mission," now the conversation emphasizes "missional church." If the former formulation (church and mission) tended to introduce a dichotomy between church and mission with the temptation of giving precedence to one over the other, the "missional church" formulation leads to a different focus. It perceives the church as being missionary in its very nature. Subsequently, every context is also perceived as a missional context where the mission can be done. Every congregation becomes a missional congregation, called to participate in God's mission within that very context.

While missional ecclesiology as described above sounds logical, I am still concerned about the fact that such a perception of mission overlooks the necessity of crossing geographical frontiers. Much has already been discussed earlier (see 2.8.1). The ongoing conversation on reconnecting church and mission should take into account God's *glocal* mission as it has been amply demonstrated by some authors.[160]

2.8.3 Study and Teaching of Mission: Preparing People for Mission *in* Context

Without doubt, the ongoing conversation on theory and practice of mission has consequently influenced the teaching of mission which in general prepares people for mission in context. As surveyed in the next chapter (3.3), training institutions have struggled to accommodate missiological education in context, moving from "mission studies" to either "intercultural

---

158. Newbigin, *Open Secret*, 121.
159. Van Gelder, "Missiology," 27.
160. Van Engen, "Glocal Church," 15; Engelsviken, "Church," 67.

studies" or "ecumenical studies." This discussion is expanded in the next chapter (see 3.3).

2.9 Some Significant Conclusions

2.9.1 Mission and Missiology: Beyond Mere Practical Perspective

This literature survey on missiology has revealed that throughout various periods the issue of mission has not been only a practical one. It was concomitantly approached as a theoretical and scientific reflection on mission practice. Using different categories of thought, inspired either by the Scripture or by philosophy, mission theorists and practitioners have significantly marked the implementation of God's mission. There has been a variety of mainstreams in mission reflections and practices. Through this survey, one could capture the main two streams: ecumenical and evangelicals. They represent two ways of thinking and doing mission. However, even within a given stream, not all have an agreed single-minded point of view about mission. It is obvious that multi-polarization of views has characterized the theory and practice of mission throughout centuries and across different contexts.

In his treatment of "the goal and purpose of mission," Johannes Verkuyl had discussed the various positions which punctuated the theory of mission in the nineteenth century and the beginning of the twentieth century.[161] One cannot easily understand mission and missiology in any context of Protestant missionary work while ignoring the findings of Verkuyl. According to the author the following goals made the essential of mission engagement:

1. The goal of saving individual souls with its many variations.
2. Ecclesiocentric goals emphasizing church planting (*plantatio ecclesiae*) as the main purpose of mission.
3. The three-self formula which stressed the goal for mission of building up the corporate life of churches (self-governing, self-supporting, and self-propagation).
4. Church growth as the ultimate goal of mission. (McGavran and Fuller Seminary).

---

161. Verkuyl, *Contemporary Missiology*.

5. The goal of forming a Christian society (the Christianizing of society; need to Christianize all people; people must be made Christians) (Gustave Warneck).
6. The goal of the "social gospel" (from the United States as a reaction to the exclusive emphasis of some on individual conversion and of others on the ecclesiocentrism), seeking to bring the kingdom of God into reality in social affairs.
7. The goal of improving the macrostructures (call for mission to join the worldwide cooperative struggle for better social structures and greater human rights) to fight against economic exploitation, political and racial oppression.
8. The kingdom of God as the goal of *missio Dei* (bringing the kingdom of God to expression and restoring his liberating domain of authority). For Verkuyl, that is what God intended for the world to which he has revealed himself in Jesus Christ.[162]

2.9.2 Mission: Its Purpose, Methods and Locus

The debate on missiology has gone along with the goal of God's mission in the world and the ways and means God chooses to achieve this goal. Two major questions arise from the debate: What should be the main purpose of mission and how should it be done? Verkuyl observes that mission methods (or means) have been often perceived through a fourfold division:[163] (1) means of communicating the gospel, (2) means of fulfilling diaconal responsibility, (3) means of establishing fellowship, and (4) means of serving the cause of righteousness and justice.

---

162. Ibid., 197.
163. Ibid., 205.

Table 2.5 Summary of the Debate on Mission Purpose and Methods

	Means of Mission	Activities	Role
1	Proclaiming the gospel of God's kingdom	-Theological education -Bible translation and distribution -Radio, television, and literature -Planning for mission	-Ensure preparation for pastoral and missionary work -Provide translation, distribution and use of the Scripture -Reach through media and literature -Stimulate gospel proclamation through mobilization of God's people
2	While fulfilling diaconal responsibility	-Education -Social-medical services -Other types of services (diaconia) -Church participation in movements for national development	-Prepare people to fight against ignorance -Ensure the close connection between word and deeds in order to liberate the whole person -Include disaster help, refugee help, help for political prisoners, aid to victims of unjust power -Participate in the whole process of development
3	Through fellowship (*koinoia*)	-Fellowship of the Christian congregation and peaceful Christian presence	-Ensure increasing contact and fellowship between Christians and adherents of other religions
4	With the intentional purpose of contributing to justice	-Quest for justice	-Equip and train God's people for the fight for justice

Source: Condensed from Verkuyl's *Contemporary Missiology: An Introduction*.

The above aspects of mission theory (sections 2.9.1 and 2.9.2) are not explicit enough about the mission locus. The question is, where should mission be done? In the context of the present study, the question on "mission field" is meaningful because it allows to check whether or not a given church actually involves in God's glocal mission. While in some periods the mission locus was "over there" (foreign mission), in other periods the mission field was "right here" (home mission). In his biblical theology of the church's mission, Christopher Wright highlighted the fact that the mission field is done from "here" (by attracting others to God) and from "there" (by reaching out through the proclamation of the gospel).[164] Wright's treatment follows the traditional evangelical discourse of mission involvement. The literature survey in this chapter has shown that the current tendency while speaking of "missional church" is to emphasize home mission. However, it is noteworthy that these variations of mission purpose, methods and locus are perceptible through the two main streams of ecumenicalism and evangelicalism.

2.9.3 Ecumenical and Evangelical Differences

The major difference between the two streams relates to hermeneutics, how they approach the Scripture.[165] As Bosch has pointed out, there has been an apparent dualism between eternal and temporal, soul and body, individual and community, religion and culture, evangelization and social involvement, vertical and horizontal, salvation and liberation, proclamation and presence, religious and secular, church and world.[166] One could even speak of evolution and revolution.[167] Ecumenicals start their missiological reflection from the context of suffering, poverty and injustice. They tend to draw their reflections and conclusions from the prophetic declarations of the Old Testament and the ministry of Jesus among the poor. Themes like "God's kingdom," "salvation today," "shalom," "*missio Dei*," etc., don't have the same apparent meaning that one could easily guess. These themes are used to promote social

---

164. Wright, *Mission of God's People*.

165. A good summary of the difference between ecumenicals and evangelicals is provided by Bosch (*Witness to the World*, 35) and H. L. Pretorius et al. (*Reflecting on Mission*, 48–55).

166. Bosch, *Witness to the World*, 35.

167. Kane, *Understanding Christian Missions*, 116–127. Kane finds "evolution" in evangelical understanding of the primary motive for mission. Evangelicals have related it to the Christ's command (Matt 28:19–20). They have also found it in the conviction that, if we do not do mission work, the people who have not heard the gospel will perish eternally. They finally have found the motive for mission in the character of God (*missio Dei*). This evolution has characterized evangelical theology of mission. On the other side, Kane perceives a revolution in the ecumenical theology of mission. According to him, ecumenical theology concerns directly to wrong structures of society: racial discrimination, migratory labour, economic and political exploitation, etc.

liberation, and salvation becomes the liberation of poor and other marginalized people. Evangelicals, on their side, start their discourse from the text, the Scripture, focusing on forgiveness of sin, faith, justification, redemption, etc. It was in 1974 during the world congress on evangelization that, under the influence of people like John Stott, the social aspects officially integrated the evangelical theological discourse. Whereas ecumenicals stress the deed as the best way to mission, evangelicals would prioritize the word, that is, the proclamation of the gospel. Therefore, even if both streams use the same concepts – such as mission, *missio Dei*, missiology, salvation, world, church etc., – their meaning wouldn't be necessary the same.

Although missiological reflection has been classified as being either ecumenical or evangelical, other wings – Roman Catholic, Orthodox, Pentecostal and Charismatic – can relate to these two major streams. This study has been undertaken from an evangelical perspective, but while learning from the positive aspects of the ecumenical focus. As said above, many evangelicals have moved from being purely "spiritual-salvation" radical to more balanced perspective while stressing the inspiration and the authority of the word of God, and valuing the nature and mission of the church in the accomplishment of God's mission. It is then the conviction of this author that the church is the channel through which God's multifaceted wisdom will benefit to people of all nations and social categories (cf. Eph 3:10). The church is a primary agent of God's mission.[168]

2.9.4 Missiological Education as the Missing Link

One of the significant insights for this chapter, even considered as its starting point, was the discovery of "mission education" as a missing link in the common treatment of missiology. Until now, the prevailing definitions of missiology do not highlight the fact that, as a science or discipline, missiology encompasses the educational aspect. If the truth is that people of God perish due to the lack of knowledge (Hos 4:6a), that God can reject someone due to the refusal of God's knowledge (Hos 4:6b), and that people in God's mission should be transformed by the renewal of their mind or intelligence (Rom 12:1, 2), missiological education becomes even pressing need today. This discovery is so important and meaningful that during the history of

---

168. Wright, *Mission of God's People*.

mission and missiology explored in this chapter, people of "knowledge" have been both a blessing and a threat to God's mission. When, due to the extreme human knowledge, the mission underwent hard times, the same way, through knowledge, mission got relief.

One example is the confrontation of 1930s on whether or not mission could be done with proclamation of the gospel inviting people of other faiths to embrace the Christian faith. Another example is the debate about *missio Dei* which occurred since 1952. When, due to the extreme human knowledge, the mission experienced the rejection of "ecclesiology" in missiological discourse at the expense of the world which should set the agenda for mission, valuing secular and non-Christian organizations, through knowledge, the recovery of "missional ecclesiology" has made the mission agenda of these days. There is a need to promote missiological education to prevent people from being confused. For instance, the concept of "missional church" in the ongoing conversation has brought confusion to many African scholars today. The term "missional" has become a *passe-partout* word, most often employed incorrectly by many uninformed users.[169] Without taking into account its main Western source and context of its creation, many African users may not realize its main implication that the setting of a local church in the West makes the context of mission today.

The question is, if that is the case, who is supposed to do mission work in such a new context of West? Western people themselves only or non-Western (in our case African) people also? If both actors (Western and Africans) apply, the term "missional" would have two meanings. On the one hand, applied to Western (doing mission in the West), "missional" would be about "local mission." On the other hand, applied to Africans (going to the West), "missional" would designate "global mission." Therefore, to be faithful and consistent to the concept of *missio Dei*, the adjective "missional" should apply to both local and global mission of the church. As discussed in this chapter, the use of a word can bear various meanings, and education is needed to prevent the church in African and its scholars to always serve

---

169. During the period of data collection for this study, I came across several cases of inappropriate and confusing use of "missional." One example is when a topic for a thesis reads like this: "An analysis of *missional* work of [name] in 1750 in India" or "Mobilization to *missional* involvement in [name of the church]." One could wonder what the term "missional" would mean in these two cases.

as the promoters of the carbon copies of our brothers and sisters of other contexts. This enduring admonitory statement by Alan Tippett would be the best way to conclude this chapter:

> Missiology is not a static thing. It grows. It adapts. It relates to the ever-changing world. Yet in every new situation it must also retain its own internal integration . . . No person can ever know all there is to know about missiology, because it is always an ongoing entity, relating afresh to new form of social, cultural and other kinds of change. This will continue until the end of the age.[170]

The next chapter focuses on the understanding of some important conceptual and philosophical considerations in secular and theological education in order to better brainstorm the nature of the expected missiological education needed to fully address the research problem of the present study.

---

170. Tippett, *Introduction*, xvi.

CHAPTER 3

Conceptual and Philosophical Considerations in Missiological Education

3.1 Introduction

Whereas the preceding chapter explored the trends in missiology as a scientific reflection on Christian mission throughout various periods and theological traditions, this chapter focuses on the educational aspect of missiology. The previous chapter contended that missiological education has not attracted much attention and related literature is not as bourgeoning as that of theory and practice of mission. If one tries to find interconnection between mission education and mission practice, the main questions would be: *To what extent has a* missio Dei *or the lack of it in the whole of theological education influenced missiological education and mission practice? Through which educational and conceptual frameworks has missiological education been offered? To what extent is missiological education and research really serving the churches?* Some aspects of the first question were addressed in the previous chapter, and the remaining aspects along with the two other questions make the essential of investigation in this chapter.

3.2 The Concept of Missiological Education

For some scholars, "missiological education" might not be an appropriate wording while discussing the issue of training people for church ministries. For instance, when the project for this study was presented and discussed at its early stage, suggestions were given to simply replace "missiological education" with "theological education." Therefore, the title of the present study would have been *Transforming Missiology: An Alternative Approach to Theological Education*. The suggestion contended not only that "theological education" is the common wording for the process of preparing people for the church ministries, but also that missiology represents only a small parcel within such a process. As one can observe, the above suggestion raises the whole issue of whether or not missiology can be perceived as an independent or dependent discipline in theological corpus. This section mainly addresses the following two questions: What is "missiological education" and why is it necessary to use such a phrase? How have scholars understood, conceived and offered missiological education?

3.2.1 Understanding Missiological Education

As already stated in chapter 1 (section 1.7.4), the concept of missiological education is preferred to that of theological education due to the main reason of staying focused. While theological education encompasses the traditional academic corpus of biblical theology, systematic theology, historical theology and practical theology, missiological education would simply emphasize the study about mission. For the purpose of this research, missiological education is the process by which the church, through its training institutions, prepares God's people to accomplish God's glocal and holistic mission at the tertiary educational level. It is, however, important to observe that, due to the below discussion, this provisional definition is questionable and susceptible to further readjustment. The question is, what is it that makes something *missiological* education or *missiological* reflection?

Edgar raised the same question while discussing the issue of "the theology of theological education." To conceptualize an education that is *theological*, Edgar observes that scholars and educators would diverge or converge in what makes the focus of such an education. At least six foci determine what people would emphasize while defining the essence of a given education, namely content, purpose, method, ethos, context and people. Applied to the education that is *missiological*, these features become clear criteria of categorization among institutions which provide missiological education.

The *content* relates to the education that is specifically about missiology, about mission. The difference will then depend on whether the focus is on

God's mission (*missio Dei*) or on the mission of the church (*missio ecclesiae*). The *purpose* is about the expected outcomes of the education that is missiological, that is, whether to produce missiologists, missionaries or missional leaders. The *method* has to do with the process of educating, whether it is through academic research or the student's personal search. The *ethos* relates to the DNA which permeates the educational process, whether spiritual commitment or intellectual curiosity. The *context* refers to the locus or setting from and through where the education takes place, namely the academy, the church, or the wider community. The *people* are about whether the faith of those involved in the education defines and orients its content.

It is then obvious that while some missiological theorists and educators would put the emphasis on one or other of these features, still all could agree that the particularity of their missiological education is significantly defined and determined by what they think of its content, purpose, method, ethos, context and people. Thus, missiological education includes all the above and it takes the colour that these features instil into the concerned missiological perspective. Later in this chapter, some case studies are presented and could even serve as reference terms for any evaluative work which purposes the in-depth examination of the type of missiological education offered in one or another setting.

3.2.2 Missiological Education in Theological Curriculum

The place of missiology in the theological curriculum has prompted debates among scholars. Following the tremendous work by Myklebust, some conference papers and published articles on the issue have enriched the debate.[1] The difficulty to allocate mission studies within the theological corpus is due to historical, theological, cultural and philosophical factors. The preceding chapter, and this one, provide accounts on how the situation which occurred in the past has made a history of mission studies being sometime in the center or in the periphery of the preoccupation of both the church and theological institutions, and most of time absent from the preoccupation. This situation was also conditioned by theological convictions about the conditions of humanity and non-Christian religions in the light of God's salvific work. The cultural heritage was equally critical since it characterizes

---

1. Myklebust, *Study of Missions*, vols. 1 and 2.

the profession and practice of faith, being like a message in an envelope in which God's written revelation passes from one generation to another. Finally, the philosophy (or worldview) that people hold about present and future life becomes a compelling determinant for mission engagement in theory or practice. Literature that discusses the place of missions in theological curriculum takes into consideration one or more of these four factors. However, not much has been said about the relationship between missiology and theology as academic disciplines.

Attention is given here to the fact that the relationship between missiology and theology would help address the issue of locating missiological education in the theological curriculum. This is still an ongoing discussion among scholars, but an important concern for missiologists as far as the future of their discipline is at stake. For instance, recently while wondering whether or not missiology could serve as the "queen" of theology, Nussbaum submits that the compartmentalization between theology and missiology would simply become an ungodly obstacle to the spread of the good news of Jesus.[2] For him, there is a need for new conversation on the matter. Though Nussbaum's observation might hold some truth, one could also allege that such a conversation is an old one, but depending on the context, it can be either recurrent or a new one. It can even take other perspectives. While in some stances the suggestion would be that of making missiology as dependent discipline, other contexts would plead for its independence, still others would recommend its integration into each traditional discipline of theology.[3] In an earlier discussion, Bosch had already provided a lengthy elaboration of how mission could permeate the whole of theological curriculum, affecting systematic theology, church history, practical theology, biblical theology and ecumenics.[4] For him, missiology should become both "synoptic discipline" by integrating the theological curriculum and "catalyst discipline" by maintaining a relative independence.

---

2. Nussbaum, "A Future for Missiology," 57.
3. Bosch, *Transforming Mission*, 489–492.
4. Bosch, "Mission in Theological Education," xiv–xxx.

Consequently, the same way there was a question whether or not theology could be the queen of sciences,[5] there has been a concern to determine whether or not missiology should be considered as the queen of theology. For some reasons stated below, I prefer to use terminologies which provide more options such as daughter, mother and sister. Bosch gives account of how the common understanding in the past perceived mission as being mother of theology.[6] That means the work of mission generated theology. Such a statement should not pose any problem since both history of church and of missions provide sufficient evidence on the fact that theology proceeded from the work of mission. It is important to mention that Bosch talks about "mission and theology" but not "missiology and theology."

There is a need to expand the discussion by focusing on missio*logy*, which, as demonstrated earlier, is a discourse about mission, similar to theo*logy* being a discourse about God. The question is not about which relationship should exist between theology and mission, but on the extent to which the relationship between theology and missiology would have influenced the theory, the study and the practice of mission by students of theological institutions. In fact, if missiology was considered a daughter of theology, its status and role would not be the same as if it was understood as its mother or sister. If discussed in terms of the theological corpus, the immediate perception would be that theology is mother of missiology. Nevertheless, while brainstorming this reality, one could reach the point where the relationship between missiology and theology needs more clarification. The above-mentioned three possibilities – daughter, mother or sister – emerge

---

5. The medieval university system was designed to produce clerics. Thereafter in high middles ages (1000–1300) the modern university system came to the existence with the immediate consequence that the education moved from monasteries and cathedrals to become a public matter. Theology was then the queen of the sciences because most education was for the church, and the subjects of study culminated in theology. Also, theology was perceived as originated "from divine revelation rather than natural observation or deduction" (Edgar, "The Theology of Theological Education," 208). To be of value, a subject had to enable theological thought. As a queen, theology had the pre-eminence and could easily dismiss any subject of *science* going against *faith*. Since the Enlightenment period, with *reason* replacing *revelation* as a channel of knowledge, theology had to justify its place in the academia. At the present time theology holds a lower status in the modern world, and the science is recognized as the real princess of the modern age.

6. Bosch, *Transforming Mission*, 6.

from this kind of reasoning and would constitute the reason why missiology has been struggling to find a stable place in theological academia.

1. Missiology being the *daughter* of theology simply means that one could not speak of missiology without aligning it within the theological corpus. From this perspective, missiology is perceived as not existing by itself and not having a status of a full and independent discipline. In this line, one could refer to the statement that "missiology is applied theology."[7] According to the authors, missiology is "deed" (practical side) and theology is "belief" (theoretical side). What people do (missiology) reveals what they truly believe and value and whatever they may say (theology). To expand their thought, the authors argue:

> As evangelical Christians, theology is simply an account of what we believe God has revealed to us in his Word about the things he regards as essential for us to know regarding the ultimate questions of life. Missiology is a description of what we believe we have been called by God to do in the world and how we believe we ought to do it. As followers of Jesus, we regard ourselves as under the authority of God. *Therefore, theology should control missiology, and our missiology should flow from our theology.*[8]

2. Missiology being the *mother* of theology is equal to the fact that one could not speak of theology if there was not missiology. Theology would have come to the existence due to missiology, that is, study on the mission of the church. Even without using the word "missiology," theology proceeded from the outcome of a reflection about what the church was intended to be and to do on the earth. It is actually a "missiological" reflection which could be implicit, not having a well-articulated curriculum, but its outcome was the need to establish studies in theology. Therefore, missiology can be seen as mother of theology.

3. Missiology being the *sister* of theology means that both disciplines have a common ancestor but each having its particular purpose. The ancestor could be the church through which both disciplines have emerged and to

---

7. Pratt, Sills, and Walters, *Introduction*, 67.
8. Ibid., emphasis added.

which they apply their findings and owe their existence. Therefore, if they are not twins, missiology would then be either old or young sister to theology. Being old sister means that there was an implicit missiological reflection on what should the church do to prepare people for the ministry (theology). Being young sister means that an explicit discipline of missiology came late after the establishment of studies in theology.

Though literature on the future of missiology as a discipline does not exactly discuss the issue in these "parental" or "familial" terms, there is no doubt that the relationship between missiology and theology will determine the future of missiology. In his introduction to issues in missiology, Edward C. Pentecost attempts to draw the relationship between missiology and other disciplines, including theology. Though his concern was to demarcate theology from disciplines of social sciences, he suggests that theology, like these other disciplines like anthropology, sociology, psychology and communications, be in the service of missiology.[9] Theology is then perceived as being part of a multiplicity of disciplines which contribute to the field of missiology. Conn states that "bad theology produces missionary decline."[10] The situation is worth considering when one thinks of Bosch's admonition that "Every branch of theology – including missiology – remains piecework, fragile, and preliminary.[11] There is no such thing as missiology, period. There is only missiology in draft." People at Fuller Theological Seminary, the *alma mater* of the modern missiological education in the United States, would say that missiology is dynamic but not static.[12] If for E. Pentecost missiology is put at the core as it receives the service of theology and other disciplines, the above statement by Bosch distils the idea that missiology is one of the branches of theology. Elliston expresses this interplay, pointing to how theology and missiology most often appear to be in conflict of interest despite their shared mandate regarding God's mission: "theology and missiology are then inextricably linked with missiologist considering theology to be a subset of missiology. And, the theologian often considers missiology as a

---

9. Pentecost, *Issues in Missiology*, 14–16.
10. Conn, "Missionary Task," 2.
11. Bosch, *Transforming Mission*, 498.
12. Martin, *Means of World Evangelization,* Tippett 1987.

subset of theology."¹³ The author suggests that theology be understood as "the outworking of people's thinking about how to interpret God's revelation and his action among them as God is working to accomplish his mission."¹⁴

This volatile status of missiology becomes alarming in the African context. Kasdorf's observations about the state of missiology in Africa (from 1968 to 1993) is revelatory of a persisting malaise.¹⁵ Of the seventy-six theological schools in Africa, thirteen have created a chair or department of missiology, with eleven of them are located in South Africa alone. I believe that the reason for such a malaise may be twofold: (a) The concept of missiology tends to be regarded as having imperialistic and Western overtones, and (b) many government-sponsored institutions have substituted the departments of theology/missiology for departments of religious studies. Kasdorf concluded his discussion with five questions, of which the fourth is still valuable today. This question is: "Will missiology be able to sustain its present status of recognition as an academic discipline by the worldwide church when it is being ignored by the secular academics and marginalized by theologians and other academicians at the seminary level as Myklebust's research points out?" Myklebust had actually concluded in his extensive research on the study of missions in theological education that the main problem lies in the ambiguity to subject matter of missiology.¹⁶ Missiology is still in need of more clarification about its nature and its task. Therefore, Kasdorf's question and Myklebust's conclusion should resonate loudly to both theological institutions and missiologists in Africa in general, and in Francophone Africa in particular, given the fact that the issue on mission involvement of the church needs to be elucidated.

In a recent study Amanze identifies various types of associations through which theological education has been promoted in Africa.¹⁷ While some of these associations promote theological education from an ecumenical perspective, others promote the theological education of specific ecclesiological ideologies. Other associations focus on theological education as the study of

---

13. Elliston, *Introduction*, 5.
14. Ibid.
15. Kasdorf, "Current State of Missiology," 64.
16. Myklebust, *Study of Missions*, vols. 1 and 2.
17. Amanze, "History and Major Goals," 346–367.

religions, and still others promote missiology through theological education, the latter being considered as a channel through which the mission of the church becomes the core of the preoccupation. However, as far as mission studies are concerned, this last category finds audience in English-speaking countries of the continent while in Francophone Africa a strong and stable association for mission studies is still missing.[18] In such a context, the question about the relationship between missiology and theology might shed some light on the relevance of missiological education in theological corpus. De Gruchy alerts that when theological education departs away from its missiological orientation, it loses touch with the world and it turns inwards.[19] De Gruchy's statement is reminiscent of what Bosch had already pointed out while saying that "just as the church ceases to be church if it is not missionary, theology ceases to be theology if it loses its missionary character."[20] James Scherer had put it well in a balanced way that, "though missiology should strive to be the most charismatic of all [theological] disciplines, it should also the same time be confident of its own validity and urgency while being flexible and humble to learn from other disciplines."[21] The following section explores the relevance of such statements.

3.3 Contemporary Models of Missiology in Theological Education

The term "theological education" may be interpreted in different ways.[22] It could designate "Christian education," that is the formation of religious identity and character within the Christian community. It could also be "laity

---

18. Réseau de Missiologie Evangélique pour l'Afrique Francophone (REMEAF) founded in Bangui, Central African Republic in 2007 is the only professional association which could fill the gap. According to its website, REMEAF was founded during a consultation held at Faculté de Théologie Évangélique de Bangui, 2–3 March 2007 under the leadership of Dr Moussa Bongoyok, the then Head of the Department of Missiology. Participants to the consultation included among others Abel Ndjarareou, Kwame Bediako, Moussa Bongoyok, Philippe Dikoufiona, Nupanga Weanzana and Mossai Sanguma. The latter two are from the DRC. Unfortunately, since the inception of REMEAF, not much has been done to promote missiology and missiological education in the context of Francophone Africa.
19. De Gruchy, "Theological Education," 43.
20. Bosch, *Transforming Mission*, 494.
21. Scherer, "Mission in Theological Education." 151.
22. Markham, "Theological Education," 158; Balia and Kim, *Edinburgh 2010*, 151.

formation," helping the non-clerical body for church ministry. It could also relate to "ministerial training," the specialist education for those entering the professional ministries of the church. Carried out in the African context, this study focuses on "ministerial training," an education which purposes the training of church ministers through schools or faculties of theology. As Amanze observes, theological institutions exist in Africa to meet the need for well-trained church ministers.[23] The majority of graduates of these institutions serve either as full-time or as part-time ministers in their churches. However, theological education is then vital, not only to churches in the African context, but also to the future of world Christianity.[24]

The nature of theological education is not monomorphic but takes on different forms. While some theological institutions are denominationally affiliated seminaries, others are non-affiliated schools of theology, still others are attached to affiliated and non-affiliated universities either under the faculty of theology or through the department of religious studies. Regardless of the form that it takes, theological education prompts many questions. For instance, while reviewing *The Handbook of Theological Education in World Christianity*, Oxley[25] pinpoints some crucial preoccupations relevant to this study on missiological education and which can be paralleled with the six features mentioned previously by Edgar:[26]

1. *People*: Who is theological education for – everyone, or those chosen to perform special functions within the life of the church?
2. *Content*: What do we learn – a tradition, skills, attitudes, relationship?
3. *Purpose*: When do we need theological education – before exercising our ministry/discipleship, or while we practice?
4. *Context*: Where is the primary location of theological learning – the academy, or where we live out our faith in church and community?
5. *Method*: How do we learn theologically – traditional academic study or reflective practice?

---

23. Amanze, "Paradigm Shift," 122.
24. Werner et al., Handbook of Theological Education, xxv.
25. Oxley, "Review," 432.
26. Edgar, "Theology of Theological Education," 215.

6. *Ethos*: Why do we learn theologically – equipping people for the existing ministries and institutions of the church or transforming people so that the church may be transformed?
7. What makes theological education ecumenical – the variety of students and faculty, content and style of curriculum?

An important question that Oxley didn't raise, much more crucial even for this study, is whether or not theological education is a guarantee for a fruitful ministry. In fact, some studies have shown that "the better the theological education, the less effective the congregational leadership."[27] Studies and experience have proved that some congregations managed by graduates of well-applauded training institutions were not launching effective and fruitful ministries.[28] Earlier in the preceding chapters, the same concern was raised as to know if missiological education is a guarantee for mission involvement of graduates and their churches. The outcome of this research would probably provide some contextualized conclusions based on the strict setting of the study.

In general, as already stated above, missiology (or mission studies) has always been provided in the context of and through theological education. At Edinburgh 1910 World Missionary Conference, two of the eight commissions dealt respectively with education in relation to the Christianization of national life (Commission III) and the preparation of missionaries (Commission V). The conclusion was that "theological education is an indispensable element of any Christian mission, both past and future."[29] The book authored by W. H. T. Gairdner in December of the same year of the Conference of Edinburgh 1910, provides a detailed account and a clear interpretation of the whole conference. Introducing his account on the Commission V, Gairdner sketches a summary of the discussion in the precedent days and highlights the importance of "the men sent (missionaries) and the church that sends (missionaries' home churches)":

> If this be the task before the Church; if the evangelization of all the world, the Christianising of the nations by a gospel

---

27. Markham, "Theological Education," 157.
28. Padilla, *New Alternatives*; Messes, *Calling Church*; Harkness, "De-Schooling"; Naidoo, *Between the Real*.
29. Werner, "Theological Education," 92.

> presented in its fullness [sic!] and its universality, by an education as profound as spirit and as wide as life, through daughter-churches raised to the measure of the stature of the fulness [sic!] of Christ: if THIS be the task before the Church, *then what manner of men must they be who are sent to set their hands to it, and what manner of Church must that be which sends them!*[30]

The Conference of Edinburgh 1910 underscored the importance of the preparation of the missionaries (being sent or to be sent) and the nature of church that sends them as strategic stakeholders for the fulfilment of its mission. How the church is led and how it acts in terms of mission involvement, becomes very critical. In other words, theological education and missionary preparation were perceived as key ingredients for mission involvement of the church. Such a reaction derived from the observation that missionary preparation was not generally viewed as being part of theological curriculum. In many cases, it would be a separate sort of training outside the formal theological corpus.

A century later at the Edinburgh 2010 Conference, one of the eight commissions focused on "theological education and formation." Of seven questions assigned to this commission only two didn't deal directly with church mission involvement. The first question reminded of the preoccupation of the Conference of Edinburgh 1910: "How can every member of the people of God be motivated and empowered for mission?" Another question came in a twofold formulation: "How can the study of missiology become an integral part of the theological curriculum? How can mission perspectives be integrated into every theological discipline?"[31] The report stated that with the interlinkedness of church, Christian mission and theological education was highlighted in many publications in the twentieth century, its concrete implementation remains a constant task for all churches and theological institutions.[32] One of recommendations was to set up a working group within International Association for Mission Studies to explore common strategies and joint action about theological education for the mission of the church.

---

30. Gairdner, *Edinburgh 1910*, 215, emphasis original.
31. Balia and Kim, *Edinburgh 2010*, 266.
32. Werner and Kang, "Theological Education," 159.

Conceptual and Philosophical Considerations in Missiological Education 117

At Cape Town 2010 Conference, the third congress of Lausanne Movement, evangelicals rang the same bell calling action through partnership within the body of Christ. The section through which the call was substantiated had the title "theological education and mission." For the participants, "theological education is part of mission beyond evangelism." Therefore, "the mission of theological education is to strengthen and accompany the mission of the church." Subsequently, the partnership requires that, on one hand, church and mission agencies leaders acknowledge the missional nature of theological education, and on the other hand, theological educators ensure that academic activities must serve the mission of the church in the world. The commitment concludes with a strong appeal to theological institutions to conduct a "missional audit" of their curricula, structures and ethos as to ensure that they truly serve the needs and opportunities facing the church with contextual relevance.[33]

Despite such a resonance from both wings – ecumenical and evangelical – there is always divergence in their focus. While the preoccupation of the ecumenical document of Edinburgh 2010 was entitled "theological education and *formation*," the evangelical document has labelled the Cape Town 2010 preoccupation more precisely as "theological education and *mission*." Consequently, though the preoccupation about the relatedness of theology and mission may apply to both sides, the ultimate objective of theological education may not be the same. Whereas Edinburgh 2010 speaks of "theological education and formation," Cape Town 2010 is concerned with "theological education and mission." It is all about either "formation" or "mission." A collective panel of both sides could bring more light on the relatedness between these two key concepts.

As previously discussed, theology and missiology correlate. Hence, missiology is not to be seen as a non-theological branch of studies even when managed as an independent department or a faculty (school, institute, or center). However, depending on the location, the tradition or the philosophy of each training institution, missiology has been undertaken, not without reasons, through different names. These names include "mission studies program," "ecumenism, science of mission, and religious studies," "school

---

33. *Cape Town Commitment*, 2010.

of world missions," "intercultural studies," and "world Christianity." As Verkuyl has observed, the selection of a name for a discipline is crucial because it displays what one perceives as the most distinctive feature of his/her field of study.[34] Various names assigned to the discipline of missiology undoubtedly reflect the beliefs and the philosophy which underpin and condition the learning and training process within each related institution. The following lines review some case studies. Although they represent a very limited sample, these models contain major elements of the whole spectrum of missiological education at tertiary level.

3.3.1 Mission Studies

While some scholars perceive mission as "all that is done by the church and by Christians to serve God,"[35] others would understand it through five general tasks regarding economic, social, religion, political and juridical concerns.[36] "Mission studies" is then a generic and common name to designate training for Christian mission. When Gustave Warneck, even his precursors, battled for a training program which could focus on the work of the church throughout the world, the general idea was to provide the science of mission in order to reach out to the world with the gospel.[37] He placed the theology of mission at the heart of the classical theological disciplines.[38] Regardless of the connotation that such a training could bear, as discussed in the previous chapter, it was all about preparing harvest workers who would across geographical frontiers to preach the gospel and to save souls.

In the same line, "mission studies" serves as label for current scholarly institutions. The Oxford Centre for Mission Studies (OCMS) based in Oxford, England, is an example. Committed to train "mission scholars and practitioners to become a key resource to the church in mission in contemporary contexts of complexity and diversity," the centre exists to "equip leaders, scholars and institutions to bring holistic mission effectively and intelligently to the nations" (website). Its research degrees program

---

34. Verkuyl, *Contemporary Missiology*, 1.
35. McKim, *Westminster Dictionary*, 175.
36. Ferguson and Wright, *New Dictionary*, 435.
37. Pierard, "Gustav Adolf Warneck," 1157; Verkuyl, *Contemporary Missiology*, 1.
38. Terry et al., *Missiology*, 3.

consists of two stages, namely the pre-university "OCMS Stage" and the University Stage. The OCMS stage extends from admission into OCMS up to registration with Middlesex University, London, for a research degree. The first stage is a period of induction into mission studies research with the purpose of helping students identify areas of study and get ready for university registration. The second stage allows candidates to continue, finalize and defend their research projects through Middlesex University. While most candidates join OCMS as "formal students" (for degree-based studies on holistic mission), others study as "research associates" (for independent research on some aspects of holistic mission). OCMS then aims at developing postgraduate training institutions in the Global South from an evangelical perspective. Its programs allow students to remain active in their ministries throughout their studies as to ensure that their research is culturally relevant and contextually informed.

OCMS organizes conferences, and publishes the journal *Transformation: An International Journal of Holistic Mission* along with imprint versions of Regnum Books, in order to promote mission theology and strategy in the growing churches of the Majority World. In doing so, the Centre hopes to give voice to those from the South and to make this voice be heard in other parts of the developing world. For instance, through its publishing house, Regnum International, the Centre has initiated and coordinated the Edinburgh 2010 Series which has released twenty-eight volumes.[39] According to the editors, these publications were initiated to reflect the ethos of Edinburgh 2010 and to make a significant contribution to ongoing studies in mission. The hope is to encourage conversation between Christians of different traditions and collaboration in mission.

Uppsala University, Sweden, can be mentioned here as another example. Missiological education is provided under the name "Studies in Church and Mission" to prepare those who plan to become priests, pastors, teachers or those who want to pursue a career in the cultural sector (website). Through the threefold framework of church history, ecclesiology, and mission studies, students focus on the study of the Christian church in its different confessional forms in different eras and contexts. They also pay attention to the

---

39. Contributors to these 28 volumes were recruited among scholars from all over the world representing Ecumenicals, Evangelicals, Roman Catholic, Orthodox and Pentecostals.

reciprocal influence between church and society, putting the emphasis on the driving forces behind the development of confessional identities and on the ecumenical movement. This taught master program values greater unity between Christian groups, and as one can realize, the accent is put on critical and speculative reflection. Students analyze the church as expanding movements in present time as well as in the past and its encounters with cultures, political systems and different religions. The emphasis is put on the interreligious dialogue and non-European interpretations of Christian faith.

3.3.2 Ecumenism, Mission, and Religious Studies

"Ecumenism, mission and religious studies" originated from Germany. The University of Hamburg is mentioned here due to the fact that one of the two pioneers of mission studies in the DRC, namely Mushila Nyamankak, was an alumnus of this institution. He completed his studies in New Testament in 1983 at the University of Hamburg. Once back home, he attempted to establish a new department of "Ecumenism, Science of Mission and Religious Studies" within the Congo Protestant University but the project would not be accepted until in 1997, when the governing board authorized the creation of a new department under the above name.

This survey focuses on the Academy of Mission at the University of Hamburg that was established in the 1950s as a place for the theological formation of missionary candidates (website). However, due to the change of the world context in the 1960s, its function also changed and the Academy became a theological institution providing theological education in a global perspective. Today, it contributes to the development of intercultural education in the field of Protestant theology, helping students from Africa, Latin America, Asia and Oceania work through their doctoral research projects. In addition, the Academy of Mission is also a place where international conferences take place, hoping to be a laboratory for ecumenical theology where subjects relevant for the Protestant world are discussed. Domains of interest for research and conferences include the dynamics of charismatic and evangelical movements in global and local perspectives, globalization, questions of justice and peace. All admitted candidates are obliged to reside in the facilities made available by the Academy in order to share in life in the Academy community and to attend all required lectures and conferences.

The Academy awards scholarships to non-Western theological students preparing a doctoral research project in Protestant Theology at Hamburg University under the condition that the proposed topic is accepted by a professor in the Faculty of Protestant Theology. Besides the requirements of mastering one of the classical languages (Hebrew, Greek and Latin) and German, the study program comprises two phases. The first phase of two years is devoted to completion of the German language culminating in the presentation of a research project. The second phase of two more years focuses on writing a complete dissertation either in German or English under the guidance of a supervisor. Once accepted, the dissertation is published in the series "Studies in Intercultural Theology at the Mission Academy" (SITMA).

At Lund University, Sweden, the Faculties of Humanities and Theology provide missiological education through the Centre for Theology and Religious Studies under the name "Church and Mission Studies" (website). This taught program is undertaken at the first (bachelor) and the second (master) cycles. Students are required to take several courses in traditional theological curriculum including "Missiology and Ecumenics."

The Ecumenical Institute at Bossey, Switzerland, is another example in this category. Founded in 1946, this institute is described as an international centre for encounter, dialogue and formation of the World Council of Churches (WCC). It brings together people from diverse churches, cultures and backgrounds for ecumenical learning, academic study and personal exchange (website). It specializes in ecumenical theology, missiology and social ethics. The teaching staff represent diverse theological, cultural and confessional backgrounds. The institute and its diplomas are recognized by the University of Geneva. These include a one-year Master of Advanced Studies in Ecumenical Studies (MAS in Ecumenical Studies), a non-residential five-year Doctorate in Theology (with mention Ecumenical Studies) conducted jointly with the Autonomous Faculty of Protestant Theology of the University of Geneva.

3.3.3 School of World Missions

The concept of "world missions" has always been understood as "the efforts of Christian churches, groups, and individuals to proclaim the Christian gospel throughout the entire world."[40] The denomination "school of world missions" is to be understood in that sense. It was the innovation of Fuller Theological Seminary, founded in the United States in 1947. According to Ralph Winter, the School of World Missions was a "mid-course correction" to get back to the initial idea that the founder Charles Fuller had about creating a School of Evangelism.[41] The original vision of Fuller was to train evangelists and missionaries to spread the faith.[42] It is important to mention that the School of World Mission was founded within Fuller in 1965 during a period when an increasing number of global ministries were established throughout the world and that movement needed well-trained workers.[43] Based on that premise, the following purposes of the School of World Mission were designed:[44]

1. Prepare men to fulfil the Great Commission in the midst of change peculiar to our age.
2. Provide a theology of missions for all seminary students looking toward a pastorate.
3. Bring Christian nationals to the school as students and teachers to provide opportunities for mutual exchange.
4. Develop a team of research specialists to study and provide a center of thought and information regarding World Mission

Church growth was the key concept of this school. Even the US Center for World Mission that Ralph Winter founded in 1976 after having left Fuller's School of World Mission, aligned with the same vision of preparing people for evangelism and mission throughout the world. Such a vision for global outreach was the *leit motiv* of any US-based schools of theology and their related training institutions abroad bearing the name "school of world mission" or "center for world mission." This orientation was mostly common within the so-called evangelical fellowship. Through its faculty members Fuller's School of World Mission has influenced the Lausanne

---

40. McKim, *Westminster Dictionary*, 306.
41. Quoted in Parsons, "History and Impact," 56.
42. Ibid.
43. Ibid., 54.
44. Ibid.

Congress in 1974 in a special way.[45] In 2003 Fuller changed the name of this school from "School of World Missions" to "School of Intercultural Studies" (Fuller Seminary's website).

3.3.4 Intercultural Studies

Since 2003 the School of Intercultural Studies (SIS) has become the new name for missiological education in the United States and in other related institutions throughout the world. Again, as for "School of World Missions," the SIS has found its first place at Fuller Theological Seminary before being duplicated in other schools related to the Association of Theological Studies in North America. The school's name was changed to address the concerns of many graduates that, in a changing global environment, the school's former name created obstacles for their work. The program is conceived to serve as a resource for the growing non-Western Christian missionary movement with the conviction that God is calling "Christians of every continent and culture to the task of making Jesus Christ known and loved throughout the world" (Fuller Seminary's website). Based on the assumption that in each situation the church is to be shaped in a way that affirms and utilizes the most positive aspects of the culture without forcing people to become "foreign" in order to become followers, the school intends to equip students as "servant leaders who mobilize the global church for the purpose of God" (website).

At Fuller Seminary, the SIS strives to prepare students holistically to serve a world in need, whether the students' mission field is an unreached group of people, an urban neighbourhood, or the marketplace. Faculty members are missiologists, committed to "a gospel-centered curriculum that is in tune with diverse shifting global realities" (website). The training programs include Master of Arts in Intercultural Studies, Master of Theology in Missiology, Doctor of Ministry in Global Ministry and Doctor of Missiology in order to prepare students for intercultural ministry, international development and other missionary vocations. Courses include the theological, historical and biblical basis of the Christian faith; they also include studies in the areas of theory of intercultural ministry, evangelism, the growth of the church, non-Christian religions, leadership development, globalization and international development. Delivery methods include

---

45. Ibid., 63.

experiential learning, lectures, readings and research. A PhD in Intercultural Studies is offered through the Fuller's Center for Missiological Research and provides candidates the opportunity to design, develop and complete a research project under the guidance of faculty advisors. Candidates undergo a tutorial-driven process that integrates a wide range of missiological disciplines. Through the Global Research Institute post-doctoral non-Western Christian scholars spend six months at Fuller Seminary to research and write materials to further the intellectual and spiritual mission of the church in their own geographical areas.

Students are comprised of missionaries, mission organization leaders, local church pastors, lay leaders in mission and professional tentmakers. Through intercultural studies, students are trained to meet the challenge of ministering in an increasingly complex, multi-ethnic and multinational world. Those studying international development could also hold positions in peace-building, child rights and transformational development.

As said earlier, many institutions related to the Association of Theological Seminaries (ATS) like Asbury Theological Seminary and Biola University, provide missiological education through the label "Intercultural Studies." In 2003, Dallas Theological Seminary organized a department of "world missions and intercultural studies" with the purpose of "focusing the attention of all seminary students on Christ's mandate to make disciples among all nations."[46] A comparative study could be done to surface the commonalities and divergences which exist among them, and to what extent the same spirit which characterized the same institutions while using "School of World Missions" would prevail or not.

3.3.5 World Christianity and Mission

Boston University is known for adopting the study of "World Christianity and Mission" (WCM) as the name for its mission studies program (website). The study at WCM is done through Boston Theological Institute (BTI)[47] and provides students with the opportunity of having access to other

---

46. Dallas Theological Seminary Catalog, 2003.

47. BTI is an association of ten university divinity schools, schools of theology and seminaries in the Greater Boston area, United States. Enrolling in one institution allows the students to study at all of them. According to its website, the BTI "enables faculty, students and the public at large to engage in robust interreligious dialogue, learning, and community."

institutions. In addition to taking courses with the faculty in the School of Theology, students are encouraged to take courses in other departments such as Anthropology, Religious Studies, History, Theology and Sociology. Due to its cross-disciplinary nature, the study at WCM can be pursued through three different PhD programs at Boston University, namely (1) PhD in History and Hermeneutics with concentration in Mission Studies; (2) PhD in Practical Theology with concentration in Evangelism and Missiology; and (3) PhD in Missiology offered in conjunction with Gordon-Conwell Theological Seminary. In addition, the Graduate Division of Religious Studies offers a PhD in Religious Studies which includes the study of world Christianity through its texts and traditions. Therefore, the study of WCM at Boston University is not done in a single way. It provides prospective students with three possibilities.

According to Dana L. Robert, director of the Center for Global Christianity and Mission through which the School of Theology offers the study in WCM at Boston University, the rationale of such a program is due to the new landscape of Christianity. Having become a worldwide faith with believers distributed across the continents, world Christianity requires studies which support and understand the global Christian community through critics, reflection, faithful witness and thoughtful engagement with multiple cultures (website). She had already stated elsewhere that "for international students, the study of world mission becomes a way to analyze the histories of their own forms of Christianity."[48] Hence, missiological education at Boston University emphasizes research and critical analysis in world Christianity, while being provided only at doctoral level.

At the University of Edinburgh, Scotland, mission studies are offered in the School of Divinity through the Centre for the Study of World Christianity which offers taught Masters and supervised research degrees at the Masters and PhD levels. However, because an appropriate Masters level degree is recommended as a prerequisite for doctoral studies, PhD students usually audit some Masters classes in the Centre or other areas of divinity at the beginning of their studies. Their areas of interest include the history of Christian missions, new missionary movements from the Global South,

---

48. Robert, "Mission Study," 200.

Pentecostalism, current missiological issues such as inculturation, ethnicity, gender and interfaith relations (University of Edinburgh's website). The Centre was established by professor Andrew Walls, former missionary in Sierra-Leone, and current core staff includes Brian Stanley. The late Kwame Bediako from Ghana was one of the alumni of the Centre.

3.3.6 Missiology

Some universities keep the word "missiology" on the name of their department, research group or degree.[49] The UNISA has a Department of Christian Spirituality, Church History and Missiology offering programs through three research areas, namely (1) Christian Spirituality; (2) Church History; and (3) Missiology. Missiology is then defined as "the systematic and critical study of the missionary (world changing) activities of Christian churches and organisations" (website). Mission is understood at UNISA as "the cutting edge of a Christian community, that is, its attempts to change the world through projects of evangelism, healing, teaching, development or liberation" (website). This department is well-known due to the fact that it was initiated and chaired by the late David Bosch, and thanks to its distance learning, the students come from various countries within and outside the continent. Missiology at UNISA is mainly open-learning and modular-based degree at undergraduate (bachelor) level including a structured MTh, with another entirely research-based MTh and doctoral programs.

From the university's website, this department exists to do the following:
1. Develop quality scholarship that integrates research, teaching and organic participation in communities.
2. Foster interdisciplinary and interreligious cooperation.
3. Design teaching in such a way that students have to engage with their communities.
4. Provide interactive learner support.
5. Encourage participation in the disciplinary societies in Africa and the world.

---

49. The situation is the same at the North-West University, Potchefstroom Campus, South Africa (www.nwu.ac.za). However, besides the fact that Fuller (or any other institution) offer programs in Intercultural Studies, some of their degrees bear the word "missiology" (e.g. Doctor of Missiology). Redcliff College in England offers a Master of Arts in Contemporary Missiology (www.redcliffe.ac.uk). Though using the description "World Christianity and mission," Boston University offers a PhD in Missiology.

North-West University, Potchefstroom Campus, South Africa, is another institution which offers mission studies under the name "missiology," a research-based degree at master and doctoral levels. At bachelor level of theological corpus, a few subjects on mission are taught as a part of the whole curriculum. The focus of the program lies on the "understanding and reaching out to people from different backgrounds with different philosophies of life who do not know the Lord or his Word, and developing a sympathetic apologetic and holistic way to answer their questions and views from the Gospel" (website). The threefold objective of the study program includes (1) furthering the Reformed approach to holistic mission, (2) studying the church in mission and new church planting in different contexts, and (3) building out Christian apologetics in the light of global trends. From the above formulation of the nature and the purpose of the study program, one can easily notice the evangelical orientation of missiological education at North-West University through which the present research is undertaken.

3.3.7 Synthesis

These few case studies indicate that some theological and missiological educators are aware of the need for educating the church for its mission and are offering various solutions to fill the gap. From the above accounts, one gets an idea of how missiological education has been diversely provided in and through the current context of theological education. This survey did not intend to be an in-depth and critical examination of theological and philosophical foundations, curriculum content and the outcomes of these programs. While surveying data available mainly through Internet search related to the nature, purpose, activities, and expected learning outcomes, some broad conclusions can be drawn.

While some models of missiological education embrace altogether formal (curriculum based), non-formal (through seminars, conferences, discussions), and informal (through communal and fellowship living, mentoring, accountability) teaching-learning strategies, others emphasize only one or two of these strategies. Whereas some develop an explicit curriculum (with academically defined study subjects and expected outcomes), others are characterized by implicit curriculum (using mostly non-formal and informal activities). While some use taught programs, others focus on research programs and still others use online or distance programs. Some combine two of these delivery methods, taught and research programs, or online and research programs. Whereas some models admit students for full-time study programs, others organize the learning through a part-time mode. While some stress rigorously theoretical and scientific activities, others stress on being prepared to impact mission reflection and practice on the ground, still others try to combine both approaches. Whereas some interpret missiology as current developments in world Christianity and interreligious dialogue, others consider it as channel to teach mission-related topics as well as methods of mission. While some prepare students at undergraduate, graduate and postgraduate levels, others focus on doctoral level only. Whereas some envision mission from a holistic perspective of liberating the all human beings, others emphasize the priority of preaching the gospel to save souls, still others combine both aspects as they also put more weight on either one. While some design their programs specifically for Majority World scholars and church leaders, others offer programs in a non-designated way, allowing candidates from any part of the world to take their studies.

Irrespective of these variations, the general feature is that these missiological programs are provided directly or progressively in and through the context of accredited affiliated or non-affiliated theological institutions. However, while some of these programs have been initiated as appendixes (or external body) to the existing theological institutions, others emanate directly from a given theological institution. To help surface some aspects overlooked by this survey,[50] an in-depth analysis could take into account the Edgar's six features discussed earlier, and the typologies of theological education and philosophies of education that follow.[51]

---

50. Since any scientific study ought to have its object and methods, these variants certainly suggest the change in both content of the discipline and the approach to the discipline. For instance, writing a history of Christianity in Central Africa is obviously a matter of church history for an African theologian according to the prevalent theological structure. The same work would become a matter of mission history for a European theologian. While analyzing the thoughts of a Congolese theologian is an issue of missiology in a German context, the same study would be a matter of systematic theology for a Congolese scholar according to the prevalent theological structure (Dehn and Werner, "Protestant Theological Education," 583).

51. Edgar, "The Theology of Theological Education," 208–217.

3.4 Missiological Education in the Light of Typologies of Theological Education

3.4.1 From Athens Typology to Antioch Model

Some authors have engaged in discussion about the nature and the purpose of theological education and about what it is that constitutes excellence in theological education.[52] The use of typologies has been common to these authors as an attempt to clarify the debate. In *Between Athens and Berlin: The Theological Education Debate*, Kelsey introduces a dual typology to synthetize and organize various points of view. The general characteristic is the geographic representation of approaches of theological education. Kelsey uses Athens and Berlin to respectively portray the classical model and the vocational model of theological education. In his *Reenvisioning Theological Education*, Banks adds the typology of Jerusalem to describe the missional model of theological education. In an article entitled "The theology of theological education," Edgar suggests the typology of Geneva to depict the confessional model of theological education.[53]

The essential of the debate lies on what scholars think of how, through which context, for what purpose, for which learning outcomes and through which teaching-learning process, theology and theological education are understood and practiced. Typology here is to be understood as an approach to or a model of theological education. Table 3.1 provides a summary of the typologies' functionality.

---

52. Kelsey, *Athens and Berlin*; Banks, *Reenvisioning Theological Education*; Edgar, "The Theology of Theological Education."
53. Edgar, "Theology of Theological Education," 208–217.

Table 3.1 Typologies of Theological Education

Symbol, Context, and Model	Purpose (Goal)	Expected Educational Outcomes	Learning Ethos (DNA of the Educational Process)	Theology Is Then Perceived As . . .
Athens *Academy* Classical model	Transforming the individual (Spiritual formation for personal development)	The production of transformed graduates (Holiness, moral, spiritual transformation)	Classical education through *Theologia* (not knowing about God, but knowing God)	Intuited wisdom
Berlin *University* Vocational model	Strengthening the church (Ministerial training for a rational ministry practice)	The production of theoretically aware and practically effective ministers	Reflective practice through *Scientia* (research and scientific rigor)	Way of thinking and applying theory to life and the church
Jerusalem *Community* Missional model	Converting the world (Missional end in order to transform the world)	The production of graduates who live for mission	Reaching the ends of the earth through *Missiology* (that transforms the learning process but not only the content)	Missiological (or missional)
Geneva *Seminary* Confessional model	Knowing God (Confessional training while informing through the tradition)	The production of graduates who know God through a particular tradition	The maintenance of tradition through Doxology (using the creeds, confessions, the means of grace)	The process of knowing God

Source: Drawn from the Works by Kelsey, Banks, and Edgar.

As one could observe, these approaches are Western-based and none of them holds the monopoly of excellence and of the whole purpose of the education that is *theological*. Each approach represents a reduced parcel of the entire edifice. Unfortunately, as Banks argues, his two models are irreconcilable and theological educators are in need of producing a negotiated scheme. Nevertheless, Edgar is correct to contend that many theological programs today, even in Africa, are a mix of these models and the nature of the mix makes a particular program distinctive. Even the contemporary models of missiological education surveyed in the previous section, provide programs offered through one or another of these typologies and mixing elements from these models.[54] The mix could be about the context, the purpose, the expected outcomes and learning process. For instance, a Baptist theological institution could be of the Geneva model while combining elements of Athens, Berlin and Jerusalem. Therefore, not only the mix makes it distinctive, but also the emphasis put on one or another element of the context, the purpose, the expected outcomes and learning process. For that reason, one could suggest a fifth typology that combines these elements because it appears that no single model encapsulates the whole picture of theological education. While reviewing Kelsey's book, Molyneux concludes with a concern for African theological educators:

> Theological educators in Africa, reading the book, will however be gratified to realize that the problems that they grapple with (overarching purpose of theological education, curriculum content, the balance between theory and practice, the concern to do justice at one and the same time to the source and also the multiple demands of contemporary pluralistic society) – all these are not peculiar to them but are being wrestled with by their colleagues in other parts of the world.[55]

For the purpose of this study, there is a need for another typology, instead of being content of the fact that the challenge is general and not peculiar to Africa. Not striving to find solutions to the educational problems in Africa shouldn't be seen as gratification. Therefore, following the same "tradition" of

---

54. Edgar ("Theology of Theological Education," 217) has provided a survey questionnaire which could be used to outline the nature of the prevailing education. Though mostly focused on theological education, the survey could also be adapted as to apply to missiological education.

55. Molyneux, "Book Review," 128.

geographic representation (or symbol), this researcher submits that Antioch could better serve as an illustration of the fifth model (fig. 3.1).

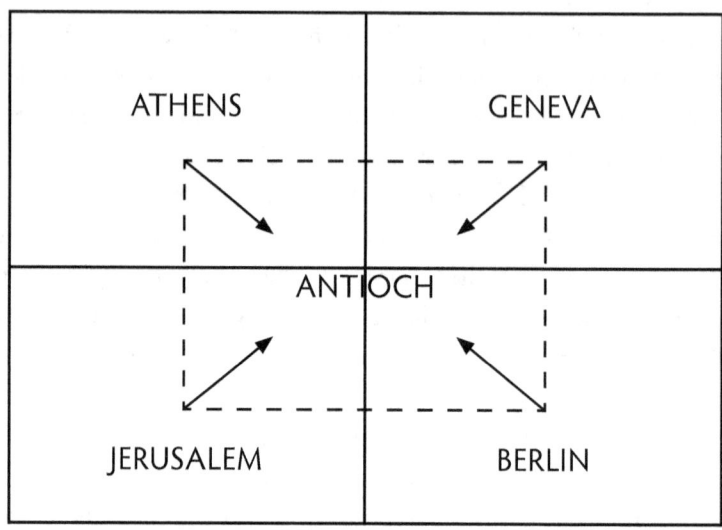

Figure 3.1: The Fifth Typology of Theological Education

As far as missiological education is concerned, the typology of Antioch conveys the purpose of providing education for God's glocal mission better. Jerusalem was not really a good model for reaching out to the world as Banks's typology might suggest. The mission engagement of the church in Jerusalem was not intentional (Acts 8:1–4); it was rather prompted by the persecution. Antioch is known as the point of departure of the missionary movement of Paul and others. The church in Jerusalem sent out Peter and John to Samaria (Acts 8), followed by the team of Paul and Barnabbas to Antioch (Acts 11) only to witness what the Holy Spirit had already accomplished respectively through Philippe and other disciples who fled the persecution. The model of Antioch also stresses the multicultural nature of the church which existed in that city, though from various origins, members of the Antioch church were opened to the voice and direction of the Holy Spirit for God's mission. Interestingly enough, Paul and Barnabbas who just arrived from Jerusalem, were allowed by the church members to be their representatives in the mission field (Acts 13:1–4). Their identity was not a

Conceptual and Philosophical Considerations in Missiological Education 133

pretext for undermining them as it could have occurred elsewhere in the context of tribalism and ethnicity.

Missiological education in the Antioch model would combine some elements of models from Kelsey, Banks and Edgar (table 3.2).

Table 3.2 Antioch Model of Missiological Education

Symbol	Antioch
Model	Transforming education
Context	Higher education: Community of learning and serving
Purpose (Goal)	Knowing God for his mission Personal development for God's mission Strengthening the church for God's mission Challenging any mission-mindless tradition
Expected Outcomes	The production of transformed graduates The production of theoretically aware and practically effective graduates The production of missiophiles (with love for God's mission) The production of graduates who know non-denominational God
Learning Ethos	Personal experience Applied reflection Missional theology Denominational identity in the service of God's glocal mission
Theology Is . . .	The process of experiencing God for his glocal mission Thinking about what God's mission purposes and applying theory to the context Missional (that is for the sake of *missio Dei*) Evaluating and orienting tradition in the light of God's mission
Missiological Education Is . . .	The process through which the church and its educational institutions prepare learners for God's glocal and holistic mission through theory, training and practice of mission

In the Antioch model, the context of education is higher education, a community of learning and serving which combines in priority elements of university, academy and community. The context of seminary which stresses ecclesial specificity comes at the end to serve as a case study at the service of the whole of God's glocal mission. A denomination or confessional community is not the end of God's mission. Instead, it is a means or a channel for God's glocal and holistic mission.

The purpose of knowing God becomes meaningful only as the knowledge allows the learners to know what God does in general and what he purposes to accomplish for the humanity and the whole creation through the church. The expected outcomes are illustrated through the production of graduates who are transformed in mind and character, being theoretically aware of God's glocal mission and practically effective for the sake of God's mission. The learning process includes personal experience, applied reflection, missional identity in the service of God's glocal mission. The theology becomes then a process of experiencing God, thinking about what his mission purposes, applying theory according to the context, and challenging the ecclesiastic traditions for the sake of *missio Dei*. As already said, even in this model (typology or approach), a given missiological program may hold its distinctiveness based on the extent to which it emphasizes one or another element of the context, the purpose, the expected outcomes and learning process.

Therefore, using one or another learning process, an institution can be *missiological*, but more or less classical, vocational, missional and confessional as it emphasizes personal development, reflective practices, denominational identity, or strengthen the churches for God's glocal mission. Such a situation might enclose or disclose the real face of a given missiological education.

3.4.2 Another Face of Theological Education in the African Context

The promotion of theological education in Africa resulted from the initiative of the International Missionary Council (IMC) which established the Theological Education Fund (TEF) during its General Assembly held in Achimota, Ghana, from 28 December 1957 to 8 January 1958. The purpose was to raise the level of theological education in the Third World.[56] It is historically safe to say that TEF emanated from the Edinburgh Conference of 1910 as Protestant missionary societies and other church leaders met to discuss the urgency of reaching out to the world in their generation. IMC

---

56. Ward, "Theological Education Fund," 137.

served as the continuation committee and through some of its gatherings (e.g. Jerusalem in 1928 and Tambaram in 1938), participants lamented the level, scope and quality of ministry training in the so-called "younger churches" (i.e. churches from Majority World countries). There was a deep concern regarding the state of the church ministry and about the growing awareness of the urgent need for reform in its training. From several regional studies commissioned by IMC on the state of ministerial training, the one in Africa was published in 1954.[57] Shortage of personnel, lack of infrastructures (buildings, libraries, well-structured programs) and of training materials were among the findings. It was then clear that nothing could satisfy Africa other than making its theological education comparable to that in Europe and America.[58]

According to Berquist, the consensus was that the national churches of the Majority World could best raise their standards of ministerial training by duplicating the patterns of the Western theological seminaries.[59] The truth is that the prevailing theological education in Africa even today is a kind of carbon copy of the Western system. However, one could ask how a purely African theological education would look. This researcher does not see any problem in the fact that the Western type of theological education, the existing one and the only one available at the hand of missionaries, could serve as a working framework. The problem is how it could be contextualized in light of the local situation and needs preparing the church and its members for God's glocal and holistic mission.

As mentioned above, TEF has to be regarded as one of the outcomes of the Edinburgh Conference of 1910 through its concern of building up local church leadership in order to accomplish the fourth and missing *self* out of the so-called three-self formula (self-administrating, self-supporting, self-propagating). The need was for self-theologizing to help the younger churches to contextualize their ecclesiastical organization, teaching and thinking. Moreau observes that contextualization has garnered attention and controversy even among evangelicals.[60] Some authors, mostly from the

---

57. Bates et al., *Survey*.
58. Ward, "Theological Education Fund," 139.
59. Berquist, TEF," 244–246.
60. Moreau, "Comprehensive Contextualization," 406.

evangelical stream, perceive the role played by TEF negatively, being a source of cultural theologies based on a loss of biblical authenticity.[61] These cultural theologies include Liberation Theology in its various forms (Minjung Theology in Korea, Black Theology, Theology of Ontology and Time, Third Eye Theology, Theology of the Pain of God, Water-Buffalo Theology and Yin-Yang Theology). Other authors, from ecumenical side suggest that the WCC should "reinvent an institution like the TEF tradition to serve the purpose and role TEF fulfilled."[62]

As far as Africa is concerned, theological education has gained its importance due to the growth and the need of churches. The growing churches have infused the need for more advanced theological education.[63] It is generally known that the main aim of theological education in Africa is to provide and secure ministerial formation of church members. People enter theological institutions to be trained for church ministry. According to Pobee, rather than being only a scientific quest, theology in Africa is also a service to the church's mission.[64] Nevertheless, Pobee's insight doesn't automatically solve the problem because the concept of *mission* has often been relativized.

Depending on the theological tradition through which it is offered, theological education can be in the service of evangelism essentially, or in the service of social, economic and political engagements as well. In general, while the evangelical theological education serves the church's mission of proclaiming the gospel, ecumenical theological education would probably include all activities which serve the social interests of human beings. Whereas the first educational orientation stresses the individual's well-being and the vertical relationship with God, the second emphasizes the collective well-being and the horizontal relationship of peace among people. The real problem arises while positing only on one or another of these two extremes. Therefore, one could detect more positions between the two extremes, either moving closer to evangelical tradition or to ecumenical tradition.

The above remark makes it clear that theological education in Africa is not only one, as the title of this section may have suggested, but it is plurality. It

---

61. Hesselgrave, "Will We Correct," 126.
62. Pobee, "Stretch Forth," 344.
63. Amanze, "Paradigm Shift," 122.
64. Pobee, "Stretch Forth," 344.

is not only influenced by both the Western culture of individualism and the African culture of community as Pobee argues, but it is also shaped by various confessional legacies inherited from Western denominations.[65] For instance, in the *Handbook of Theological Education in World Christianity*, which is made up of three parts, an entire third part deals with theological education from denominational and confessional perspectives. The long list includes theological education in Orthodox churches, in the Roman Catholic Church, in the Anglican churches, in Lutheran churches, in Reformed churches, in Methodist churches, in Baptist churches, in evangelical theological schools and in Pentecostal churches.[66]

Even in such a categorization, the reality on the ground may reveal a variety of hybrid theologies. Among the reasons, for instance in the DRC, one can suggest the fact that Protestant missions have worked in partnership to provide theological education with the possibility of promoting one's own theology. Amanze notices the same trend elsewhere in Africa when he indicates that "the need for well-trained church ministers necessitated the ecumenical cooperation of the churches in a particular country or region."[67] Another reason relates to the books and other training materials available which are actually a product of various theological traditions but perceived by African users as being from one indispensable source. One can even find with amazement many students from Protestant theology using books produced by Catholic scholars as valuable tools for their own Protestant theology. Without doubt, theological education in Africa becomes a mixture of cultural and confessional expressions which might not make the task easy. It is a multiform artefact which necessitates to be revisited and re-oriented. Pobee is somehow right to argue that theology in the African context is not a finished product, but an edifice under construction.[68]

A final observation relates to the role of the African theology in regard to mission engagement of African churches. One of the recent accounts of the African theology with its conjunction to theological education is authored by Amanze of the University of Botswana. In an article entitled

---

65. Ibid., 339.
66. Werner, D., et al.
67. Amanze, "Paradigm Shift," 122.
68. Pobee, "Stretch Forth," 339.

"Paradigm Shift in Theological Education in Southern and Central Africa and Its Relevance to Ministerial Formation," the author describes the changes that have taken place in theological education in post-independent Africa.[69] He argues that, having been Euro-centric, theological education during the colonial period failed to address the pressing challenges of colonial oppression, poverty, patriarchy and those related to political, cultural, social, religions and economic issues. It was rather a male-dominated, anti-cultural and Western-oriented theology.

After having provided the historical account of the origin and expansion of the church in Africa, the role of theological education and the nature of the curriculum of traditional theology and its failures, Amanze briefly evokes the various theologies that are currently taking shape in Africa. In this regard, the author underscores the place of African theology in both theological education and the church. He then proposes that African theological discourse should address the following issues, namely: (1) the need to take African culture seriously; (2) the demand made by women in church and society for equal opportunities in the ministry of the church; (3) the need for the church to play an active role in the fight against HIV and AIDS; (4) the need to fight against global warming and depletion of natural resources; (5) the need to develop a theology of liberation for those who are oppressed; and (6) the need for the churches to engage in socio-economic development.[70]

A close look at the job description that Amanze and many other African theologians design for African theology depicts it as a theology without global mission. Amanze's article displays the root cause of African theology not being a missional theology. For instance, after having observed that in the past theological education tended to emphasize the exclusive nature of Christianity at the expense of other, he rejoices on the fact that "there has been a more move towards a multi-faith approach in theological education" and that "people have become aware that the different religions prevalent in Africa today are to stay."[71] He then submits that there should be a multi-faith theological curriculum in order to forge peaceful coexistence and to enhance

---

69. Amanze, "Paradigm Shift," 120–131.
70. Ibid., 125.
71. Ibid., 129.

religious tolerance.[72] He proposes furthermore that the course syllabi should cover the life of the founders of the different religions, their teachings, beliefs, rituals, practices, sacred places and symbols and the relation of each of these religions with other religious groups. While the content of such syllabi is recommendable, the critical question still is that of the ultimate purpose of doing these studies. If for Amanze and others, the purpose is to promote and enhance religious tolerance, then such a simplistic motivation would cover this implicit implication: "No more evangelization of people of other faiths!" Therefore, such a theology would simply be a new version of Hocking's point of view that shook the mission enterprise with the publication of his book in 1932 as already discussed in chapter 2 (section 2.5.2).

Amanze's submission contradicts the strong conclusion of his article that "theological education contributed tremendously to the growth and expansion of the church in Africa."[73] How could Amanze expect the church to experience the growth and expansion without a passion for mission and evangelization? Which kind of theology would have prompted such growth and expansion if not a theology that is intentionally missional? If today there is a need for a new African theology, a compromising theology, shall people continue to dream for the growth and expansion of the church in Africa or rather for the euthanasia of the church of Africa? It then becomes clear that African theology has not much contributed to the engagement of African churches to God's glocal mission. In another article, the same author has demonstrated that few training institutions in Africa promote missiology through theological education.[74] Such a theology will certainly lead to the weakening, if not the euthanasia, of the African church. One could perceive an urgent need for bringing back missional theology into theological education in Africa. Bevans is right in asserting that "what missiology is claiming today is that there cannot be just a theology any more: all theology has to be missiological . . . A missiology in a world church can only be a theology for a world church; a theology for a world church can only be a missiology in a world church."[75] There should be a clear philosophy of theological

---

72. Ibid., 130.
73. Ibid., 131.
74. Amanze, "History and Major Goals," 346.
75. Bevans, "From Edinburgh to Edinburgh," 10.

education that is missional for our African theology to become a missional African theology.

3.5 Missiological Education in the Light of Philosophies of Education

Any teaching-learning process is a result of a given or a mixture of philosophies of education. Therefore, educational philosophy conditions the curriculum (what is taught), instruction (how curriculum is taught) and assessment (how learning is measured).[76] Throughout the history, classical philosophies of education have prevailed due to variety of situations, worldviews and beliefs. As Jones points out, a brief sketch of the philosophers' worldviews would demonstrate how their beliefs about education influenced the teaching and learning cycle regarding curriculum, instruction, and assessments in education today.[77] While some philosophies are based on an ideal (idealism) or a reality (realism), others are articulated around the age (andragogy) or the gender (feminism), still others on the personality or the morality, and others on the process or the result (reconstructivism), even on religious convictions. For the strict purpose of this study, the focus is put on learning theories of adult education as discussed by contemporary educators and educationalists. This choice is dictated by the age of the beneficiaries of missiological education, and also by the interest of examining the outcomes of such an educational program with special reference to the current international trends in higher education. The conviction is that the result of missiological education would depend on what is taught, how it is taught, and how learning is measured. With this in mind, the following four themes are explored, namely learning theories of adult education, threefold mission of higher education, the transformative purpose of higher education, and the Bolognization of educational system.

3.5.1 Learning Theories of Adult Education

Education has traditionally been perceived as a pedagogic relationship between the teacher and the learner; the teacher decides what the learner

---

76. Gutek, *Historical and Philosophical*.
77. Jones, "Teaching and Learning Cycle," 1.

needs to know, and how the knowledge and skills should be taught. For example, discussing the urgency of shaping the academic enterprise in the context of Christian education, Sanderson has this to say: "It must be clearly understood *that the primary role is the teaching role*. One of the threats we face in Christian higher education is the temptation of trying to become all things [both teacher and scholar]."[78] This general understanding of the primary role of teaching, but not researching, is common in many places. It emphasizes the learning approach which is based on the priority of the teaching responsibility of the instructor even at higher education level. With Malcolm Knowels'research on andragogy, there has been a revolution in education on how people learn.[79] However, different individuals have different understandings of andragogy. While some consider andragogy as a pedagogic discipline, others view it as an autonomous science within the framework of the general sciences of teaching and learning, still others perceive andragogy as a method, skill, theory, or model of adult learning.[80] As Peterson and Ray observe, there were also three other meanings for adult education, namely (1) the *process* by which adults continue to learn after completing formal schooling; (2) *organized activities* for adults offered by a variety of institutions to accomplish specific educational objectives; and (3) a *movement* or *field* related to this learning.

Knowles' initial theory didn't answer the question, "what is adult about adult education?" Also, there was no clear idea on what can or cannot be considered as adult education.[81] As a result, there was semantic confusion. While contradicting Knowles, Mohring even suggested that *andragogy* could rather be replaced by *teleiagogy* because the Greek word *aner*, from which andragogy derives, means adult male and not adult of either sex, while *telios* is the Greek word for the English adult.[82] He also argued that despite its roots in the word *pais*,in antiquity, the common understanding of the

---

78. Sanderson, "Shaping the Academic Enterprise," 383, emphasis added.
79. The title of the 1970 edition presents andragogy and pedagogy in an antagonistic way. The book was revised and updated in 1980 under the title *The Modern Practice of Adult Education: From Andragogy to Pedagogy* in which Knowles took another direction of seeing andragogy and pedagogy as steps in a process (teaching-learning continuum).
80. Klapan, "Andragogy."
81. Clair, "Andragogy Revisited," 4.
82. Mohring, *Andragogy and Pedagogy*, 6.

word *paideia* had to do with culture and the education not only of children but also of adults.[83] Mohring's proposition failed to win the battle, and as many other neologisms, has disappeared from common use. However, more works have expanded the discussion on how teaching could and should be provided. It has been noticed that Knowles has finally moved from perceiving andragogy as the antithesis of education for children to conceiving it as the idea of a continuum through which someone (any learner) moves from one level of educational commitment and performance to another.[84] The following statement that Knowles made ten years after the first edition of the same book is eloquent:

> So I am at the point now of seeing that andragogy is simply another model of assumptions about learners to be used alongside the pedagogical model of assumptions, thereby providing two alternative models for testing out the assumptions as to their "fit" with particular situations. Furthermore, the models are probably *most useful when seen not as dichotomous but rather as two ends of a spectrum*, with a realistic assumption in a given situation falling in between the two ends. For example, taking the assumption regarding dependency versus self-directedness, a six-year-old may be highly self-directing in learning the rules of a game but quite dependent in learning to use a calculator; on the other hand, a forty-year-old may be very dependent in learning to program a computer but completely self-directing in learning to repair a piece of furniture. *As I see it, whenever a pedagogical assumption is the realistic one, then pedagogical strategies are appropriate, regardless of the age of the learner – and vice versa.*[85]

As Knowles proceeds in his reasoning, he suggests that the andragogical process involves the following phases which must drive the education processes:[86]

---

83. Ibid., 5.
84. Clair, "Andragogy Revisited," 3; Peterson and Ray, "Andragogy and Metagogy."
85. Knowles, *Modern Practice,* Rev. ed., 43, emphasis added.
86. Ibid., 59.

1. Adult learners need to know why they need to learn something; there is a need to formulate directions of learning (objectives).
2. Adult learners need to learn experientially; there is a need to develop a design of activities.
3. Adults approach learning as problem-solving; there is a need to conduct a diagnosis (planning) and rediagnosis (evaluation) of needs for learning.
4. Adults learn best when the topic is of immediate value; there is a need to establish a climate conducive to adult learning.

In this study, pedagogy and andragogy are not seen in Knowles's initial dichotomist way, but rather as a continuum in the training-learning process of either gender. Discussion takes into account various educational philosophies which have affected and are still affecting the teaching-learning process. Among the most prominent educational philosophies of adult learning experience, one can mention *gogical* formulations of educational approaches. Besides Knowles's *andragogy*, some educationalists have suggested many other neologisms ending by *gogy* to which Courtenay and Stevenson have referred as *gogymania*. Peterson and Ray have discussed the evolution of these neologisms showing why some of them survive while others disappear. A word or phrase ceases being a neologism either by disappearing from common use or by aging. While pedagogy and andragogy are no longer neologisms due to their age, many of other newly crafted educational terms could not survive and have disappeared from common use. Some of them didn't gain the status of neologisms. For instance, *metagogy*'s trademark was cancelled in 2010.[87] Another example is Mohring's *teleiagogy* mentioned above.

Reynolds and Stringer, and Peterson and Ray, indicate some of these approaches from selected authors:[88] *gerogogy* (Lebel in 1978), *humanagogy* (teaching human beings by Knudson in 1979), *geragogy* and *eledergogy* (teaching old adults by Yeo in 1982), *synergogy* (students-interdependent learning by Mouton & Blake in 1984), *anthrogogy* (by Trott in 1991), *ergonagy* (by Tanaka and Evers in 1999), *heutagogy* (by Hase and Kenyon in

---

87. Peterson and Ray, "Andragogy and Metagogy," 84.
88. Reynolds and Stringer, "Pedagogy to Heutagogy," 1–23; Peterson and Ray, "Andragogy and Metagogy," 84. All these authors are quoted in Peterson and Ray ("Andragogy and Metagogy," 85) where one could get related bibliographical details.

2000), *metagogy* (teaching about teaching by Lavoie in 2000) and *ubuntugogy* (by Bangura in 2005). Being affected by the same *gogymania*, Reynolds and Stringer ended up by introducing their concept of *mesagogy* as a transitional stage between pedagogy and andragogy that would embody the struggle both teachers and learners experience in moving beyond pedagogical assumptions and techniques.[89]

The whole issue is about the relationship which exists and should exist between the instructor and the learner and the development of the teaching-learning process. Table 3.3 summarizes, on the one hand, the evolution of the contribution of the instructor, moving from close support to synergy via moderate support and the consulting role. On the other hand, it highlights the contribution of the learner's moves from receiving to synthesizing via accepting and internalizing. According to Reynolds and Stringer, educational approaches move from making the learner passive to active, from making the learner dependent to independent.[90] This continuum in the teaching and learning process has been the research subject for theorists of adult education.

Based on Grow's Staged Self-Directed Learning (SSDL) model, Laton et al. provide an explanation of the student progression.[91] According to these authors, *receiving learners* are accustomed to *pedagogical methods*. Pedagogy being the art or science of educating children, whereby the educator assumes responsibility for deciding what will be learned and when it will be learned.[92] This practice implies that students have neither the means nor the ability to learn on their own. As pedagogy connotes teacher's authority and control, the students' role is to acquire basic facts and concepts presented by the instructor. At this stage, they are *dependent learners*. They learn through such methods as rote memorization, reading assignments and attending lectures. They are dependent upon the instructor and are generally passive learners with limited development. Most often, they have little self-confidence in their ability to apply the information. They may not be motivated to learn and might be dissatisfied or frustrated with the current situation of their learning process.

---

89. Reynolds and Stringer, "Pedagogy to Heutagogy," 1–23.
90. Ibid., 6.
91. Ibid., 9, 10.
92. Hinchey, *Becoming A Critical Educator*.

Table 3.3 Teaching and Learning Continuum: Moving from Pedagogy to Heutagogy

Instructor Contribution →				★
Close Support	Moderate Support	Consulting Role	Synergetic Venture	
			HEUTAGOGY	
		ANDRAGOGY		
	MESAGOGY			
PEDAGOGY				
		Teaching and learning continuum		Learner Contribution
Receiving Learners	Accepting Learners	Internalizing Learners	Synthesizing Learners	

Source: Adapted from Laton, et al. *From Pedagogy to Heutagogy: A Teaching and Learning Continuum.*[93]

Accepting learners are accustomed to *mesagogical methods*. Mesagogy is a model that introduces a stage of development between pedagogy and andragogy. From *meso* in Greek, it refers to middle or intermediate. Hence, mesagogical learners are beyond pedagogical learning – being largely dependent upon the teacher – and are focused on *becoming* andragogical, motivated largely by their own needs and desires to learn. Students exhibit emerging self-confidence and motivation. They comprehend the relationship of facts and concepts taught. They are interested learners. Although still dependent upon the instructor, these learners show some interest in learning and application. They now accept the teacher's instruction and advice as applicable to them.

Internalizing learners are accustomed to *andragogical methods*. According to Cyr, after European adult educators had developed andragogy as a new

---

93. Laton et al., "From Pedagogy to Heutology," 6.

theoretical model of adult learning in 1960s, Malcolm Knowles introduced and expanded the concept to North American adult education literature in 1968.[94] He then compared andragogy (the art and science of helping adults learn) with pedagogy (the art and science of teaching children), which was the traditional teaching method for all learners, regardless of age, prior experience, or developmental level. This educational concept was introduced as a new way of approaching adult education and provided distinctions between how adults and children learn. Subsequently, andragogy, and the principles of adult learning that were derived from it, transformed face-to-face teaching and provided a rationale for distance education based on the notion of self-directedness.[95] At this stage students have taken personal control of learning. Although still dependent upon the instructor for some information, these learners prefer to interact with the teacher and take direct responsibility for *how* learning will be conducted, *what* learning will occur and *why* learning is important. They seek to apply learning, integrating new concepts and values into their mental schema. They are *involved learners* and as such they are confident, committed, and motivated to learn because they now recognize the validity of the information and how it applies to their particular situation.

Synthesizing learners are accustomed to heutagogical methods. Heutagogy emerged in Australia in 2000 and is learner-centered as opposed to teacher-centered learning.[96] The triggering argument for the rationale of heutagogy has been summarized by Hase and Kenyon: "People know how to learn; they did it from birth until they went to school. It's a question of helping them remember how to do it. We need to help people have confidence in their perceptions and how to question their interpretation of reality, within a framework of competence."[97] The key concept of heutagogy is *self-determined* learning. It assumes that people have the potential to learn continuously through their lifespan and in real time by interacting with their environment. Therefore, a heutagogical approach recognizes the need to be flexible in the learning where the teacher provides resources but the learner designs

---

94. Cyr, "Overview."
95. Hase and Kenyon, "Moving from Andragogy."
96. Blaschke, "Heutagogy," 67.
97. Hase and Kenyon, "Moving from Andragogy," 7.

the curriculum, not just the learning process, by negotiating the learning.[98] This stage is characterized by students' expectation of success. They are *self-directed learners*. They have developed to the point of accountability for their decisions and actions, as well as the creation of new and unique applications of learned concepts. Full responsibility for determining sources, flow, content, and outcomes of the learning experience is assumed by the learners. The student-instructor relationship (if an instructor is needed) is now one of interdependence, where challenges are met through mutual inquiry.

Ingalls identified seven steps in the development, organization and administration of programs applicable to any adult learning situation (be it a higher education lecture-room, a project team in the workplace, or a volunteer committee within a community agency, table 3.4).[99] The focus here, however, is the higher education lecture-room.

The evolution, even the revolution, which one could perceive in these various approaches focuses on the training-learning process. It is based on a desire to go beyond the simple acquisition of skills and knowledge as a learning experience. As the student moves from one cycle of study to another, or depending on the expected outcomes of a subject or a field of study, it becomes evident that the choice of a given approach should be appropriately rationalized. These approaches can undoubtedly apply to theological education in general and to missiological education in particular if provided for the purpose of preparing students for the cause of *missio Dei*. Questions that arise may include the following: Does missiological education in a given context exist to teach students through pedagogical, mesagogical, andragogical or heutagogical approaches? Which result should be expected as the outcome of missiological education while using one or another of these approaches? To what extent does the missiological curriculum help students move from one step to another in the teaching-learning continuum? These questions require more inquiry on the transformational role of the nature, purpose and outcome of higher education as the attention should be directed to how these approaches can be used to teach factual knowledge, to enhance attitudes and to develop skills.

---

98. Hase and Kenyon, "Heutagogy."
99. Ingalls, *A Trainer's Guide*.

Table 3.4 Ingalls's Seven Steps in Managing Adult Education

Actions	Steps
Organization	**1. Setting a climate for learning** -Need of accessible, physically and psychologically comfortable surroundings -Need a sense of organizational structure (e.g. lesson plan and agenda)
	2. Establishing a structure for mutual planning -Need to be taught the skills to work collaboratively -Need to promote interaction
Input	**3. Assessing needs, interests, and values** -Need to commit to something which meets their interest -Need to clarify values
	4. Formulating objectives -Steps 1–3 help adults find problem, and from step 4 they move to problem-solving
	5. Designing learning activities -For adults, learning is an internalizing process; learning only what is wanted and in response to their needs, interests and values.
	6. Implementing learning activities -The steps 1–5 are simply an intellectual exercise -Step 6 is where the learning process reaches its peaks
Output	**7. Evaluating results (reassessing needs, interests and values)** -There are two sides of evaluation: the hard (quantitative) and the soft (qualitative) -Evaluating knowledge (capacity to demonstrate what has been acquired), experience (capacity to communicate personal learning experience), and power (capacity to relate knowledge and experience; application of knowledge to real life)

Source: Captured from Ingalls' *A Trainer's Guide to Andragogy*.

3.5.2 Threefold Mandate of Higher Education

Given the fact that missiological education in the context of this study is conducted at tertiary level – the level of adult learners – it is important to capture some perspectives about the *raison d'etre* of a university as they might apply to missiological education. If provided and managed for the purpose of *missio Dei* and how the church has to join God in his mission, missiological education is expected to be a fruitful enterprise. One way of distinguishing between fruitful and unfruitful higher education institutions, relates to what extent the higher education institution not only pays attention to providing teaching, promoting research or serving the community, but also how these objectives are actually implemented in the training-learning process. While some higher education institutions could be described as teaching-universities (teaching-only institutions), others would stand for research-universities (research-only institutions), while still others would be known as community-oriented universities. If standing alone, none of these three categories represents the ideal university. In fact, when the University of Bologna was established in 1088 in Italy, being known as the first university in the history of Europe, people probably did not anticipate the evolution that it was about to experience in both its nature and functions.[100] As Mugabi has put it, not all the three functions of teaching, researching and serving the community were in the agenda of the University of Bologna.[101]

From the earliest medieval period, universities were perceived as teaching-only institutions which focused on interaction between the *master* (instructor) and the *scholar* (student), the latter strongly depending on the former. At the beginning of the nineteenth century, mainly through the influence of the Humboldtian University of Germany,[102] research emerged as a second function of the university, promoting the learner's freedom. Later on, with the founding of land grant universities and colleges in the United States, the mission of the university was broadened into community engagement. At the beginning of the twentieth century, community engagement gained further importance when six civic universities were established in six provincial cities in England – Birmingham, Liverpool, Leeds, Sheffield, Bristol and Manchester – to promote scientific research, practical professional training,

---

100. Sanz and Bergan, *Heritage*.
101. Mugabi, "Institutional Commitment," 187.
102. It was established by Wilhelm von Humboldt and was based upon Friedrich Schleiermacher's liberal ideas about the importance of freedom, seminars and laboratories. Like the French university model, it involved strict discipline and control of every aspect of the university.

more open access and regional development.[103] Therefore, the ideal university is not judged by a label that is glued on a notice-board or a brochure. Instead, it depends on whether the university keeps these three functions in "constant tension with each other at different levels."[104] In the context of this study, one could raise the concern of finding out how theological institutions value and manage such a tension.

The crucial question might be about the understanding of these three functions. Teaching, research and service to the community might not be understood the same way. Sanderson previously mentioned for her statement of prioritizing teaching, was correct to suggest that suitable definitions of scholarship must be explored as an important first step.[105] By "scholarship" Sanderson was actually talking of research. Her preoccupation applies to the other two functions, namely teaching and service to the community. They require a clear understanding.

Skip Bell's research on the Seminary Professorate in Association of Theological Seminaries (ATS) provides a tangible example on how higher education institutions implement the above threefold function of a university in mission studies.[106] ATS forms a community of schools, commonly called seminaries, sharing a collective vision for graduate theological education. Many ATS seminaries are part of a university community, while others exist independent of any linkage to a university. At the time of Bell's research, defining and applying criterion for scholarly research when considering rank advancement was problematic. The purpose of his research was to surface criteria for rank advancement in graduate theological education used in the United States and Canada by ATS seminaries. ATS seminaries were selected, twenty with linkage to a university and twenty independent of such an affiliation. The sampling took into account diversity of region, size, student body and denominational tradition. Through the literature survey, the researcher identified three major trends of how professors on the one side, and the seminaries on the other, consider teaching, research and service to community for rank advancement. The questionnaire was

---

103. Mugabi, "Institutional Commitment," 187.
104. Altbach et al., *Trends*, 139.
105. Sanderson, "Shaping the Academic Enterprise," 384.
106. Bell, "Research Priorities."

returned by 159 seminary professors from 39 ATS member schools. Fifty-seven respondents served seminaries affiliated with a university and 102 from non-affiliated seminaries. Among the variables were departments of mission studies and other departments of theology.

The result was eloquent. In the department of missions or ministry (as Bell called it), according to respondents' perception, the emphasis given by seminaries in rank advancement decisions scored 53.3 percent for teaching, 26.2 percent for research and 20.5 percent for service, when in other departments, the score was of 51.7 percent for teaching, 28.2 percent for research and 20.1 percent for service. The inference from Bell's research is that the departments of missions or ministry within ATS seminaries valued more teaching than research or service. It was the same in other departments, though their appreciation for research was a bit higher than in the department of missions or ministry. Although the research was mainly about rank advancement, another aspect of the inquiry revealed the importance that ATS seminaries assigned to the three components of the mission of a higher education institution.

Further research could be carried out to address some missing aspects in Bell's research. For instance, to determine to what extent the teaching-learning approaches (pedagogy, mesagogy, andragogy and heutagogy) used to prepare students were effective enough to achieve the expected learning outcomes. Research could also be done to determine the extent to which the research projects were either quantitative or qualitative and how their outcomes were in the service of the community. Furthermore, to triangulate Bell's research, both students and deans of academic affairs could be selected as respondents. As direct beneficiaries of their professors' performance, students would have contributed with input whether or not the training was mostly teaching-based, research-based or service-based, and if any of these priorities was needed. Deans of academic affairs would have provided the researcher with official data to determine the reasons of their emphasis on one or another criterion among the three. To check the fruitfulness of the department of missions, research could be done to assess its outcomes given the fact that these seminaries seem to not keeping the three functions in balance. What is true is that, although these three functions are not kept in balanced, they still are in constant tension. ATS seminaries have directly, through exchange programs, or indirectly, through their alumni, influenced many theological institutions throughout the world. By 2005 when Bell's research was carried out, almost all ATS seminaries had changed their mission programs from being schools of world mission to intercultural studies or world Christianity. This change has also affected many ATS-related theological institutions around the world. Research could be done to actualize and confront Bell's findings with current international trends dictated by the Bologna Process whose influence is tangible in many countries in the world. In many countries of Francophone Africa, theological institutions are required to align their training programs with the Bologna Process for accreditation.

3.5.3 The Transformative Purpose of Higher Education

The etymological meaning of education conveys the idea of impacting and acquiring knowledge through teaching and learning.[107] Thus, education denotes the process of both putting new knowledge into the learners and helping them come out of themselves. However, as Shaw observes, education is first about learning rather than teaching.[108] Applied to theological education, it is about a maturation process in students so that they can in turn facilitate the same process in others.[109] According to Sidorkin, education is a set of methods to make learning more efficient, faster and more focused than it would have occurred naturally, learning that is enhanced, organized and structured.[110] For Reardon, education is that process by which new ways of thinking and behaving are learned; as such a very significant component of the transition-transformation processes, the process by which what might be and what people themselves can become, could be glimpsed.[111] From these definitions, one can depict education as a transformative process by which the learner and his/her community are affected for the best. Unfortunately, the experience has shown that the existing educational efforts have not

---

107. Microsoft Encarta, *Encyclopedia*.
108. Shaw, Transforming Theological Education.
109. Plueddemann, "Towards a Theology," 57.
110. Sidorkin, "On the Essence," 523.
111. Reardon, "Human Rights."

always succeeded. That is why the concepts of "outcomes-based education" and "problem-based education" have emerged.

In higher education, this process can be done either as in training for "a specific profession" through practical professional training or in "scientific training" through scientific apprenticeship.[112] While some theorists and commentators conceive education in a dualistic perspective of theory/science versus practice/profession, the conviction here is that, if undertaken to achieve well-oriented and thoughtful actions, higher education in the context of this study should not be carried out neither as visionless professional studies nor as an impractical scientific exercise. Puett thinks that traditional methods of education have not typically aimed to affect constructive social change due to the fact that they tend to promote assimilation rather than transformation.[113] Only the intellectual needs of students, rather than the emotional and spiritual dimensions are stressed. In many locations in Africa, transformative education seems not to occupy the essential place. A holistic approach suggested by Puett would be an alternative to the current educational system. Education must be a tool of transformation and not of mere assimilation.

Two inferences can be drawn from the above observations. On the one side, visionless professional studies are provided to students without helping them to develop a personal vision and the skills relative to their professional integration; students take training programs which cause them to desperately apply for jobs in which their performance would not even fit. On the other side, an impractical scientific exercise would simply provide students with theoretical knowledge which fails to address the actual needs and struggles of the community; students take training programs to propose sophisticated answers to non-asked questions. Therefore, the necessity of providing vision-based professional training or practical scientific studies rests at the core of education for community transformation. Such an education would certainly aim at raising proactive transformers of unfruitful paradigms rather than producing mere conformers to the existing paradigms.

---

112. Van der Walt, *Transformed*, 131–133.
113. Puett, "On Transforming," 263.

Using Van der Walt's above categories, at least three kinds of higher education can be laid out, namely (1) higher education for practical professional training, (2) higher education for scientific apprenticeship, and (3) higher education for combined training strategies.[114] In other terms, while some training institutions would target the "hand" (acquisition of skills), and others the "head" (acquisition of knowledge), still others would embrace both "hand" and "head." For rare cases, the focus on the "heart" (formation of the character) would hardly make the educational agenda. Therefore, the fourth type of higher education institutions is missing in many secular educational systems in the world, which includes the formation of students' character. In general, this has been mostly promoted by Christian-based training institutions due to their stress on the ethical side of the personality formation.

Nevertheless, it is also appropriate to observe that the fact of being a Christian-related institution does not de facto make it a setting for community transformation. Much needs to be done in the process. It requires a strong cultivated sense of responsibility, engagement and accountability within and outside the learning community. Sanderson proposes that the students must actively engage in conversation with instructors in the classroom or in the offices, but also outside the campus with the entire community.[115] To cultivate a transformative learning community, this suggestion will require more work to create structures that bring not only students and instructors together, but also the rest of the community, along with scheduled events that address needs and meet the interest of many stakeholders (e.g. church, secular society, parents, students themselves, etc.). Sanderson is correct to assert that the Great Commission compels man to enter the world which will receive Christ at the hands of graduates who are prepared to live and work anywhere in the world to where Christ leads them.[116] Engagement with the community is the way to transform it. But such an aspiration requires another manner of educating.

---

114. Van der Walt, *Transformed*, 131–133.
115. Sanderson, "Shaping the Academic Enterprise," 385.
116. Ibid., 389.

3.5.4 The Bolognization of the Educational System

The Bologna Process or Philosophy of education is the educational reform which started within the context of the European Union in 1999 when ministers of education met at Bologna, Italy.[117] Suffice it to precise that only twenty-eight of the signatories were ministers (Ireland's signatory was a civil servant); not all the signatories represented countries (Belgium provided both Flemish and Walloon representatives) and most importantly, the Bologna meeting had been preceded by a meeting of ministers from France, Germany, Italy and the UK held at the Sorbonne in 1998.[118] The main objective was to harmonize the educational system within the European Union and, by 2010, to create a common European Higher Education Area and to ensure transparency and accountability in the educational system. This reform was planned in three phases, Bologna I dealing with bachelor programs (of three years for 180 credits), Bologna II addressing the master programs (of two years for 120 credits) and Bologna III relating to doctoral programs (from a minimum of three years for 180 credits).[119] In this process, the workload is defined through a framework comprised of two semesters per year. One semester covers 60 credits and one credit is composed of 25 to 30 hours divided between contact hours and research hours. According to prescriptions of the Bologna reform, the learner should spend more time working alone or in group than attending a magisterial lecture. Therefore, of 25 to 30 hours, the lecture has to likely take 10 hours and the remaining 15 or 20 hours are devoted to the student's personal or collective directed activities.

---

117. European Communities, *ECTS Users' Guide*. The six action lines of the Bologna Declaration were designed to promote the mobility of teachers, researchers and students, to ensure that teaching was of a high quality and to embed a European dimension into higher education. These action lines are: (1) the introduction of easily recognizable and comparable academic degrees and a shared diploma supplement to improve transparency; (2) a system based essentially on a first three-year cycle and a second two-year cycle (master's level) built on the first; (3) the European Credit Transfer System (ECTS) so that credits can be accumulated and transferred; (4) the elimination of obstacles to freedom of movement to enhance mobility; (5) cooperation on quality assurance; and (6) increase the European dimension of study in higher education.

118. McMahon, "Impact."

119. European Credit Transfer System (ECTS) is a system that allocates credits to course units describing the student's workload required to complete them. Credits reflect the quantity of work each course requires in relation to the total quantity of work required to complete academic study.

Both *pros* and *cons* evaluative works on the Bologna Process have been carried out within and outside Europe. Speaking of possible negative effects of the Bologna Process, McMahon highlights the most dramatic change facing those countries that previously had long (five years) first degree cycles leading to a master degree and that have required to introduce a bachelor degree program of three-years duration. This significant shortening of degree program undoubtedly affects the scope and/or the quality of the degree. Consequently, when taken in conjunction with the requirement that the first degree must have relevance to the labour market, one can expect that employers in many countries will experience a radically different type of university graduate starting employment. To overcome such a situation, the Bologna agenda recommends compulsory internships and integration of professional-oriented courses into the first cycle.

Though there is no official position in the United States for the equivalence of the new European bachelor's degree, there are indications that US graduate schools are likely to be opened to the new three-year degrees and that they are willing to consider candidates with strong academic records.[120] A survey conducted in 2005 by the Council of Graduate Schools revealed that 78 percent of the institutions that responded, indicated that they would consider holders of three-year degrees for admission to graduate programs under specific conditions, while 22 percent require four-year degrees.[121] As for doctoral programs, Altbach indicates that although the United States borrowed the basic concept of doctoral studies from Germany in the nineteenth century, adapting it to meet American conditions, the United States, has not been much influenced by other countries.[122] Instead, the influence flows largely from the United States to the rest of the world. Nevertheless, as authors have argued, it is true that the impact of the Bologna agenda will continue to gain adhesion and produce rejection.[123]

From the literature one can also see in the Bologna Process a mixture of educational strategies from both Europe and North America in order to make the European educational system more competitive both within and

---

120. World Education Services, *Understanding and Evaluating*.
121. Ibid., 3.
122. Altbach, United States," 268.
123. McMahon, "Impact"; Gleeson, "European Credit Transfer."

outside the Union. Besides the quality assurance to monitor and ensure the quality of the teaching-learning activities from internal and external perspectives,[124] other key concepts include outcome-based education and problem-based education, whereby the teaching-learning process moves from subject-oriented courses to content-oriented modules, and from teacher-centered education to learner-centered education.[125] These concepts are discussed in further sections below. Meanwhile, it is important to stress that, though it originated from the European Union, the Bologna Process is not limited solely to Europe as McMahon's article tends to show.[126] Due to the tied relatedness between European nations and their corresponding past-colonized countries, this educational system has strongly affected Sub-Saharan African nations in general and those in Francophone Africa region in particular. Accreditation of any training program, including theological education, has even been subsumed to adherence to the Bologna Process. Bernhardt speaks of "Bolognization of theological education" and demonstrates how in his German context, all theological programs had to align with this educational agenda.[127]

In the East African Community (EAC)[128] where I have been active in the educational reform meetings on behalf of my university, the Act which integrated Inter-University Council for East African Community (IUCEA) set at its core an education for transformation. The general observation is that IUCEA's documents on harmonization of higher education system and on

---

124. The term quality assurance refers to all the policies, ongoing review processes and actions designed to ensure that institutions, programs and qualifications meet specified standards of education, scholarship and infrastructure. According to European Association for Quality Assurance in Higher Education (*Standards and Guidelines*), standards and guidelines include internal and external assessment of the training-learning activities. Guidelines for internal quality assurance within a higher education institution include six features: (1) Policy and procedures for quality assurance; (2) Approval, monitoring and periodic review of program and awards; (3) Assessment of students; (4) Quality assurance of teaching staff; (5) Learning resources and student support; (6) Information systems; and (7) Public information.

125. European Communities, *ECTS Users' Guide*.

126. McMahon, "Impact."

127. Bernhardt, "Bolognization," 584. "Bolognization of theological education" is borrowed from "Bolognization of theological education in Germany and Switzerland" by Bernhardt (Ibid., 584–593).

128. EAC includes six countries, namely Kenya, Tanzania, Uganda, Rwanda, Burundi and South Sudan.

quality assurance are mostly the carbon copy of those produced in the context of the Bologna Process in Europe. The argument is that there is no need for reinventing the wheel. For instance, according to the Act, the roles and functions of IUCEA include "promoting internationally comparable higher education standards and systems for sustainable regional development."[129] From this statement of roles and functions, IUCEA articulates its mission as to "promote strategic and sustainable development of higher education systems and research for supporting East Africa's socio-economic development and regional integration."[130] These statements can be easily paralleled with those postulated in the context of Europe. Therefore, the International Leadership University (ILU) located in Burundi, and where I served as academic dean and quality assurance director, had to comply with some specific requirements related to the Bologna Process to keep its membership with IUCEA. However, for various unjustifiable and justifiable reasons including a lack of libraries and infrastructures, reluctance to change, lack of qualified instructors, Internet inaccessibility and dominance of the English language, many countries in Sub-Saharan Africa are still reluctant to accept the Bologna Process. Some of these reasons are discussed by McMahon in the context of European countries and they can apply to the African context as well.

In the DRC which makes the locus of this study, the situation is not different.[131] The prevailing higher education system was initiated and organized based on the Belgian model of three cycles of *Graduate, Licence* and Doctorate (table 3.5). The first three-year cycle of *graduate* inaugurates the tertiary level of post-secondary studies. Admitted to this cycle are candidates who have successfully passed the state examination, a system which started in 1976. The second two-year cycle of *licence* builds upon the first cycle and gives the right to further studies. Most often, not all graduates of this cycle are admitted to the next level of studies. The majority of university-educated graduates, active in both public and private workplaces, belong to this category which is considered key for doctorate studies. The third cycle is

---

129. Inter-University Council for East Africa, *East African Qualifications*.
130. Ibid.
131. Apindia, "La réforme," 102–110; Nyama, "L'université Congolaise," 71–78; *Journal Officiel*.

Conceptual and Philosophical Considerations in Missiological Education   159

doctorate, comprising two stages, namely the first stage of two-year theoretical and research seminars passed upon presentation of a research document of up to 200 pages, and the second stage of three to five years consecrated to thesis research, writing and defence of not less than 400 pages. Some students are even encouraged to produce a doctoral thesis in two or three volumes. While the Bologna Process requires a minimum of eight years to complete a doctoral program, the above-described program would expect a candidate to cover a minimum of ten years.

Table 3.5 DRC Educational System Compared to French Old System and the Bologna Process

Years	French Old System		DRC Current System	Bologna Process	ECTS credits
10			Doctorate		
9					
8	Doctorate		DEA	Doctorate	180 6 semesters
7					
6					
5	DEA	DESS	Licence	Master	120 4 semesters
4	Maîtrise				
3	Licence		Graduate	Bachelor	180 6 semesters
2	DEUG				
1					
SECONDARY SCHOOL					

Source: Drawn from various documents cited in this section.

As displayed in table 3.5, among challenges that the current educational system in the DRC poses, three major challenges can be highlighted here. First, this system of "Graduate-Licence-DEA-Doctorate" no longer exists elsewhere, not even in Belgium from where it originated. When students move to other countries, they always face the challenge of integrating the educational system of the new milieu, in most cases, being obliged to start from scratch. There is loss in terms of years, energy and consideration. Second, the above-described educational system emphasizes a theoretical approach, most of the time relying on out-dated scientific productions of the West where professors were educated. There are proved stories about course notes of more than thirty years still being repeated and used by professors. In rare cases, a bibliographical list of core texts is provided; where such a list exists, books used in many cases are more than thirty years old. Third, this system has hindered initiatives to embrace important educational reforms, including the Bologna Process whose international impact, even over the Belgian system, is obvious. More than twelve years since the Congolese Ministry of Higher Education has suggested the educational reform in 2004, and regardless of the recent Bologna-carbon copy of official instructions released in 2014,[132] the implementation of this new educational system has not yet gained the adhesion of higher education institutions in the country. Meanwhile, the tendency in the prevailing situation is to evaluate education based on quantity (extended duration of studies, big number of courses to be taken, number of pages of dissertation, etc.,) rather than on quality and innovation. Further chapters (5 and 6) of this study will demonstrate whether or not the same situation applies to theological education in general, and to missiological education in particular. Meanwhile, discussion on major concepts which characterizes the Bologna Process sheds some light on the concern.

3.5.4.1 Outcomes-Based Education

The concept of a curriculum traditionally included two elements which are (1) the content or what the students studied, and (2) the examinations which were designed to assess the extent to which the students had learned the content. This concept has expanded to include the learning methods and educational strategies adopted and later to include the aims and objectives of the program. According to Gleeson, outcomes-based education (OBE) means "clearly focusing and organizing everything in an educational system around what is essential for all students to be able to do successfully at the end of their learning experiences."[133] It is an approach in which decisions about the curriculum are driven by the outcomes the students should display by the end of the course. It is a "results-oriented thinking" rather than an

---

132. Journal Officiel.

133. Gleeson, "European Credit Transfer," 1; Spady, *Outcome-Based Education*, 2.

"input-based education" where the emphasis is on the educational process and where educators are happy to accept whatever is the result.[134] According to Spady, the key elements of sound OBE include the definition of outcomes, the design of curriculum, the delivery of instruction, the documentation of results, and the determination of advancement.[135]

OBE has been subject to critics. Several educators and educational theorists have questioned the validity and effectiveness of OBE. Speaking from his Australia context, Berlach found in OBE an obsession with accountability where everything requires proof, speaking in terms of outputs (or exits) rather than inputs, focusing not on content to be acquired, but on outcomes to be achieved.[136] Holt states that OBE advocates misunderstand education because education is not a product defined by specific output measurers; it is rather a process of the development of the mind.[137] Schlafly puts it even more strongly saying "Outcome-based education is not education; it is experimentation. It is not academic; it is psychological."[138] Berlach also adds the following:

> Few teachers, I would venture to say, joined the profession with the idea of becoming indentured servants to the OBE agenda. Not only has their job description changed but with it, their status. What students want has somehow become more important than what teachers want. OBE is all about the "stakeholders," not about teachers. The "stakeholders" rather than the educational providers, are now the educational experts.[139]

The truth is that traditionalists will not perceive OBE positively since it suggests the paradigm shift regarding the role of instructor and student, the teaching-learning process and environment, curriculum design and development and the responsibility of other stakeholders.

One of the features of the Bologna Process is the emphasis on competences – the expected outcomes or the result of the training-learning activities. In

---

134. Harden et al., "Introduction."
135. Spady, *Outcome-Based Education*, 8.
136. Berlach, "Outcomes-Based Education."
137. Holt, quoted in Berlach, "Outcomes-Based Education."
138. Schlafly, quoted in Berlach, "Outcomes-Based Education."
139. Berlach, "Outcomes-Based Education," 1.

a joint quality meeting held in Dublin in 2004, the complete set of shared "Dublin Descriptors" was set out to differentiate the three Bologna cycles of bachelor, master and doctorate while indicating the progression steps between them.[140] Given the need of having a framework of comparable and compatible qualifications, and drawn upon national frameworks of various countries, these descriptors are the fruits of a long process and are based on five competences, namely (1) acquiring knowledge and understanding; (2) applying knowledge and understanding; (3) making judgements; (4) making insightful communication; and (5) learning skills (table 3.5). As one can observe, the focus is on acquiring and applying theoretical knowledge through critical thinking with ability in communication and learning skills.

Subsequently, in outcomes-based education, "product defines process."[141] It is about "product before process."[142] For instance, while planning for a missiological training program, the question should be, "What sort of missiologist, missionary or missional leader will be produced?" rather than "What should be the education process?" Therefore, the educational outcomes are clearly articulated and they determine the curriculum content and its organization including the teaching methods and strategies, the courses offered, the assessment process, the educational environment along with the curriculum timetable and its evaluation framework.

---

140. Joint Quality Initiative, "Shared Dublin Descriptors."
141. Harden et al., "Introduction," 8.
142. Gleeson, "European Credit Transfer," 1.

Conceptual and Philosophical Considerations in Missiological Education 163

Table 3.6 The Dublin Descriptors of Three Cycles

Cycles / Competences	Bachelor 3 Years – 180 Credits	Master 2 Years – 120 Credits	Doctorate 3 Years – 180 Credits
Acquisition of knowledge and understanding	have demonstrated knowledge and understanding in a field of study that builds upon and their general secondary education, and is typically at a level that, while supported by advanced textbooks, includes some aspects that will be informed by knowledge of the forefront of their field of study	have demonstrated knowledge and understanding that is founded upon and extends and/or enhances that typically associated with bachelor's level, and that provides a basis or opportunity for originality in developing and/or applying ideas, often within a research context	have demonstrated a systematic understanding of a field of study and mastery of the skills and methods of research associated with that field
Applying knowledge and understanding	can apply their knowledge and understanding in a manner that indicates a professional approach to their work or vocation, and have competences typically demonstrated through devising and sustaining arguments and solving problems within their field of study	can apply their knowledge and understanding, and problem-solving abilities in new or unfamiliar environments within broader (or multidisciplinary) contexts related to their field of study	have demonstrated the ability to conceive, design, implement and adapt a substantial process of research with scholarly integrity

Making judgements	have the ability to gather and interpret relevant data (usually within their field of study) to inform judgements that include reflection on relevant social, scientific or ethical issues	have the ability to integrate knowledge and handle complexity, and formulate judgements with incomplete or limited information, but that include reflecting on social and ethical responsibilities linked to the application of their knowledge and judgements	have made a contribution through original research that extends the frontier of knowledge by developing a substantial body of work, some of which merits national or international refereed publication – are capable of critical analysis, evaluation and synthesis of new and complex ideas
Communication	can communicate information, ideas, problems and solutions to both specialist and non-specialist audiences	can communicate their conclusions, and the knowledge and rationale underpinning these, to specialist and non-specialist audiences clearly and unambiguously	can communicate with their peers, the larger scholarly community and with society in general about their areas of expertise
Learning skills	have developed those learning skills that are necessary for them to continue to undertake further study with a high degree of autonomy	have the learning skills to allow them to continue to study in a manner that may be largely self-directed or autonomous	can be expected to be able to promote, within academic and professional contexts, technological, social or cultural advancement in a knowledge based society

Source: Based on Joint Quality Initiative, *Shared Dublin Descriptors*.[143]

---

143. Ibid., 3, 4.

3.5.4.2 Problem-Based Education

The guiding principle here is an education that addresses the real problem faced in and by the community. An education that lacks to deal with the real issues or challenges of the society will simply result in becoming a sterile academic exercise. It will rather prepare students to provide sophisticated answers to non-asked questions. Such a reality has prompted scholars to underscore the value of problem-oriented learning (POL) or problem-based learning (PBL). Cunningham and Cordeiro define it as "an instructional approach that uses typical problems of practice as the context for an in-depth investigation of core content."[144] For Savery it is "an instructional (and curricular) learner-centered approach that empowers learners to conduct research, integrate theory and practice, and apply knowledge and skills to develop a viable solution to a defined problem."[145] These definitions underscore the fact that PBL is an instructional approach, but not an end in itself. As such, it needs contextualization and actualization to fit the learners' needs and interests. It requires a strong sense of commitment and sufficient participation on both sides of the instructor and the learner who must move from theory to practice. According to Dolmans reviews conducted in the early 1990s and since 2000 demonstrated not only that students and instructors were highly satisfied with PBL, but they also demonstrated that PBL stimulates students towards constructive, collaborative and self-directed learning.[146]

There has been a concern, however, to determine the superiority of PBL over traditional curricula. Reports on a systematic review and meta-analysis on the effectiveness of PBL used in higher education programs have not proved convincing evidence. Despite this lack of evidence, PBL has been adopted and utilized in various contexts, from elementary schools to universities and professional training centers, within different disciplines of studies.[147] However, research has revealed that failure to achieve the expected learning outcomes is due to several factors including the following:[148]

---

144. Cunningham and Cordeiro, *Educational Leadership*, 354.
145. Savery, "Overview," 12.
146. Dolmans et al., "Problem-Based Learning."
147. Torp and Sage, *Problems as Possibilities*.
148. Savery, "Overview," 11.

1. confusing PBL as an approach to curriculum design with the teaching of problem-solving;
2. adoption of a PBL proposal without sufficient commitment of staff at all levels;
3. lack of research and development on the nature and type of problems to be used;
4. insufficient investment in the design, preparation and ongoing renewal of learning resources;
5. inappropriate assessment methods which do not match the expected learning outcomes defined in problem-based programs; and
6. evaluation strategies which do not focus on the key learning issues are implemented too late.

Several authors have identified important elements which characterize PBL, including the following:[149]

1. Students must have the responsibility for their own learning.
2. The problem simulations used in problem-based learning must be ill-structured and allow for free inquiry.
3. Learning should be integrated from a wide range of disciplines or subjects.
4. Collaboration is essential.
5. What students learn during their self-directed learning must be applied back to the problem with reanalysis and resolution.
6. A closing analysis of what has been learned from work with the problem and a discussion of what concepts and principles have been learned are essential.
7. Self and peer assessment should be carried out at the completion of each problem and at the end of every curricular unit (for both cognitive and motivational self-regulations).
8. The activities carried out in problem-based learning must be those valued in the real world.
9. Student examinations must measure student progress towards the goals of problem-based learning.

---

149. Quoted in Dolmans et al., "Problem-Based Learning"; Savery, "Overview."

Conceptual and Philosophical Considerations in Missiological Education 167

10. Problem-based learning must be the pedagogical base in the curriculum and not part of a didactic curriculum.

A summary of these characteristics is done by Dolmans et al. through a set of four learning principles. They maintain that PBL has the potential to prepare students more effectively for future learning because it is based on four modern insights into learning, namely constructive, self-directed, collaborative and contextual. Therefore, the learning activity should be the following:

1. A constructive process in which students actively construct or reconstruct their knowledge networks. When trying to explain the phenomena in the problem students should determine what they already know about the problem, what they do not yet know and which questions still need to be answered, and which ones require study.
2. A self-directed process whereby learners play an active role in planning, monitoring and evaluating the learning process. Teachers are facilitators who stimulate students towards self-directed learning.
3. A collaborative process in which two or more learners interact with each other and, in some circumstances, some types of interactions occur that have a positive effect. Motivational and cognitive self-regulations of each group members influence tutorial groups.
4. A contextual process which takes place in a given context or in a well-located situation. The context is taken into account for application.

For this study, one could wonder about the relevance of PBL in missiological education. If missiology is an applied science as discussed previously, this instructional approach could help students lead their churches toward God's mission.

3.5.4.3 From Subject-Oriented Courses to Content-Oriented Modules

The basic principle of the Bologna reform is that "orientation toward content and acquiring competence is to replace conveying knowledge of subjects in isolation."[150] Instead of focusing on traditional subjects, the learning process emphasizes the acquisition of skills and competences generated by a well-defined content of a module. For instance, in classic Protestant theological corpus, the most important subjects are Old and New Testaments, church history, history of theology, systematic theology and practical theology. In most programs the theological curriculum is made up of these subjects. Now, with the Bologna philosophy, the curriculum is made up of modules, each module being a unit of study. Modules are built upon one another. While some modules are compulsory, other are electives or optional. Optional modules allow students to pursue their own interests as they also strive to develop their personal emphasis according to their area of research or concentration.

The study under the Bologna system is much more structured than in the previous practices. For each module the following features are to be well-defined: The module description (nature, rationale and purpose), the prerequisites (foundational learning), the content, the goals for learning (expected outcomes), the forms of instruction (showing clearly the instructor's and learner's specific role) and the type of assessment (formative and summative).

3.5.4.4 From Teacher-Centered Learning to Learner-Centered Apprenticeship

A detailed comparative discussion about teacher-centered and learner-centered approaches is conducted in a collective document entitled *Student Centered Learning: An Insight into Theory and Practice* edited by Attard. According to this document teacher-centered learning has to be organized by others who make the appropriate associations and generalizations on behalf of the learner.[151]

The work by Barr and Tagg on paradigm change shows the difference between "instruction paradigm" and "learning paradigm" whereby the mission and purposes of education, criteria for success, teaching/learning structure, learning theory, and nature of roles of instructor and student take different forms and orientations (table 3.6).[152] For the authors, education should be aimed at transformation of the learners in order to make them

---

150. Bernhardt, "Bolognization," 587.
151. Attard, *Student Centered Learning*, n.p.
152. Barr and Tagg, "From Teaching to Learning," 13–25.

agents of transformation. Though their work was based on undergraduate education, the authors' suggestions are likely to be relevant to any level of tertiary education.

Table 3.7 Comparing Educational Paradigm – From Teaching to Learning

Instruction Paradigm	**Learning Paradigm**
Mission and Purposes Provide/deliver instruction Improve the quality of instruction Achieve access for diverse students	*Mission and Purposes* Produce learning Improve the quality of learning Achieve success for diverse students
Criteria for Success Quality of entering students Quality and quantity of resources Quality of faculty, instruction	*Criteria for Success* Quality of exiting students Quantity and quality of outcomes Quality of students, learning
Teaching/Learning Structure Time-held constant, learning varies Covering material End-of-course assessment Degree equals accumulated credit hours	*Teaching/Learning Structure* Learning held constant, time varies Specified learning results Pre/during/post-assessments Degree equals demonstrated knowledge and skills
Learning Theory Learning is cumulative and linear Learning is teacher-centered and controlled The classroom and learning are competitive and individualistic	*Learning Theory* Learning is a nesting and interacting of frameworks Learning is student centered and controlled Learning environment and learning are cooperative, collaborative and supportive
Nature of Roles Faculty are primarily lecturers Faculty and students act independently and in isolation Teachers classify and sort students	*Nature of Roles* Faculty are primarily designers of learning methods and environments Faculty and students work in teams with each other and other staff Teachers develop every student's competencies and talents

Source: Based on Barr & Tagg, *From Teaching to Learning*.

3.5.4.5 Field Education

Field education has been discussed by scholars in the context of theological education. On an empirical study conducted about the purpose and shape of theological field education within theological education, Beisswenger reported of forty-two people who responded to a questionnaire with the following result:[153]

> 42 percent indicated the integrating of academic study with practical issues of ministry;
>
> 14 percent indicated the development of skills for the work of ministry;
>
> 14 percent indicated the integrating of what students know with their personhood, life in the spirit, and professional skills in the work of ministry; and
>
> 5 percent indicated the development of pastoral identify and appropriate sense of pastoral authority.

As one can infer from these findings, for many, the primary purpose of field education in theological education is to integrate academic study with practical issues of ministry which include professional skills and personal spiritual life. The research also asked the respondents if they could anticipate changes in field education in the next decades. The concept of integration as the primary goal persisted. The integration was understood in the context of the research as "bridging the gap between academic perspectives and ministerial perspectives."[154] However, Beisswenger suggests that further research was needed to determine whether the integration does serve as the governing purpose and goal in field education.[155] Beisswenger's suggestion applies to the context of this research on missiological education. The question would then be, "Is field education important for missiological education? If yes, what is the primary purpose of field education in missiological education? How can field education be undertaken?"

---

153. Beisswenger, "Field Education."
154. Ibid., 53.
155. Ibid., 51.

Even without an empirical research on the issue in the context of the DRC, one could already answer to these preoccupations based on the following general comments provided by participants to Beisswenger's research:

> Field educators perceive a problem of fragmentation within theological education. The student's academic studies are not clearly related to their social existence in ministry. Knowledge learned in the classroom is not closely related to the requisites for situations of ministry. The knowledge in the classroom, it appears, needs to be related to the tasks of preaching, caring, educating, administering, and advocating.[156]

As stated in the first chapter, the same observation has triggered the present research. The assumption was that if Protestant theological education in the DRC was really in the service of God's glocal mission, the CCC and its related *communautés* would have been more active in the mission field at the global context than they are today. Undoubtedly, one of the reasons would be the lack of relatedness of academic studies to the social existence in the ministry of students. This situation would have caused theological education to be irrelevant for the mission of the church. The problem of fragmentation between knowing, being and doing is permanent in any setting. This problem has prompted models of theological education in Berlin, Athens, Jerusalem, Geneva and Antioch as already discussed earlier in this chapter (section 3.4.1). Therefore, field education is perceived as a way to address the recurring issue of fragmentation within theological education. The same problem can apply to missiological education as well. In fact, the critical questions would be to know if field education will appear in a given missiological curriculum as one of the important teaching units, in which form will it be, how it will be designed and assessed by the instructors, and how it will be undertaken by students.

3.6 Concluding Considerations

The literature survey carried out in this chapter investigated key features of a productive education, taking into account both conceptual and philosophical

---

156. Ibid., 53.

elements. Such a purpose emerged from the findings of the preceding chapter where missiological education for *missio Dei* was identified as one of key determinants for both theory and practice of mission. Therefore, the chapter included literature from both secular and theological educators focusing on higher education with application to missiological education. The findings of this literature review can be sketched in the following two categories: (1) missiological education and theology, and (2) missiological education and higher education.

3.6.1 Missiology in the Context of Theological Education

Missiology has always been offered in the context of theological education, either in the setting of a seminary or within a university-affiliated program. The survey of the literature has prompted some significant insights.

1. Understanding missiological education as a process which is done through an intended content, a purpose, a method, an ethos, a context and a people. These features are defined by the providers of a given study program, and make a missiological discourse different from other discourses. The question remains to know what is that makes a discourse really missiological. The answer to this concern will justify the *raison d'être* of missiology and its related educational activities.

2. Missiological education in theological education has been subject to several studies whose findings have shown that theological institutions tend to lose missional essence. Instead of being in the service of the mission of the church, the prevailing theological education in many instances failed to assign an honorable place to missiology. The question is still to know the relationship which could be developed between missiology and theology. Is missiology mother, sister or daughter of theology? The answer to this question will certainly determine the future of missiology and missiological education regarding its place within the theological corpus.

3. Contemporary models of missiology in theological education have been designed in various ways in different countries and institutions. In general, research centers established in a context of university, are the channels through which missiological

education is provided in many places, focusing on graduate and postgraduate levels. Missiological education becomes more a research-based study program than a traditional coursework. The critical question is whether such a model can be duplicated and fruitful in contexts like in the DRC where the traditional coursework is still the common approach to education.
4. Missiological education and typologies of theological education constitutes a strategic approach to a study program which purposes the involvement in God's glocal and holistic mission. Unfortunately, the existing typologies have proved insufficient to the training of people for God's glocal mission. This gap has called for a new model, and a proposition of the Antioch model was made.

3.6.2 Missiology in the Context of Higher Education

Because missiological education is undertaken in the framework of higher education, the following conceptual and philosophical features are determinant as they underscore the importance of productive education:

1. Learning theories of adult education have undergone a continuing development which caused educationists to deconstruct and construct existing theories. The truth however is that an adult teaching-learning process requires an appropriate curriculum, methods and learning settings. Consequently, missiological education shouldn't be provided without these requirements.
2. The threefold mandate of higher education relates to providing teaching, promoting research and serving the community. Experience has shown that many institutions have the tendency of uplifting one or two of these mandates at the expense of others. To be relevant and fruitful, missiological education should use these three mandates as a three-leg chair to install a mission-mindset in the life of students and their respective churches.
3. The transformative purpose of higher education underscores the fact that an educational activity which fails to bring transformation loses its *raison d'être*. This transformative endeavour is concerned with the students, the instructors, the

training institution itself and the community in which the institution is established and from which students come. The question is to know whether missiological education could apply its transformative purpose in a given context.

4. The Bolognization of higher education has become a must and missiological education is not exempted. Experience has learned that the implementation of the Bologna Process has been delayed in many places for several reasons. The critical question, even for this study, is to know how missiological education can be "bolognized" (without being Europeanized, or becoming irrelevant to the context of a given country), without losing the ultimate purpose of promoting God's glocal mission.

The following chapters will explore the above preoccupations through historical (ch. 4) and empirical (ch. 5) surveys before proposing a model of missiological education (ch. 6) that takes into account all these preoccupations.

Part III

Missiology and Missiological Education in the DR Congo

CHAPTER 4

Mapping the Historical Roots of the Protestant Missiology and Missiological Education in the DR Congo

4.1 Introduction

The previous chapter discussed the conceptual and philosophical considerations in missiological education. It was demonstrated that missiology in general, and missiological education in particular, is underpinned by doctrinal and philosophical exigencies while also being influenced by both international and local contexts. This chapter focuses on the particular context of the DRC, the immediate setting of the present study. It is an historical survey and a missiological analysis of the Protestant work in the DRC as it may have paved the path for missiology and the missiological education along the way. It is an attempt to provide a broad description of the various forms that missiology and missiological education have taken in the history of the Protestant Missions and Church in the DRC in order to better understand and interpret the current situation of missiology and missiological education in the country. While exploring these historical features, effort is made to stick to the main subject under consideration, "the historical roots of the Protestant missiology and missiological education in the DRC," highlighting key facts, events, institutions and people as they would have influenced the missiological threefold lines of conceiving, teaching, and doing mission. This objective aligns with our working definition of missiology as being a scientific and applied reflection on how mission is and should be conceived, taught and done.[1]

The chapter could otherwise have been entitled "The study of missions in theological education"[2] or "Missions and theological education."[3] For several reasons including our working definition of missiology, the use of the word *missions* as it is explained shortly below, the fact that this chapter is an attempt to move beyond mere theological education, and also due to historical realities of the DRC, I prefer the formulation "the historical roots of the Protestant missiology and missiological education in the DRC." If missiology encompasses "conception, training, and doing" of God's mission, then the missiological education would only be a parcel of the whole package to the extent that the conception and the doing of mission influence the training for mission.

Three sets of questions undergird our investigation:

1. **The theory of God's mission**: What is actually God's mission? To describe the Protestant missiology as a reflection on the **theory of God's mission**, two important guiding questions are: "What is the nature and the purpose of the church according to you, your mission society or your church?" "How could the nature and the purpose of the church be described?"

2. **The practice in God's mission**: How should God's mission be accomplished? To describe the Protestant missiology as a reflection on the **practice of God's mission**, two important guiding questions are: "What are the methods and strategies used by your mission society or church to accomplish the purpose of the church?" "What could be the effective methods and strategies to accomplish the supreme task of the church?"

3. **The training for God's mission**: How should the training for God's mission be provided? To describe the Protestant missiology as a reflection on the **training for God's mission**, two important guiding questions are: "What are the methods and content used by your mission society or church to teach about the nature

---

1. See chapters 1 (section 1.7.3) and 2 (section 2.2.2).
2. Myklebust, *Study of Missions*, vols. 1 and 2.
3. Conn and Rowen, *Mission and Theological Education*.

and the purpose of the church?" "What could be the effective methods and content to teach about the nature and the purpose of the church?"

In fact, what someone conceives is relatedly taught in one way or another, verbally or through actions. What Protestant missionaries and nationals in the DRC have said and done in regard to the nature and the purpose of the church is actually an important part of the teaching they would have provided, intentionally or not. All the same, what someone teaches consequently would come from what that very person thinks and does. What Protestant missionaries and nationals in the DRC would have taught about the nature and the purpose of the church certainly proceeded from their conception and practice of mission. As matter of fact, "the study of missions in theological education" (Myklebust) or "missions and theological education" (Conn and Rowen) in the particular context of this study cannot be well-captured without considering the prevailing missiology of the time, both at global and local level. As it will clearly appear in this chapter, the story about missions, church, and mission-related courses in the DRC has actually been a developmental process which cannot be understood separately if someone hasn't to distort the whole picture of the subject under study.

Thus, the purpose of this chapter is to trace the development of Protestant missiology in the DRC as to facilitate the comprehension of how missiological education (or mission-related courses and programs) closely related to the historical facts and events which punctuated the nature and the task of Western missions and their related national churches. Writing an historical account of several missions and churches in one chapter requires tact, concentration, and discipline as long as materials to be sorted out come by thousands. For such a limited research scope, only key insights can be selected. Effort is made to capture the conception, the teaching and the practice of mission throughout the long period of the formal missionary presence in the DRC (1878–1970) and then during the national leadership of the national church (1970–2016). So far as the DRC makes the essential of this study, data will be integrated to this chapter only if they would contribute to the description of the nature and the task of Western missions and their related national churches.

4.2 Important Terminologies

Before moving forward, it is now important to clarify the use of *mission, missions, missionary(ies), mission-related courses,* and *church* in the particular context of this chapter on the DRC. Besides their general use, the above terms bear specific meanings. In the history of church in the DRC, *mission* was mostly used to designate Western mission organizations or the mission station where missionaries settled. In this chapter, I will use *Mission* (with capital letter and sometime in plural) for that purpose. The *Church* (with capital letter always in singular) will be used to designate the national church which resulted from the work of Missions. However, various local churches which made the national church will be identified by either *local denominations* or *communautés*. The use of local denominations is important because each Mission which usually represented one or more Western mainline churches (Baptist, Methodist, Presbyterian, Reformed, etc.) has produced at least one or more related local denominations. For instance, there were two distinct Methodist church in Katanga and Kasai provinces, while Mennonite church was found in Kasai and Bandundu. These local denominations were officially entrusted administrative autonomy in February 1960 due to the political situation and events which accompanied the independence movements in the country. The church in the DRC got its "autonomy" before the political independence was given to the country on 30 June 1960. With this "precipitated" autonomy,[4] nationals took over the leadership of the work from Missions, and the inherited work became *Eglises* (churches). Therefore, there was transfer of legal papers between Mission and *Eglise* (Church). For instance, "Mission Evangélique en Ubangi" (MEU)[5] became "Eglise Evangélique de l'Ubangi" (ECU).[6] These *Eglises* bore the status of denominations and, later, changed the name to *communautés* when, not without

---

4. I use this term provisionally and with prudence because from my understanding of the history, already in 1938, nationals were invited to hold their first Protestant Christian Convention in parallel to Missionary conference, twenty-two years before the independence. However, one can also research on the reason which triggered the organization of that Convention, and whether these Conventions continued or not.

5. Mission Evangélique en Ubangi means Evangelical Mission in Ubangi.

6. Eglise Evangélique de l'Ubangi means Evangelical Church in Ubangi.

reason, all Protestant churches in the DRC united under one *Eglise du Christ au Congo*[7] in 1970. Much details will be given about it in this chapter.

Though this study doesn't understand the work of biblical mission as the exclusive responsibility of Western Christians, in order to be consistent with the history, the word *missionary(ies)* in this chapter will be used only for Western missionaries. Later, in subsequent chapters, distinction will be made by using other terms like "Western missionaries" and "Congolese missionaries," etc.

Due to the fact that the use of *missiology* as an academic discipline was not common in the DRC before 1990s, I prefer to use *mission-related course(s)* or *programme(s)*. The point is that though not using the academic controversial concept of *missiology*, courses related to evangelism, world religions, or alike, were provided in Bible Schools or Institutes initiated by both Missions (before 1960), or in partnership (between 1960–1970), or by churches/ *communautés* (after 1970).

To be well-captured, the history of the Protestant missionary work in the DRC can be traced through some existing frameworks as in any account of the history of missions. Nevertheless, authors diverge in their subdivision of the treatment of the history of Missions. Some frameworks are reviewed before selecting one to be used for the particular purpose of this study.

4.3 Discussion about Frameworks to Understand the Missionary Work in the DRC

4.3.1 An Analysis of Existing Frameworks by Some Authors

Any researcher wishing to grasp the evolution of Protestant missions in the DRC from a missiological perspective would find the book *Zaïre: Midday in Missions* by McGavran and Riddle as a valuable tool. The book was published in the context of the celebration of the centenary of *Protestant* presence, but not *Missions* presence, in the DRC. As said earlier, the use of "Missions presence" couldn't be politically correct in an environment where "missions" were believed to cease existing a decade earlier, since the last meeting of the Congo Protestant Council (CPC) in 1969. Also because

---

7. The Church of Christ in Congo.

missionary enterprise has been charged of collaborating with colonialism. Nevertheless, an objective historical account of Protestant missions in the context of the DRC would probably paint a different picture.

McGavran and Riddle suggest a framework of four stages in order to apprehend and sketch the real situation of missionary work in the DRC and in any land: exploration, occupation, people movements, and completion.[8] What they call "exploration" is actually more than mere investigation. It includes preliminary activities of identifying a land and starting the first evangelistic and humanitarian services. For some missions in the DRC, this period could last longer than twenty years. During the second stage of occupation, a permanent location is found and developed. More missionaries are recruited to join the work, and different services are established. The third period of people movement inaugurates the era during which tribes and clans come to faith, having churches amidst them in small villages, schools develop and national leaders multiply, occupying position of authority.

The final stage is completion – when the work of Christianization of a country is completed by making a great part of the population Christian. In McGavran and Riddle's words, it's during this period that "nationals are sent abroad to play their part in world evangelization." In this stage, the church of Christ bears two forms: institutional form (the national denominations) and dynamic form (missionary society). As they conclude their description of stages, McGavran and Riddle make a challenging point about some missionaries and nationals' tendency to confuse the difference between these stages ignoring that each of them has its realities and requires a particular way of conducting affairs. One can question this categorization of conceiving the national church as *static* and the mission society as *dynamic*. Many people might find in this categorization the root of lack of mission mindset of most mainline-related churches in Africa; while Western missions are seen dynamic, involved in God's mission worldwide, the national churches accept the call of being static, institutions which have to keep what has been inherited from missionaries.

---

8. McGavran and Riddle, *Zaire*, 26.

Though not specifically dealing with the DRC, Alan Johnson provides another framework worth considering in tracing the history of missions.[9] He speaks of emerging paradigm and also suggests four stages, moving from pioneer to participation via paternal and partnership stages. During the first two stages (pioneer and paternal), the reality of the missionary is done within the respective context of unreached people and reached people. Meanwhile, the author thinks that it might be natural [sic] to undergo a parenthetical period of paternalistic stage. Once the paternalistic stage has been over, two more stages come across (partnership and participation). The stage of partnership and that of participation give opportunity to both parts to play a role in the common business of the Kingdom.

These two four-stage models of understanding the missionary work by McGavran, Riddle and Johnson raise some crucial questions in the context of the DRC where over fifty mission groups from different geographical, ecclesiastical and doctrinal backgrounds finally came to unite under the consultative umbrella of the CPC: How similar, different or interchangeable are these frameworks? If used in one given country, like the DRC, how should we date each stage? To which extent are these two models relevant to our understanding of the development of missiology and missiological education in the DRC and its impact on the mission engagement of the Church?

These questions could be addressed elsewhere in a different work. The context of this chapter imposes that only the third question be examined. The study is more concerned about the work generally done by Protestant missions in the DRC than other studies could focus on a particular mission group. The history teaches that more than fifty missions reached DRC in different periods and they established their works in different "mission fields" or different grounds following the comity policy.[10] In the process,

---

9. A. Johnson, "A Model," 136.

10. The comity generally represented a "gentleman's agreement whereby one mission agreed not to intrude in the territory or interfere in the work of another mission in the same country" (Kane, *Understanding Christian Missions*, 156). This policy had a positive effect on the missionary work in terms of unity and cooperation, but it has left a negative effect on the missionary involvement of nationals in mission beyond their direct environment. Bradley N. Hill ("Rethinking Comity," 175–178), a former missionary to the DRC couldn't hesitate to state that once invaluable tools of efficient evangelization without conflict, the comity policy finally became counterproductive. It only served to perpetuate the religious disorder inherited from Western denominationalism. Comity-related churches remained "rigidly immobile

one or another group of missionaries certainly would have experienced one or another of the four grounds of Jesus's parable (cf. Matt 13:4–8). Some would have scattered seed "along the path," others "on rocky places," still others "among thorns," and the luckiest "on good soil." McGavran and Riddle recognize that their first stage for some missions in the DRC took eight years while others endured for twenty years.[11] This is the reason for authors to finally admit that they could not set the beginning and the ending times of any of their four stages because "there is a wide variation in dates [. . . of stages] since no two regions of Zaïre are exactly the same in point of development."[12] Explaining why missions preferred Western part of the country, Alfred Stonelake finds the reason in difficulties missions encountered in moving to other parts of the country: "Difficulties of travel . . . coupled with the unfriendly attitude of the natives."[13] Several years later, giving an account of the situation of Protestant missions in 1960s, Crawford reports that while some missionary structures dissolved, others were in the process of reducing their involvement, and others in the process of integrating into the national churches.[14] Therefore, it is fair to contend that stages in missionary work were not the same for all mission groups. Since this study does not deal with one single mission group, McGavran and Riddle's stages do not seem applicable to our effort of describing the missionary work in the DRC as a whole with implications for the missiological education in the country.

The same observation applies to Johnson's scheme. As far as mission societies in the context of the DRC are concerned, it is even difficult to distinguish when one could speak of partnership or participation between Missions (in their diversity) and the Church in Congo (in its diversity as well). For instance when the CPC made the decision to found the CCC,

---

within their walls of comity" (Hill, "Rethinking Comity," 179). Klaus Fiedler (*Story of Faith Missions*, 365) observes: "Because the whole country was divided up by comity agreements, missionary work would have meant working abroad, but the churches could not afford that, and the indigenous church principle, as applied by faith missions, meant that 'white' money could not be used for black missionaries." Also Robert P. Beaver (*Ecumenical Beginnings*).

11. McGavran and Riddle, *Zaire*, 26.
12. Ibid., 68.
13. Stonelake, "Missionary Situation," 314.
14. Crawford, *Protestant Missions* (1969), 17.

another group of missionaries and nationals decided to set up the *Conseil des Eglises Protestantes au Congo* (CEPCO)[15] in February 1971 because they were more interested in their own autonomy rather than in an organic unity.[16] Up to now some churches, like Seventh-Day Adventist, have never been members of the CCC. Likewise, some other churches, even though members of the CCC, as the denomination connected with the Baptist Missionary Society, would prefer to use on its official letter headline only the mention "Culte Protestant au Congo" instead of "Eglise du Christ au Congo, *Communauté* . . ." as required by the constitution of the CCC. Thus, Johnson's scheme can work in a context of a single group as he states himself that his diagram "illustrates the new missiological framework within the *context of a single people group.*"[17]

The third framework to understand missionary work could be that of using the two kinds of missions: denominational missions and interdenominational missions. In his published doctoral research, Klaus Fiedler identifies two eras in missionary movements anywhere in the world.[18] The era of denominational classical missions inaugurated by William Carey in 1792 through his *An Enquiry into the Obligation of Christians to Use Means for the Conversion of the Heathen*, and the era of interdenominational faith missions inaugurated by Hydson Taylor in 1865. Fiedler would even prefer to call them otherwise as respectively "classical missions" and "post-classical missions," the latter, called also "faith missions," being the main concern of his book.[19]

Thus, according to the author, two missionary traditions have set the path to all missionary movements. The first is based on the initiative of William Carey who went to India, and the second relates to the work of Hydson Taylor who went to China. Mission through the first model, denominational, is attached to a given denomination. The Baptist Missionary Society (BMS) becomes the prototype of denominational missions, whereby the missionary engagement is well organized within the denomination which

---

15. Council of Protestant Churches in Congo.
16. Garrard, "Protestant Church," 134.
17. Johnson, "A Model," 136, emphasis added.
18. Fiedler, *Story of Faith Missions*, 9.
19. Ibid., 10.

sends its sons and daughters overseas to perpetuate the work started at home. In this way, there is the Baptist Church in Great Britain, and there should be the Baptist churches through the work of Baptist Missions outside of Great Britain, in India, the DRC, Kenya, etc. On this line come Methodist, Reformed, Presbyterian, Lutheran, Mennonite, etc.

Similarly, Mission through the second model, interdenominational, is not attached to one single denomination. China Inland Mission, now Overseas Missionary Fellowship, becomes the reference of interdenominational missions, whereby mission engagement is undertaken by faith, without too much prior organization in terms of financial support as it is mostly the case with denominational missions. A group of missionaries, coming from different local churches and denominations coalesce for mission adventure outside of their countries. They serve in different capacities and churches are not necessary named after a mainline traditional church at home.

If Fiedler's framework coincided in other countries, the situation in the DRC was different. Mission organizations which served in the DRC were either "denominational missions," "non-denominational missions" or "interdenominational missions."[20] As Stonelake observes, the Livingstone Inland Mission (LIM), a non-denominational mission group, not BMS, reached the country first in February 1878.[21] The founders of LIM, H. Grattan Guinness and his wife,[22] were inspired by Hudson Taylor's thinking of world mission and his experience in China.[23] Within a year the mission was rapidly set up and the first missionaries were recruited and deployed to Congo. This conglomerate of missionaries could not last longer and, six years later, split into two different groups. There were the American

---

20. Further in his book, talking about the "comity policy," Fiedler (*Story of Faith Missions*, 192) recognizes that "Zaire, in particular, with its plurality of classical missions, faith missions, non-denominational missions and denominational evangelical and Pentecostal missions, had an extremely well-functioning comity system."

21. Stonelake, "Missionary Situation," 314; *Congo Past and Present*, 35.

22. Dr H. Grattan Guinness was the founder of the non-denominational East London Institute for Home and Foreign Missions in 1872, and the pioneer of this organization in the DRC was H. Craven who landed at Banana a few days after Grenfell and Comber of BMS had left. He settled on a hill-top at Palabala, a month or so before the arrival of the first permanent missionaries of BMS. According to Stonelake (*Congo Past and Present*, 35), efforts to carry the gospel into the interior were a first pursued by the LIM.

23. McGavran and Riddle, *Zaire*, 52.

Baptist Foreign Missionary Society (ABFMS) on one side, and the Swedish Covenant Mission (SCM) on the other side. Still they all were influential members of the CPC which was transformed into the CCC several years later. The BMS joined the game six months later. The reality is that in the DRC interdenominational mission preceded the denominational mission.[24] Also, they didn't even come as classical or post-classical, nor "with faith" and "without faith." They were all challenged by the discovery and left their respective countries by faith as God was providing.

To some extent, Fiedler's framework could be a good way to understand the missionary work in the DRC if each Mission group kept its identity of being "denominational" or "interdenominational" from home country. However, given the widely accepted aspect that Protestant missions in the DRC have decided to work in a spirit of unity, bringing together denominational, non-denominational and interdenominational missions, one could not easily notice the difference between the three groups. As early as in 1902, missionary held their first Conference of Protestant missionaries, attended by missionaries representing the eight mission societies of that time.[25] The shared idea was to provide a platform "not only for spiritual inspiration and worship, but also to discuss common problems connected with their work and how best, collectively, they could serve Christ and Congo."[26] This unity was also forced by the climate of antagonism faced on ground; antagonism conspired by Roman Catholic missions and the Belgian government against Protestant missions. Authors have documented this unfortunate situation.[27] These realities "helped to draw the Protestants of Congo closer together."[28] For these various reasons, the agenda of the first Conference of Protestant

---

24. For instance, taking the example of the London Missionary Society (LMS) and the American Board of Commissioners for Foreign Missions (ABCFM), Kane (*Understanding Christian Missions*, 151) observes that "the earliest society [in the 19th century] were interdenominational."

25. While Coxill ("Protestants," 274) reports that participants represented eight mission societies, McGavran and Riddle (*Zaire*, 66) contends that there were rather seven mission societies. What is true is that not all mission societies were represented.

26. Coxill, "Protestants," 273.

27. Stonelake, Missionary Situation, Anet, "Congo Native," "Protestant Missions"; Lerrigo, "Protestant Missions"; Coxill, "Protestants"; Davis, "Educational Development"; Slade, *English-Speaking Missions*; Carpenter, "Whose Congo?"

28. Coxill, "Protestants," 275.

missionaries included issues such as "education, native evangelists, polygamy and the church, uniformity in translations, relations with the government, etc."[29]

One might straightaway observe that the conference went beyond mere fellowship by tackling the issues related to mission methods and strategies, and doctrinal problems. These issues and problems could compromise both the missionary work that time and the future of the church in Congo. Though back home from their respective denominations missionaries could have held some different points of view, the context and realities of their work on ground in the DRC imposed to the majority of them another conduct of more openness and cohabitation. For instance, the Evangelical Free Church from the United States started its work in the DRC in 1922 before being joined by the Evangelical Covenant Church in 1937. Though being different denominations in the United States, these two churches made one denomination in the DRC until the year of their split in 1970 resulting in two national denominations, Communauté Evangélique du Christ en Ubangi (CECU) and Communauté Evangélique de l'Ubangi-Mongala (CEUM). The latter is my church of origin through which I heard about Jesus and have served as pastor for dozens of years before being set apart for an interdenominational ministry in 2003. I attended the theological school started by the above two American denominations with my colleagues of the other church. We used the same books on "evangelical" doctrines and pastoral ministry upon the completion of our theological studies. We then duplicated the same teachings in our respective local denominations.

The above-described situation was a common experience in several places in the country to the point that the nationals were not as aware as their missionaries could be about some particularities in the identity of their related Western missions. The implication is that the differentiation of "denominational missions," "non-denominational missions" and "interdenominational missions" was not apparent except for the interdenominational ministries which didn't own local churches. Among them one can name Campus Crusade for Christ, Scripture Union, Bible Translation Society, etc. These were actually interdenominational in the context of the DRC. The remaining

---

29. McGavran and Riddle, *Zaire*, 66.

represented local denominations such as different branches of Baptists, of Mennonites, of Methodists, of "Evangelicals," etc.

The above three frameworks, though useful in some cases and for other purposes, do not seem applicable to the present study. The next section describes our working framework.

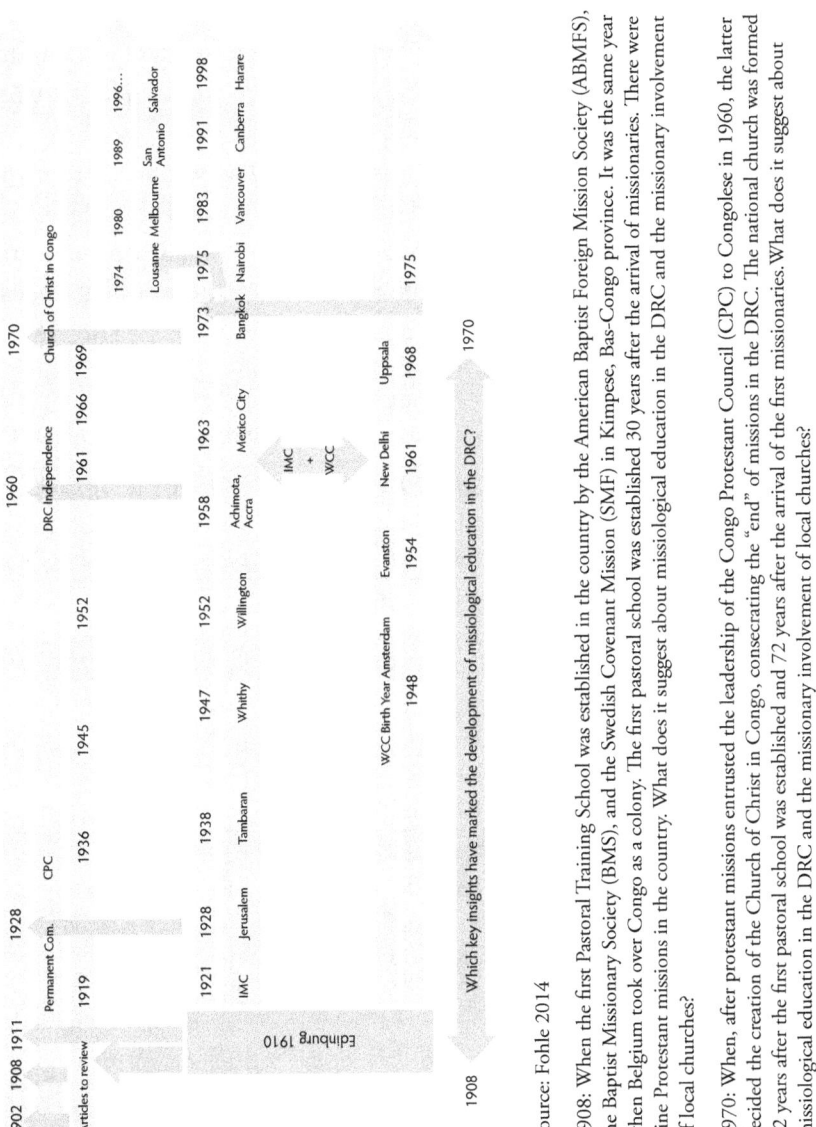

Source: Fohle 2014

1908: When the first Pastoral Training School was established in the country by the American Baptist Foreign Mission Society (ABMFS), the Baptist Missionary Society (BMS), and the Swedish Covenant Mission (SMF) in Kimpese, Bas-Congo province. It was the same year when Belgium took over Congo as a colony. The first pastoral school was established 30 years after the arrival of missionaries. There were nine Protestant missions in the country. What does it suggest about missiological education in the DRC and the missionary involvement of local churches?

1970: When, after protestant missions entrusted the leadership of the Congo Protestant Council (CPC) to Congolese in 1960, the latter decided the creation of the Church of Christ in Congo, consecrating the "end" of missions in the DRC. The national church was formed 42 years after the first pastoral school was established and 72 years after the arrival of the first missionaries. What does it suggest about missiological education in the DRC and the missionary involvement of local churches?

Figure 4.1 Matching Protestant Mission Work with Global Mission Trends

4.3.2 Toward a New Framework to Understand Missionary Work in the DRC

As one seeks to understand the missionary work in the DRC and its implication for the missiological education in the country, and in regard to the above discussion, the idea of thinking of a new framework surfaces. Taking into account the realities of missionaries' struggles which caused them to consider openness and cohabitation as best strategies for missionary work, also knowing that the global trends influenced the missionary work in the DRC as they were in other part of the world, a framework made of crucial global and local events could be useful (fig. 4.1).

In addition to the frameworks discussed in previous section, there might exist others. Mission historians could think of general world historical events working plan, like colonial period, World War I and II, independence, etc. Others might consider Missions-State or Missions-Church relations, when others, as in this study, would relate the missionary work in the DRC to the global mission history (table 4.1).

Table 4.1 Possible Time Frames to Understand Missionary Work in the DRC

Periods	*FRAMEWORK 1* Missions-State Relations	*FRAMEWORK 2* Missions-Church Relations	*FRAMEWORK 3* Missions and Global Mission Trends
1	1878–1908 Under Free State (the rule of King Leopold II)	1878–1902 From one mission to several missions working in solo to the 1st Congo Protestant Conference of missions	1878–1908 From the 1st mission to the 1st pastoral training school
2	1908–1948 Under the Colonial non-friendly Belgian government	1902–1924 From the 1st Congo Protestant Conference of Missions to the CPC	1908–1911 From the 1st pastoral training school to Congo Continuous Committee (influenced by Edinburgh 1910)

3	1948–1960 After the recognition of Protestant schools (toward the independence of the country)	1924–1928 From the CPC to the mission 50th anniversary (1878–1928)	1911–1928 From Continuous Committee to the mission 50th anniversary (1878–1928) 1928: IMC Jerusalem
4	1960–1970 The first decade of the independence of the country (transitional period for mission); CPC under Congolese leaders	1928–1960 From the 50th anniversary to the transfer of leadership	1928–1952 From the mission 50th anniversary to 1952: IMC Willingen, Germany
5		1960–1970 From the transfer of the leadership to the birth of CCC	1952–1961 From IMC Willingen conference to the merge of IMC and WCC at New Delhi
6			1961–1970 From the merge of IMC and WCC at New Delhi to the birth of CCC

The point at stake in this section is to demonstrate the importance of setting the framework of understanding the development of missiology and missiological education in the DRC. The main argument is that, as we have already demonstrated in the previous section, not all frameworks can help understand what, why and how the missiology and missiological education would have taken one or another form in the history of missions in the DRC. The truth is that in one single document, different chapters or sections can be produced through different frameworks. One can even see it in the above-mentioned Crawford's documents. Later on in this chapter, another framework will be used to discuss the missiology and missiological education in the DRC during the post-missions period (1970 to present). In the history of missions in the DRC, besides what has been previously discussed, the following framework can be considered.

4.3.3 Time Frame Referring to Missions and Global Mission Trends

As far as the missiological education in the context of Protestant missions in the DRC is concerned, the framework which refers to global mission trends presents several advantages. One of the main advantages relates to the fact that Protestant missions in the DRC from the beginning were motivated by and linked to global mission trends, and along the way, the missionary work in the DRC was influenced and affected by the global mission trends. It has been reported that the discovery of David Livingstone by Henry Morton Stanley made the DRC internationally known. Not only the person of Livingstone was the most important event, but also what Stanley discovered during his trip in the interior of the DRC and on the Congo River. For him, it was a rich land one could prefer to visit or to settle in, a land of "heathen" people. Writing from a Baptist context probably for Baptist constituents, Stonelake sees this situation as a divine providence for God's mission in the DRC:

> The commencement of missionary work in Congo coincided with the discovery by Stanley of the course of the river. It is a significant example of God's over-ruling providence that the Baptist Missionary Society in September 1877 publicly accepted the challenge of Mr Robert Arthington to begin work in Congo, only three weeks before the proclamation of Stanley's discovery did so much to prepare the way for its accomplishment.[30]

Historically, the BMS was preceded by Livingstone Inland Mission, rapidly formed due to Stanley's report.[31] The same, the work in Katanga province by the Garanganze Evangelical Mission, a non-denominational mission, was motivated by the news about Livingstone.[32]

Even after the first Protestant missionaries had arrived, their work was not done without international awareness, mostly as, according to authors, missionaries faced the rude treatment of natives by both King Leopold II (up

---

30. Stonelake, "Missionary Situation," 314.
31. Falk, *Growth*, 375.
32. McGavran and Riddle, *Zaire*, 52, 55.

to 1908) and by the Belgian government (from 1908 to 1938).[33] Protestant missionaries rang the bell and their sound was heard, attracting the attention of worldwide political powers and civil societies around the world. It then becomes obvious that Protestant missionaries realized that their mission went beyond the simple fact of preaching the salvation. It should not be an exaggeration to guess that the teaching on the responsibility of the church of Christ, according to the majority of Protestant missionaries that time, entailed different aspects including the fact of helping natives to enjoy freedom. As we will discuss further, the question could also be raised whether the natives' freedom should be the final end of the missionary work or not. Subsequently, the missionaries' theology of mission is to be understood in light of the context of their work.

Throughout the years, the Protestant missionary work in the DRC was closely enlightened, if not influenced, by the World Mission Conferences, a direct result of the Edinburgh Conference in 1910. Stonelake makes it clear: "In 1911 a local Continuation Committee was formed, in order that Congo might linked up with the World Missionary Conference, Edinburgh 1910. Any action taken by this committee has to be submitted to the General Conference for approval."[34] What Protestant missionaries in the DRC started in 1902 through their first General Conference in Léopoldville (Kinshasa) is developed through global mission gatherings held outside of the country, in Edinburgh (1910), in Jerusalem (1928), in Tambaran Madras, India (1938), in Whitby, Ontario, Canada (1947), in Willingen, Germany (1952), in Achimota, Accra, Ghana (1957–58), and in Mexico City, Mexico (1963). The General Assemblies of the WCC held in New Delhi, India (1961) and in Uppsala, Sweden (1968) had also a significant impact on the Protestant missionary work in the DRC (see fig. 4.1).

Suffice it to say that the framework which is used to explore the development of missiology and missiological education during the period of Western missions in the DRC is the framework which uses glocal mission trends as *fil conducteur* (guidelines). It will be demonstrated that the understanding of the nature and the task of the Church and Missions was not only what

---

33. Stonelake, "Missionary Situation"; Anet, "Congo Native," "Protestant Missions"; Lerrigo, "Protestant Missions."

34. Stonelake, "Missionary Situation," 326.

missionaries initially brought from their home churches, but also a mixture of newly acquired insights through new encounters: what they had learned before joining the mission field, what they gleaned from their experience on ground, what they continued to discover through readings and conferences, etc. From my own experience of serving as missionary in the Central African Republic and now in Burundi along with my ministerial visits in many places of the world, it would not be an exaggeration to state that the understanding of mission task by Protestant missionaries didn't remain static. One can also observe the same change in their teaching. For instance, in a thoughtful article published in 1936 on the future of Protestant missions in the DRC, P. H. J. Lerrigo reports on the following life-changing account in the life and ministry of some missionaries:

> The older and more thoroughly organized missions have made serious efforts both to co-ordinate their work and to keep in touch with the government, but some of the newer missions pursue their course with little regard for the programs and practices of other missions and pay a minimum of attention to the government itself . . . Many of those even whose preconceived theories laid no emphasis whatever on education *have come to realize that the training of mind and heart is part of the gospel message*, and are asking for counsel on how they may best develop the educational services which they find it impossible to avoid establishing for the peoples in the areas where they work.[35]

This kind of account on the transformation of missionaries' mindset is inevitable in the whole history of missions all over the world. Even the apostle Peter underwent the same transformational experience in his mission work. The most of his obvious experience resulted from his encounter with Cornelius. After having seen God's work in Cornelius's life with a direct impact on his household, Peter couldn't hesitate to confess: "I now realize how true it is that God does not show favouritism but accepts men from every nation who fear him and do what is right" (Acts 10:34, 35 NIV). Mission and missiology should bring transformation.

---

35. Lerrigo, "Protestant Missions," 231, 232, emphasis added.

Another account is from John Gration who served for several years with African Inland Mission in the DRC and in Kenya. Gration shares his experience of how he gained a new perspective on the contextualization of the gospel message in these terms:

> I recognized that I had delivered many prepackaged boxes of biblical truth to my Zairian students . . . Furthermore, the delivery system fostered a mentality of theological dependency that matched the colonial context. Through my deepening understanding of what contextualization was saying to missions and churches alike . . . I had no choice but to return to the church in Zaire with this new word.[36]

The literature review which follows will probably trace these realities. Based on the reasons yet to be stated below, the main literature to review is made of papers or articles written by Protestant missionaries who served in the DRC, or by some mission statesmen who worked closely with Protestant missions in the DRC. To keep the study focused, only documents connected with the local and global mission trends will be reviewed. This work is an attempt to set the tune for further in-depth works relating either to one particular denomination, or one province in the DRC, or one particular theological institution, or for a very limited or extended time frame, etc. Here, the focus is on Protestant missions from the time they set up the first pastoral training school in 1908 followed by the establishment of a permanent committee in 1911 due to the influence of the Edinburgh Conference held in 1910. This section will conclude with the eve of the official proclamation of the CCC in 1970.

4.4 Protestant Missions, Mission and Missiological Education in the DRC (1878–1970)

4.4.1 From One Mission to Several Missions: Revisiting *Their* History

The Protestant missionary work started in the DRC in February 1878 through the Livingstone Inland Mission, a mission society rapidly formed

---

36. Gration, "Willowbank to Zaire," 297.

as response to Stanley's report on his discovery of David Livingstone and the rich land of Congo.[37] As the word spread out, several other mission societies followed the step, representing denominational, non-denominational and interdenominational bodies until 1969 when, according to Bokeleale missions as institutions ceased to exist.[38]

The use of *their* on the subtitle is significant. I don't pretend to trace the historical steps without facing some hesitation. The hesitation on telling the story of someone else is a normal feeling when the objectivity is required at its maximum. Consequently, the major duty here is to review the missionaries' story in order to revisit their history and to learn what has been thought and done in regard to missiology and missiological education. In one of his important books entitled *Changing the Frontiers of Mission*, Wilbert R. Shenk, the historian of missions, states that "although they were frequent participants in discussions of missionary principles, missionaries contributed little to the literature of mission theory."[39] Where Shenk's observation applies, the reason is obvious. Whether missionaries were not academically qualified enough to attempt such a demanding enterprise of coining theoretical insights, or simply because, though being academically well-equipped, the enormity of the task on ground along with all the struggles they faced, time and the context of the work could not allow them to "waste" time in theorizing. Nevertheless, so far as the Protestant missionaries in the DRC are concerned, Shenk's observation does not apply. Most published books and articles used in this section originated from missionaries. In a paper published when the missions were described as being under attack, Ralph D. Hyslop wonders whether the picture painted in missionary literature about missions, mostly written at headquarters of mission boards, could be the same if it was produced by missionaries on the field or by national pastors and laymen.[40] His wonder is legitimated by the fact that a report from eyewitnesses would generally be more reliable than a second-hand account from a distant author.

---

37. Stonelake, "Missionary Situation," 314; Coxill, "Protestants," 273; Falk, *Growth*, 374.
38. Bokeleale, "From Missions to Mission," 433.
39. Shenk, *Changing the Frontiers*, 41.
40. Hyslop, "Missions," 460.

Here emerges also the debate about whether missiology as a reflection on mission comes before or after mission.[41] To put it differently, could a missionary be treated as missiologist or not? Which kind and size of a writing (published or unpublished) can be recognized as an authorized channel of mission theory: a one-page original reflection paper from a mission practitioner or a hundreds-page researchable thesis from a scholar? Shenk, and theoreticians of research methodology, would probably answer in affirmative for both cases since in any scientific research, the primary sources, or first-hand accounts, are mostly recommended regardless their size. Just after having made the above statement, Shenk acknowledges that although many missionaries were not able to produce mission theories, some of them, like John L. Nevius who served as missionary in China was among the few mission theoreticians.[42] Some Protestant missionaries who served in the DRC are to be counted among them. Most of us probably remember the book *Missionary, Go Home!* by James Scherer as one of the books on mission theory in 1960s. Maybe, not many know that another book, *Missionary, Come Back!* by Arden Almquist, a missionary to the DRC, was released few years later as another face of the same mission coin. While in *Missionary, Go Home!* the cry was that the national church should be handed over to the local leadership, through *Missionary, Come Back!* the cry came out to insist that the church, being Lord's new family, needs God-given gifts from both Western and African Christians. The latter book promotes the mission theory of a responsible, but brotherly partnership in mission.

While recognizing that sometime missionary literature, be it from the mission field or from the headquarters of mission boards, was either informational or promotional, still one can use and cross-check them as to get meaningful insights about the overall scenario. The conviction here is to learn from missionaries' own story. Therefore, the effort is made to keep track of what missionaries have written, as long as the content sheds some light on their understanding of mission and mission-oriented education before objectively making any assumption. Moreover, the plan is to first of all understand the educational background of missionaries, their mutual

---

41. Winter, "Missiological Education," 169–185.
42. Shenk, *Changing the Frontiers*, 42.

comprehension of mission and missionary task, some key spotlights of their mission-oriented training ministry, and the essential legacy of their work to the national church.

The review of the following literature constitutes the backbone of this section. If one desires to let Protestant missionaries who served in the DRC speak of their story, there are two valuable sources of information: Interviewing with them or reading their writings (letters, journals, articles, and books). Because at this stage, the first source is not available, most of them having been with the Lord, or for rare of the surviving their memory has been weakened, the most available source are their writings. Two significant writing sources are the *Congo Missions News* (CMN) and the *International Review of Missions* (*IRMs*) launched both the same year in 1912. While the former was a local periodical for specifically the Protestant work in the DRC until 1972 when the government regulation in the country prohibited the publication of religious journals,[43] the latter was, and still is, a well-appraised international platform for discussion about mission(s).

4.4.2 The Significance of the Congo Missions News and Other CPC Publications

Speaking of the nature and the content of the *Congo Missions News* (designated from now as *CMN*), Stonelake contends that this periodical was "highly valued by the missionaries as a medium of fraternity and help in mutual service."[44] He also adds that the *CMN* has been perceived by missionaries as "a means of securing a consensus of opinion on the ordinary problems of missionary work, and of obtaining the benefit of the experience, council and help of the missionaries of long standing, it is invaluable."[45] Later in his book on *Congo: Past and Present*, Stonelake shared the reaction from a South African professor, J. du Plessis who applauded *CMN* in the following friendly words: "Your paper is in many ways unique. Though missions in South Africa are now more than one hundred years old, we have not attained to the happy position of possessing a paper which represents the views of

---

43. Irvine, *Church of Christ*, vi.
44. Stonelake, "Missionary Situation," 326.
45. Ibid., 327.

all the missions on the field."⁴⁶ Du Plessis' reaction was published in *CMN* (41:13). However, it is not unimportant to note that *CMN* was "prepared especially for missionaries and their supporters."⁴⁷ Therefore, one could see in it as an instrument for marketing and fundraising rather than pure scientific platform for objective and impartial discussion. Therefore, someone who searches first-hand (though sometimes subjective) information about what Protestant missionaries in the DRC used to think, say and do about mission and the mission-related training, had better drink from the *CMN* fountain. Unfortunately, I was not able to find copies of this important collection at the headquarters of the CCC. The Internet search through WorldCat.org revealed however that a collection of *CMN* was available in forty universities and colleges around the world including Yale University, University of Chicago, Boston University, and Harvard University. A good collection can be found in two universities and one institute in South Africa with a restricted access.⁴⁸

Besides *CMN*, the following publications pertaining to the work of Protestant missions in the DRC are worth mentioning, and researchers willing to collect first-hand data will find in them as valuable sources of information.

1. *Message of the Congo Jubilee and West Africa Conference*, Léopoldville, 15–23 September 1928.
2. *Christ and the Congo: Findings of Conferences Held under the Leadership of Dr John R. A. Mott, Chairman of the International Missionary Council*, Léopoldville, Mutoto and Elisabethville, 1934.
3. *After Sixty Years 1878–1938: Report and Findings of Conference Held at Léopoldville, Congo Belge, to Celebrate the Diamond Jubilee of the Foundation of Congo Protestant Mission*, Léopoldville, 1938.

---

46. Stonelake, *Congo Past and Present*, 63.
47. Coxill, "Protestants," 275.
48. According to SACat, the national catalogue of South Africa *Congo Mission News* can be found at the following three institutions: (1) University of Pretoria, Merensky Library, for issues of 1914–1935; (2) South African Institute of Race Relations, Johannesburg, for issues of 1929–1956; and (3) University of the Witwatersrand, Waternweiler Library, Johannesburg. The search on WorldCat indicates that at least ten other libraries in the world hold this journal.

4. Series of *Congo Protestant Council Minutes*, each year from 1940 to 1970, except the year 1946 which had two minutes.
5. E. M. Braekman, *Histoire du protestantisme au Congo*. Bruxelles: Librairies des Eclaireurs
6. Unionistes.
7. D. A. McGavran and N. Riddle, *Zaire: Midday in Missions*, Valley Forge, PA: Judson Press.

4.4.3 The Significance of the International Review of Mission(s)

For the evident reason of tracing the connection between the Protestant missionary work in the DRC and the global mission trends, the *International Review of Missions* (designated from now as *IRM*) is selected as the most official and reliable source of information since these articles were either presented during the World Mission Conferences or just submitted to the editors through scrutiny of the CPC. Since the first World Mission Conference held in Edinburgh, 14–23 June 1910, mission societies were challenged not only to reach out the whole world with the whole gospel in their generation, but also to profit from the benefit of the unity. At Edinburgh, one of the biblical references was John 17:21 ("That all of them may be one . . . so that the world may believe"). In the DRC, the call has fallen on a good soil. Reference has already been given to what Stonelake has reported, that "in 1911 a local Continuation Committee was formed, in order that Congo might linked up with the World Missionary Conference, Edinburgh 1910."[49] Concluding his report on the Protestant missions in the DRC, Stonelake's words show the link between the two entities, "Congo" and "Edinburgh":

> It is earnestly to be desired that an influential deputation may be sent to represent the Edinburgh Conference at the next Congo conference in November 1921, in order to examine the conditions at first-hand and to help the missionaries to solve the problems and face the tasks with adequate forces of workers and equipment.[50]

---

49. Stonelake, "Missionary Situation," 326.
50. Ibid., 330.

Another evidence of the link "Congo-Edinburgh" comes from H. Wakelin Coxill. Writing as the secretary of the CPC in 1945, Coxill almost repeats Stonelake's remark on the common feeling among missionaries in the DRC: "In 1911 the Congo Continuation Committee was formed, probably the first field committee to link up with the Continuation Committee of the Edinburgh Conference of the 1910."[51]

The first issue of *IRM* was launched in 1912 under the editorship of Oldham who defined the primary purpose of this newly initiated journal as a way to "further the serious study of the facts and problems of missionary work among non-Christian peoples, and to contribute to the building up of a science of missions."[52] For that very scientific reason, the editor insisted that *IRM* had the ambition of being more than a collection of papers. It tended to be an "organ of a comprehensive, systematic, and united effort to study missionary problems" by promoting "Christian fellowship and foster the spirit of readiness to learn from one another."[53] Another crucial function of *IRM* was to serve present and future missionaries, and to stimulate authors to learn from the past and to engage in a scientific enterprise of producing thoughtful papers through which the journal had to:

> . . . study and sift the vast body of experience that has been accumulated in different mission fields, and make it available for the direction of present work; to aim at reaching large guiding principles, based on a thorough and fearless examination of the facts; and to test all methods with a view to securing the highest efficiency.[54]

Authors have demonstrated the significance of *IRM* as "a means of international exchange of ideas and information within the new discipline of 'missionary science,'"[55] in advancing "learning about mission strategy, methods of evangelization and mission theology."[56] Brian Stanley observes that *IRM* brought a fresh orientation in missionary periodicals. While most

---

51. Coxill, "Protestants," 274.
52. Oldham, "Editor's Notes," 1.
53. Ibid., 5, 6.
54. Ibid., 2.
55. Stanley, "Edinburgh 1910," 149.
56. Skreslet, "Missiology," 160.

missionary publications were produced with the primary function of informing and rallying support for missions, *IRM* was designed primarily for the benefit and edification of the mission professionals themselves.[57] This reality highlights the significance of *IRM* as a channel through which missiological reflections were developed and disseminated, not only by great scholars of the time, but also by practitioners who were on ground. In 1987, *IRM* celebrated its 75th anniversary. The celebratory issue of *IRM* was released, and Philips Potter, one of the former editors, wrote a review of some important articles published from the inception of the journal in 1912, mentioning only articles written by influential scholars such as Roland Allan, Kenneth Latourette, Emil Brunner, Hendrik Kraemer, etc. In a recent article released during the celebration of *IRM*'s centenary, Andrew Walls confronts Potter's attitude through an article entitled "Missions or Mission? The *IRM* after 75 Years" in which he provides a section on "What was and was not reviewed in 1987."[58] The following statement from Walls shows that other contributions, including those from the Protestant missions in the DRC, were ignored despite amount of insights they contained:

> Mission societies underwent convulsive experiences such as the withdrawal of missionaries from China, and a short period in Congo evoked comparisons with the Boxer Rising. The winds of change in Africa, where there often were slow transitions from missionary to national church leadership, blew with a strength that became irresistible.[59]

In 1969 the CPC held its last joint "Missions-Nationals" meeting which consecrated the end of missions in the DRC as the initiative to form the CCC started. With this decision, the *Congo Missions News* couldn't survive. The very same year the *International Review of Missions* also made the decision to drop "s" from "mission."[60] Therefore, *International Review of Missions* [*IRM* with "s"] became *International Review of Mission* [*IRM* without "s"].[61]

---

57. Stanley, "Edinburgh 1910," 149.
58. Walls, "Missions or Mission?" 181–188.
59. Ibid., 185.
60. International Review of Mission.
61. Though the official abbreviation could be either *IRM* or *IRMs* to stress the change, I however prefer to use *IRM* for all issues published before and after 1969 to avoid confusion.

This change was actually the result of a long theological discussion which started at the World Missionary Conference at Willingen, Germany, in 1952. The discussion continued throughout the years at Achimota, Ghana, in 1958, when the agreement was made to merge the International Missionary Conference and the World Council of Churches. The first merged meeting of New Delhi in 1961 followed by Mexico City, Mexico, in 1963, were enough to bring change. The common theological conviction was that the mission has its origin in the triune God and belongs to him, though he uses the churches and the missions or sending agencies as instruments in the interim period. These temporal instruments should be ready to submit themselves to changing realities and needs. *Missio ecclesiae* (man-made missions) should be ready to concede its right to *missio Dei* (God-made mission). The church receives its existence from God's mission and receives its responsibility of world mission from the same God.[62] This concept did not go without misunderstanding and critics.[63] The second chapter of this study has already discussed them.

Pastor Jean Bokeleale Itofo, who served as the general secretary of the CPC (1968–1970) prior to being elected the first president of the CCC,[64] could entitle his article published in *IRM* in 1973, "From Missions to Mission." The first paragraph of his article is revelatory of the connection between the Protestant realities in Congo and the global mission trends:

> It is quite some time now since the *International Review of Missions* became the *International Review of Mission*. The change in thinking revealed in this change in name characterizes also some of the thinking of the Church of Christ in Zaire (Protestant church), for since 1969 Protestant **missions** have ceased to exist in Zaire. At the General Assembly of the former Congo Protestant Council in that year, Zairian churchmen decided that after almost a century of missionary endeavour

---

62. Hogg, "Teaching of Missiology," 488; Gunther, "History and Significance," 528–530.

63. Glasser, "Conciliar Perspectives"; Engelsviken, "Missio Dei."

64. Pastor Jean Bokeleale Itofo has served as the president of the CCC for 22 years (1970–1998) and died in 2002, four years after he stepped down from the leadership of the CCC.

in their country, missions as institutions no longer had any reason to exist, and the Church in Zaire had to assume its responsibilities for the true **mission** of the Church to evangelize the Zairian people.⁶⁵

Much will be said about the significance of Bokeleale, his ministry and thoughts, in relation to the development of missiology and missiological education as one can already see some spotlights from the above quote. For the moment, suffice it to stress the link "*CMN-IRM*." One might be impressed by the permanent reference to the Edinburgh Conference and the frequency of news about Protestant missions in the DRC in this leading missionary journal of the post-Edinburgh. George W. Carpenter, a former missionary in the DRC, was even the secretary of the IMC which was established in 1921 as a continuing committee of the World Missionary Conferences.

The following articles are selected due to the light they shed on this study. With reference to the framework used to understand the missionary work in the DRC, one might detect the relationship between these articles, the global mission trends and the understanding of mission, missionary task, and the training for the missionary task of the church. Along the way, other books and articles written by missionaries or nationals on the missionary work of this period (1908 to 1970) are used to supplement with any valuable information.

1. "The Missionary Situation in Congo," a 16-page article published in the *International Review of Missions (IRM)* 8, (1919): 314–330, authored by Alfred Stonelake.⁶⁶ The paper was prepared after the Edinburgh Conference of 1910, after Protestant missionaries in the DRC have already initiated their General

---

65. Bokeleale, "From Missions to Mission," 433.
66. According to the editor of *IRM* (1919): 422, Rev Alfred Stonelake went to DRC as missionary with the Baptist Missionary Society in 1900 and "has taken a leading part in connection with the recent successful development of cooperation among Congo missions." Referring to the recommendations of the World Conference of Missions in Edinburgh (1910), Stonelake proposed to the General Conference of Protestant missionaries in the DRC that a continuing committee be established. The permanent committee was launched in 1911 before being transformed into the Congo Protestant Council in 1928 following another World Conference of Missions held the same year in Jerusalem (McGavran and Riddle, *Zaire*, 66).

Conference in 1908 and their permanent committee in 1911, and also in the context of World War I (1914–1918).

2. "Congo Native and Belgian Administration," a 10-page article published in *IRM* 30, (1921): 196–206, authored by Henri Anet.[67] This article coincided with the establishment of the International Mission Council (IMC) in 1921 to serve as continuation committee for the World Mission Conferences (WMC). Delegates to WMC were representing National Missionary Councils around the world, and later on National Christian Councils. In the case of the DRC, these two councils are respectively the Congo Protestant Council and the Church of Christ in Congo.

3. "Protestant Missions in Relation to the Future of Congo," a 7-page paper published in *IRM* 25, (1936): 227–234, authored by P. H. J. Lerrigo[68] This article was published between the two World Mission Conferences held in Jerusalem (1928) and in Tambaran, Madras, India (1938). For the first time in the history of WMC, one-third of the audience was made of the delegates from younger churches. In Tambaran, the stress was on indigenization, the call for local theology. Lerrigo's article can shed some light on how missionaries were thinking of the nature and the future of the work they initiated in the DCR.

4. "Protestants in the Belgian Congo," a 6-page article published in *IRM* 34, (1945): 273–279, authored by H. Wakelin Coxill.[69] This article was published in the context of World War II,

---

67. According to the *IRM*'s editors (1921): 293, Rev Henri Anet held a doctorate in Social Sciences from Brussels University. By the time he wrote this paper, he was pastor of the Belgian Church and General Secretary of the Société belge de Missions protestantes au Congo. This paper is the result of an extensive survey the author made on Protestant mission work in the Congo and as he was acting as "agent de liaison" between Protestant missions and the Belgium government.

68. According to *IRM*'s editors (1936): 286, Rev P. H. J. Lerrigo, MD, was by the time of the publication of his paper, the Home Secretary of the American Baptist Foreign Mission Society. He had an experience of medical mission service in Belgian Congo. His article was written following his visit to the DRC. Editors add: "The problem of which he writes – the status of the non-Roman missions – is a pressing one."

69. According to editors (1945): 351, Rev H. Wakelin Coxill was the General Secretary of the Congo Protestant Council by the time his article was published.

between Tambaran (1938) and Whitby, Ontario, Canada (1947). On the world political side, nations were divided, causing destruction and lost in terms of human beings and infrastructures. On the religious side, mostly for delegates to the Whitby conference, the call was a new "Pentecost" of unity, raising awareness for world mission as it was in Edinburgh.[70] This article will shed light on the unity of the Protestant missionary work in the DRC and Missions' position vis-à-vis the colonial government. Coxill was the second General Secretary of the Congo Protestant Council, and it has been said that his service "was especially valuable in relating Protestant missions to the colonial government during the years after World War II" and due to his leadership, the colonial chartered and subsided Protestant schools in 1948.[71] Moreover, his article shows the connection of his vision for the Protestant Missions and Church in the DRC with the overall spirit of the World Mission Conferences of his time. He would say, "The Congo Protestant Council has a great responsibility . . . It must continue to foster and encourage true Christian fellowship and understanding and seek to help not only missions, but the whole Church of Christ in Congo to move forward and upward . . . seeking to relate the Church of Christ in Congo to the great Church of Christ in all the world."[72]

5. "The Church and Its Missionary Task in Congo," an 8-page article published in *IRM* 41, (1952): 301–309, authored by H. D. Brown.[73] This article was published the same year of the Willingen conference, Germany (1952) where the concept of *missio Dei* emerged as a new way of thinking mission. There was a shift from "missions" to "mission," a preparation to the change even in the name of the *International Review of Mission*(s) in

---

70. Gunther, "History and Significance," 524.
71. McGavran and Riddle, *Zaire*, 66.
72. Coxill, "Protestants," 279.
73. The editors didn't provide the information about the author who was speaking from his on-the-ground experience as missionary.

1969. Mission societies were criticized in several places as being at the service of the colonialism. For instance, all missionaries were expelled from China; and the independence movements started in several countries in the world. Willingen made clear to churches that "mission is an essential part of their innermost being."[74] Enlightened by such a statement and the spirit of his time, Brown's article is a courageous indictment of the missionary work in the DRC.

6. "Co-operation in Christian Literature Production in Belgian Congo," a 6-page article published in *IRM* 54, (1954): 414–420, authored by George W. Carpenter.[75] This article was published between the Willingen (1952) and Achimota, Accra, Ghana (1957/58). It was in Ghana that the decision of integrating Missions within the Church was made. The theology of *missio Dei* in Willingen had already paved the path, "mission" shouldn't be thought as a human movement, but as God's sovereign initiative. Everything human should disappear and leave its place to divine. While "missions" (with "s") were seen as connected with the colonization, only the "Church" was God's instrument to accomplish his ultimate "mission" (without "s"). The decision was made to merge the International Mission Council with the World Council of Churches, the former representing "missions" and the latter representing the "Church." It was during this conference that Evangelicals took the decision to quit any meeting organized by the World Council of Churches.[76] The Lausanne Movement which took place in 1974 was preceded by some conferences by evangelicals in 1966 and 1968. Hopefully, Carpenter's article will shed some light as to how this spirit would have influenced the Protestant missions in the DRC.

---

74. Gunther, "History and Significance," 528.

75. Rev George W. Carpenter, was then missionary in the DRC with the American Baptist Foreign Mission Society. While in the DRC, he was in charge of Christian literature, production and distribution for the Congo Protestant Council (Coxill, "Protestants," 278).

76. Gunther, "History and Significance," 531.

7. "Educational Development in the Belgian Congo," a 7-page article published in *IRM* 43, (1954): 421–428, authored by Orval J. Davis.[77] The context of Davis's article is the same as the previous article by Carpenter. The author provides an overview of educational system in the Belgian Congo from elementary primary school to the emergence of university-level program initiated by Roman Catholic through Louvanium. He furthermore discusses how the prevailing landscape of educational system was a challenge to Protestant missions in the process of preparing the eve of the Church of Christ in Congo. He then stresses the necessity of cooperation among Protestant missions as they were obliged to meet prescribed standards set by the government.

8. "Whose Congo?" a 14-page article published in *IRM* 50, (1961): 271–285, authored by George W. Carpenter.[78] This article was published the same year during the General Assembly of WCC in New Delhi, India (1961). At the international level, there was already division between "evangelicals" and "ecumenicals." This article may provide some light on the implication of such a climate in the local setting.

9. "Protestant Missions in Congo 1960–1969," a 9-page article published in *IRM* 55, (1966): 86–95, authored by John R. Crawford.[79] The article was published after the World Mission Conference of the WCC held in Mexico City, Mexico in 1963. With its theme of "God's Mission and Our Task," this conference strived to consolidate the result of the preceding conferences, Willingen (1952), Achimota (1957/58) and New Delhi (IMC/WCC) in 1961.[80] The slogan was "mission in six continents," not at all a duty of "foreign missions." This article may also

---

77. According to *IRM*'s editors (1954): 480, Orval J. Davis was missionary in the DRC with the Evangelical Christian Covenant Church by the time he wrote this article.

78. According to *IRM*'s editors (1961): 371, Rev George W. Carpenter, PhD, was formerly missionary in the DRC with the American Baptist Foreign Mission Society, and by the time he wrote this paper he was the secretary of the IMC.

79. The editors didn't provide the information about the author.

80. Gunther, "History and Significance," 531.

Mapping the Historical Roots 209

provide some light on the implication of such a climate in the local setting, as discussion to terminate Protestant missions in the DRC was already in the agenda of meetings on the Congo Protestant Council.

These writings and more others will be surveyed in order to surface some roots of missiology and missiological education in the DRC.

4.4.4 Educational Background of Missionaries

The reality in any educational system is that instructors teach the way they were taught and only what they know. One cannot give what he/she doesn't have. Such a reality is also applicable in the context of mission, missiology and missiological education in the DRC. Protestant Missionaries who served in the DRC were mostly from North America (USA and Canada), Great Britain, and Scandinavia (Sweden and Norway). Some Belgian missionaries came but without a lasting work, except the fact that a liaison office was established in Belgium in 1922 to assist Anglos-Saxon and Scandinavian missionaries to learn French and other subjects such as the history of Belgium and the Congo, colonial legislation, African ethnography and Bantu linguistics.[81] Such an opportunity came after almost half century since the missionary work had started in the country in 1878. It is possible to imagine the outcomes of the missionary work in those years in regard to the intellectual development of Protestant Christians in comparison to Catholic Christians.

Undoubtedly the best way to trace the educational background of missionaries would be to understand the context of the educational system of their respective countries of origin. Some authors have produced valuable works on the issue.[82] Therefore, this section deals with the question to sketch the educational background of missionaries prior to joining the DRC and its implication to the promotion of mission, missiology, and missiological education. The question is important because the understanding of mission and missionary task by nationals would also depend on what missionaries conveyed through their life and ministry. As said previously, what missionaries have said and done in regard to the task of the church is actually an important part of the teaching they would have provided, intentionally or

---

81. Anet, "Protestant Missions," 420.
82. Myklebust, *Study of Missions,* vols. 1 and 2; Beaver, "American Protestant."

not. All the same, what they would have taught about the task of the church certainly proceeded from their conception and practice of mission.

Some writings lament the level of missionaries who served in the DRC, implying that the outcomes of their work would have depended on the efficiency or the level of their own education. The issue becomes more interesting, even challenging, when one comes across the recommendation made by Dr John R. Mott to the Congo Protestant Missionary conference held in Léopoldville (now Kinshasa), in 1934. According to Stonelake, one of Mott's recommendations was a "suitable preparation of missionaries for the task."[83] Mott arrived at his recommendations after having attended a series of regional missionary conferences in Congo during which he collected data. His observations included the fact that "the missionary program in Congo has seemingly failed to produce an adequate native leadership" and "worldwide renown men."[84] One wonders if missionaries could do more than what their academic capability had allowed. The following warning statement from Coxill made some years after Stonelake's book is also revelatory of the prevailing malaise:

> While it is of first importance that all missionaries have these spiritual qualifications that are essential in all truly Christian undertakings, other qualifications are also required to enable God's servants to serve the people of Africa today. *The best possible training of missionary candidates* should be sought. Africans are demanding higher standards of education and of living. Missionaries must be able to help them to attain such standards with love, sympathetic understanding and ability.[85]

Seven years after Coxill's admonition, Brown conducted what himself called "a critical examination of the Church in Congo."[86] Without directly and openly pointing to the responsibility of missionaries, this critical examination demonstrates "the patent weakness" of the Church, which is

---

83. Stonelake, *Congo Past and Present*, 66.
84. Ibid., 79.
85. Coxill, "Protestants," 279, emphasis added.
86. Brown, Church and Its Missionary Task," 301.

actually the fruit of the missionary work. Nevertheless, Brown concluded with a revelatory appeal about the educational background of missionaries:

> There is thus much still to be done before the Church in the Congo achieves adult stature. It is incumbent on the mission boards to help strengthen the growth of the Congo Church *by sending missionaries whose training and convictions* give them an adequate conception of the place and function of the Church and who will bring to the native Church gifts of evangelism, teaching and administration.[87]

The above situation applied to many places. Kane notes that directors of mission societies believed that mission fields in Asia deserved the better educated candidates than in Africa.[88] The main reason was their conviction that China and India had more sophisticated people with superior cultures, and Africa was without history and civilization. Subsequently, "second rank" missionaries were sent to Africa when the better educated ones were entrusted the work of mission in Asia. He furthermore observes that missionaries from Germany and Scotland were much better trained, having university educational level, the same as the early missionaries from the East Coast in the United States. They were therefore able to establish some prestigious educational institutions on the mission field, especially in the Middle and Far East. On the other side, missionaries from England and many of so-called "faith mission" and non-denominational from the United States were not so well-educated, being in general laymen, not ordained ministers. Missionaries with a higher education were sent to Asia, while those with less education found their way to Africa.[89]

Referring to literature produced during this missionary era of 1960s, one could immediately evoke an issue of *IRM* which featured the problematic questions of missionary preparation, on the one side, and of theological training, on the other hand. Because this section is more concerned with the first preoccupation, two articles by H. A. Wittenbach and A. R. Tippett

---

87. Ibid., 309, emphasis added.
88. Kane, *Understanding Christian Missions*, 151.
89. Ibid., 154.

are worth mentioning.⁹⁰ Wittenbach reported on the increasing insistence by leaders of the national churches that missionary recruits should receive training in the new country to which they were called, and by the church with which they were called to serve. The author mentioned that the same issue was already raised during the meeting of the IMC at Tambaran in 1938 where participants recommended that "the national and regional Christian Councils of the receiving countries explore ways of providing supplementary missionary training on the field."⁹¹ Even at the Willingen meeting of the IMC in 1952 the recommendation was that missionary training must include preliminary training from home country before sailing, on the mission field during the first term of service, and in their home countries again during the first furlough.

While reflecting on "probing missionary inadequacies at popular level," Tippett indicated that these inadequacies were caused by and were perceptible through three areas: (1) The prevailing curricula which focused more on mental exercise and failed to match the training with its ultimate validity and applicability in a missionary ministry.⁹² For instance, courses on "world religions" or "comparative religion" couldn't help the future missionaries to really deal with what they were about to face on the ground. They had to discover for themselves by trial and error. (2) The prevailing curricula were based on the questionable quality of basic texts for study which failed to address and appreciate the real problem. For example, the course on "child psychology" was taught to missionaries when on the mission field they were mostly dealing with adults. (3) The prevailing curricula failed to facilitate the identification of future missionaries with the people to whom they were sent out. According to Tippett, that reality was reflected in the manner in which new missionaries set about their task when they arrived on the field. Very few could realize to what extent their first years on the mission field were part of their previous training period.

In the DRC, missionaries underwent training on the mission field only to acquire a sound knowledge of the local language and some issues related

---

90. Wittenbach, "Training," 405–410; Tippett, "Probing Missionary Inadequacies," 411–419.

91. Quoted in Wittenbach, "Training," 405.

92. Tippett, "Probing Missionary Inadequacies."

to the culture, religions and customs. However, this training was mostly designed and provided by older missionaries. As Wittenbach reported, new missionaries in this formative period used to live in a predominantly Western community and not among the people with whom their service was to be given.[93] It is undoubtedly true that such a training program, if designed and offered by nationals, could have had a different accent. In the same way missionaries' educational background and worldviews had conditioned their interpretation of African culture, religions and customs, nationals' worldviews could also have provided a more balanced perspective. As far as the context of the Protestant missionary work in the DRC is concerned, such an undertaking was not possible at a certain point for some evident reasons. One reason could be the aforementioned presumption that Africans were not civilized and knowledgeable enough to offer any intellectual and developmental insights to missionaries. To use Tippett's formulation, they didn't have the mental capacity to comprehend the academic concepts of their more educational missionaries.[94] The Catholic priest and missionary in the DRC, Placide Tempels, developed the Bantu philosophy in 1949 to contradict such a view. On the Protestant side, George W. Carpenter, formerly missionary in the DRC with the ABFMS, wrote the following remark while serving as the secretary of the IMC:

> Yet the will and the capacity are there [in the people of Congo]. They are an element of strength in the African character which the West had consistently under-rated, perhaps partly because centuries of African slavery etched the idea of African inferiority so deeply in the white man's mind that he has not yet been able to rid himself of it. In the case of many Congolese this first-rate human endowment has been moulded, matured and liberated by the influence of the Christian gospel. This is true both of Roman Catholics and of Protestants, for the grace of God is not confined to any one channel.[95]

---

93. Wittenbach, "Training," 408.
94. Tippett, "Probing Missionary Inadequacies," 411
95. Carpenter, "Whose Congo?" 280.

One could also evoke another reason of the assumption that nationals were not educated enough to hold any theological and ecclesiological articulated belief. Even for Protestant missions, this assumption was not totally absent. For a long time, nationals couldn't be part of major decisions about the Protestant work in the DRC. It is reported that nationals gathered for the first time in a general assembly in 1938; sixty years after the Protestant work started in the country in 1878.[96] This reality prompted Molo to observe in a doctoral thesis that the CCC was designed by missionaries without the active participation of nationals. Nationals were however obliged to inherit and lead a church that they didn't design its structures.[97] Therefore, missionaries couldn't expect to further their training on the mission field under the mentorship of nationals.

One thing is certain that many missionaries rather took opportunities to further their studies during the furlough in their countries of origin. As it was noticed in the previous chapter (section 3.3), many institutions (i.e. Fuller Seminary) provided continuing education to missionaries and mission leaders. Without doubt, in such a context where missionaries had a limited educational background, the debate on missiology and missiological education would be done at a lower level, inferencing discussion themes only from the daily practice of mission activities, learning "by trial and error."[98] However, one could find the specific case of the Protestant missions in Congo slightly different. As demonstrated in previous sections, there was a close relatedness between Protestant missions in Congo and the global trends (through Edinburgh and its related international structures like IMC). Reports and reflections from Congo missionaries were published in the influential mission journal *IRM*. Some of Congo missionaries held administrative and leadership positions at IMC. Such a reality could imply that some missionaries would have gone through an appreciable education. Therefore, inferences on missiology and missiological education could be easily drawn from either their mission experiences or their reflective reports. Nevertheless, in regard to what the aforementioned authors have contended, the general impression is that the majority of Protestant missionaries who

---

96. Mahaniah, *L'impact*, 23.
97. Molo, "Quest," 109.
98. Tippett, "Probing Missionary Inadequacies," 412.

were based in the DRC didn't foster missiology and missiological education for and at global level.

4.5 Some Roots of Missiology and Missiological Education in the RDC

4.5.1 Protestant Missiology in the DRC: Theory and Practice of Mission

The main concern here is how Protestant missionaries who served in the DRC would respond to the questions: "What is the supreme task of the church according to you or your mission society?" "What should be the supreme task of the church?" "What are the methods and strategies used by your mission society to accomplish the supreme task of the church?" "What should be the effective methods and strategies to accomplish the supreme task of the church?" This section combines both theory and practice of mission because they are actually twins. Theory leads to practice, and the practice applies the theory.

Writing about "The missionary situation in Congo," Alfred Stonelake drew the landscape of missionary work in the DRC. He made a point that despite the fact that there were about fifteen mission societies, with various stages of development and progress, Protestant missions shared in many respects a common policy: "They are distinctly evangelical, preaching 'Christ and him crucified' in the language of the people or in one of the *lingua franca* considered effective for the purpose. All the missions demand public confession of sin, repentance towards God, and faith in our Lord Jesus Christ."[99] Commenting on the church life, the author stated that the standard of church membership was high and mighty forces were at work "for the evangelization of that dark land."[100] Along with the proclamation of the gospel, Protestant missions in the DRC promoted also education. Stonelake to add: "Education must necessarily have a prominent place in any mission work among backward races. Whenever a native preacher goes into a village to settle he conducts an elementary school, in which reading,

---

99. Stonelake, "Missionary Situation," 317.
100. Ibid., 318.

singing, memorizing and often writing play an important part."[101] Stonelake observed that, "It is safe to say that nearly all our missions have failed to recognize sufficiently the value of agriculture . . . [which could] foster the principle of self-support for the work of the Church."[102] He furthermore added that "It is a discouraging fact that our Protestant missions have never more than touched the great centres [cities] of Congo."[103] For the author, the battles are not won in small villages but at the strategic points of greatest importance. He also pointed out the fact that, as regards Islam influence, "the whole outer portion of our field is still untouched by Protestant effort."[104] Apart from the pejorative and judgemental linguistic style of Stonelake ("dark land" and "backward races"), one could derive from these statements the same theology of mission which prevailed at Edinburgh 1910 where "the evangelization of this generation" was the motto. It is noteworthy that the missionary work included both evangelization and education though much was still to be done.

A few years after Stonelake's writings discussed above, Henri Anet authored two articles on "Congo Native and Belgian Administration" and "Protestant Missions in Belgian Congo." Anet was pastor of the Belgian Church and General Secretary of the Belgian society for Protestant missions in Congo based in Brussels. He was concerned with the mistreatment of natives in general, and Protestant missions in particular by the colonial government. He reported that a commission of seven members was formed in 1908 "to watch in all the territory of the colony over the protection of the natives and the betterment of their moral and material conditions."[105] Of the seven members of the commission two were Roman Catholic bishops and two Protestant missionaries. From their meeting of 1919, the commission urged the government to take measures to stop the progress of diseases, apply methods of social hygiene, to help and favour the work of the missionaries who were perceived as auxiliaries of the medical service.[106] However, the

---

101. Ibid.
102. Ibid., 321.
103. Ibid., 328.
104. Ibid., 329.
105. Anet, "Congo Native," 198.
106. Ibid., 202.

reality on the ground is that Protestant missions didn't enjoy the same treatment as the Roman Catholic Church. In his second article, Anet provided an account on Protestant missions in which he noticed that equal treatment was relatively granted to both Roman Catholic and to Protestant missions.[107] One could also learn from this article that there was cordial collaboration between the Protestant missions and the authorities before the founding of the Independent State in 1885. This relation changed when Protestant missionaries protested against the abuses regarding the system of forced labour that the Independent State adopted as a way to address its financial situation. It is safe to say that some Protestant missions in the DRC included some humanitarian services in their evangelical activities.

This reality is discussed in articles by P. H. J Lerrigo and Wakelin Coxill. Lerrigo made a visit to the DRC and his article was published as a report to his experience while visiting Protestant missions. He contended that "the future of Congo will depend less upon economic and industrial factors than upon the development of the life and character of its people."[108] For Lerrigo, these two elements constitute the task of missions: the development of life and the development of character of people. Based on what he experienced during his visit, he then recommended that a conference between the government and Protestant missions be held to address the following issues: (1) relation missions and government should be developed; (2) Protestant education philosophy and system should be reformed through a more unified system; (3) the question of finance to be solved due to depression which characterized the world; and (4) the status of Protestant natives as "foreigners" should change. The question was however to know if missionaries were qualified for such a dialogue. The general impression was that some mission societies denied the fact that the training of mind and heart was part of the gospel message.[109]

The truth is that the mission theory of the Protestant missions in the DRC underwent a gradual development due mainly to local circumstances and to global imperatives. Their mission theory was not static. Things became even clearer as the time came to pass, as local needs became more

---

107. Anet, "Protestant Missions," 415.
108. Lerrigo, "Protestant Missions," 227.
109. Ibid., 232.

obvious, and as the global trends prevailed. Lerrigo observed: "One of the handicaps of the past has been the lack of coherence in the evangelical movement in Congo: the difficulty of inducing groups of diverse origins to see eye to eye in major matters of policy."[110] The initiative of the Congo Protestant Conference of missions in 1902 which culminated in the formation of the Congo Protestant Council (CPC) in 1924 was an effort to bridge the aforementioned incoherence.[111] Writing in 1945 as the secretary of the CPC, Wakelin Coxill provided not only a global overview on the nature and task of this institution, but also a discussion on the life of missions and the church with a proposition of new strategies for mission work. He indicated that by establishing the CPC missionaries sought occasions to get together, not only for spiritual inspiration and worship, but also to discuss common problems connected with their work and to find how they could serve Christ and the Congo.[112] The responsibility of the CPC included to help the mission work together, view the field and task as a whole, and encourage one united Protestant church in the country.[113] As one goes through this article, insights on theory of mission become clearer. The author called for new methods and strategies in doing mission: literature, medical service, education, leadership training, and women ministry. Although these services were carried out even in the past, Coxill's proposition was to encourage Protestant missions to go extra mile, and for those who used to focus only on evangelization, to embrace and develop these new strategies. He then concluded with a plea that the CPC ought to help not only the missions, but the whole CCC to "move forward and upward in the knowledge and love of Jesus Christ and in effective service for him."[114]

The world context after two world wars can be perceived as root cause of such an insistence to get the national church (or people) on board. Commenting in the *International Review of Missions* 37 on a book entitled *Knowing the Africa* published in 1947, Newell S. Booth, bishop for Africa of the Methodist Church (USA), insisted that "If missionaries are to be

---

110. Ibid.
111. Stonelake, "Missionary Situation," 326.
112. Coxill, "Protestants," 273.
113. Ibid., 275.
114. Ibid., 279.

successful in realizing the goal of their work, cooperation with the African in the development of the Kingdom of God, it is essential that they should know the African."[115] After having recognized the importance of other parts of the world as they became so attractive in terms of mission personnel and funds, Booth reinforced his plea: "But the fact remains that for a wise strategy in building the ecumenical Church of Christ, strong in all the world, Africa should be given a higher priority than she has enjoyed in mission counsels in the past."[116] Coxill and Booth's concerns about missionary work in Africa and the future of the church in Africa distil the general malaise that the continent underwent for several decades. In the previous section (4.4.4), mention was made of the quality of missionaries sent to Africa in comparison to those sent out to Asia for instance. In their respective pleas, the above-mentioned authors also mentioned the fact that the deployment of missionaries had to do with funds and services, such as education, medical program, literacy, etc. For them, much was needed to be done for Africa.

It was in this general context that H. D. Brown, another missionary based in the DRC, released his "critical examination of the Church" with the main purpose of "understanding its weaknesses" for the task ahead.[117] Brown proposed to conduct an examination of the Protestant church (in singular). It is clear that the examination was about the result of the work done by the Protestant missions, but not the work of the Protestant church itself since it didn't yet exist as an autonomous entity. Everything was still under the direction and control of missionaries. Brown recognized that by the time he was writing his article the existing local churches "were under the oversight of a missionary sent from a foreign country."[118] His final recommendation made it clear: "It is incumbent on the mission boards to help strengthen the growth of the Congo church by sending missionaries whose training and convictions give them an adequate conception of the place and function of the Church and who will bring to the native Church gifts

---

115. Booth, "Mission Priorities," 93.

116. Ibid. It is important to remind that Booth's article was published the same year of the birth of the World Council of Churches, slightly before it was officially launched during Amsterdam 1948.

117. Brown, "Church and Its Missionary Task," 301.

118. Ibid., 302.

of evangelism, teaching and administration."¹¹⁹ In other words, the work examined by Brown was actually the fruit of the work done by foreign missionaries. Therefore, the title of his article "The Church and Its Missionary Task in Congo" could otherwise be framed. The best title could have been, "The Protestant missions and their missionary task in Congo."

Despite this important observation, Brown's reflection is commendable because it sheds some light on the prevailing theory and practice of mission. For instance, the author defined missionary as "every activity in which the gospel is preached and men are called to a life of repentance, faith and Christian action."¹²⁰ For him, African pastors, evangelists and catechists deserved to be called "missionaries" due to what they did through preaching the gospel and calling people to repentance. He however observed that "while there is definitely a missionary activity in the Congo church, it is confined to the borders of each station and often within that station area, tribal divisions remaining separate."¹²¹ The mission by Africans was strictly local. He also indicated that the common policy among missions working in the Congo was to throw the support of the evangelistic aspect of the ministry to local people while education and medical service were entrusted to foreign missionaries. In other words, if missionary work existed in the Congo church, it was about preaching within the immediate area of the preacher. If there was any local financial participation to mission, it was to support the pastoral workers. For the author, "behind this [situation] lies a general ignorance of the Scriptures . . . the ministry is poorly trained, the people are still less instructed, and so nothing can be done until some force from the outside can work effectively."¹²²

The following observation by Brown speaks more than any comment:

> The factors contributing to the failure of the Congo Church to be missionary are many. First we may cite the fact of an untrained ministry. Very few Congo pastors have had more than nine years' schooling at the very most, and the great majority of them have had five years or less . . . The Congo Church is

---

119. Ibid., 309.
120. Ibid., 302.
121. Ibid.
122. Ibid., 304

weak in oecumenical vision. Only the few, well-instructed [sic!] African leaders realize anything at all of what is taking place in the Church as it exists all over the world . . . The Congo Church is weak not only in oecumenicity but in any comprehension of the world outside . . . Lack of awareness of the world's great needs, making it impossible to appreciate the resultant call for Christian service, contributes to the lack of the missionary witness in the Congo Church."[123]

The above assessment by Brown not only shows the reasons for the Congo church to be mission-mindless, but it also surfaces the conception of what mission was in theory and practice. Preaching was not a new understanding of mission, but the addendum from Brown was the global aspect of the Christian mission. For him the mission of the Congo church shouldn't only be local, but also global. The only one problem is that the Congo church was trained only for the local aspect. For him, preaching, education, and medical services were the responsibilities of the Congo church to be performed inside and outside the country. This revolutionary understanding of the Church and its missionary task was not common in the DRC. It was a point of view of the minority. As Brown pointed out, a general ignorance of the Scripture was the root cause of the situation. As matter of fact, even if Brown didn't state it clearly, this ignorance came from the foreign missionaries. This assumption is confirmed by what he finally suggested that the Congo church needed "missionaries whose training and convictions give them an adequate conception of the place and function of the Church and who will bring to native Church gifts of evangelism, teaching, and administration."[124] Without doubt, had Brown's conception of mission be promoted, the CCC would have been active in both local and global mission.

Later after Brown, George W. Carpenter and John R. Crawford produced valuable accounts of the general landscape of the mission theory promoted in the DRC.[125] Their two articles were written during the transitional period of after independence when foreign missionaries were already obliged to

---

123. Ibid.
124. Ibid., 309.
125. Carpenter, "Whose Congo?"; Crawford, "Protestant Missions."

leave the country. For that reason, ideas contained in these articles should be understood as either the continuation of what already existed as described above, or as wishes which could or not occur. Carpenter's reflection was more on the responsibility of the church to form the consciousness of people of a given nation. He stressed the notions of "freedom," "self-control," "liberation" and "the kingdom of God." These notions matched with the context of dismantlement of colonialism and independence of formerly colonized nations. In general they were speculative concepts which characterized the missionary and missiological vocabulary after the meeting of IMC at Willingen in 1952. The following statement from Carpenter reveals his conception of the mission of the church:

> The Church, as bearer of this gospel, is not called to align itself with the coercive structures of society as one more instrument of social control. Its concern is rather to widen the area of human freedom and deepen its content, to help men and women make wise choices and decisions as children of God and responsible members of society. Its power lies not in the organizational leverage it can exert, but in the common commitment of the whole people of God scattered throughout society and their capacity for spontaneous action together.[126]

One could find in Carpenter's reflection a brand new and uncommon theoretical construction. Far from helping the Congo church to do mission as per Brown's above proposition, Carpenter's reasoning is actually a local-centered mission that the CCC retained as the leadership moved from Western missionaries to African church leaders. Coming to Crawford, the structure of his article perpetuated the traditional threefold mission of the church: (1) evangelistic work, (2) education and training, and (3) medical and relief work. He concluded his article with an ambiguous observation:

> The missionary picture in Congo is no longer as encouraging as it was five or ten years ago . . . The important thing, however, is that the Church is in Congo, and will remain there, even if every missionary has to leave. The Church exists, proclaims the

---

126. Carpenter, "Whose Congo?" 284.

gospel and ministers in the name of Christ. We may not expect
that the Church in Congo will do everything the missionaries
have tried to do, or do it with the same technical and theological skill. But we may expect that the Church will seek to be
obedient to the will of God . . . The future is uncertain. We
may suppose that missionary effort will continue in many areas,
probably in most. Medical will probably diminish; educational
work will grow. Theological schools will continue to raise their
standards . . . The details of the future are in the hands of God.[127]

The above lines summarize the legacy of the Protestant missions. When the CCC came to the existence in 1970, the concept of mission was glued to what foreign missionaries left behind: mission as preaching the gospel and, depending on the possibility, doing some education and medical services, but in the local context. Without doubt, such an understanding and practice of mission made the content of the training corpus.

4.5.2 Protestant Missiology in the DRC: Training for Mission

The main concern here is, how Protestant missionaries who served in the DRC would respond to the questions: "What are the purpose, the content and the methods used by your mission society to teach about the supreme task of the church?" "What should be the purpose and the content, and the effective methods to teach about the supreme task of the church?"

Writing in 1937, Stonelake informs that *Ecole des Pasteurs et Instituteurs* founded in 1908 at Kimpese was the highest type of Protestant school in Congo.[128] The purpose of the school was to train "those actually engaged in and pledged to the work of *educational evangelization*" (emphasis added). The study schedule allowed students to take classes for three hours in the morning and one-and-a-half hours in the evening for five days (Monday to Friday) a week, nine months per year. Though the author didn't explain what he meant by "educational evangelization," the general motivation for training local people was to make them preachers of the gospel in their immediate context. The following quotations from former missionaries in

---

127. Crawford, "Protestant Missions," 95.
128. Stonelake, *Congo Past and Present*, 108.

Congo disclose Stonelake's idea. An excerpted paragraph of an official circular of the CPC stated:[129]

> These young churches have grown so that they are pleading for more adequate light and leading. They want to know how to organize their village and church life on a Christian basis, but do not know how. The time has come for missions to change their methods, and to lead out, rather than send out alone, trained teachers, and help plant them in their own soil. We must ever put our main emphasis on the education of the native heart-life by putting first the preaching and teaching of the gospel of the Cross, the availability of the kingdom to all, and the fact that abundant and eternal life is not derived from economics and schools, but from a living faith in the living Christ.[130]

Stonelake, one of the leading mission leaders of that time, provided the following comment on the same issue:

> The great need of the churches is for Christians of more disciplined intelligence and more sustained application, such as the three-year course of teacher-training is calculated to produce. Indeed, there should be such an institute as Kimpese in each province. This matter is a part of the present spiritual challenge, and it is urgent.[131]

In his published report as the secretary of the CPC in 1945, Coxill depicted the landscape of educational activities of Protestant missions:

> For their part, the Protestant missions realize that they have much to do, as have the Roman Catholics, to improve the quality of their work, particularly in the field of education. The standard now attained by some of the missions at many different centres is good, considering the present development of the Congo, but that of other missions is decidedly poor. The

---

129. Congo Protestant Council, 15 September 1936, quoted in Stonelake, *Congo Past and Present*, 147–148.
130. Stonelake, 147–148
131. Stonelake, *Congo Past and Present*, 145.

> Church of Christ in Congo suffers on this account, and more and more missionaries are alive to *the fact that evangelism alone, in such a country as the Congo and at such a time as the present, is not enough.* The Congo Protestant Council is seeking to help and advise missions in their educational programmes, but the problem resolves itself into one of personnel and adequate funds. The Protestant missions need immediately far more men missionaries, *many of them fully qualified in educational work . . .* If our churches are to be strong and self-propagating, both pastors and lay members must have opportunity for growth and training. *Christian schools form the natural agency for it.*[132]

As already discussed in the previous section, Brown's article stigmatized the fact that the training of nationals was not adequate for the intended work and that it was a way to only prepare mission-mindless people.[133]

> The factors contributing to the failure of the Congo Church to be missionary are many. First we may cite the fact of an untrained ministry. Very few Congo pastors have had more than nine years' schooling at the very most, and the great majority of them have had five years or less. This detracts not all from their discipleship and devotion, but *it seriously limits their horizons and effectiveness in sharing with the foreign missionary in the missionary task.*[134]

According to Carpenter, though there were over three hundred ordained Protestant pastors in the DRC, not one of them had had full theological training equal to that of a European or an American could receive.[135] As one goes through the above Brown's overall examination of the church and its missionary task in Congo, several points to ponder become transparent. However, it is important to remember that Brown's examination was actually on missionary work in Congo rather than on the church in Congo. He actually evaluated the work that Missions were transferring to the local church.

---

132. Coxill, "Protestants," 277–279, emphasis added.
133. Brown, "Church and Its Missionary Task," 303.
134. Ibid., emphasis added.
135. Carpenter, "Co-operation in Christian Literature Production," 79.

Suffice it to highlight the following insights: (1) There was "untrained ministry." Though there could be some training around there, according to Brown, the training was not appropriate to the global mission of the church; (2) The training offered was not only poor in terms of breadth, but also in terms of missionary vision; the training focused on a local ministry of preaching to immediate audience.

In 1953 the IMC commissioned an interdenominational team to evaluate the work of preparing Africans for the leadership of the church. The report released by the commission under the title *Survey of the Training of the Ministry in Africa* reported numerous weaknesses and problems in the preparation of Congolese leadership.[136] Crawford makes it clear that the tendency at the beginning of missionary work in the DRC was poor, not harmonized, and the process of transferring the leadership to nationals through training was not speeded up. The following statement sets it without complaisance:

> Increasingly, the evangelization of the people has been entrusted to Congolese Christian. It is natural that a Congolese, prepared for and dedicated to the task, can reach his own people far more effectively than a foreigner. Training for the pastoral task, however, has varied markedly from mission to mission. Originally working for apart from one another, most of the Protestant missions have been woefully lacking in intelligent foresight in preparing men to take over from themselves the functions of preaching and pastoral at a reasonably high level (about nine year's total schooling) were the Institut Morrison in the Kasai and the Ecole de Pasteurs et Instituteurs at Kimpese.[137]

The above paragraph is excerpted from Crawford's section on Protestant witness in Congo during the colonial period (1908–1960). In light of the above statement and of the overall history of the Protestant missions in the DRC, seven important insights are worth mentioning: (1) The reason of the training was to help students reach out to their own people; (2) The training was actually a "pastoral" training, but with the purpose of reaching out to their own people; (3) The training for the pastoral task varied from one

---

136. Bates et al., *Survey*; Crawford, *Protestant Missions* (1969), 14.
137. Ibid.

mission to another; (4) Whereas some schools were founded by one mission, others were initiated by a group of missions; so, the training also varied from one group of founders to another; (5) While some schools were started by one Missions, they later on became a joint effort of several Missions; (6) Missionaries have changed their mindset, from working separately to serving through joined venture in training nationals for the preaching and pastoral ministries; (7) Though some Missions could organize some training programs, the "high level" (about nine years of total schooling) waited for a long time before being initiated.

The aforementioned school was founded in 1908, thirty years after the arrival of the first missionaries in 1878. The *Ecole de Pasteurs de Kimpese* (EPK) was a joined effort of the American Baptist Foreign Mission Society (ABFMS), the Baptist Missionary Society (BMS), and the Swedish Covenant Mission (SMF). While the extension of EPK to Kinshasa has become the *Univeristé Chrétienne de Kinshasa* (UCKIN), the site of EPK in the province of Bas-Congo, serves today the *Université de l'Alliance Chrétienne* (UAC). These two universities were also included in this study. Though Crawford mentions only two schools, the history teaches that other schools were founded along the way. For instance, the Disciples of Christ Congo Mission (DCCM) founded *Institut Chrétien Congolais* (ICC) in 1927 at Bolenge (Mandaka). One year later, the Congo Balolo Mission, CBM, (a Swedish Baptist Mission) founded in 1919, and the Evangelical Mission in Ubangi, MEU (from the Evangelical Free Church of America), founded in 1922, joined DCCM to enlarge the school into *Institut Chrétien Congolais* (ICC). Today, the site of ICC serves the *Universié Protestante de l'Equateur* (UPE), one of the selected universities for this study.

It was in 1928, when meeting for the celebration of the fiftieth anniversary of the Protestant missionary work in the DRC that the Congo Protestant Council (CPC) initiated the discussion about establishing a higher education institution. According to Munayi, the project faced many challenges including the monopoly of the government regarding the provision of higher education and the lack of resources within Protestant missions to carry out such a project.[138] It was after fourteen years that B. C. Hobgood,

---

138. Munayi, "Enseignement universitaire protestant."

missionary with the Disciples of Christ Congo Mission, raised the same question in a letter addressed to the CPC in 1942. The same answer was given as in 1928. Twelve years later, in 1954, due to the aforementioned survey of the IMC, the CPC finally made a decision to start a Protestant University which opened in 1956. The discussion to establish the faculty of theology for the ministry of the church arose in 1958, the decision was formally made in 1959, and the first class opened in 1960. One can tell from this account that the issue of training more qualified people for the church ministries was not easy to handle. It took eighty years (1878–1958) for the issue to be responsibly discussed and addressed. Out of around forty Protestant mission societies which operated in the DRC, only four were committed to found a faculty of theology at higher education level. Despite the recommendation of Dr John Mott in 1934 (see section 4.4.4) to produce an adequate native leadership, the majority of Protestant missions seemed reluctant to the project. Research could be done to find out the profound root causes of such a situation.

When the CCC was officially born in 1970 succeeding to the CPC, the above-mentioned faculty of theology known today as Protestant University of Congo (PUC) had graduated less than three students with such an advanced degree for the church ministries in the whole country.[139] It is safe to state that the legacy of Protestant missions in terms of preparing Congolese for God's glocal mission was poor, and the CCC, its related *communautés* along with theological institutions reflect today the outcomes of such a legacy.

4.6 Protestant Church, Mission and Missiological Education in the DRC (1970–2016)

4.6.1 Understanding the Legacy of Protestant Missions in the DRC

One could set differently the period of the eve of the National Church in the DRC, choosing for instance 1960 (when Missions entrusted the responsibility of CPC to nationals) as the starting year. The very historical

---

139. Munayi, *Les vingt-cinq*.

fact is that the autonomy entrusted to the national church was, in the sight of observers, an interim responsibility until when all Protestant churches made the critical decision to unite under one national church in 1970. Prior to that, Missions were still holding some critical and final decisions, mostly for the matters pertaining to their possessions. Nationals could operate as watchmen, keeping missionary possessions on place and dealing with other matters relating to the maintenance of the church life. One can without hesitation guess that this transitional period was a time of frustrations on both sides, and sometimes a time of confrontation between the two parts. In his article entitled *Protestant Witness in Congo*, John R. Crawford assigns to the period of 1960–1967 the somewhat emotional title, "Witness in Chaos."[140] The following comment shows that Crawford wrote his paper sometime in 1970 but before the birth of the CCC,[141] describing what he calls "disparate picture of Congo Protestantism:"

> The day of the younger churches has come. Certain of the older missionary structures have dissolved; others are in the process of reducing or integrating into the national churches. Various churches hold their assemblies and make decisions; some invite missionaries as observers, others as voting members. There remain a few regions where foreign missionaries definitely hold the guidelines; there are more, and larger, areas where Congolese make decisions, and the missionary seeks to implement.[142]

The aforementioned situation couldn't be otherwise for those, as McGavran and Riddle advise, would have confused the realities of the four stages of Missions.[143] According to Mahaniah, the CPC in which key leaders were nationals played a *consultative role* between 1960 and 1970, whereas by 1970, the newly born, the CCC, was entrusted the *executive function*.[144] Before 1970, nationals worked as members of consultative body. After 1970,

---

140. Crawford, *Protestant Missions* (1969), 17.
141. In his undated paper, Crawford says on page 21: "The meeting of the Congo Protestant Council in 1969 indicated a new trend in the life of Protestant work in Congo."
142. Ibid.
143. McGavran and Riddle, *Zaire*, 26.
144. Mahaniah, *L'impact*, 25.

they acted as members of an executive association. That day, after a meeting which went until 4:00 a.m., the official declaration was "Today, the Mission is over, and the Church is born!"

By saying that the Church is *born*, one would hope that they didn't say the Mission has *died*! However, taking into account the climate in which the meeting was held and the time it took for the final decision to be taken late [*and* early!] at 4:00 a.m. for a non-stop meeting, one can reasonably guess that even if the statement was "Mission is *over*," the spirit of the declaration could be "Mission has *died*." Later in an article published by *IRM* in 1973, the president of the CCC simply said, "For since 1969 Protestant missions *have ceased to exist in Zaire.*"[145]

Writing during the chaotic period as stipulated above, Crawford explains the real climate which conditioned the birth of the CCC:

> Within the disparate picture of Congo Protestantism appear several diverse tendencies, with consequences and implications which are not yet analyzed. One is a leaning towards an organic union of major churches desired and initiated by Congolese church leaders, with some serious discussion taking place. There is also a tendency to overleap traditional "comity" agreements, with the result that several churches may find themselves working side by side in almost every urban center. Tribal patterns occasionally are repeated in ecclesiastical structures. (The BMS work has divided into three distinct churches on tribal and geographical lines.) There is a continued dependence on the mission societies, particularly for educational leadership and funds.[146]

Another paragraph provided by Crawford demonstrates the existing real status of Missions after the birth of the CCC:

> The meeting of the Congo Protestant Council in 1969 indicated a new trend in the life of Protestant work in Congo. An overwhelming expression of opinion and desire on the part of the Congolese Christians indicated their own feelings

---

145. Bokeleale, "From Missions to Mission," 433, emphasis added.
146. Crawford, n.d., 20.

concerning the desire that the mission organizations be fully integrated into the life of the National Church and its various branches. Following this, several of the major Protestant mission organizations have become fully integrated into the life of the local churches and the transfers of legal personalities to the Congolese churches are in the processes of being made . . . Increasingly, missions will be operating within the scope of and under the leadership of Congolese Christians.[147]

This reality of whether Mission was "*over*" or "*died*" would undoubtedly have affected the theology of mission of the CCC, because at a time the idea of *mission* included both *mission organization* and the task of being a *church in mission*. The first [mission organization] came to the existence in the DRC in 1878 because of its understanding of the church as a Christian community for *and* in mission. Therefore, when the first [mission organization] is rejected, the second [church in mission] cannot survive. Undoubtedly, such an understanding of mission *and* church couldn't go without influencing the missiological education and the missionary involvement of the local denominations.

At the global level, as mentioned in chapter 2 (section 2.6.2), the integration of the IMC into the WCC in 1961 brought a change to the landscape of mission theory and practice. IMC represented Missions and WCC represented churches. With the fusion of IMC and WCC, Mission was diluted into the Church and became one of its commissions. Therefore, IMC became the "Commission of Evangelism and World Missions." It was during this global environment that the CCC was officially proclaimed in 1970, after a long process of difficult transition.[148] Missions had to disappear as to leave the place to the national Church.

---

147. Ibid., 21, 22.

148. Due to the visit and recommendation of Dr John R. Mott in 1934 conferences of the CPC, the phrase "Native Christian Church" became officially "Church of Christ in Congo" in 1942. When an amendment was made to the constitution of the CPC to change the article 2, the amendment statement was: "The words, Church of Christ in Congo without quotation marks be substituted for the words Native Christian Church." Although the name "Church of Christ in Congo" was introduced in 1934, the year 1942 is when this new name was officially inserted into the constitution, the year 1942 being its official birthday. (See the Preamble to the Constitution of the Church of Christ in Congo of 1979).

The leadership for the future of this newborn church was then entrusted to [or taken away by?] pastors and laypeople over everything that missionaries initiated and developed. As days and years have passed, several questions arise about the nationals' understanding of the nature and the task of the church according to the reading of the Scripture. Forty-six years (1970–2016) of grassroot church leadership and management, forty-six years of accountability, forty-six years of continuing the *mission* entrusted to disciples on the Mount of Olives (Acts 1:12) more than two millennia ago, forty-six years of taking over the work (*and* its spirit) that Western missions entrusted to the national Church on that year of 1970. How have been the mission-related training activities? Waiting for the findings of empirical research in the next chapter, the attention here is directed to some historical trends which characterized the foundation of the CCC. These trends will facilitate the comprehension and the interpretation of the forthcoming data of empirical investigation.

4.6.2 From Several Churches to One Church: Revisiting *Our* History

If the use of *their* history was meaningful in the previous survey on Protestant missions (4.4.1), that of *our* history here is not naïve. I feel part of the story. Having given my life to Christ and having participated in God's mission during this period, I feel a sense of responsibility to revisit *our* history that is still made. With humility, the urgent task for those who decide to invest in reconstructing the history of the CCC will be to check and double-check information from available documentation and some personal experiences before objectively drawing conclusions. The scope of this study doesn't allow more space for such an undertaking. It is however important to briefly sketch important guidelines for the task.

The history of the CCC cannot be understood without taking into account the legacy of Protestant missions as described in the previous sections. The remaining parts of the history flow out of the preceding account. The formation of a national church is to be understood as a turning point in the process of getting local people involved in God's glocal mission. However, the nature of the church put in place has influenced its task. Historians will discover that the situation changed depending on how the conception of ecclesiology also varied. Molo has conducted an outstanding study on the issue. Suffice it to observe that the first period of seven years (1970–1977) of the existence of the CCC was a transitional period of establishing a national church. One could then identify three eras in the post-mission history: (1) The ante-Episcopalian era under pastor Bokeleale (1970–1977); (2) the Episcopalian era under Bishop Bokeleale (1977–1998); and (3) the post-Bokeleale Episcopalian era (1998 to present).

The installation in May to June 1977 of pastors Bokeleale Itofo, Boyaka Inkomo and Assani Baraka as bishops by a bishop from the Lutheran Evangelical Church of Germany has brought a new wave of understanding and leading the CCC.[149] Introducing the Episcopalian system implicated that the church is *one* under a centralized hierarchy in which officials are not delegated by their churches of origin. Consequently, before 1977, nationals working within the structures of the CCC used to have the status of "church-mandated officials." They were selected and recommended by their churches of origin to hold any available position in that national executive association.

After June 1977, officials could join any structure of the CCC even without being selected and recommended by their churches of origin. This practice resulted in the broken unity which was inspired by the 1970 meeting, the day the CCC was born. Some *communautés* decided to quit the association. Further studies can be done to find out whether the situation has changed along the way or not, and how it would have influenced the missiological education and the missionary involvement of local denominations. Besides the approach used further in chapter 5 to map missiology and missiological education in the context of theological institutions, two more settings can be suggested. The first possibility is to explore issues about the mission of the CCC using its official documents such as constitution and minutes of the meetings of the National Synod. The second possibility could be to explore the historical development of the department of mission in the structures of the CCC and its related *communautés*.

4.7 Concluding Remarks

This chapter dealt with the historical development of missiology and missiological education in the DRC. The prevailing frameworks in mission

---

149. Mahaniah, *L'impact*, 26.

studies couldn't help capture such a development due to the diversity of Protestant missions and their establishment in the country in different periods. A threefold framework based on time frame was suggested, that takes into account Mission-State relationship, Missions-Church relation, and Missions and global mission trends. The impact of colonization, Edinburgh 1910, and decolonization affected the way of understanding the mission of the church by Protestant missionaries who were based in the DRC. The same impact affected the mission practice and the promotion of training for the mission of the church of Christ. To reconstruct the historical development of missiology and missiological education, writings by missionaries served as valuable sources of information. Threefold lines of missiology defined in chapter 2 as mission theory, practice and education were used as *fil conducteur* to capture such a development. In the process of retracing missiology and missiological education within the CCC, in both missionary (1878–1970) and post-missionary (1970–2016) eras, one should take seriously the following questions into account:

1. **The theory of God's mission**: What is actually God's mission? "What is the nature and the purpose of the church according to you and your *communauté*?" "How could the nature and the purpose of the church be described?"
2. **The practice in God's mission**: How should God's mission be accomplished? What are the methods and strategies used by your *communauté* to accomplish the purpose of the church?" "What could be the effective methods and strategies to accomplish the supreme task of the church?"
3. **The training for God's mission**: How should the training for God's mission be provided? "What are the methods and content used by your *communauté* to teach about the nature and the purpose of the church?" "What could be the effective methods and content to teach about the nature and the purpose of the church?"

This chapter has made it clear that in general, the legacy left by the Protestant missions to the Protestant church in Congo didn't allow missiology to be well-articulated and missiological education to be part of the prevailing theological curriculum. While Western missionaries had some understanding of God's *global* mission, a vision which was not much communicated during their ministries on the mission field, the emerged national church simply inherited a vision of God's *local* mission. The CCC and its related 82 *communautés* have not been intentionally present in world mission at global level. Two more important concluding remarks need to be highlighted here, namely (1) some technical and critical problems in reconstructing the historical facts and events, and (2) profound root causes of the current status of missiology and missiological education in the DRC.

4.7.1 Problems to Expect in Reconstructing the Historical Facts and Events

The task of reconstructing the historical development of Protestant missiology and missiological education in the DRC becomes even more arduous due to some practical and technical problems any researcher would encounter. While practical problems refer to facts and events which cannot be well-captured unless the social, cultural and political backgrounds are understood, technical problems are facts and events which required scientific rigor in focusing on the subject under consideration. It is then important to layout these different problems a researcher would certainly encounter while retracing the historical facts and events on Protestant missiology and missiological education in the context of both Missions and Church in the DRC.

4.7.1.1 The Problem Related to the Reliability of the Source of Information

The first set of problems relates to the reliability of the source of information. Generally speaking, two sources are worth mentioning: the written source and the oral source. These sources pose both practical and technical challenges to any historian of mission on one side, and to the historian of church on the other side.

The written historical accounts have been mainly produced by Western missionaries and also, in some extent, by local researchers. While available literature by Western missionaries was mostly produced in English, French and Swedish, covering the time frame of 1878 up to 1970s, the literature authored by Congolese can only be retraced after 1960s, mostly done in French, trade languages (Lingala, Swahili, Kikongo, Tshiluba) and vernacular languages (more than 400). However, these accounts need to be understood with caution as to preserve the fairness of the information. One can identify at least two tendencies within each of the above two categories of writers, be it Western missionaries or Congolese. While some missionaries could strive to produce research and evidence-based accounts, complying with the scientific rigor, others would probably have offered non-documented stories for their home countries in order to secure their support. For the first case, the written accounts usually comprise detailed bibliographical references which allow cross-checking, whereas the latter falls short of written evidences.

Orality has been proven to be most available source of information in Sub-Saharan Africa. The situation in the DRC is not different. First-hand accounts are provided orally by those who witnessed historical facts and events which punctuated the life of mission and the church. Among the accredited informers one can enlist peasants who worked in the compound of missionaries, some as cooks, other as cleaners, still others as transporters. From the compound, the same people happened to be key leaders in the church, serving as catechists, deacons, or teachers. They knew what the real life of missionaries was, and could even participate in some hidden agendas of missionaries' decisions. For some hard situations, they could even be used as *bouclier humain*, being put in front of hard decisions which were initiated by missionaries. One or another tribe could be advantaged or disadvantaged when it comes to task distribution, favour sharing, ministerial training, leadership development or appointment. They might have known why such ethnic group would have been more favoured than others; for which reasons people were trained in one or another school (biblical, theological or secular).

Therefore, in reconstructing the history of missiological education, the researcher should be aware of these realities. Depending on the scope and perspectives of the research, the researcher ought to overcome language barriers either by learning them or by requesting the service of the natives. One of key preoccupations relate to the way informers make the difference between missiological education and any other kind of education (biblical, theological and secular) in those past days.

4.7.1.2 The Problem Related to the Availability of the Source of Information

Due to several reasons, including series of wars that the country has undergone, the written sources are not always easy to access locally. For instance, in researching for this study, I couldn't find the *Congo Mission News* in any of church offices in Kinshasa. Unlike the above remark, oral sources also represent a big challenge to the historian of missions and of the church. As the generally known saying by Apante Ba contends, "Once an African elder passes away, a library has been burned." There is a serious problem of the availability of the source of information while researching for the development of missiology and missiological education in the DRC. But such a problem can be overcome by using some techniques adopted in this study.

4.7.1.3 *The Problem Related to the Interpretation of the Information*

The interpretation of a historical fact might depend on the educational background and the penchant of the interpreter. For instance, while retracing the historical development of missiological education, some prerequisites are needed on missiology and its different concepts. Otherwise, one wouldn't see missiological education during the period preceding its implementation in the DRC in 1990 when Nzash U Lumeya started his Centre Universitaire de Missiologie in Kinshasa. The penchant also can disorient the understanding of historical facts as they would have occurred in one or another situation. For instance, while compiling data on the split of a mission organization or a local denomination (or church), the selection and categorization of the information can be biased if the researcher or the informer are tempted to take the side of one or another part. The following problem (4.7.1.4) can also serve as example of this kind of historical problem.

4.7.1.4 *The Problem Related to a Plurality of Western Missions and Local* **Communautés**

There was a multiplicity of Western mission organizations working in the DRC to the point that groups within the Mennonite, Baptist or Methodist traditions could be two or more; some from the same country of the origin, others from different countries of origin. Some divisions which occurred in missionaries' countries of origin affected their work in the mission field, either by causing the split of missionary groups or through the abandonment of the missionary work started in the DRC. Whereas some were divided from their country of origin, others experienced the split while serving in the DRC.

Similarly, there was, and the situation is still occurring, a multiplicity of local churches (*communautés*) originated from either the work of Western missions or simply due to division within the *communauté*. This situation might put the researcher in a position of confusion while trying to decide on an important information. For instance, the Mission Evangélique en Ubangi (MEU) worked in the Northern part of the DRC, in three administrative districts of Mongala, North-Ubangi and South-Ubangi. Historically, MEU was founded in 1922 by Titus Johnson, an American missionary, who separated from African Inland Mission (AIM) in the North-Eastern part of the DRC. Instead of going back to his country, the missionary decided to initiate an independent mission which became MEU. His first mission station was built in 1922 in Karawa, in North-Ubangi. Later on, the work expanded to South-Ubangi, with a mission station built in Tandala, in 1924. In the United States, Johnson was member of the Evangelical Free Church. Due to the consequences of the World War I, the Evangelical Free Church was no longer able to support the work in the DRC and searched for partnership. The Evangelical Covenant Church (ECC) joined MEU in 1937 and was assigned the North-Ubangi as mission field, taking over Karawa which historically started in 1922. The Evangelical Free Church (EFC) remained in Tandala mission station which started in 1924. The two missions organized joined projects including a Bible Institute and a Seminary. The latter is where I went for my undergraduate studies.

Along the way, conflict occurred between missionaries of the two branches, Tandala and Karawa, which also involved local people. In 1970, MEU was divided in two local denominations: Communauté Evangélique du Christ en Ubangi (CECU), working with the Evangelical Free Church and based in Tandala; and Communauté Evangélique de l'Ubangi-Mongala (CEUM), connected with the Evangelical Covenant Church, based in Karawa. Coming back to my point on the problem facing the historian of mission and church in the DRC, the following situation becomes difficult to handle by the historian. In 1997, there was a debate because the local denomination affiliated with the EFC, now in Tandala (which was started in 1924) organized its seventy-fifth anniversary when Karawa (which started in 1922) was no longer part of the EFC since ECC took it over in 1937. In an unpublished document I wrote in 1997, I raised the question to know whether the EFC could or not "own" this anniversary. What would be the best way to give a historical account? Should it be the anniversary of MEU or of the work of Titus Johnson in the DRC? Or, should it be simply considered as the anniversary of Karawa mission station? In both case, who should be part of the enjoyment? Only CECU which was connected to EFC, the original church of Titus Johnson? Or only CEUM which related to ECC, the US-based denomination that took over Karawa mission station from EFC? Similar stories can be found in many places in the DRC.

4.7.2 Profound Root Causes of the Current Status of Missiology

The theoretical and historical findings of chapters 2 to 4 prompt the argument that there are more profound causes which would have contributed to the current situation of missiology and missiological education in the DRC. One could discern the following five root causes: (1) historical legacies; (2) theological convictions; (3) educational realities; (4) ecclesiastical structures; and (5) economic and political factors.

4.7.2.1 Historical Legacies

As discussed in this chapter, the Protestant missions that pioneered the work in the DRC have left a legacy of poor and belated leadership development of nationals despite countless encouragements of the Edinburgh 1910 conference and its continuing committee, the IMC. Two factual evidences can be mentioned and sketched here.

First, it took thirty years for mission societies to set up the first pastoral school at Kimpese. The Protestant work started in the DRC in 1878 and the first school was established very late in 1908. In addition, the quality of the training was so low that Brown, one of the missionaries in the DRC, could not hesitate to observe that the first factor, which contributed to the failure of the Congo church to be a missionary, is the fact of an untrained ministry.[150] By the time he published his article, "very few Congo pastors have had more than nine years' schooling at the very most."[151] The eve of the first faculty of theology in 1959 was the fruit of IMC's Theological Education

---

150. Brown, "Church and Its Missionary Task," 303.
151. Ibid.

Funds project as proposed in Bates's report.[152] One could also observe that this newly established training institution was structured according to the existing fourfold pattern of theological education which ignored everything about mission. Historians have indicated that the purpose of that theological institution was to prepare qualified ministers to serve the church in its work of serving people of Congo. The general secretary of the newly formed CCC, pastor Bokeleale could state that "the true mission of the church [in Congo] is to evangelize the Congolese people."[153]

The second evidence of the historical legacy could relate to the educational background of missionaries who served in the DRC. Many of them, if not the majority, have been themselves of low educational background in mission studies. Section 4.4.4 of this chapter provided some evidences of it. Since one gives only what he or she possesses, the missionary legacy for missiology and missiological education could not be expected to be beyond the capacity of missionaries themselves. For instance, after his visit to the DRC in 1934 where he attended two Protestant missionary conferences, Dr John Mott came to the conclusion that Protestant missions in the DRC failed to speed the process of transferring the leadership to nationals and to raise internationally renowned people (section 4.5.3). The general impression and legacy is that "mission" was for Western missionaries and "church" for nationals.

4.7.2.2 *Theological Convictions*

Theological convictions would have played an important role in the state of missiology and missiological education in the DRC. Much of that situation could derive from the opposing coexistence of ecumenical and evangelical streams at both international and local levels. The historical legacy of theological convictions can be described according to two main periods.

The first period of ante-WCC can be set from 1910 to 1948. This period was one of shared theological conviction that the supreme task for the mission of the church was to reach out to the world with the message of the gospel. Since the Conference of Edinburgh in 1910, this conviction was generally shared by missionaries, by leaders of younger churches on

---

152. Bates, *Survey.*
153. Bokeleale, "From Missions to Mission," 433.

the mission field and by leaders of missionary societies in the West. During this period, the IMC was an asset for the promotion of such a conviction. As already demonstrated in chapter 2 and then in this chapter, there was a close relatedness between the Congo Protestant Council (CPC) and the IMC. Though the spirit of unity characterized the Protestant work in the DRC due to several reasons, including the fact that Protestant missions were constantly under the threat of the colonial regime and the Roman Catholic Church, some structures of the Protestant missions were modelled after the recommendations of the Conference of Edinburgh 1910 and its continuing committee. Many Protestant missionaries based in the DRC published their reflections in the *IRM(s)*, which was edited by the IMC. Some among them were involved in the leadership and managerial positions of the IMC.

The second period started in 1948 when WCC came to existence, and mostly when the WCC and the IMC emerged in 1961. This period was the starting point of the bipolarization of theological convictions about mission. While evangelicals would continue with the spirit of the Conference of Edinburgh 1910, ecumenicals would rather shape new directions for missions, which actually were already insinuated by the Conference of Edinburgh 1910. Literature has shown that alongside the preoccupation of evangelizing the whole generation, some participants also raised the concern of social engagement by the church as being part of its mission. The radicalization of the ecumenical movement against the proclamation of the gospel as being the essential element of missionary enterprise came to comfort theological teachings of mission that value humanization as the purpose of mission. These two points of view influenced mission, missiology and missiological education at both international and national levels. This bipolar reality came to its pick when finally evangelicals set for the creation of what has become "Lausanne Movement" in 1974. In the DRC, these two convictions, ecumenicalism and evangelicalism, have also polluted the climate of understanding and of collaboration. Though the constitution of the CCC promotes neutrality regarding these two theological convictions, the ecumenical movement has been the most influential organization for the CCC and its services.[154] The related theological trends have left a legacy

---

154. Eglise du Christ au Congo, *Procès verbal*, 1994.

of not having an agreed point of view about mission, missiology and missiological education in the country.

4.7.2.3 Educational Realities

Educational realities have meaningfully influenced the state of mission, missiology and missiological education in the DRC. Besides what has been said earlier about the educational background of missionaries (section 4.4.4), which might have shaped the theory and practice of mission, one could point to the general standard of the educational system in the DRC. Beginning from the earlier context of colonialism up to the post-colonialism period, authors have lamented the low quality of the Protestant educational system. While the Catholic educational system was said to be of high quality, the Protestant system could not prepare students to hold an influencing leadership position at both local and international levels. Authors have attributed this situation to the colonial policy, which favoured Catholic missions and granted them subsidies for their educational programs. It was only and painfully in 1948 under international pressure that the Protestant educational programs were granted some subsidies.

Such a legacy affected the complete intellectual environment of the Protestant missions. One could probably find in this environment the reason of the delay in transferring the leadership to nationals. As discussed earlier (section 4.5.2), authors indicate that the formation of the first Protestant theological institution in 1959 was the result of a long and painful process, which would even affect the relationship between missionaries and nationals. This climate of misunderstanding caused nationals to have a bad image of whatever falls under the label of "mission," including "mission studies" which were easily interpreted by many as being an instrument of the Western imperialism. How could a Protestant theological institution in such an atmosphere plan any department or training program about "mission" or "mission studies"? Therefore, if there could have been a better way of speaking of "mission," the only possibility would be to promote the ecumenical understanding of mission as reminded in the previous section (4.7.2.2). Mission is humanization, liberating people from political oppression and social inequalities, valuing the local culture and living in peaceful relationship with people of other faiths without any attempt of converting them.

In addition, educational philosophies and practices influenced also the teaching-learning process. Education was perceived as a means of indoctrinating effort, which discourages independent thought or acceptance of other opinions. Even at the higher education level, the educational approach was teacher-centered rather than learner-centered, subject-oriented rather than content-oriented, pedagogy-oriented rather than andragogy-oriented. These concepts were amply explored in chapter 3 (section 3.5). In such an educational environment, students are mostly dependent on whatever instructors conceive and impart. If there is nothing of "mission" or "missiology" in the instructor's mindset, nothing different could be expected from the graduates of such a learning system, and from the church that they would serve after their studies.

4.7.2.4 Ecclesiastical Structures

In the DRC the understanding of mission and missiology, the practice of missiological education cannot be well-captured without taking into account the debate, which punctuated the formation of the CCC. In his doctoral thesis, Molo amply surveyed and analyzed this debate, demonstrating how the ecclesiastical structures that were adopted in 1970 shaped a unique ecclesiology of the Protestant church in the DRC. As one revisits missions and church history in the DRC, it becomes obvious that the post-missionary Protestant missions and church were actually the result of what started during the missionary era through the creation of the CPC whereby mission societies of various ecclesiastical traditions came to work together. The debate centred on the question whether the unity of the church in the DRC could be "structural" (with consultative role) or "organic" (with executive role). While the first suggests that the CCC is a consultative federation of autonomous churches, the second insinuates that churches from various traditions should keep their autonomy but under one official representative leadership comparable to the Roman Catholic Church.

Recent accounts of this debate can be found in the official documents of the CCC.[155] These documents report on the negative implication that the debate has on mission engagement of the CCC and its related *communautés*. For instance, during the celebration of the thirtieth anniversary of the CCC

---

155. Eglise du Christ au Congo, *Procès verbal*, 1996; 1997a; 1997b; 1999.

held in Kinshasa, 1–8 October 2000, the theme was *Unité de l'Eglise du Christ au Congo, Paix et Développment* (The unity of the Church of Christ in Congo, Peace and Development). Eight presentations were delivered by professors of the Faculty of Theology of the PUC. As the formulation of the theme and of each presentation suggests, none of these eight presentations dealt expressively with "mission" of the church. Furthermore, it was during the meeting of the National Executive Committee of the Church of Christ in Congo held on the same occasion, that Dr Diafwila who went with his family to serve in Canada was judged as deserter rather than being considered as missionary.[156]

Subsequently, a closer look of the history of the relationship between missionaries and nationals would rather suggest another interpretation about the coexistence or non-coexistence of "mission" and "church." As already discussed previously (section 4.6.1), what was at stake was whether or not the "mission" (missionaries' institution) could coexist with "church" (nationals' institution). With the foundation of the CCC in 1970, the final decision was that mission organization was over and the church organization took over. This decision had undoubtedly affected the theology of mission. In the nineteenth century and the first half of the twentieth century, mission included both "mission organization" and the task of being a "church in mission." The "mission organization" from the West came to the existence in the DRC in 1878 due to the understanding that the church *per essence* is a community *for* and *in* mission. Therefore, if "mission organization" is dismantled, the concept and reality of "church in mission" becomes questionable. This questionability is so real that the concept "mission" could not bear a clear meaning within the CCC and its related *communautés*. For instance, the words *mission intérieure* (home mission) and *mission extérieure* (foreign mission) which existed in some earlier versions of the constitution to define the mission of the CCC disappeared from the recent versions.[157] For a long time the department of evangelism and life of the church did not explicitly include the word "mission" until as recently as 1998. Even with the inclusion of "mission," a close survey of the minutes of the CCC

---

156. Eglise du Christ au Congo, *Procès verbal*, 1999, 16–17; 2000, 17.
157. See Eglise de Christ au Congo, *Constitution*, 1970, 2004, 2014.

about its nature, ministries and projects indicate that "mission" is not the preoccupation for many church leaders and members. The structures of the church do not provide conditions for mission involvement of the church.

Another aspect is the missionless bureaucratization of the church structure where, as Crawford had observed, the ablest men were removed from the pastorate into administrative positions.[158] It is however noteworthy that the administration per se was not a bad thing. It was needed in a period when Western missionaries were departing from the country. The church needed a capable and fruitful managerial leadership to ensure its future. Unfortunately, as in any other human situations, the focus on administration without equal attention on God's glocal mission caused the CCC to become a more "maintenance-church" than a "missional-church." Similar observation could also be made of the focus on the implicit suggestion of Crawford to concentrate on pastorate as far as, according to Brown, the pastoral ministry was mostly focused on local scope.[159] In general, both pastoral and administrative ministries in the context of the DRC were more for local mission than glocal mission. The focus was only on the local ministry of the church instead of being on both its local and global ministries together.

4.7.2.5 Economic and Political Factors

Economic and political factors have influenced the state of mission, missiology and missiological education in the DRC from the beginning of the missionary work to date. Writing after the independence of the DRC, Crawford observed that economic factors and status played a part regarding recruitment to the ministry.[160] According to the author, these factors caused the church to suffer from a lack of consecrated and well-trained men. After independence, many catechists left their work to seek better life in cities. Even today, the church ministry is not a paying service except when focusing on the prevailing prosperity gospel. Theological education in general and missiological education in particular, is not an attractive field of study based on the reason that it does not ensure financial and material return. The situation could not be otherwise since the human tendency has been

---

158. Crawford, "Protestant Missions," 93.
159. Brown, "Church and Its Missionary Task," 303.
160. Crawford, "Protestant Missions."

often to concentrate on current difficulties and problems. Disciples faced the same problem when the Samaritan harvest was ready (John 4). Jesus and his disciples had the choice between focusing on their famine and take time to eat or lifting up their eyes to watch and minister to the Samaritan harvest. Jesus taught a missiological lesson to his disciples that amidst difficulties and challenges of their daily life they should not forget to lift up their eyes, to see and to minister to the harvest (John 4:35).

In the DRC, Protestant work had always faced challenges, which caused the church to focus on them with the temptation of overlooking God's glocal and redemptive mission. Apart from the experience of Western missionaries during their pioneering work under the unfriendly colonial regime, the CCC underwent the same temptation of side lining the global aspect of God's mission. A good look at official documents such as the minutes of meetings of the CCC and its related *communautés* would lead to the conclusion that most often these meetings focused on challenges, difficulties, and problems faced locally.[161] One could even find the same trends through different versions of the constitution of the CCC, moving from mission as proclamation of the gospel throughout the world to social engagements as the true mission of the church.[162] Various themes of national meetings of the CCC from 1971 to 2015 display clearly the same orientation.

The economic and political situations have caused the DRC to continually being a contrasting place of wealth with economically, socially and politically unstable population. Recurrent army conflicts and wars since the independence have hindered the development of the country and that of its population, destroying any hope one could attempt to expect and keeping people in a pessimistic environment. This situation has then become both psychological and normal. The affected psychology of the inhabitants of the country – including church leaders and members – has put them in an environment where abnormal becomes normal. In such an environment, the church is likely tempted to abdicate its God-given vision of doing mission both locally and globally. The church and its training institutions would probably focus on theologies which concentrate on daily struggles losing

---

161. Eglise du Christ au Congo, *Procès*, 1996, 1997, 1999.
162. See Eglise de Christ au Congo, *Constitution*, 1970, 2004, 2014.

sight on the fact that these human struggles have their root cause in sin. As mentioned earlier, the prevailing theologies promoted on the continent (African theology, Black theology, Reconstruction theology, etc.,) have been more "revolutionary" theologies rather than being "evolutionary" theologies that could lead the church to join God in his glocal mission (but not only local). There is a need of transforming the prevailing theology into missional theology.

Using the research questions introduced in the first chapter (section 1.3) along with arising themes discussed in the theoretical literature review (chs. 2 to 4), the next chapter explores specific trends of missiology and missiological education in theological institutions in the DRC as far as God's glocal (both local and global) mission is concerned.

CHAPTER 5

Missiology in Theological Education in the DR Congo: Empirical Investigation and Findings

5.1 Introduction

The interest for this study arose from an observation on the reality of the DRC as being a less "missionary-sending country" at the global level, while housing several tertiary theological institutions and churches in full bloom. The assumption was that missiology and theological education in such a context needed to be revisited. If graduates had a training which encompasses a personal and profound inner conviction for *missio Dei*, they would realize the power of *transforming* missiology. While being subject to change, their missiology would also be an activity susceptible to bring change to their life and churches. Whereas some literature states that mission engagement in the history has been the fruit of revival rather than that of formal theological education, others recognize the crucial role that theological institutions might have in the process of mission articulation and engagement.

Through the review of theoretical, educational and historical literature, the preceding chapters (2 to 4) explored and discussed how the prevailing perception of missiology and missiological education in various historical contexts (including the Protestant mission in the DRC) was determinant in the theory, training, and practice for mission. Therefore, the purpose of this concurrent mixed method study was to better understand how the prevailing missiological training programs in the DRC align with the preoccupation of providing missiological education for God's glocal mission. The key question was about how the prevailing missiological education in the DRC aligns with the purpose of *missio Dei*. To address such a preoccupation, some sub-questions were formulated as they help tackle some specific aspects of the central question.

This chapter describes the research design to surface the current situation of missiology and missiological education in the DRC. It also displays, interprets and analyzes the findings. As John Creswell suggests, it is important in research to clearly state the nature of the study to avoid any unintended confusion.[1] The following lines elaborate more on the nature of this research.

5.2 Research Design

The study is prominently a qualitative inquiry done through case study using the descriptive method. Authors relate the qualitative research to two fundamental beliefs, namely (1) events must be studied in natural settings, that is, understanding requires field-based research; (2) a researcher cannot understand events without understanding how they are perceived and interpreted by the people who participate in them.[2] It is important to substantiate such a choice before getting to the procedures of data collection and analysis.

5.2.1 The Nature of This Research

In his book entitled *Introduction to Missiological Research*, Edgar Elliston indicates that missiological studies can be descriptive, experimental or evaluative.[3] He also observes that while the first and the third are used extensively in missiological research, the second is used less often. Nevertheless, descriptive research is neither the private hunting ground of the discipline of missiology, as Elliston assumption tends to assert,[4] nor specifically for practical theology.[5] Being a scientific method which purposes the description of one or more characteristic of a group of people, as Smith recognizes it,

---

1. Creswell, *Research Design*, 3rd ed., 74.
2. Tuckman and Harper, *Conducting Educational Research*, 388.
3. Elliston, *Introduction*, 67.
4. Ibid.
5. Smith, *Academic Writing*, 225.

descriptive research can apply to other scientific disciplines as well because it is about "making reality known."[6]

Authors contend that in some cases, descriptive research requires quantitative data, and in others it uses qualitative data.[7] One could observe that these types of research can also be undertaken through mixed approaches which use data collected through both quantitative and qualitative methods even in a single work. Nevertheless, the reality is that a mixed approach would always be either prominently quantitative (QUAN+qual) or qualitative (QUAL+quan).[8] It is not possible to have pure quantitative research without integrating some elements from qualitative, and vice versa.[9] As Tuckman and Harper put it, "no researcher can ever carry out a totally systematic (qualitative) or totally objective (quantitative) study."[10] This study is based on a prominently qualitative mixed method.

Creswell identifies six major strategies in collecting data for a mixed method research, and these strategies are of two categories, namely those which allow the investigators to collect quantitative and qualitative data in phases (sequentially), and those which help them collect both quantitative and qualitative data the same time (concurrently).[11] This study used one of the following three concurrent strategies. The *concurrent triangulation strategy* which gives the same priority to both quantitative and qualitative inquiries, and data analysis is done separately before comparing data results. The *concurrent nested strategy* gives the priority only to either one of quantitative or qualitative inquiries, and the analysis of findings is done based on the priority, either quantitatively or qualitatively. For the *concurrent transformative strategy*, the priority can be equal between the two methods in data collection

---

6. Ibid., 226.

7. Vyhmeister, *Quality Research Papers*; Elliston, *Introduction*, 67.

8. Creswell, *Research Design*, 2nd ed., 213. QUAL+quan stands for "prominently qualitative research using some elements of quantitative inquiry"; and QUAN+qual means "prominently quantitative research using some elements of qualitative inquiry."

9. Johnson and Onwuegbuzie, "Mixed Methods Research"; Creswell, *Research Design*, 3rd ed.

10. Tuckman and Harper, *Conducting Educational Research*.

11. Creswell, *Research Design*, 2nd ed., 213–219. They are (1) sequential explanatory strategy, (2) sequential exploratory strategy, (3) sequential transformative strategy, (4) concurrent triangulation strategy, (5) concurrent nested strategy, and (6) concurrent transformative strategy.

and analysis, but in practical application, the priority may be given only to either one of quantitative or qualitative inquiries. Due to its purpose, this study used concurrent nested strategy. The qualitative and quantitative data collection was done in the same phase (concurrently), having the qualitative method as priority and quantitative method with less priority, being embedded (nested) within the predominant qualitative method.

In this perspective, the descriptive approach collected data through interviews, questionnaires, a survey and case studies in order to explain the phenomenon through journalistic questions ("who," "what," "when," "where" and "how"). Therefore, though prominently being of qualitative nature, this study benefited also from some quantitative insights through questionnaire and statistical data from published documents.

Creswell outlined the characteristics of qualitative research, and the following features are summarized to substantiate how I strived to comply with them:[12]

1. Qualitative research takes place in the natural setting of the study. For this research, I visited some universities and had interaction with participants of the study.
2. Qualitative research uses multiple methods that are interactive and humanistic. It adopts and uses one or more strategies of inquiry as guide for the procedures in the study. As stated further, data collection for this study was done using different methods while taking into account ethical considerations.
3. Qualitative research is emergent rather than tightly prefigured. Caution was taken during this study to closely watch significant aspects of the research outcomes arising from the research.
4. Qualitative research is fundamentally interpretive. Effort was deployed to not take any aspect of the outcome for granted as far as the research problem and purpose were concerned.
5. Qualitative research views social phenomena holistically. Without involving to detailed account and analysis, arising matters were, however, approached with consideration of the theological and historical background surveyed in the precedent chapters.

---

12. Creswell, *Research Design*, 3rd ed., 181–183.

6. Qualitative research allows a systematic reflection on who has been researched on, his or her biography and how it shapes the study. The conviction for this research was that people, including their actions and declarations, constitute crucial elements to facilitate the understanding of the issue under consideration.
7. Qualitative research uses complex reasoning that is multifaceted and simultaneous. The study had already engaged in theological, philosophical and historical reasoning in the precedent chapters. The same spirit continued in this and the remaining chapters.

Without expanding their list Tuckman and Harper assign five characteristics to qualitative research:[13]

1. The natural setting is the data source, and the researcher is the key data-collection instrument.
2. Such a study attempts primarily to describe and only secondary to analyze.
3. Researchers concern themselves with process, that is, with events that transpire, as much as with product or outcome.
4. Data analysis emphasizes inductive methods comparable to putting together the parts of puzzle.
5. The researcher focuses essentially on what things mean, that is, why events occur as well as what happens.

While conducting this study caution was made to comply with these guidelines either while reviewing literature in the precedent chapters or in collecting and analyzing data for the empirical investigation reported in this chapter.

5.2.2 Understanding Descriptive Research Applied to This Study

Authors have discussed the purpose, characteristics, values and limitations of descriptive research. Speaking from missiological perspective, Elliston indicates that descriptive research in missiological studies generally serves to develop theory.[14] For the author, developing theory means describing what has been or is true in a situation while providing an explanation of the

---

13. Tuckman and Harper, *Conducting Educational Research, 387.*
14. Elliston, *Introduction,* 68.

phenomena. The process also includes showing from the patterns of what has been described how to predict what is likely to happen in the future and to suggest a basis for action based on the description of the phenomena. According to Isaac and Michael, descriptive research serves four main purposes, namely (1) to collect detailed information that describes existing phenomena; (2) to identify problems or justify conditions and practices; (3) to make comparisons and evaluations; and (4) to determine what others are doing with similar problems or situations and benefit from their experience in making future plans and decisions.[15] Therefore, theoretical outcomes of descriptive research should serve (1) to explain the phenomena under study; (2) to provide bases for action; and (3) to provide bases for testing theory.[16]

A given missiological situation might require more than one research method in order to fully understand the issue. Descriptive research "allows the combination of multiple methods in order to describe better the situation."[17] Therefore, descriptive research is supported by a wide range of methods which include historical research, survey research with questionnaires and interviews, participant observation, ethnographic descriptions, applications of grounded theory, exegetical studies, case studies and theological research.[18] Some of the above listed methods have contributed to the present study, namely theological research in chapter 2 and 3, historical research in chapter 4, and case studies with questionnaires and focus groups in this chapter. As said previously, the aim of this study was to better describe the phenomena related to missiology and missiological education in the DRC in order to surface theory that could be used to either solve the problem or be tested in further research.

Leedy has identified the following characteristics of descriptive research to which the present study strived to conform:[19]

1. It deals with a situation that demands the technique of observation as the principal means of collecting the data. Preceding chapters (1 to 4) were designed to generate in-depth

---

15. Isaac and Michael, 197 quoted in Smith, *Academic Writing*, 226.
16. Elliston, *Introduction*, 69.
17. Ibid., 68.
18. Ibid.
19. Leedy, *Practical Research*, 187.

insights which could facilitate the observation process applied in this chapter.
2. The population for the study must be carefully chosen, clearly defined and specifically delimited in order to set precise parameters for ensuring discreteness to the population. Further in this chapter, effort is done to meet this requirement.
3. It is particularly susceptible to distortion through the introduction of bias into the research design. Particular attention should be given to safeguarding the data from the influence of bias. This chapter provides details on the validity and reliability of instruments used in the research.
4. Although it relies upon observation for the acquisition of the data, that data must then be organized and presented systematically so that valid and accurate conclusions can be drawn from them. Based on the research questions formulated in the first chapter, the structure of the result presentation, interpretation and analysis will be organized accordingly.

Authors have also pointed out some limitations of descriptive research of which I was aware. For instance, based on a medical-related perspective, Grimes and Schultz caution that there are things that descriptive studies can and cannot do, one of them being the fact that they are concerned only with description without regard to causal or other hypotheses.[20] From practical theology perspective, Smith echoes the voices of other authors contending that descriptive research cannot be used for prediction and control purposes; neither to establish a causal relationship between variables.[21] Reflecting on missiological research, Elliston indicates that the issue is mostly on the generalizability of the findings if the research used case studies, interviews, etc.[22] Based on these observations effort was made in this study to consider the question "why" and to make any prediction or generalization with caution, leaving further studies the possibility of testing the emerging theory. The study focuses on exploration, description and critical analysis

---

20. Grimes and Schultz, "Descriptive Studies," 145.
21. Smith, *Academic Writing*, 229.
22. Elliston, *Introduction*, 68.

based on the theological, philosophical and historical discoveries of the precedent chapters.

5.2.3 The Choice of Case Study

This study was based on case studies, which are defined diversely. While some authors define case study "straightforwardly"[23] as "an intensive analysis of an individual unit stressing developmental factors in relation to environment," others do it in a "highly problematic" way.[24] An illustration of the latter is derived from the Penguin Dictionary of Sociology, which defines a case study in the following terms:

> The detailed examination of a single example of a class of phenomena, a case study cannot provide reliable information about the broader class, but it may be useful in the preliminary stages of an investigation since it provides hypotheses, which may be tested systematically with a larger number of cases.

As Flyvbejerg demonstrates, this definition echoes the prevailing judgement of undervaluing case study.[25] There have been five misunderstandings about case studies, which Flyvbejerg has examined and refuted. He brightly demonstrates that the misunderstandings below which have been adopted for a long time should be abandoned.

1. General, theoretical knowledge is more valuable than concrete case knowledge. The author has demonstrated that "predictive theories and universals cannot be found in the study of human affairs. Concrete case knowledge is therefore more valuable than the vain search for predictive theories and universals."[26]
2. One cannot generalize on the basis of an individual case; therefore, the case study cannot contribute to scientific development. The author has demonstrated that "one can often generalize on the basis of a single case, and the case study may be central to scientific development via generalization as supplement or alternative to other methods. But formal generalization is

---

23. Flyvbejerg, "Case Study," 169.
24. Ibid.
25. Ibid., 175.
26. Ibid.

overvalued as a source of scientific development, whereas 'the force of example' and transferability are underestimated."[27]
3. The case study is most useful for generating hypotheses, while other methods are more suitable for hypotheses testing and theory building. The author has demonstrated that "the case study is useful for both generating and testing of hypotheses but is not limited to these research activities alone."[28]
4. The case study contains a bias toward verification, that is, a tendency to confirm the researcher's preconceived notions. The author has demonstrated that "the case study contains no greater bias toward verification of the researcher's preconceived notions than other methods of inquiry. On the contrary, experience indicates that the case study contains a greater bias toward falsification of preconceived notions than toward verification."[29]
5. It is often difficult to summarize and develop general propositions and theories on the basis of specific case studies. The author has demonstrated that "it is correct that summarizing case studies is often difficult, especially a concerns case process. It is less correct as regards case outcomes. The problems in summarizing case studies, however, are due more often to properties of the reality studied than to the case study as a research method. Often it is not desirable to summarize and generalize case studies. Good studies should be read as narratives in their entirety."[30]

Given the purpose of this research, the debate on the above misunderstanding and Flyvbejerg's examination and conclusions are crucial to raise here. The choice of case study to discuss the critical issue of the present study should not be underestimated as Flyvbejerg has amply demonstrated. Instead, it provides the opportunity to discuss the issue in-depth with the possibility of understanding more deeply the unit under consideration in

---

27. Ibid., 179.
28. Ibid.
29. Ibid., 190.
30. Ibid., 195.

order to make thoughtful conclusions and generalizations. Table 5.1 below highlights the strengths and weaknesses of case studies.

Table 5.1 Strengths and Weaknesses of Case Study

Strengths	Weaknesses
Depth	Selection bias may overstate or understate relationships
High conceptual validity	Weak understanding of occurrence in population of phenomena under study
Understanding of context and process	Statistical significance often unknown or unclear
Understanding of what causes a phenomenon, linking causes and outcomes	
Fostering new hypotheses and new research questions	

Source: Adapted from Flyvbejerg.[31]

It is in the light of these strengths and weaknesses that one could stress the need of opting for complementarity between case study and statistical methods, knowing that what the former cannot achieve, the latter will.[32] The mixed methods – the combination of some elements of qualitative and quantitative research approaches – originated from the need of making greater sense out of the numerical findings. However, this new solution has prompted controversies among researchers. Creswell identifies eleven key controversies and questions being raised in mixed method research.[33] Much of them relate to definition, philosophical debates and the procedures for conducting study. Creswell then suggests that a research can be done using a given method, and be redone using another method. On their side, Teddlie and Tashakkori have observed that in their own research, they found that information gleaned from narratives generated by participants and

---

31. Ibid., 179.
32. Ibid.
33. Creswell, "Controversies," 101–133.

investigators often proves to be the most valuable source in understanding complex phenomena.[34]

As the debate continues, the option in this study is to use the case study of the DRC while benefiting from some elements of quantitative inquiry wherever need is, in order to reach a more comprehensive understanding of the issue under consideration.

5.2.4 Research Questions

In the first chapter, the research questions were simply listed without being substantiated. This section explains what the study exactly purposed to discover. What are different specific aspects of the problem for which the study purposes to get answers? Why is each of these aspects important for the research? These questions are addressed, not only as to stick to the particular focus of the study, but also in order to maintain the harmony between the chapters of the study and to progressively shed more light on the issue under consideration (table 5.2).

Designing research questions for qualitative research is different from quantitative research. Quantitative research uses "why" or "to what extent" to pose questions with words which assume directional orientation such as "affect," "influence," "impact," "determine," "cause" and "relate."[35] The findings of literature review explored in the precedent chapters along with the purpose of this study, called for the revision of the research questions as to relate them to the qualitative nature of the research. The explorative purpose of the present study was to build theory about missiology and missiological education in the context of the DRC. Future research could then undertake to test it through a more quantitative study.

---

34. Teddlie and Tashakkori, "Mixed Methods Research," 137.
35. Creswell, *Research Design,* 2nd ed., 107.

Table 5.2 Schematic Presentation of the Research

	Research questions	Aim and objectives	Research method
Central question	How does the prevailing missiological education in the DRC align with and contribute to the purpose of God's global and holistic mission?	The main aim of this study is to make a missiological evaluation of the missiological education provided by Protestant universities in the DRC as to determine to what extent it contributes to mission engagement of graduates and their churches.	This historical, theological and educational study is done from the perspective of the evangelical tradition.
Q.1	Through which paradigms of theology of mission and for which reasons missiological education has been provided in the DRC?	Based on Scriptural revelation, to study and evaluate the arguments of the selected Protestant universities.	Literature analysis, survey, and focus group are done to evaluate past and present points of view.
Q.2	To what extent has a *missio Dei* vision or the lack of it in the whole of theological education influenced missiological education and mission practice?	To determine, study and evaluate the extent to which the selected Protestant universities would contribute to *missio Dei*.	Literature analysis, survey, and questionnaire are done to ensure analysis, interpretation and synthesis.
Q.3	Through which educational and conceptual frameworks have missiological education been offered in the DRC?	To determine, study and evaluate the arguments of the selected Protestant universities.	Literature analysis, survey, and focus group are done to evaluate past and present points of view.
Q.4	To what extent is missiological education and research really serving the churches in the DRC?	Through statistical studies, to determine and study the level of relatedness of mission education on church engagement in God's global mission.	Questionnaire and documentation analysis.

5.2.5 Research Instruments

The first chapter briefly sketched the information about the research plan. The intention here is to move a bit deeper regarding the data collection. As mentioned earlier, authors suggest that in a qualitative studies the researcher spends a considerable time in the natural setting gathering information. For this study, data were collected through participant observation, documentary research, questionnaires, some informal interviews and focus groups.

5.2.5.1 Participant Observation

The research was conducted through participant observation. Creswell defines this method as a process through which the researcher collects data by "taking field notes on the behaviour and activities of individuals at the research site," recording activities at the research site either in an unstructured or semi structured way.[36] The present study did not seek to explore behavior as per Creswell's definition, but to surface the state of missiology and missiological education in the DRC theological institutions. It was necessary to approach some leading Protestant theological institutions.

Neuman insists that some factors should be taken into account for the selection of the site and the information to observe.[37] He then underscores three factors relevant to choosing a field research, namely richness of data, unfamiliarity and suitability.[38] For this study, I ensured that data were rich enough to provide needed information, that new unknown data were discovered to broaden the understanding, and appropriate data were accessed to make the research relevant. With regard to the procedures of observation, Neuman indicates that researchers of qualitative studies pay attention, watch and listen carefully as they use all the senses, being sensitive to what is seen, heard, smelled, tasted or touched.[39] The researcher himself becomes an instrument that absorbs all sources of information. To avoid possible disruption that technology often causes or questionable impressions people could have had, I did not audiotape or videotape any interaction with people

---

36. Creswell, *Research Design*, 2nd ed., 185.
37. Neuman, *Social Research Methods*.
38. Ibid., 352.
39. Ibid.

but managed a notebook to jot down any interesting and relevant verbal or written information.

Based on some specific criteria to be explained below, I visited five Protestant theological institutions. The first institution was the PUC, which, as already explained in the first chapter, makes the backbone of this research. Besides previous occasions I used to visit this University to use the library, to give a conference, to attend thesis defence and to connect with faculty members, I spent three months in Kinshasa, from May to July 2015. During that time of research, participant observation occurred. Activities included using the library, attending thesis defences specifically in the area of mission studies, conducting two focus groups with bachelor (*licence*) and master (DEA) students, interacting with professors and research teams and getting some official documents (meeting minutes, program handbooks, etc.).

The focus group was conducted through a conference on *Missiologie comme une discipline en et de transformation: défi aux institutions théologique protestantes avec référence à la République Démocratique du Congo* (Missiology as a transforming discipline, challenge to Protestant theological institutions with reference to the Democratic Republic of Congo).

I spent also three to five days visiting four more institutions. On the occasion of the celebration of its twenty-fifth anniversary (1990–2015), the *Centre Universitaire de Missiology* (University Centre for Missiology), located in Kinshasa, launched a conference and I was invited to speak on *Pour une évaluation quantitative et qualitative d'une formation missiologique de niveau Universitaire* (Conducting a quantitative and qualitative evaluation of a training program in missiology at university level). During that time, I learned many things about the institution through questions asked and suggestions made by participants, mostly students and alumni.

From 17 to 20 October 2015, on his request, I was given opportunity to visit the campus of Université Libre des Pays de Grands Lacs (Great Lakes Free University) located in Goma, the Eastern part of the country. This university doesn't offer programs in mission studies, and by the time the research was done, the general impression was that of reluctance to missiological education. The focus group session was conducted through a conference on *Missiologie comme une discipline en et de transformation: défi aux institutions théologique protestantes avec référence à la République*

Démocratique du Congo (Missiology as a transforming discipline, challenge to Protestant theological institutions with reference to the Democratic Republic of Congo). The conference was attended by theology students and faculty members. Other informal contacts and interactions were made by either students or faculty members.

Under the same conditions, similar activities (observation, conference, focus group, informal interaction) were conducted in Bukavu, in two more Protestant universities. From 3 to 5 December 2015, I visited Université Evangélique en Afrique (Evangelical University of Africa) and from 5 to 7 December 2015 the visit took place at Université Libre des Pays de Grands Lacs (Great Lakes Free University) located in Bukavu. More visits could have been done in other places if the financial capability allowed. However, some colleagues helped administer the research questionnaire in such areas as Université Méthodiste du Katanga (Methodist University of Katanga) near Lubumbashi, Université Shalom de Bunia (Bunia Shalom University), Université Evangélique de l'Alliance (Alliance Evangelical University) in Boma, and Université Protestante de l'Equateur (Protestant University of Equator), near Mbandaka, and Université Protestante au Coeur du Congo (Protestant University in the Heart of Congo), in Kananga.

5.2.5.2 Documentary Research

Two documentary sources, primary and secondary, were used to collect data. Elliston specifies that, while secondary sources are those written about the subject, primary sources are the subject or participants.[40] In educational research, journals and books are primary sources because they contain the original work, or raw materials.[41] In historical research, primary sources include text and other media, oral history, relics and quantitative data.[42] Missiology being an interdisciplinary field, this study combined missiological research, educational research and historical research on how the Protestant theological institutions of Congo view and practice missiology and missiological education. Program handbooks, websites, minutes of meetings, journals and books were consulted when available.

---

40. Elliston, *Introduction*, 31.
41. Tuckman and Harper, *Conducting Educational Research*, 53.
42. Gall et al., *Applying Educational Research*.

5.2.5.3 Questionnaires

As indicated previously, this study is prominently qualitative using concurrent nested strategy. Based on the fact that authors recognize the importance of mixing method procedures by integrating some elements from other types of research, for instance QUAL+quan, it was useful to design a research questionnaire without however giving to "QUAL" and "quan" equal priority. Although the questionnaire is a technique of quantitative research, it was used in this study to help get greater understanding on the issue under consideration. As Creswell states, "this model [concurrent nested strategy] uses one data collection phase during which both quantitative and qualitative data are collected simultaneously . . . It helps gain broader perspective as using the different methods as opposed to using the predominant method alone . . . The data collected from the two methods are mixed during the analysis phase of the project."[43]

Speaking of what questionnaires and interviews measure, Tuckman and Harper state that these data collection methods allow the researcher "to measure what someone knows (knowledge or information), what someone likes and dislikes (values and preferences), and what someone thinks (attitudes and beliefs)."[44] In this study, the questionnaires helped to collect data from geographical areas I could not reach in order to complement the data collected through the documentary method. For instance, it was not possible to visit the Alliance Evangelical University in Boma, Western Congo; the Methodist University of Katanga in Mulungwishi, Southern Congo; the Protestant University of Lubumbashi, Southern Congo; the Protestant University in the Heart of Congo in Kananga, Central Congo; the Protestant University of Equator in Bolenge near Mbandaka, Nord-Western Congo; Bunia Shalom University in Northern-East Congo; and the Methodist University of Maniema, Kindu, South-Eastern Congo. Therefore, through email, some colleagues helped administer the questionnaire.

The questionnaire was designed using open-ended questions to allow respondents to express their ideas and opinions. Wherever a non-open-ended

---

43. Creswell, *Research Design*, 2nd ed., 218.
44. Tuckman and Harper, *Conducting Educational Research*, 387.

question was asked, the possibility of sub-open-ended question was provided (see appendices A and B).

To ensure the reliability of the questionnaire, a pilot-test was taken by a group of students in Burundi, and by theology students in Kinshasa. Clarification was provided to improve the understanding of unclear questions.

5.2.5.4 Some Informal Interviews and Focus Groups

Creswell indicates that in qualitative research, interviews encompass options like face-to-face (one-on-one, in-person interviews), telephone (researcher interviews by phone), and group (researcher interviews participants in a group).[45] This study collected data mainly through focus groups with students following conferences, and through informal interviews with available professors to get their feedback on the discussion of the conference.

5.2.6 Population

In social science research, the research population represents a set of individuals, cases or objects which make the setting of the research.[46] In general, a research population consists of individuals, cases or objects with some common observable characteristics. For instance, Christian universities make a population. Even within a population, one can also find a particular population that has some characteristics that differentiate it from the other population. For instance, Protestant universities with the characteristic of being Protestant within a population of Christian universities, differ from Catholic universities, which also form part of the population of Christian universities. There are then two kinds of population in a given research project, namely the *target population* (Protestant universities) and the *accessible population* (Protestant universities offering missiological education). Because it is often impossible to study the whole of the *target population*, researchers usually identify and define an *accessible population* through *sampling*, for example, Protestant universities that offer missiological education at master and doctoral levels.

---

45. Creswell, *Research Design*, 2nd ed., 86.
46. Mugenda and Mugenda, *Research Methods*, 41.

5.2.6.1 Target Population

The target population is "the population to which a researcher wants to generalize the results of a study."[47] In this research, the Protestant universities in the DRC were the target population. More than twenty Protestant higher education institutions (faculties of theology and universities offering theological education) operate throughout the country. This category makes the target population, but not the accessible population. Due to limitations in terms of finance and time, the intention was not to visit and conduct participant observation in all of them. However, the results of the research can be generalized to any Protestant university of any category within the DRC mostly due to the following three reasons.

The first reason of generalizability relates to the fact that the Church of Christ in Congo (CCC) serves as an umbrella to the Protestant denominations in the country. All eighty-two denominations are members of CCC and meet regularly either for the National Executive Committee or for the National Synod (General Assembly of CCC). Organizational structures, which operate within CCC are duplicated at each denominational level. These structures include department of evangelism and mission, department of theological education, etc. They serve as channels for collaboration and action between Protestant churches. This situation develops a context for collaboration and provides an opportunity for easy access to data. For instance, while conducting this study, I enjoyed the opportunity of doing participant observation in the headquarters of the CCC in Kinshasa, interacting with key church leaders from many provinces of the DRC, and using the archives and exploring minutes of important meetings of the CCC. Records of the Protestant educational system were available through minutes and other documents.

The second reason is the existence of the Association of Theological Seminaries (ATS) whose office is housed by the Protestant University of Congo (PUC). This association is made of Protestant theological institutions serving in the DRC and in other countries in the Central African region. The rector of PUC serves as chairperson of ATS. It was easy to get in touch

---

47. Ibid.; Tuckman and Harper, *Conducting Educational Research*, 267.

with him and to access documents and minutes, which provided important qualitative data.

The third reason is the organization of the educational system in the DRC. As mentioned in the previous chapters, regardless of its nature (public, private or religious-based) every higher education institution is regulated by the ministry of higher education. Since 2004, the educational reform process has harmonized the study programs for all fields of studies, including theology, but not missiology. It was, therefore, easy to access the study programs for theological education.

5.2.6.2 Accessible Population

As indicated above, the accessible population derives from the target population based on clear definition and criteria. There should be a rationale for defining and identifying the accessible population for a research project. This rationale must be based, not only on some theory, or previous studies or professional experience, but also on the research context and the researcher's experience and reality.[48]

The PUC was the accessible population and served as a platform for a grounded research. From its inception in 1959 as the first university-level Protestant institution, the PUC has served as *alma mater* for theological education in the country, along with the reputation of being the unique higher education institution, which provides mission-related studies at doctoral level for all Protestant churches in the country. Eighty-two Protestant denominations work under the umbrella of the CCC and are scattered throughout the country. Some institutions train candidates from two to five of these denominations, and almost all faculty members of these institutions are alumni of the PUC. Therefore, and in addition to three reasons described in the previous section on the target population, insights derived from this university are likely to be representative of the landscape of theological education in the country.

To get the same degree of attention as that of PUC in treatment, an institution among those represented in the map (fig. 5.1) or listed in table 5.3 had to align with the following requirements: (1) missiology is recognized as a subject in its own right (separate chair/department), or is combined

---

48. Mugenda and Mugenda, *Research Methods,* 42.

with some other subjects (Systematic Theology, Biblical Theology, Church History, Practical Theology, Religious Studies, Ecumenism, etc.); (2) missiology is part of the core curriculum, or it is offered as an elective from *bachelor* (graduate) to doctorate levels; (3) the institution admits students from at least seven of previous eleven DRC provinces or from at least one-third of eighty-two denominations (*communautés*).[49] None of these institutions has met the criteria, but they were referred to, as they would have brought a particular insight into the study.

Figure 5.1 Some Key Protestant Universities in the DRC

---

49. When this research started, the DRC had eleven provinces. It was only in November 2015 that the government decided to implement the plan of decentralization of the country, increasing the number of provinces to 26. This decision has been judged as an ill-made decision due to several reasons including the fact that the election of the governors of these newly created provinces was not possible and the required infrastructures for these provinces were not available. As far as the Church of Christ in Congo is concerned, the political decentralization has not yet been completely applied to the church organization. Therefore, I could not abruptly change the design of the study.

Table 5.3 Tertiary Theological Education in the DRC

		When?			Bachelor	Master	Doctorate
		School creation	Became university	Mission studies	3+2 years (*Licence*)	2 years (*DEA*)	3 years (*Doctorat*)
1	Université Méthodiste du Katanga	1951			x		
2	Université Protestante au Congo	1959	1997		x	x	x
3	Université Shalom de Bunia	1961	2008		x		
4	Université Evangélique de l'Alliance de Boma	1976			x		
5	Université Protestante au Cœur du Congo	1996					
6	Université Evangélique en Afrique	1980					
7	Université Protestante de l'Equateur	1978					
8	Université Libre des Pays des Grands Lacs	1985			x		
9	Centre Universitaire de Missiologie	1990		1990	x		
10	Université Chrétienne de Kinshasa	1960					

The first two criteria are adapted from Myklebust in his insightful article "Missiology in Contemporary Theological Education: A Factual Survey."[50] Myklebust did not consider the educational levels, which is an important element for this study and the context of higher education in the DRC where graduate studies start from *graduate* to doctorate. The significance of the third criterion lies on the configuration of the CCC where in each province

---

50. Myklebust, "Missiology," 87.

there is at least ten denominations. Most often schools, which are started by one single denomination tend to serve its own students. This third criterion assures that the whole country is represented.

It is important to insist that the preoccupation of this research is on missiological education rather than on theological education. Though the PUC started with traditional theological education programs (systematic theology, biblical theology, church history and practical theology), it has finally added some aspects of missiological education in 1997. I explored the following: (1) historical background; (2) curriculum and the delivery systems; (3) relation to the Bologna Process; (4) reference to the threefold mission of the University; (5) educational philosophy and the learning process; and (6) theology of mission. These elements were also explored through literature analysis.

The questionnaire was designed to match the threefold aspect of missiology, namely mission theory, mission education and mission practice. Only theology students of advanced level (*licence* and DEA) and the deans of the faculty of theology received the questionnaire. Students' inputs were significant for the study since they are on the ground and are the primary beneficiaries of the educational activities.

5.2.7 Variables

Etymologically speaking, a *variable* is a quantity that can vary (e.g. from low to high, negative to positive, etc.) in contrast to *constants* that do not vary (i.e. remain constant). Assuming that the researcher X conducts research on a topic and gets data from respondents Y and Z; the respondent Y is a doctorate-holder woman from a Protestant university located in Bukavu. She speaks Swahili, English and Topoke. The respondent Z is a bachelor-holder man from a Protestant university located in Mbandaka who speaks Lingala, French, and Ngbaka. The research questionnaire is designed in French and then is translated into English. To the respondent Y the researcher administered the questionnaire in Swahili, and the respondent Z used the French version.

As the researcher processes the returned questionnaires, he/she should be aware of the variables which influence the answer. Variables are what make the difference in these two respondents. Some of the variables might be independent while others will be dependents. In the case of respondents

Y and Z, independent variables are their gender and their nationalities. The dependent variables would be their educational background and their language skills. As one can realize, these dependent and independent variables would certainly influence and affect the answers from both respondents Y and Z. While analyzing, interpreting and discussing the findings, the researcher X should make these aspects clear and take them into account.

The main variables in this research were the following: whether or not the respondents were missiology students or professors; whether or not the university had a department of missiological studies; whether or not the university is "evangelical-oriented" or "ecumenical-oriented"; and whether or not the university is a denominational-based or interdenominational-based. Some of these variables were dependent (variables that are explained by other variables), for example having or not having a department of missiological studies; being students or professors in the department of missiological studies. Other variables failed in the category of independent variables (those that explain other variables), for example being an evangelical or an ecumenical university; being a denominational or an interdenominational university; being a student that belongs to a church which emphasizes evangelization or to a church which promotes social actions.

5.2.8 Validity and Accuracy

Validity refers to the credibility and trustworthiness of instruments, data and findings in research. While "validity of data" is used for quantitative studies, "accuracy of findings" is used for qualitative studies. Authors in mixed methods advocate for the use of validity, procedures for both the quantitative and the qualitative phases of the study.[51] Therefore, the concept of validity applies to the instrument, to the data and to the findings. Researchers should sketch what they did to ensure instrument validity, data validity and finding validity. *Instrument* validity refers to the question "are the instruments that were used to measure something valid?" In other terms, was the questionnaire appropriate enough to address the research question? As one can observe, the validity of data is tied to the validity of instruments. *Data* validity refers to whether or not the information gathered can lead to a valid conclusion, for instance is it valid to conclude that English speakers are more insightful

---

51. Creswell, *Research Design,* 2nd ed., 221.

than French speakers just because the respondent Z in the above example (section 5.2.7) gave more insightful answers than the respondent Y? For the qualitative data, researchers are requested to mention the strategies used to check the accuracy of the findings.[52]

To ensure authenticity and credibility of data, I designed a questionnaire which required that the respondents (for both students and instructors) provide details of their university, names and email addresses, department within the faculty of theology and research area. To ensure trustworthiness of the findings, I asked some colleagues to administer the questionnaire before meeting for the conference and meeting the focus groups. In addition, during the gathering of focus groups, I asked participants to evaluate the questionnaire.

During the meeting of the first focus group, three reactions were received, namely the questionnaire was clear, provocative and opportune. The general impression was that the questionnaire was clear, that is, understandable. However, the questionnaire was also provocative and opportune. By provocative participants felt that the purpose of the questionnaire was to stimulate them to think and provide their personal points of view about a discipline which is not promoted by their university. It was provocative because it encountered their worries about a faculty of theology not having a department of missiology. Therefore, the questionnaire was provocative in the sense that it stimulated them towards reflection and it provided them with the opportunity of echoing their voices. Thus, the questionnaire was opportune. From that first focus group, I used these three concepts to check the reliability of the questionnaire. The question was "How did you find the questionnaire: clear, provocative, and opportune? Explain." Reactions from all focus groups were almost similar, except where the question was to know whether students were independent, dependent or interdependent in their learning process. Verbal explanation was provided for clarification.

5.3 Data Analysis

Analyzing data for quantitative, qualitative and mixed methods is not done the same way. Even for the mixed research itself where there are simultaneous

---

52. Ibid.

triangulation and sequential triangulation, one could analyze the data differently. Creswell has provided valuable details about the process.[53]

Given the nature of the selected research method – mixed method using concurrent nested strategy – data transformation was the main approach of this study. According to Creswell data transformation is the approach through which the research quantifies the qualitative data:[54]

> This involves creating codes and themes qualitatively, then counting the number of times they occur in the text data (or possibly the extent of talk about a code or theme by counting lines or sentences). This quantification of qualitative data then enables a researcher to compare quantitative results with the qualitative data. Alternatively, an inquirer may qualify quantitative data. For instance, in a factor analysis of data from a scale on an instrument, the researcher may create factors or themes that then can be compared with themes from the qualitative database.[55]

This study used the quantification of the qualitative data, drawing inferences from the occurrences of important data mentioned in the statements, interaction or in focus groups. Steps in analyzing data followed Creswell's recommendation of (1) preparing the data for analysis; (2) conducting different analyses; (3) moving deeper and deeper into understanding the data; (4) representing the data; and (5) making an interpretation of the larger meaning of the data.[56] Due to lack of the skills in using qualitative software programs (e.g. NVIVO), the process of data analysis was done manually through coding.

The first coding related to participants. A letter was assigned to each group of participants in the study as follows:

S for students within the faculty of theology;

I for instructors within the faculty of theology;

---

53. Creswell, *Research Design*, 2nd ed.
54. Ibid., 220.
55. Ibid., 221.
56. Ibid., 190.

A for educational administrators within the university; and

P for pastors (church leaders).

The second coding pertained to important themes related to the four research sub-questions formulated in the first chapter:

RQ1 – paradigms of theology of mission;

RQ2 – Theological education and *missio Dei*;

RQ3 – educational and conceptual frameworks; and

RQ4 – missiological education and research.

5.4 Ethical Considerations

Although this research did not involve sensitive issues, I ensured that participation in the conference and in the focus groups be voluntary. It was the same for the research questionnaire, which was administered by some colleagues and assistant researchers as to avoid influencing the responses. It was clearly set to respondents that their names will not be mentioned in the final report of the study. Wherever I went for conference and for meeting the focus group, permission was duly granted by the authorities of the university. The process was facilitated by the recommendation letter that the North-West University issued to serve the purpose of this study.

5.5 Findings Presentation and Interpretation

As already mentioned, data collection was done mainly through participant observation, documentary research, questionnaires and using focus groups. Participant observation was conducted in five sites, namely the PUC, the University Centre for Missiology, the Free University of Great Lakes Goma, the Free University of Great Lakes Bukavu and the Evangelical University in Africa. The documentary data came mostly from the PUC which serves as *alma mater* of theological institutions in the DRC, with official information from the Ministry of Higher Education of the DRC. The questionnaire was administered to theology students in advanced degrees (*licence* and DEA) and to some theology professors. The questionnaire was sent to nine other universities, and the research team on the ground helped administer the questionnaire. The focus groups gathered in the above listed institutions where I delivered academic conferences to theology students and professors as a strategy of data collection. Qualitative data collected lead to the following conclusions corresponding to the four sub-questions announced in chapter 1 (section 1.3) and schematized earlier in this chapter (section 5.2.4).

5.5.1 Paradigms of Theology of Mission

The first research question was to find out key paradigms of theology of mission of leading theological institutions which offer some degrees in missiology or mission studies in the DRC. In chapter 1 (section 1.7.7) "theology of mission" was defined as the biblical and theological justification of mission work. Such a definition leads to more specific questions such as "Why does the church exist?" "Why does the church engage in mission?" "What then is 'mission'?"

The research questionnaire contained the two following questions which aimed at getting more precise reactions on the issue: (1) Give two biblical references which, according to you, better justify the existence of *communautés* of the CCC. (2) Which activities should the department of mission of these *communautés* perform and where should these activities be done? During the meetings of the focus groups, a straightforward question was the following: "From your point of view, why does the church exist?"

The biblical texts as reported in table 5.2 were suggested though there was no sub-question asking the respondents their interpretation of the concerned passages. However, while reading them, one can imagine the message behind. While some provided two biblical references, others, due to practical reasons yet to be explored, could only provide one biblical reference. Some others could not provide any biblical reference. To get more insights, another question was asked where the respondents had to comment on the mission engagement of the churches in the DRC. These comments could provide more hidden thoughts. Still, some respondents failed to add any comment (table 5.4).

Table 5.4 General Perception on the Biblical Justification of the Existence of the Church

Biblical references	Comment on the mission engagement of the churches in the DRC
UPC – N(10)	
Matt 9:35 and Matt 19:21	*Communautés* should "have"[sic] *missio Dei* and holistic mission; no conflict.
Matt. 28:19	Mission engagement should take into account the current societal situation.
Matt 28:19–20	Need for contextualized mission for the salvation of the whole person.
Matt 28:16–20	Pastors work for their personal interests rather than for the mission of the church.
Acts 1:8 and 2 Cor 5:20	Need for unity and partnership among church in order to achieve holistic mission.
Matt 28:19–20 and John 4:34	There is confusion between evangelization and mission. Holistic mission needed.
Matt 28:19–20 and Acts 1:8	Budgeting for mission projects because church is born from and for mission.
John 17:21	*Communautés* don't have the vision for mission; need for appropriate training.
Other universities	
Mark 1:35–39	ECC should reflect on the mushrooming of prayer rooms (Eastern Congo).
Matt 28:19 and 1 Tim 1:3	To revisit its way of doing mission; not "maintenance mission."
2 Tim 4:1–6 and Isa 61:1ff.	Encourage members for mission; send people to missiological schools.
Matt 28:19–20 and 2 Tim 4:1–5	All *communautés* should involve in mission.
1 Cor 12:4–11	*Communautés* should teach a gospel that liberates the whole person.
Matt 28:19–20 and John 17:18	No comment.
Matt 28:16–20 and Matt 10:1–3	No comment.

No biblical passage (5 respondents)	Four no comment; one comment: "Tribalism is a problem."
Matt 28:18–20 and Acts 1:8	*Communautés* shouldn't plant churches where other churches already exist.
Mark 1:17 and Matt 13:47–50	*Communautés* don't know how to care about missionaries.
Gal 2:1–10 and Luke 9:49–50	They should promote the universality of the church against tribal churches.
Matt 28:18–20 and Luke 10	They should avoid "pastoral ministry of maintenance."
Matt 28:19ff (?)	No comment.
Matt 28:18ff and Mark 28:1 (?)	Mark 28:1 (?) – Go throughout the world; contextualize our message.
Matt 28:16ff	Missiology could have been a part of all departments of the *communauté*.
Matt 28:16–20 and John 10:10	ECC should go to all corners of the DRC to reach the unreached with the gospel.
Matt 28:19–20 and Acts 1:8	No comment.

To justify the existence of the church, respondents refer mostly to the New Testament, quoting Matthew 28, one of the most quoted biblical chapters in mission. There is no reference to other most quoted passages like Mark 16:15–20, Luke 24, John 20:21. References from other books of the New Testament are not commonly used in mission discussion. These include Matthew 13:47–50, Mark 1:17, 35–39, 1 Timothy 1:3, 1 Corinthians 12:4–11, Galatians 2:1–10, etc. It could have been interesting, time allowing, to get respondents' interpretation of these biblical texts with regard to the nature and the mission of the church. Most interesting is a quote from Mark 28:1 probably due to confusion with Matthew 28:18ff. quoted by the same person. One reference from the Old Testament relates to Isaiah 61:1, the foundational source of Jesus's mission statement in Luke 4:17–21. It magnifies the work of the Holy Spirit and the mission of liberation. It is also interesting to note the difference between respondents from PUC, the so-called alma mater of theological education in the country, and those from other universities. There is no reference to Old Testament from PUC respondents, most of them quoting Matthew 28 and one quoting Acts 1:8. While also being attracted by Matthew, some respondents from other universities seem to struggle with the issue of biblical justification for the existence of the church. There is obvious lack of precision in the citation of biblical passages. It is important to observe that these respondents are from universities which do not have a department of missiology although they offer some courses on evangelization.

To triangulate the finding of table 5.2, a list of actions to be undertaken by the church was provided and participants had to tick on all assertions that were applicable. Table 5.3 illustrates the trends which exist within Protestant universities as far as mission activities are concerned.

Table 5.5 Actions That the Church Is Supposed to Perform as Part of Its Mission

Actions that a church from the DRC should accomplish to demonstrate its *raison d'être*	N(10)
UPC	
Evangelization in other provinces within the DRC	9
Evangelization in urban cities within the DRC	6
Evangelization in rural villages within the DRC	6
Evangelization outside the DRC	7
Church planting in other provinces within the DRC	8
Church planting in urban cities within the DRC	4
Church planting in rural villages provinces within the DRC	6
Church planting outside the DRC	6
Social actions (education, medical services, development/relief) in other provinces within the DRC	6
Social actions (education, medical services, development/relief) in urban cities within the DRC	4
Social actions (education, medical services, development/relief) in rural villages within the DRC	9
Social actions (education, medical services, development/relief) outside the DRC	5

Table 5.5 indicates that three trends are mostly suggested to be taken by the departments of mission: (1) evangelization in other provinces within the DRC; (2) church planting in other provinces within the DRC; and (3) social actions in rural villages within the DRC. Their vision of mission of the CCC echoes what Bokeleale has already said several years before: "The Church in Zaire had to assume its responsibilities for *the true mission of the Church to evangelize the Zairian people.*"[57] The difference here is that church planting in other provinces within the country and social actions in rural villages are highly recommended than in Bokeleale's statement. In addition, as Molo has brightly demonstrated in his thesis, Bokeleale could not recommend that a *communauté* initially established in one province could move to other provinces to plant churches.[58] This point of view even appears in table 5.4 where one comment reads, "*Communautés* shouldn't plant churches where other churches already exist." During the gathering of the focus groups, the following comments were made as responses to the questions: "Why does the church exist?" and "Which other activities could the churches undertake as mission endeavour?"

- "Training people for environmental care and management."
- "Funding projects such as farming and literacy."
- "Caring for environment and ecology."
- "Caring for street children, young mothers, and unemployed youth."
- "Performing social action for Pygmies." (A marginalized people who live in the forest in eight countries of the central African region.)
- "Caring for the whole person."
- "Bringing light to the world by assuming the prophetic role against injustice."
- "Reminding political authorities of their role of ensuring human rights and freedom."
- "Working for the liberation of oppressed people."

---

57. Bokeleale, "From Missions to Mission," 433, emphasis added.
58. Molo, "Quest."

One could perceive in these comments a strong orientation to the work of the church within its direct milieu and focusing on social actions involvement. This creation focus is reminiscent of the second aspect of *missio Dei* discussed in chapter 2 (section 2.6.1).

5.5.2 Theological Education and *Missio Dei*

The purpose of the second research question was to find out the extent to which *missio Dei* vision or the lack of it in the whole of theological education has influenced missiological education and mission practice in the DRC. In chapter 1 (section 1.7.6) *missio Dei* was defined as "God's glocal and holistic mission to save humankind in Christ through the sent church." Central to this definition is the preoccupation about the role of the triune God (Father, Son, and Holy Spirit) and the church, and the geographical sphere of such a mission. In addition, as far as theological education is concerned, an important concern relates to the typology of theological education which would better serve God's mission (see ch. 3, section 3.4).

The research questionnaire contained three questions to allow respondents to elaborate more on their understanding of the relationship between God's mission and theological education focusing on the place of missiology in theological education: (1) What is the state of missiology in your faculty of theology? (2) From your point of view, which mission-related courses could have been added to the prevailing theological curriculum to allow students to engage in God's mission? (3) Which actions should be taken by the department of mission of each *communauté* within the CCC in relation to God's global and local mission?

At the Protestant University of Congo (PUC) the answer about the state of missiology was clear because this university organizes a department of Mission Science, Ecumenism and Religious Studies. Founded in 1959 as a faculty of theology, this institution became "Protestant Faculties in Congo" due to the launching of other programs like Faculty of Management and Administration and Faculty of Law, before getting the status of a full-chartered university in 1990. PUC grants degrees at bachelor (*licence*), master (DEA), and doctorate levels despite the fact that it has not yet formally integrated the Bologna educational system. Degrees are still *graduate* (3 years), *licence* (2 years), "DEA" (2 years) and *Doctorat* (3 years) in theology.

The department of Mission Science, Ecumenism and Religious Studies was created in 1997 after several attempts by Professor Mushila Nyamankank who was appointed as the first head of the new department.[59] Being an alumnus of Hamburg University in Germany from where he graduated in New Testament in 1983, Mushila wanted his University back in the country to add this new department to the traditional theological departments as it was in Hamburg University. It was after fourteen years of struggle that he could convince the university's authorities to allow the existence of this new department whose objective was to help students learn how to address issues that their churches face in the society. Thereafter, Mushila became the Dean of the Faculty of Theology while chairing the department of Mission science, Ecumenism and Religious Studies. It has been said that this department experienced growth and expanded its influence during Mushila's deanship.

The program handbook contains details which not only distil the organization of the teaching-learning process, but also the educational philosophy of this study program. According to the educational system in the DRC, the first two cycles of study, *graduate* and *licence*, do not grant specialized degrees. However, at *licence* level, every student gives an orientation to his or her studies. For instance, one could choose Old Testament or Mission Science, Ecumenism and Religious Studies. During these two years the student takes all courses scheduled to all students regardless their study orientations. Among these courses two or three relate to each theological study (Old Testament, New Testament, Systematic Theology, Church History, Practical Theology, and Mission Science Ecumenism and Religious Studies). At DEA level students take some research seminars on their specific area of studies. DEA and doctorate programs are mainly research-based.

Several monographs (*mémoires de licence*) and theses (*thèses Doctorales*) have been produced by the students of the department of Mission Science Ecumenism and Religious Studies. Unfortunately, I could not find neither Mushila's own thesis (said to be written in German) nor any of the students' works in the university library except a recent thesis presented by Kalombo under the supervision of Mushila. After his retirement, Mushila assigned all his courses to Kalombo who could be considered Mushila's successor, not

---

59. Much of the following information derives from a personal interaction I had with Mushila Nyamankank in Kinshasa on 11 May 2015.

in administrative matters, but in perpetuating the teachings of his mentor. In addition, I had several opportunities to attend the defence of works produced by *licence* students in June 2015. Prior to attending the defence, I was granted the opportunity of meeting with *licence* and DEA students whose studies were done within this department. A research questionnaire was administered to them by one of my facilitators and I conducted the focus group discussion.

Besides the PUC, other universities were either included in the research questionnaire administration or I visited some others. As said earlier, during these visits, focus group discussions were conducted with *licence* students who have completed three years of *graduate* and were at that time studying either in the first or second year of *licence*. It is important to mention that only one institution, Centre Universitaire de Missiologie (CUM), grants degrees in missiology at bachelor (*licence*) level. PUC and three other universities[60] offer courses in mission at *licence* level but they grant degrees in theology (not in missiology). Therefore, in the DRC one university (CUM) offers mission programs and grants degrees in missiology at bachelor (*licence*) level. One university (PUC) offers in a department of mission science degrees at bachelor (*licence*), master (DEA) and doctoral levels but grants degrees in theology. Four more universities with each a department of mission (or missiology) offer degrees in theology at either bachelor (*licence*) level only (Université de l'Allicance Chrétienne) or at bachelor (*licence*) and master (DEA) levels.

When going deeper into the inquiry about the relatedness of *missio Dei* and theological education, one could get the impression that most theological institutions in the DRC are in need of strong expression of such a relatedness. Several conceptual and philosophical considerations of chapter three (precisely from section 3.3 to 3.5) have shown that the presence or the absence of a vision for *missio Dei* in a curriculum is likely to affect the outcome of theological education in regard to the mission involvement of the graduates. Even at a theoretical level, this outcome can be noticed through the students' reflection. As displayed in table 5.3 above, respondents seem to minimize the global aspect of God's mission as they mostly focus

---

60. These are Université Shalom de Bunia, Université Méthodiste du Katanga in Mulungwishi, and Université de l'Alliance Chrétienne in Boma.

on "mission within the DRC." In addition, as said previously (see section 5.5.2), the attraction to the creation focus of *missio Dei* gives the impression that the redemption focus (missional ecclesiology) is still an option to explore. This situation can also be shown through the biblical justification of the mission work of the church (table 5.4) where respondents' vision of God's mission is limited to the same few selected verses.

Table 5.6 Universities Offering Some Programs in Mission Studies as of December 2015

Universities	Bachelor (Licence 3+2 years)	Master (DEA 2 years)	Doctorate (3 years)
Université Protestante au Congo	Yes (2 years)	Yes	Yes
Centre Universitaire de Missiologie	Yes (5 years)	No	No
Université Shalom de Bunia	Yes (2 years)	No	No
Université de l'Alliance Chrétienne	Yes (2 years)	No	No
Université Libre des Pays de Grands Lacs	No	No	No
Université Méthodiste du Katanga	Yes (2 years)	Yes	No

5.5.3 Educational and Conceptual Frameworks

The third research question was about identifying key elements of educational and conceptual frameworks through which missiological education has been offered in the DRC. In chapter 1 (section 1.7.4), "missiological education" was defined as "the process by which the church through its training institutions prepares God's people to accomplish God's glocal and holistic mission." Aspects of definition raise the following preoccupations: (1) Can missiological education lead to mission engagement of graduates and their churches? (2) Through which educational approach such a result can be expected (teacher-dependent, self-dependent or interdependent learning)? (3) What are the prevailing philosophies of theological education?

The research questionnaire was designed in such a way that students could give their points of view about the educational approach through which they took their studies. In chapter 3 (sections 3.5.1 and 3.5.4.3), the discussion on the adult teaching-learning process was concluded with the note that this process can be teacher-dependent, self-dependent or interdependent learning. Table 5.7 below indicates the major trends.

Table 5.7 Perception of Students on the Prevailing Educational Approach

Educational approach	N (52)
Teacher-dependent learning The students depend on what the instructor proposes through the course syllabus and notes. He/she then explains before assigning some homework to students who will finally sit for an exam. Therefore, students are too dependent.	39
Self-dependent learning The students make their own course notes out of the course syllabus produced by the instructor who will however provide some explanations of the course. The students will be assigned homework and sit for the final exam. Therefore, students are somehow independent.	11
Interdependent learning The instructor and the students discuss the course syllabus and the students conduct personal research to provide course notes before producing a personal reflective paper and sitting for the final exam. Therefore, students and the instructor are plus or minus interdependent.	2

Table 5.7 indicates that the prevailing educational approach is teacher-dependent learning through which students mostly rely on what instructors propose through the course syllabus and the notes they provide. Responding to the same question, one professor mentioned that in a few cases they encourage students towards a self-dependent learning process. This comment from a professor could justify the score of 11 out of 52 respondents (table 5.7) in students' perception. Nevertheless, in general, the teacher-dependent process is mostly used and students depend largely on the instructors. Instructors cannot teach more than they know. As far as *missio Dei* is concerned, what instructors know about it, and the conviction that they have about it, will eventually determine what they will deliver to the students. At a university which did not have a department of missiology, I met a professor of theology after the conference to get his feedback. The following comment is eloquent:

I am trying to discover new things. What I know is that there is internal (home) mission, and there is external (foreign) mission. The problem that your discipline raises is to know "what is the definition of missiology today?" "What distinguishes mission to evangelization?" "What is the broad: is it theology which includes missiology, or missiology which includes theology?" What you are doing through this kind of conference is good because making yourself known to others who don't know is already enough.

If asked to talk about missiology, mission or missiological education, this professor would simply share what he knows as summarized in the above quote. Students would only know what their professor tells them if they are teacher-dependent. Without doubt, the outcome would be different if the educational approach promotes "self-dependent learning" or "interdependent learning."

Respondents were also asked to provide comments about their perception of the educational approach of their university. The following comments were given by those who thought that "teacher-dependent" was the common learning practice within their faculty:

- "Students depend on instructors' points of view because it is said that students' points of view are not taken into account."
- "Students depend on instructors because they are the ones who have the knowledge."
- "Students cannot do any research unless they receive a bibliography from the course syllabus provided by the instructors."
- "It is unavoidable to depend on instructors because they are the ones who know how and where to lead the students."
- "Because this is the way courses have been always taught."
- "This is a traditional methodology which doesn't allow student to self-direct and self-evaluate through participation in the design of the course and the learning process."
- "Because we have many courses in a short time frame."
- "Because students don't have sufficient time for research."

It was also important to know whether missiological education can lead to mission engagement of graduates and their churches, or if it could bring any change in regard to the conception and the practice of missiology. During a focus group session, the participants reflected on the question, "If missiology had its birthplace in the DRC and if it was well-managed, what could have happened with reference to the following features?" I provided a worksheet to each group of five to seven members. Participants were all *licence* (bachelor) and master (DEA) students in the department of missiology, and their reflections were based on their personal experience. This group discussion was held after I had delivered a speech on "missiology as a transforming discipline" with reference to the Francophone Africa in general, and to the DRC in particular.[61] Compared with the responses to the research questionnaire returned before the conference, the results of the group discussion display a big improvement in their thinking. They became more aware of the issue with the conviction that, if undertaken through a certain educational philosophy and approach, the outcomes of missiological education could have been different (see table 5.8). My research assistant and I could clearly observe such a transformation in their reflection.

---

61. Lygunda, "Missiologie comme."

Table 5.8 Perception of Students on Possible Outcomes If Missiology Was Well-Promoted in the DRC

Missiological Features		Possible Outcomes
Missiology	The discipline of missiology…	**Could have:** -been mandatory in all theological education -become a department in each faculty of theology -led to the setting of a regional office for missiological studies -experienced a breakthrough -been valued in each theological institution -consistent content (but not an instable content) -led to academic publications on the subject -led to regular academic and professional conferences
Provide Quality Teaching	Courses on missiology…	**Could have:** -been well-designed and scheduled -been taken into account in theological institutions -been allocated more credit hours -been specific enough (but not confused with other study areas) -been dynamic (but not static, without improvement) -been more practical (rather than too speculative) -been well-designed (well-articulated and well-elaborated) -been more contextualized -been taught by various missiologists (not the same people)
Provide Quality Teaching	Instructors of missiology…	**Could have:** -been all missiologists (who are qualified in this field of study) -been ready to become missionaries -been mission-minded theologians (using their areas of expertise for mission; e.g. NT at the service of mission like David Bosch) -been scholars of this field of study (missiology) -been given opportunities of professional development -been fully committed to the promotion of this discipline -been members of professional associations of mission studies -helped the CCC for its mission engagement -published books and articles in missiology

Provide Quality Teaching	Students of missiology…	**Could have:** -been men and women of mission calling -been sent out for mission work of their respective churches -been on the ground to transform the community -been more attracted to study under this department -been cared for by their churches -had an impact on the ground (due to their practical skills) -been many in this department, with a clear vision of the future -been more interested to missiological studies -influenced their churches towards mission engagement
Promote Incentive Research	Research in missiology…	**Could have:** -been deepened (well-undertaken with in-depth reflections) -led to scientific interaction between scholars (instructors and students) -led to many publications (valuable books and articles) -been more advanced and promoted -been well-oriented according to missiological various areas of research -led to publications of international audience -led to effervescence for missiological research projects -led to theological institutions acquire well-equipped, appropriate and updated library in missiology -led to easy access to the electronic library in missiology
Serve Meaningfully the Community	Protestant churches in the DRC…	**Could have:** -become mission-minded churches -become laboratories for mission and for missiology -been transformed and committed to *missio Dei* -become active in mission -been well-informed and trained about mission -become more committed to and competitive for mission -become missionary churches -led ECC to have more impact both inside and outside the country -facilitated intercultural interaction in order to minimize the prevailing climate of tribalism

To check the above statement of transformation in the mindset of participants, I asked another group of participants to provide their feedback after having listened to the speech on "missiology as a transforming discipline."

The question was, "What did you learn for the first time that you will never forget?" The following reactions came from respondents, who were all students at *licence* (bachelor) level in a university that did not have a department of missiology:

- "I now realize that missiology could be at the intersection of all theological disciplines."
- "If our university accepts the existence of a department of missiology, then it will not be a specialization at *licence* [bachelor] level because in our educational system specialization is for doctoral studies."
- "I can now say something about mission as it relates to missiology."
- "We are all called to be missionaries."
- "I can say that missiology is a hinge of all theological disciplines; it is the crossroad of other disciplines of theology."

Even if one could not agree with all these statements, the point is that due to their exposure to the issues about missiology, participants in the focus groups have gone through transformational experience. At least their way of perceiving missiology has been transformed after a 2-hour conference and a 2-hour focus group session.

5.5.4 Missiological Education and Research

The fourth research question was concerned with the extent to which missiological education and research really serve the churches in the DRC for its glocal mission. In chapter 3 (section 3.5.2), "missiological education" was discussed in the light of any tertiary education which has a threefold mandate of providing quality teaching, promoting research, and serving the community. Linked to such a mandate are the following questions: (1) What model of missiological education has been provided in the DRC? (2) What is the purpose of providing missiological education? (3) How are research projects helping churches to solve their daily struggles for God's glocal and holistic mission?

The research questionnaire was submitted to the faculty of theology to request the list and description of courses and to professors of theology to supplement the list of courses they would strongly recommend to their university. As indicated in tables 5.4, 5.5, and 5.6, the students' perceptions communicate the realities of teaching and research in missiological education in the DRC. In chapter 1 (section 1.2), observation was made that even the official benchmark of university programs in the DRC doesn't mention missiological studies. Courses offered at the PUC in the department of Mission science, Ecumenism and Religious Studies relate mostly to reflection on what the church can do in the society where it operates. They would mainly be oriented toward a prophetic mission of denunciating injustice and promoting freedom. In general, wherever the mission-related program exists, courses are taken as theological common courses by all theology students. It is only at the *licence* level that two or three courses are designated to those who have chosen a mission-related program.

During focus group sessions with students, the question was raised to know which department among the prevailing ones prepares students for the church ministry. Is it Old Testament? New Testament? Church history? Systematic theology? Practical Theology? According to Munayi, professor of history at the PUC, the main purpose of the faculty of theology was to train students for pastoral ministry in the local church based on the Scripture.[62] Even when this faculty became part of the university in 1990, this objective was not changed. In general, students were prepared for the church ministry. Therefore, the following question becomes worth considering: Which department better prepares students for the church ministry?

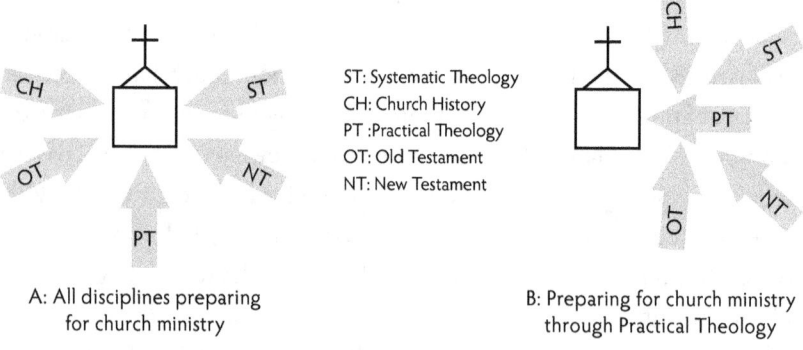

A: All disciplines preparing for church ministry

B: Preparing for church ministry through Practical Theology

ST: Systematic Theology
CH: Church History
PT: Practical Theology
OT: Old Testament
NT: New Testament

Figure 5.2 Theological Education and Church Ministry

---

62. Munayi, *Les vingt-cinq*.

During the focus group sessions students realized that the prevailing theological curriculum was either A or B (fig. 5.2). On the one hand, the scheme A means that all departments directly prepare students for church ministry. Therefore, none of the *licence* graduates could pretend to having specialization in any of the disciplines (OT, NT, CH, ST, and PT). Each department contributes to the future of church and pastoral ministries of the students. The danger is when a student overvalues his or her specialization in systematic theology or any of these other disciplines at *licence* level. As consequence to such a claim, many graduates of the prevailing theological curriculum have been reported for having unfruitful church and pastoral ministries.

On the other hand, scheme B means that the very department which prepares students for church ministry is Practical Theology. Consequently, other disciplines (OT, NT, CH, and ST) contribute to that purpose through Practical Theology. Therefore, students pursuing other disciplines of theology would be prepared for teaching and research ministries or any other duty apart from pastoral ministry. The truth is that all graduates from any of the existing theological disciplines in the DRC end up by being assigned church and pastoral ministries. This debate is still going on and more research is needed while involving professors of theology who were not in the focus group. Meanwhile, suffice it to say that the above two schemes demonstrate the focus of the prevailing theological curriculum, namely to prepare students for church and pastoral ministries within their own context.

As one could realize, missiology or mission-related studies are out of the agenda in many theological institutions in the DRC. Through the returned questionnaire, several reasons were suggested, including the following:

- "Due to the existing curriculum in our faculty of theology which doesn't provide a room for missiology or mission studies."
- "The problem is that missiology is not clearly defined to state how different it is from practical theology."
- "Because practical theology is at the core of any theological education, preparing people for church ministry."
- "Maybe due to lack of qualified professors in the area of missiology."

- "Because 'mission' is included in theology; it is one of theological disciplines."
- "The problem is that the curriculum pertaining to missiological studies has not yet been designed."
- "Missiology is not really important in our faculty of theology because it is already represented through the department of practical theology."
- "Missiology doesn't have any impact as other disciplines (or departments). It is not attractive."
- "This concern of having missiology as one of the departments is not an interesting preoccupation for the management committee and the governing council of our university."
- "Missiology is a practical discipline . . . already in practical theology."
- "Missiology is more about church . . . Practical theology has already that function."
- "Many mission-related courses have already been taught through other departments. There is no need of having a new department."
- "Missiology is a portion of practical theology, and the latter has the role of implementing what other departments teach. There is no need for having a new 'practical' department."
- "Missiology is just a course as any other course in theology. Its place is in practical theology."

Professors of theology at a university which doesn't have a department of missiology or mission-related programs returned the questionnaire with the following comments:

- "Missiology doesn't have a particular status in our faculty of theology."
- "Missiology in not perceived as one of essential disciplines of our faculty of theology."
- "Our problem is that missiology is not clearly defined to state how different it is from practical theology."
- "Missiology is rather a discipline within the department of practical theology. However, our faculty of theology is planning

to have a department of missiology but at master (DEA) and doctoral levels."
- "Missiology is taught as a discipline within the department of practical theology because we don't have qualified professors in the area. But now that we have them we will start the process of establishing a department of missiology."

Even where the department of mission-related programs exists, the following comments send out some messages:
- "Missiology is a part of the department of Mission Science, Ecumenism and Religious Studies. However, the course 'missiology' is an optional course and students have the freedom to take or not take it."
- "It is true that missiology is not yet clearly defined to state how different it is from practical theology."
- "I am not sure if we really have a program handbook on missiology in our department."
- "Missiology is a mandatory course because all disciplines of theology are linked to it."
- "Missiology is not yet well-defined; it is still confusing and not well-understood."
- "Missiology is just a 30-hour course taught only at *graduate* level, and it is a part of the department of Mission Science, Ecumenism and Religious Studies."
- "In missiology, one can learn how to reach the unreached people."

Without doubt, the above statements from students and professors distil a climate of persisting malaise about missiology, assigning to it a status of an unstable discipline. During one of the focus group sessions participants enrolled in final year of *licence* and those undertaking DEA (master) mission-related program, shared their research titles with me. It was not a surprise to observe that these research topics would be done either under practical theology or under systematic theology. There is still a preoccupation to know what is that makes a research really missiological.

5.5.5 Summary of the Findings

From the above findings, the following elements become obvious and need to be broadly highlighted:

- Many theological institutions in the DRC are still operating under the traditional fourfold pattern (biblical theology, systematic theology, historical theology, and practical theology) established by Frederick Schleiermacher in 1811 and vulgarized by missionary work of the nineteenth and twentieth centuries. Missiology is still absent in many institutions, and wherever a related program is offered there is still a need for more clarification in terms of definition, research methodology, learning outcomes, training structures, teaching-learning methods.

- Mission theory is still a critical issue to address. Many students as well as some professors are still struggling with the formulation of theology of mission, that is, a biblical and theological justification of the mission engagement of the church. While criticizing the missionary theory and practice of the past centuries, the justification of the *raison d'être* of the church by respondents is still based on the same selective and isolated biblical references such as Matthew 28 or Acts 1:8. Sometimes these biblical references are quoted only to be given another meaning. There is a hermeneutical problem.

- Mission education represents another aspect of the problem that many theological institutions face in their threefold mandate of providing quality teaching, promoting incentive research and serving the community. Almost all Protestant universities, as other higher education institutions in the country, are still having difficulty to join the Bologna Process, a new agenda for higher education despite the legal Acts (ordinances and decrees) released by the government. The teaching-learning process is still strongly teacher-centered and subject-centered.

- Mission practice from these theological institutions is, in general, assimilated to work performed by Western missionaries, charging it with some pejorative clichés such as mission being an instrument of imperialism, or a mere activity of proselytism, etc. For many respondents mission is not only preaching the gospel and planting churches, but also and mostly, it is about what the church can do to the people and to the society of its immediate context. This may include, for instance, speaking out against injustice and poverty, engaging in interreligious dialogue without the pretention of converting people of other faiths, involving in social activities such as education, development, ecology, etc.

- A direct implication of the above findings is that God's glocal mission is still a field of exploration for both theological institutions and churches. This reality is portrayed in the existing reports on theological education in Africa and in the mission engagement of African churches. While focusing on how these issues relate and apply to the DRC, the facts are important:
    - **Theological institutions in the DRC seem to have ceased to be fully in the service of God's glocal mission.** The 8th National Congress of Evangelism and Mission of the Church of Christ in Congo, held in Kinshasa 2–9 August 2015, has lamentably stigmatized this reality. As part of this study, I was invited to deliver two conference papers at national level. The first was designated to the key denomination leaders at the main office of the Church of Christ in Congo on *Leadership et engagement missionnaire de l'église: cas de l'Eglise du Christ au Congo* (Leadership and mission engagement of the church: case of the Church of Christ in Congo) (Kinshasa, June 2015). The second was delivered during the above-mentioned 8th Congress on *Quand la théologie cesse d'etre au service de l'évangélisation* (When theology ceases to be in the service of evangelism) (Kinshasa, August 2015). These papers are in the process of being submitted for publication.
    - **Missiology, which could help face and address the above challenge, has not been well-promoted** through well-designed curricula, appropriate publications and bibliographies, professional associations of missiology, fora

and conferences in missiology. However, it is an undeniable and historical fact that the DRC is the birthplace of the Protestant missiology in Francophone Africa. I produced a paper which demonstrates such a reality: *Missiologie comme une discipline en et de transformation: Défi aux institutions théologiques protestantes de l'Afrique francophone avec référence à la République Démocratique du Congo* (Transforming missiology as a challenge to Protestant theological institutions in francophone Africa with reference to the Democratic Republic of Congo). This paper was used as an introduction to the focus groups for the present study designed for students and professors of theology in many Protestant universities. The paper was finally published in the national-based theological journal of the Protestant University of Congo, *Revue Congolaise de Théologie Protestante*.[63]

- **The Church of Christ in Congo through its 82 *communautés* has not been intentionally present in the global mission.** Since its inception in 1970 as a legacy of the Protestant mission societies, this federation of Protestant churches distils a clear tendency of being more "institutional church" than "missional church." While conducting research for this study, I couldn't find official records on the mission involvement of the Church of Christ in Congo or that of its affiliated *communautés* at global level. As part of this study, I published an article on "Understanding and Evaluating the Participation of Francophone Africans in World Mission: Congolese Working in Burundi."[64]

The next chapter suggests and discusses possibilities of transforming missiology for a fruitful missiological education.

---

63. Lygunda, "Missiologie comme, 257–271.
64. Lygunda, "Understanding and Evaluating," 255–271.

Part IV

An Alternative Approach to Missiology and Missiological Education

CHAPTER 6

Towards a Transforming Missiology for a Fruitful Missiological Education

6.1 Introduction

Some meaningful indications on the initial observation which triggered this study have surfaced through the empirical investigation reported in the preceding chapter. The observed reality of the DRC was that this "well-Christianized" nation tends to be a missionless country at the global level despite the fact that it houses several tertiary theological institutions and churches in full bloom. The assumption was that a revisit of missiology in theological education would undoubtedly lead to some discoveries susceptible to build significant theories about missiology and missiological education. Therefore, the purpose of this study was to better understand how the prevailing missiological training programs in the DRC align with the preoccupation of providing missiological education for God's glocal mission. The key question was "How does the prevailing missiological education in the DRC align with the purpose of *missio Dei*?"

Four important themes related to the four research sub-questions formulated in the first chapter (section 1.3) and elaborated in chapter 5 (section 5.2.4) were generated, highlighted and discussed to address the research problem of this study. These themes include (1) paradigms of theology of mission; (2) theological education and *missio Dei*; (3) educational and conceptual frameworks; and (4) missiological education and research. The interpretation and analysis of the findings related to these themes have displayed the reality that in general much is needed to be done as to align the prevailing theological education with the purpose of God's glocal mission.

Based on the findings of the preceding chapters (2 to 5), this chapter concentrates on providing theoretical insights and analysis on transforming missiology for a fruitful missiological education. It is a missiological reflection on the need for a transforming missiology (section 6.2), on the attributes of missiology (section 6.3), on the tripartite concern of missiology (section 6.4), and on a model of study program for missiological higher education (section 6.5). Attributes designate what missiology is as a discipline; the tripartite concern of missiology conveys the idea of being a systematic reflection on the theory of God's mission, on the training for God's mission and on the practice of God's mission. The chapter intends to be a reflection to solve the research problem and to pave the path for future research. According to *Encarta*, reflection is "careful thought, especially the process of reconsidering previous actions, events, or decisions."[65] Therefore, references will be done either to the findings of the preceding chapters (from 1 to 5) or to any valuable missiological insights and inputs from other scholars and authors.

6.2 Need for a Transforming Missiology

The profound root causes of the current status of missiology and missiological education in the DRC discussed in chapter 4 (section 4.7.2) and the findings of empirical investigation displayed in the previous chapter (sections 5.5.1 to 5.5.5) convey the message that there is a need for well-structured missiological education in the country. However, such a need requires a substantiated rationale of an appropriate theoretical framework, which encompasses objectives, expected outcomes, and activities. Further sections in this chapter are intended to discuss these matters but focus is first placed on the need for a well-structured missiological program and the need for a transforming missiology.

---

65. Microsoft Encarta, *Encyclopedia*.

6.2.1 The Need for a Well-Structured Missiological Program

As mentioned previously, the official handbook of university programs was published in 2010 because of a long process of educational reform in the DRC which started in 2004. Two facts are evident about that document. First, the program on theological studies is mainly Catholic-oriented. I went to the Ministry of Higher Education in Kinshasa to inquiry more about the absence of a Protestant-based theological program. The answer was simple: "That is what we received and we assume that it comprises both Catholic and Protestant theological study program. If Protestant universities want their specific theological program to be included, they should apply for it." It is clear that even the existing theological program of Protestant faculties of theology does not exist in that official handbook, although these faculties are recognized by the government. The second fact is that even in the Catholic-oriented existing program which covers both Catholic and Protestant institutions, there is nothing about a course entitled "mission" or "missiology."

However, two other facts should be mentioned here to argue that missiology is officially recognized in the DRC. First, some Protestant universities that provide mission-related programs since 1990 (Centre Universitaire de Missiologie) and 1997 (Université Protestante au Congo) are officially accredited and their degrees granted at bachelor, master and doctoral levels have been endorsed by the government. While the first mentioned institution grants degrees of bachelor in missiology, the second grants degrees in theology, with some students focusing their research projects on mission science, ecumenism and religious studies. The second fact relates to a recent Act, *Loi-Cadre no 14/004* (11 February 2014) signed by the president of the DRC and published in the official journal (*Journal Officiel*) on 19 February 2014. Article 98 of this document gives the injunction to universities to align their study programs with the Bologna agenda. The requirement is to offer studies in three cycles of bachelor (3 years), master (2 years) and doctorate (3 to 5 years) in order to ensure mobility of students and instructors at both national and international levels. As explained in chapter 3 (section 3.5.4), the prevailing educational system in the DRC has caused many students to take remedial courses or to repeat all the courses from scratch.

Before moving any further, it is now meaningful to sketch how missiological education could function within the theological fourfold pattern and with other disciplines of social science. Figure 6.1 illustrates the interplay between the attributes and nature of missiology with other disciplines. At the core of the diagram is missiology as it displays its attributes of being a scientific and applied discipline, an interdisciplinary discipline, an intentional discipline and a discipline focused on God's glocal and holistic mission. The inner cycle of missiology comprises of other theological disciplines based on the fourfold pattern of biblical theology, systematic theology, historical theology, and practical theology. Missiology is about God's affairs; therefore, theology and theological disciplines indisputably matter. This inner cycle is followed and underpinned by social sciences in their diversity. Missiology is about God's affairs with humankind; therefore, social sciences meaningfully matter. When brought together, these ingredients allow missiology to systematically reflect on how mission has been conceptualized, how it is conceptualized, and how it should be conceptualized; how it has been taught, how it is being taught, and how it should be taught; how it has been executed, how it is executed, and how it should be executed.

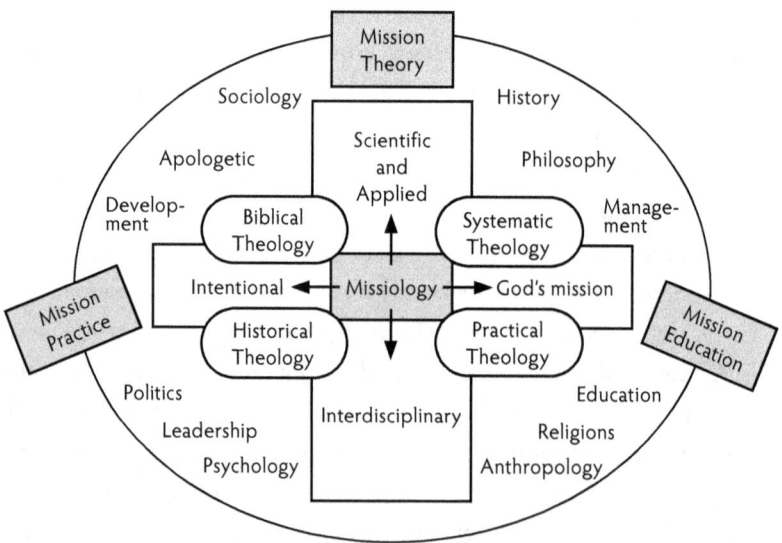

Figure 6.1 Interplay between Attributes, the Nature of Missiology and Other Disciplines

6.2.2 The Need for a Transforming Missiology

The concept of "transforming missiology" was already defined in the first chapter (sections 1.2 and 1.7.1) to highlight the fact that missiology can be changed (transformed) and it can lead to change (transformation). Acting as both verb and adjective, *transforming* simply means that the call is for God's people to assess *their* missiology to match it with the purpose of *missio Dei*. Missiology can be transformed (or changed) by either empowering some of its aspects, or modifying some of its irrelevant categories, or replacing some of its non-applicable categories. For instance, the content, the methods and the delivery systems can be transformed through empowering, modifying or replacing. There should be a possibility of transforming missiology and missiological education if they happen to no longer serve the cause of God's glocal and holistic mission.

Transforming also implies that missiology should bring change to the life of stakeholders that are instructors, students, their churches and the community. As stated elsewhere, to be of any sense, missiological education should help students "transform their churches into either mission-minded congregations or in-mission communities."[66] A mission-minded church is not necessarily an in-mission church. While the first is about "knowing about mission" or "having a vision for mission," the second is about "taking active part in mission" or "being on the mission ground." One can have knowledge *on* and *of* mission without being available to *do* mission. Moving from the first into the second conveys the reality of transformation. Therefore, the urgent task here is to call for a *transforming* missiology, which strives to equip students as future graduates with the passion for and action of making their respective churches not only mission-minded congregations but also communities in mission.

The working definition proposed in the first two chapters (sections 1.7.3 and 2.2.2) is expanded here. In the context of the DRC, the definition of missiology has been at the core of the marginalization of this discipline in the theological curriculum. Respondents to the questionnaire for this study insisted on the fact that missiology is not clearly defined to state how different it is from practical theology or any other discipline of theology. As

---

66. Lygunda, "Toward A Reconstructionist Philosophy," 19.

indicated through the literature review, this difficulty has been highlighted even in other contexts in the world. After a quick survey of literature, the proposed definition below encompasses important features of this discipline.

Although missiology is already recognized as a discipline in its own right, the issue of its nature and task has not yet reached agreed consensus.[67] Depending on the theological perspective from which the answer is provided, missiology can be a theoretical-oriented discourse or a practical-oriented reflection and even more than these two extremes. In several occasions (see ch. 2, section 2.2.2), the literature has shown a reduced interest of materials on mission education as an intrinsic nature of missiology. It then became extremely important to provide a definition which could address some of the unresolved aspects of the existing definitions both in local and global contexts. Missiology is understood here as a scientific and applied study based on the word of God and on disciplines of social sciences in order to understand and orient how God's glocal and holistic mission entrusted to the church is and should be conceptualized, executed and taught (see illustration of fig. 6.2).

As far as missiology and missiological education are concerned, and based on the above observations, there is a need to clarify the attributes and function of missiology. The following sections discuss the attributes of missiology as they appear in the proposed definition.

6.3 Attributes of Missiology

Understanding the attributes of missiology can help solve most of the preoccupations raised by participants to this study. Attributes simply refer to intrinsic elements of the nature of missiology; important characteristics which make missiology different from other disciplines. Missiology is a scientific and applied discipline, an interdisciplinary discipline, an intentional discipline and a discipline focused on God's glocal and holistic mission. The following sections attempt to elucidate them.

---

67. Scherer, "Missiology," 509; Roxborogh, "Missiology after Missions," 1; Feshman, "Group Discussion Conclusions," 80–86; Langmead, "What Is Missiology?" 67–79; Moreau et al., *Introducing World Missions*, 19.

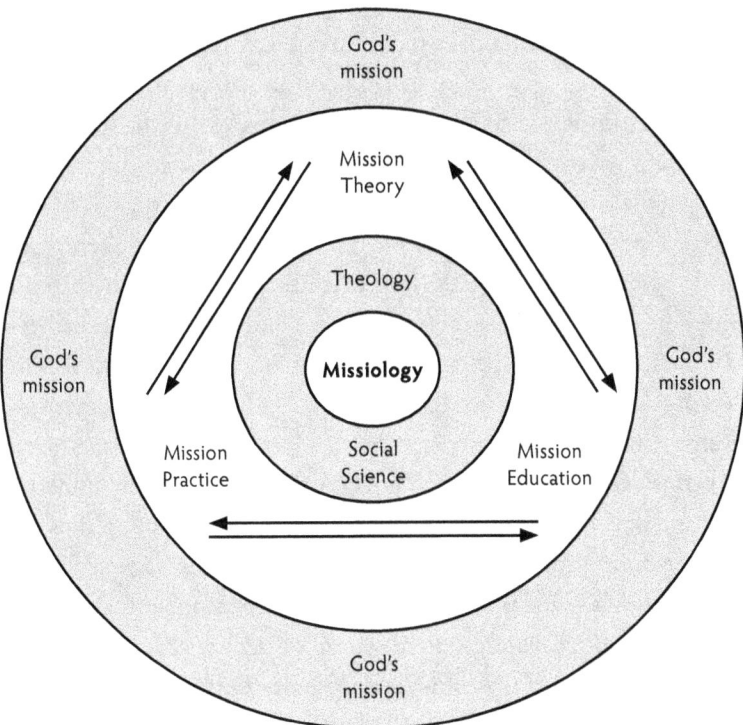

Figure 6.2 Missiology and Its Interplay with Other Disciplines for God's Glocal Mission

6.3.1 Missiology as a Scientific and an Applied Discipline

Missiology has clear object and methods, taking into account how mission is conceptualized, how it is taught and how it is practiced in various contexts. It is a discipline, which is scientific and conforms to science and its principles. It is methodical, proceeding in a systematic and methodical way.[68] Missiology is also an *academic* discipline, that is, it relates to the educational system. However, when defining academic in terms of *scholarly* discipline, *Encarta* states that it is "scholarly and intellectual, and not vocational or practical." *Encarta*'s definition of academic does not apply to the definition

---

68. Microsoft Encarta, *Encyclopedia*.

of missiology. On the contrary, authors have perceived missiology as both "scholarly and intellectual" and "vocational or practical." It is an applied science. Glasser is right to insist that if missiology is a science, it should be an applied science.[69] For Verkuyl, "all good missiology should be able to be translated into action. If there is no action, you're missing something."[70]

Missiology is a scientific discipline, which is undertaken with the purpose of applying the results to the real life of the church in the struggle of responding to the God-given mission. As such, missiology is undertaken based on object (to study what?), methods (how to study it?), sources (where to get the information?), for which reason (what are the outcomes?), etc. It has its own central questions, data to be examined and methods to be used. It is in the process of addressing these concerns that approaches to missiology converge or diverge. Chapters on theoretical (ch. 2), educational (ch. 3) and historical (ch. 4) considerations have shown how missiology is diversely understood, formed and delivered. Depending on theological conviction, philosophical orientation and historical realities, missiology has taken various forms and tasks. Tippett has made this reality obvious by contending that missiology grows, adapts and relates afresh to new form of any kind of change.[71] All this because it is an applied discipline and does not only address the question "what should we know?" or simply "what should we do?"

In a scientific inquiry, there are three kinds of questions a researcher could ask:[72] (1) Conceptual question: "What should we know?" (2) Practical question: "What should we do?" (3) Applied question: "What should we understand before we know what to do?" When focused on conceptual questions only, missiology becomes merely a theoretical, a speculative and an intellectual activity, which allows the learners to acquire and accumulate non-transferable and non-applicable knowledge. The learners may have sophisticated insights without addressing the felt needs or the problem on the ground. They may possess theoretical insights without attending to real preoccupations of the church and its mission. Theological institutions in the DRC have been criticized for not preparing students to help the churches

---

69. Glasser, "Missiology," 724.
70. Verkuyl, *Contemporary Missiology*, 3.
71. Tippett, *Introduction*, xvi.
72. Turabian, *Manual for Writers*, 8–11.

achieve their God-given mission. They have been accused of having ceased to really be in the service of the church.

If undertaken with focus on practical questions only, missiology is reduced to mere pragmatism, without a theoretical and durable foundation. The learners may perform activities without a strong theoretical basis. They can change their mind any time without solid foundation on what they do. They may be active in the ministry without stable principles, which could help the church to survive without them. Transforming missiology is not a matter of being volatile; it is rather about changing through solid basis; transforming by the renewal of mind (cf. Rom 12:1, 2). Many Protestant missionaries in the DRC were criticized for not being able to train local people on time at highly expected level. They were practitioners, but as discussed in chapter 4 (section 4.4.4), many needed solid theoretical principles. Probably due to the fact that mission has been a fruit of seasonal revival, it has been leading participants to activism. In many places, and in some hardship occasions, such an activism could not survive against critical thinking attack. In the DRC, the existence of the CPC was also prompted by the need of creating synergy to compensate for the lack of a solid theoretical foundation in some other missionaries (see, for instance, section 4.5.1).

A transforming missiology would rather require an answer to the third question, namely "what should we understand before we know what to do?" It is about combining conceptual and practical questions or practical and conceptual questions. Depending on the context and the nature of the problem, the process can go either way, providing that the theoretical part helps address the real problem, or that the practical part is supported by an insightful basis. The demonstration of this process is discussed later in this chapter (section 6.5.4).

6.3.2 Missiology as an Interdisciplinary Discipline

Missiology is an interdisciplinary discipline. It is grounded in the word of God, while also using disciplines of social sciences. It gets light from both God's revelation and human ingenuity. The danger is not only when missiology is undertaken based strictly on one of these sources, but also how these sources and tools are conceived and how their interplay is balanced. Again, chapters on theoretical (ch. 2), educational (ch. 3) and historical (ch. 4) considerations have shown how missiology is diversely understood, formed and delivered due to how people perceive and use the Scripture and the disciplines of social science. Depending on theological conviction, philosophical orientation and historical realities, missiology has taken various forms and tasks.

The understanding of what the "word of God" is has shaped the prevailing mission theories. If the Scripture is considered as "being the word of God" mission theories and their implication for God's mission wouldn't have the same meaning and implication as in the case of it being perceived as "containing the word of God." Subsequently, the presupposition one holds on the Scripture determines their missiology, missiological education and mission practice. This reality was depicted in chapter 2. The history of missions has proven that mission during one period took a different shape than in another period, different from both the preceding and following periods.

Bibliology holds a special place in missiology, specifically the teaching about authority and inspiration of the Scripture. Missiology cannot survive if undertaken while questioning the authority of the Scripture. Even while revisiting each missiological discourse that has characterized one or another period in the past, mission theory, education and practice were shaped by the biblical understanding of their promoters. The question is, "does the content of the Scripture deserve indisputable allegiance?" Depending on the period, the context and theological convictions, different answers were given and mission theory, education and practice were accordingly shaped and reshaped. This situation raises the issue of hermeneutics. How should a missiologist approach, understand and interpret the Scripture? While some missiological discourses were labelled "evangelical" or "neo-evangelical," others were known as "liberal" or "ecumenical." From this reality, various missiological wings were formed, known as "Catholic missiology," "ecumenical missiology," "evangelical missiology," "Orthodox missiology," "Pentecostal/charismatic missiology." Even within one group, one could also find subcategories. I indicated that in the DRC, one could find "evangelical-ecumenical missiologists," "ecumenical-evangelical missiologists," and "Pentecostal-ecumenical missiologists."[73] How a missiologist approaches, understands and interprets the Scripture certainly assigns a label to him or her.

---

73. Lygunda, *Missiologie*, 51.

Towards a Transforming Missiology for a Fruitful Missiological Education 309

In the DRC, Protestant theological institutions find themselves labelled either as "evangelical" or "liberal," and the way missiology is perceived and practiced depends mainly on how exegetical and hermeneutical issues are handled. In some cases, the principles of historical-critical methodology are meticulously applied, using the same categories inherited from the Enlightenment period of the eighteenth and nineteenth centuries. The Scripture is approached with critical eyes. For instance, adherents of this methodology would attempt to discover which of the statements and specific words attributed to Christ by the writers of gospel were actually spoken by him.[74] An example from one of the Protestant universities in the DRC illustrates this approach as a professor denied that Jesus was baptized by John the Baptist. The Scripture is then approached with critical eyes. In other cases, only literal-grammatical-historical methodology is used, examining the context of the text.[75]

On the other side, missiology draws insights from various cognate disciplines in order to describe the complex nature of mission. Such disciplines and sub-disciplines include anthropology, sociology, psychology, education, politics and governance, history, religious studies and apologetics, to name a few.[76] These disciplines make missiology relevant because they address the real problems faced by the real people. Using *emic* (collecting data from people inside the research setting) or *etic* (collecting data from outside the research setting) strategies, missiologist strives to understand people's realities so as to address their real problems. However, the danger arises when missiologists frame their premises mostly on these social aspects at the expense of God's revelation; or when missiological discourses proceed from mere rationalism and relativism at the expense of God's revelation and biblical faith. In chapter 2, it was demonstrated that such a challenge has shaped missiology, mission theory, mission education and mission practice.

A transforming missiology will use the principle of balance, using both *emic* and *etic*, approaching both text and context, and depending on the nature of the problem and the situation, missiologists could start their discourse

---

74. Enns, *Moody Handbook*, 23.
75. Ibid., 180.
76. A long list of disciplines and sub-disciplines are provided by many authors (see Van Engen, *Mission on the Way*, 18)

either way, i.e. from text to context, or from context to text. In the African context, African theology and other theological formulations (e.g. theology of reconstruction, Black theology, etc.) were conceived mainly as "identity theologies" which seem to have neglected God's global mission focusing rather on local and contextual struggles (see section 3.4.2).

6.3.3 Missiology as an Intentional Discipline

Missiology is deliberately based on a clear intention or purpose. It is purposefully undertaken to understand and orient the mission entrusted to the church. Missiology not only identifies problems and opportunities of thinking and doing mission; it also provides answers on how mission should be conceptualized, taught and executed. While asking "what is mission and how do people perceive mission?" missiologists go further to address another question, namely "how should mission be perceived?" The question relates to mission education in the following sense: "What is mission education and how do people provide education for mission?" This question will lead to "how should mission education be provided?" In connection to mission practice, the question "how do people involve in God's mission?" will lead to "how should people involve in God's mission?" These examples serve to indicate that missiology or missiological discourse is an intentional reflection, which aims at action and transformation and identification of the problem and it substantiates propositions to solve the problem.

A transforming missiology starts with a prevailing issue related to God's mission. Any topic could be studied by any discipline. For instance, the topic "telephone" can be differently approached and discussed by scholars of sociology, psychology, education, business, political science, mathematics, etc. It can also make the preoccupation of a missiologist as far as the telephone and its use contribute to or hinder God's mission. A missiological discourse on telephone should start with the demonstration of the extent to which it is a prevailing problem for mission with the intention to provide a solution for God's glocal mission.

In the DRC Protestant theological institutions have been criticized for not having provided enough opportunity to problem-based education. During this study, I attended sessions of thesis defence, skimmed through some *licence* and DEA monographs (*mémoires*) and journal articles published locally by some Protestant universities and received feedback during the focus group sessions. The recurrent observation is that many students, researchers and writers seem to not substantiate and match their research problems accordingly. For instance, it was obvious how DEA students of the department of Mission science, Ecumenism and Religious Studies struggled to demarcate their research topics from those undertaken in practical theology or in systematic theology. The question is, what is it that makes a research really *missiological*? Coming back to the illustration of telephone, how does a missiologist address this issue differently than the way in which a practical theologian or a systematic theologian would do it?

A transforming missiology strives for a new and fruitful orientation about the involvement of the church in God's mission relevant to the context. In the process of producing a missiological reflection a missiologist starts from the local context, takes into account the global context, learns accurately from both contexts without trying to impose the global context, learns faithfully from the Scripture and objectively from other disciplines of science and comes back to address the local issue. Subsequently, a missiology which criticizes without providing relevant alternatives, is likely to become a sterile and useless academic activity. Originality, relevance, appropriateness, accuracy, objectivity, contextualization, biblical-based and transformation are among the characteristics of a transforming missiology. Correlated with *Encarta*'s definition of these concepts, their application to missiology offers a good perspective of these important concepts.

Originality has to do with avoidance of plagiarism. Relevance stresses the idea of a missiological discourse, which has some significant and logical connection with the beneficiaries, the people from the context of the research. Appropriateness evokes the idea of fitness, being suitable for the discipline of missiology (instead of confusing a missiological discourse with discourses from any other theological discipline). Accuracy points to the necessity of the correctness (ability to avoid obvious errors and to be precise) or the truthfulness of missiological reasoning. Objectivity relates to accuracy but emphasizes the ability to perceive or describe something objectively without being influenced by personal emotions or prejudices. Contextualization has to do with the necessity of placing missiological reflection within a suitable context, which must be assessed and readjusted by the normative principles of the Scripture (biblically anchored and suitable). Transformation means that missiological discourse should lead to change in thinking and in action (Rom 12:1, 2).

In the DRC some reports lament the fact that graduates of theological institutions fail to create or lead church ministries through and for transformation. Consequently, the rate of the growth of Protestant membership and churches has been decreasing. The recent strategic plan designed by the Department of Evangelism, Church Life and Mission of the CCC (see ch. 1, section 1.1) was based on such a reality. In relation to this study, I conducted an empirical study and published an article on "Understanding and Evaluating the Participation of Francophone Africans in World Mission: Congolese Working in Burundi."[77] The result that could also be generalized to Congolese working in other countries throughout the world doesn't show any direct impact of theological education on these "auto-proclaimed missionaries." The question is to what extent theological education prepares students for transformation if the academic production is not original, relevant, appropriate, accurate, contextual, objective, biblical and transformational. A transforming missiology should take such a preoccupation seriously.

6.3.4 Missiology as a Discipline of God's Glocal and Holistic Mission

At the moment mission is a *passe-partout* word in both religion-related and non-religion-related settings. Tennent observes that "the word *mission* has lost its identity as an exclusively Christian term [. . . that it] needs very careful definition if it is to continue as a useful word for the church."[78] In chapters 2 and 3, mission in the context of religion in general, and church in particular, bore various connotations. Related to such a variety of perceptions, missiology has also become multiform. The change in the title of *International Review of Missions* is an example. From its launch in 1912 up to 1969, the letter "s" was added to the word "mission." Thereafter, due to perceptions and convictions of the theology of *missio Dei*, the journal became *International Review of Mission*, without the "s." This change affected the understanding of mission among the leaders of the CCC as well. Its first Congolese president mentioned the implication of this change:

---

77. Lygunda, "Understanding and Evaluating," 253–270.
78. Tennent, *Introduction*, 53.

It is quite some time now since the *International Review of Missions* became the *International Review of Mission*. The change in thinking revealed in this change in name characterizes also some of the thinking of the Church of Christ in Zaire (Protestant church), for since 1969 Protestant **missions** have ceased to exist in Zaire. At the General Assembly of the former Congo Protestant Council in that year, Zairian churchmen decided that after almost a century of missionary endeavour in their country, missions as institutions no longer had any reason to exist, and the Church in Zaire had to assume its responsibilities for the true **mission** of the Church to evangelize the Zairian people.[79]

Fuller Theological Seminary established the School of World Mission in 1965 before changing it into School of Intercultural Studies in 2003 (see sections 3.3.3 and 3.3.4). If a Congolese undertakes research on the history of Communauté Evangélique de l'Ubangi-Mongala (CEUM) where I was baptized and received to pastoral ministry, the work would be considered "church history." But if someone from the United States does research on the same CEUM, the work would be put under the category of either "mission history" or "world Christianity." Outside religious matters, the word mission appears ubiquitous. Terrorists can go on a mission of destroying a village or a building, though they may falsely evoke religious reasons. An employee can get a mission order to collect taxes or to undertake a business trip. In the DRC the United Nations deployed the mission of peace observation though no one can tell the outcome.

Mission is also used either to designate geographical location where missionaries established their houses, chapels and schools, or the missionary society (e.g. Baptist Mission), or the work done by Western missionaries and sometimes the fact of leaving the country of origin to minister in another country. From the findings of this research presented in chapter 5, it is obvious that many Protestant theological institutions in the DRC have not yet been able to clarify the meaning of mission. During the focus group sessions for this research, students were wondering about what mission

---

79. Bokeleale, "From Missions to Mission," 433.

really meant in the context of Africa in general, and that of the DRC in particular. One professor, known for his academic standard and knowledge, made the following statement with a perceptible sense of honesty: "I am in a discovery process; what I know is that there is internal mission and there is also external mission. However, what is really the definition of missiology today? What makes 'mission' different to 'evangelization'?"

It is important for the purpose of this study to submit that a transforming missiology is not about any kind of mission; it is concerned about God's glocal and holistic mission entrusted to the church regardless of its context. Missiology sheds the light for the work to be done both locally and globally, while treating human beings as a whole entity. In a recurrent way, one of the aspects of the missiological debate was to know whether the mission is theological, cultural or geographical. One could label these three aspects as "theological comprehension of mission," "cultural comprehension of mission" and "geographical comprehension of mission." In theological comprehension of mission, the emphasis is on perceiving mission in terms of its religious or biblical mandate. This aspect has caused a lot of discussion. When some people stress the importance of the ministry of the church, which sends its sons and daughters to preach the gospel about Christ, others would rather insist that it is God's mission, which is at work everywhere without expecting necessary the involvement of the church. The proponents of cultural comprehension of mission would focus on mission as being the ministry of the church in one or another culture. It is about cultural frontiers. The church does not have to cross geographical frontiers because it is surrounded by people from various cultures. As far as the church reaches out to those people, it does mission. The defenders of the geographical comprehension of mission would insist that mission cannot be done without crossing geographical frontiers. This perception of mission takes seriously the mention of "nations" in Matthew 28 and the geographic itinerary of Acts 1:8. For this group, geographical frontiers must be crossed as a way to accomplish God's mission.

One could easily notice strengths and weaknesses in each of these perceptions. They focus either on the content of mission or on the means through which to achieve such a mission. *Theological comprehension of mission* focuses on the content of mission. For some, it is about what God intends and does independently from human intervention of the church. For others, it is about what the church intends and does about God's mission to non-Christians. *Cultural comprehension of mission* focuses on the sociological identity of people to whom the church should minister through word and deed. It can be people from other tribes different to the major tribe which initiated the church, or foreigners joining the milieu where the church exists, or groups of special categories (seekers, street children, prostitutes, business people, etc.) because they are driven by another life culture. *Geographical comprehension mission* focuses on the necessity of ministering to God's created world, the inhabited earth (*oikoumene*). It also focuses on the content of the message to be shared with non-Christians and any other ministry to render to them. Therefore, a transforming missiology would consist of bringing together these strengths to state that God's mission is concerned with both the content and the means.

Missiology is concerned with God's glocal mission. It recognizes that mission under consideration is not a human-made business. It originates from God, but God uses people whom he calls through Christ. These people are gathered, nurtured and used in the context of a local expression of the church of Christ, irrespective of its denominational identification. In the particular case of a given local church, God's mission starts locally and proceeds globally, as from Jerusalem, Judea, Samaria to the ends of the earth (Acts 1:8). While starting at one point, the final destination is beyond local delimitations. It is about *panta ta ethne*, people of all nations, cultures and languages (Matt 28:19; Rev 7:9–17). These New Testament statements echo that of the Old Testament, where God had already revealed his concern about the whole world (Gen 11:1–10) and all nations (Gen 12:1–3). The content of such a mission is to share and demonstrate God's love which was made evident through the life, ministry and death of Jesus Christ (John 3:16; Rom 5:8). Again, this is an echo of the Old Testament (Ps 96; Isa 53). It is about Christ, the unique mediator between the sinful humankind and the holy God (2 Cor 5:10–21; Heb 8:6; 9:15; 12:24). This Old Testament truth was expressed through various acts of mediation such as sacrifice, Moses and the law, prophets, the king, priests and the temple.[80] This mis-

---

80. Sakenfeld, *New Interpreter's Dictionary,* 8.

sion is also concerned with the whole human being, body, soul and spirit. It is a holistic mission as exemplified through the teaching (Luke 4:17–21) and the ministry of Jesus (Matt 9:35; John 7:23). God is interested in the whole human being.

Be it through mission theory, mission education and mission practice missiological discourse has the mandate of pointing to such an orientation. Coming back to the example of telephone, a missiological reflection should link the telephone – its fabrication, its commercialization, its use – to the necessity and urgency of God's glocal and holistic mission.

6.4 The Tripartite Concern of Missiology

After having discussed the attributes of missiology as a discipline, it is important to elaborate more on the threefold concerns of transforming missiology with focus on important features on mission theory, education and practice. One could understand the following discussion as a way to address the critical preoccupation of how mission should be conceptualized, taught and executed as to make the discipline a transforming one.

6.4.1 Concern for a Transforming Mission Theory

The literature survey of chapter 2 has prompted some revelatory findings related to mission theory. The concept of "mission theory" or "theory of mission" can be problematic if paralleled with "mission theology" or "theology of mission." Even without much convincing explanation and evidences, authors have used these concepts interchangeably to designate the theoretical and conceptual aspects of mission. *Theory of mission* would simply mean how mission has been generally understood and conceptualized. It then addresses the question, "why and how should we get involved in God's mission?" The answer to such a question is provided using either insights from non-theological or theological materials, or combining both theological and non-theological insights. In *theology of mission* the question would be specific as, "according to the Scripture, why and how should we get involved in God's mission?" The answer to this question will mostly use biblical and theological materials. Theology of mission would simply refer to the biblical and theological justification of doing mission. Therefore, theory of mission is broader than theology of mission. I prefer "mission theory" or "theory of mission" which includes "mission theology" or "theology of mission." The main concern is "how should God's mission be understood, conceived and conceptualized?"

The findings of chapter 2 have surfaced bipolarity in mission conceptualization. While one side would perceive mission as church undertaking of proclaiming the gospel to save souls, while crossing geographical boundaries to convert people of other faiths, the other side stresses God prominence demonstrated in the presence of his people in the world to liberate oppressed ones through peaceful cohabitation with people of other faiths without necessary crossing geographical frontiers. While one side perceives the church as God's instrument to establish his kingdom in the life of believers, the other side assigns to the world the responsibility of setting the agenda for the establishment of God's kingdom on the earth. While one side tends to focus on the spiritual aspect of God's mission for humankind, the other side emphasizes the social aspect of God's purpose for his creation. This bipolarization of mission theory has characterized missiological reflections throughout generations and locations. Even in the past (see ch. 4) and present (see ch. 5) context of the DRC, the bipolarization of mission theory is perceptible. A transforming missiology should attempt to address this bipolarization by moving away from unfruitful extremism.

Far from minimizing the complexity of the task, the conviction is that if undertaken with humility and faithfulness to the Scripture through an objective hermeneutics, the mission theory is likely to be unbiased. The literature survey of chapter 2 has revealed that authors have suggested some guiding questions to elaborate the theory of mission, using "what, who, where and how"[81] or "how mission? wherefore mission? whence mission? whither mission? why mission? what mission?"[82] Drawn on literature review, Mashau makes a list of seven elements of theology (or theory) of mission which address some specific questions:[83]

---

81. Kritzinger et al., *On Being Witnesses*.
82. Anderson, *Theology*, 3–16.
83. Mashau, "Hugo Du Plessis' Contribution," 162.

1. The concept of mission: what is actually mission (salvation or humanization)?
2. The content of mission: which areas of human life should be addressed by mission (physical, spiritual or mental needs)?
3. The agent of mission: who are initiators and implementers of mission (*missio Dei, missio ecclesiae, missio humanum*)?
4. The objects of mission: who are objects of mission (to whom mission should be done)?
5. The context of mission: where is the mission field (local or global)?
6. The methods of mission: How is mission undertaken (words or deed)?
7. The movement of mission: towards which direction mission is done (centrifugal or centripetal)?

For the purpose of this study, the following three devices could be used to develop a mission theory since they substantially encompass the aforementioned guiding questions: (1) the inspiration and authority of the Scripture; (2) the nature and the destiny of human beings, and (3) the nature and the task of the church.

6.4.1.1 *The Inspiration and Authority of the Scripture*

A mission theory that disregards or distorts the inspiration and authority of the Scripture would simply be a human philosophical gesticulation which could miss the point, losing the essence of mission. While surveying literature around the debate on mission, the issue of the inspiration and authority of the Scripture laid at the core of the real problem. Glasser and Wright have done great work to remind us of the importance of Scripture as the book of God's mission (Wright) or a missionary book (Glasser).[84] The mission is what the Bible is all about.[85] There is a need of reconsidering the central place of the Scripture in missiology, providing that to not employing the common tendency of selecting some biblical passages to compose the mission theory. On the road to Emmaus and later to other disciples (Luke 24:27–47), Jesus demonstrated that the whole Scripture spoke of him as God's plan to save the humanity. As Wright points out, the reality of the Bible being the book

---

84. Glasser, *Announcing the Kingdom*, 17–28; Wright, *Mission of God*.
85. Wright, *Mission of God*, 29.

of God's mission requires that we read its content both *messianically* (Christ in the center) and *missionally* (God's mission in the center).[86] The findings of this book stated in chapter 5 have demonstrated that the use of the complete written revelation (Old Testament and New Testament) is not common among many theology students. Therefore, theological institutions are urged to reconsider their curricula as to what extent the conviction about the inspiration and authority of the Scripture make the bedrock of missiological discourse. One of the important features of mission theory would address the following questions: Which place does the Scripture occupy in our mission theory? What is the implication of accepting the inspiration and authority of the Scripture for the mission theory? What does the whole of the Scripture say about God's mission today? Linked to these concerns is the whole issue of hermeneutics in missiological discourse. Bosch and Van Engen have amply demonstrated the exigence and the relatedness of hermeneutical principles to the biblical foundation (Bosch) or theology of mission (Van Engen).[87]

6.4.1.2 The Nature and Destiny of Human Beings

A mission theory that overlooks or distorts the nature and destiny of human beings would simply miss the point about what triggered God's mission. Both the literature survey of chapter 2 and the findings of the empirical investigation reported in chapter 5 have shown how debate on mission tended to move away from the nature and destiny of human beings, promoting rather peripheral issues such as ecology, social and political liberation, the promotion of the culture, etc. Authors have shown from a survey of the Old Testament that God's comprehensive redemption includes political, economic, social and spiritual concerns.[88] Even if these issues relate to the well-being of human beings, it is however the conviction here that these concerns shouldn't make the core of mission theory. Jesus made it clear through a rhetorical question: "What good is it for someone to gain the whole world, yet forfeit their soul?" (Mark 8:37). God is more concerned about human beings themselves than other peripheral issues, which are actually the consequences of the distorted nature of human beings. Biblical

---

86. Ibid., 30.
87. Bosch, "Hermeneutical Principles," 437–451; Van Engen, "Relation of Bible," 34.
88. Wright, *Mission of God*, 268–272.

accounts flourish in showing the importance that a human being has for God, being created in the *imago Dei* as the best of the whole creation (Gen 1:30, 31). Throughout the Scripture human beings occupy a special place in God's plans and interventions to the point that the psalmist could wonder: "What is man that you are mindful of him?" (Ps 8:4). One of the important features of mission theory would address the following questions: Which place human being occupies in the mission theory? What is the implication of considering the nature and destiny of human beings as important subjects for the mission theory? What does the whole of the Scripture say about human beings with regard to God's mission today?

6.4.1.3 The Nature and Task of the Church

A mission theory that ignores or undermines the nature and task of the church would simply miss the point about what God has to do beyond human-oriented philanthropic activities. The literature survey of chapter 2 has shown how debate on mission tended to remove the church as being instrument for God's glocal mission. As discussed in chapter 2 (see section 2.6.2), authors have advocated for the euthanasia of the church for the world to set the agenda for mission. Though apparently attractive, the unspoken truth for such a suggestion is to assimilate God's mission to mere philanthropic activities. For its proponents the concept of *missio Dei* cancels any church involvement in God's mission. One could oppose this point of view with another version of the fact that demonstrates the importance of church in God's mission. From the Old Testament to the New Testament God reveals himself being in search of a special people to be used for the accomplishment of his eternal plans. There is a mission for God's people; it is the church's mission.[89] Being a new family, intentionally purposed by Christ, the church is the channel through which God sovereignly has chosen to reach out to his creation (Matt 16:18; Eph 3:10). Van Engen would suggest that as members of a local church, God's people participate in God's mission through fellowship (*koinonia*), teaching (*kerygma*), service (*diakonia*), and witness (*martyria*).[90] Goheen is right to state that ecclesiology is so

---

89. Wright, *Mission of God's People*, 20.
90. Van Engen, *God's Missionary People*, 89.

important.[91] Therefore, one of important features of mission theory would address the following questions: Which place does the church occupy in the mission theory? What is the implication of considering the nature and task of church as an important subject for the mission theory? What does the whole of the Scripture say about the church with regard to God's mission today?

As already mentioned previously, mission theory can comprise more than the aforementioned components of the Scripture, human being and the church. These components do not emphasize the strategic aspects of mission expressed through some questions such as "what, how, who, to whom, where, when, how many, how much, etc." However, the above three themes of Scripture, human beings and church can provide space to discuss these questions. Therefore, to elaborate, implement and evaluate mission theory one needs to have a clear idea of the following prerequisite questions:

1. Which place does the Scripture occupy in the mission theory?
2. What is the implication of accepting the inspiration and authority of the Scripture for the mission theory?
3. What does the whole of the Scripture say about God's mission for today? What, how, who, to whom, where, when, how many, how much?
4. Which place do human beings occupy in the mission theory?
5. What is the implication of considering the nature and destiny of human beings as an important subject for the mission theory?
6. What does the whole of the Scripture say about human being in regard to God's mission today? What, how, who, to whom, where, when, how many, how much?
7. Which place does the church occupy in the mission theory?
8. What is the implication of considering the nature and task of church as an important subject for the mission theory?
9. What does the whole of the Scripture say about the church in regard to God's mission today? What, how, who, to whom, where, when, how many, how much?

While it is one thing to elaborate theories of mission from an office desk, it is still another thing to pass them on to those who will engage either in

---

91. Goheen, *Light to the Nations*, 1–21.

implementing them or in teaching them to future generations. Mission education for transformation is important.

6.4.2 Concern for a Transforming Mission Education

Accounts have been provided on various statuses of missiology in the theological curriculum as being either a dependent or an independent discipline with some other variants such as integration or penetration (see section 3.2.2). In general, two main streams have emerged from this debate and have characterized contemporary missiological education in many places. For instance, a doctoral program can be either a Doctorate of Theology in Missiology (DTh in Missiology) or a Doctorate of Philosophy in Missiology (PhD in Missiology). While the first tends to perceive missiology as a dependent portion of theology, the second considers missiology as an independent portion within theology. The following lines summarize important aspects of the existing models of a curriculum in missiological education before providing some practical suggestions to re-envision a missiological curriculum and to re-brand missiological concentrations.

6.4.2.1 Missiology: A Dependent or an Independent Degrees-Granted Discipline

In the first approach of Doctorate of Theology (DTh) in Missiology, the student is supposed to take theological courses at bachelor and master levels through the traditional fourfold patterns of biblical, historical, systematic and practical theology before producing a research-based thesis in missiology. Few Protestant universities that grant mission-related degrees in the DRC promote this approach. Students are granted a degree in mission studies or missiology without having sufficient prerequisite courses in mission and missiology. Degrees in missiology are then granted based on an intellectual inquiry done through reading randomly or by chance, during the intensive period of writing a thesis. Through such a timely intellectual exercise, the student lacks an arena for implementation, the main purpose being the pursuit of a theoretical higher degree. Subsequently, upon the completion of their studies, doctorate holders join the faculty without possessing required tools of missiological epistemology from which they could develop courses that could intellectually, spiritually and practically challenge the students for God's glocal mission.

In this educational context, students are trained with some unstructured and mere theoretical body of knowledge, which could hardly address the actual issues and challenges that their churches face for God's glocal mission. The critical question in such an educational context is, how to initiate a transforming missiology. In other terms, how to transform missiology itself and how to make missiology a discipline that transforms. As discussed in chapter 3 (see section 3.2.2), authors have suggested the integration of "mission" into all disciplines of theology at each level of bachelor, master and doctorate. Such a suggestion means that all teaching staff would already acquire clear and harmonized insights about mission that they could insert into their respective courses. In many Francophone African countries, this solution is far from being realistic. For instance, in the DRC one couldn't expect such an expertise in "mission studies" to be found in *all* teaching staffs of a given Protestant theological institution. As discussed in the previous chapter, mission studies or missiology has been a missing link in theological curriculum. For instance, during a recent focus group session for this study, one respected professor of theology contended that "missiology is just a theological fraud; a strategy to keep Congolese away from the church responsibility of liberating people; the process of perpetuating Western imperialism." Another solution is needed and can be explored.

The Doctorate of Philosophy (PhD) in Missiology approach could be another possible venue for transforming missiology in the above-described context under the condition that missiology is undertaken with relatedness to theological disciplines. For instance, at doctoral level, the candidate could undertake missiology with the focus on one or more theological discipline, for example PhD in Missiology with focus on Old Testament, on New Testament, on Systematic Theology, on Practical Theology, on Historical Theology, on World Religions, on World Christianity, etc. Such a configuration means that these other theological disciplines serve *missio Dei*; they are in the service of God's glocal and holistic mission. Bosch and Wright, to cite only a few, can be referred to as examples. Though they did not undergo the above suggested educational approach, their contributions to missiological discourse shed some light on this proposition. Both authors have produced outstanding works in missiology, respectively *Transforming Mission: Paradigm Shift in Theology of Mission* (Bosch) and *The Mission of God: Unlocking the*

Bible's Grand Narrative (Wright). While Bosch has produced a doctoral thesis in New Testament, Wright's doctoral thesis was done in Old Testament. Bosch and Wright contributed an unusual accomplishment, which not all theological scholars can do. In the DRC the names of two scholars who contributed largely in this regard can be mentioned, namely Nzash U. Lumeya who submitted a doctoral thesis in Old Testament in the Faculty of Fuller Theological Seminary, USA, and Mushila Nyamanak who submitted a doctoral thesis in New Testament related studies in the Faculty of Theology at University of Hamburg, Germany. As I have indicated elsewhere, these two Congolese scholars have pioneered the insertion of mission-related studies into the traditional theological curriculum in 1990 and 1997 respectively.[92] Their initiatives have made the DRC the birthplace of Protestant missiology in Francophone Africa, the first country where the discipline of missiology was organized in a faculty (Nzash) or a department (Mushila) at higher education level. Again, as for Bosch and Wright, the situation of Nzash and Mushila cannot be generalized to all theologians. There is still a need of providing structured and intentional studies in missiology at all levels of bachelor, master and doctorate.

It is possible to plan for transforming missiology even in the current context of the DRC by re-envisioning the discipline according to theoretical insights gained through the literature survey of this study (see chs. 2 and 3), and by re-branding the curriculum based on the current trends in higher education as revealed through the same literature survey (see chs. 3 to 5). In the process, missiological education can be provided either as a dependent discipline, being a department among others but while penetrating the whole of the theological curriculum, or as an independent discipline, being a faculty while relating to the theological corpus. In the DRC, some Protestant universities align with the first structure, while only one, the Centre Universitaire de Missiologie (CUM), stands for the second structure. There is no place where missiology is offered through a research center comparable to those surveyed earlier in chapter 3 (section 3.3). However, as already discussed in chapter 5 and earlier in this chapter, the current status and realities of missiological education in the country call for new approaches.

---

92. Lygunda, "Missiologie comme," 268–269.

6.4.2.2 Missiology through a Department within the Faculty of Theology

Missiological education can be provided through a department within the faculty of theology, operating alongside other traditional departments of biblical theology, systematic theology, historical theology and practical theology. The question is still to know which of these departments would better serve the church for God's glocal mission. If, as it has been re-enforced in this study, theology or theological studies ought to be in the service of *missio Dei*, the above question should be reformulated otherwise. One could rather ask, "What should each department within the faculty of theology do in order to prepare students to help their respective churches involve in God's glocal mission?" Such a preoccupation would lead to two possibilities, namely either to infuse the complete theological curriculum with mission insights, or to use the department of missiology as a catalyst to influence the remaining departments through some specific mission-related courses and activities.

On the one hand, infusing the complete theological curriculum with mission insights means that each course within the curriculum should have a missional orientation. For instance, a course in Exegesis of Old Testament or Exegesis of New Testament would end up by helping students to infer some missional implications of the text given the fact that, as discussed earlier (section 6.5.1.1), the Bible is the book of God's mission. Courses in Church History or World Christianity would draw insights on mission engagement today based on the historical realities and trends. A course in Research Methodology or in any other social science-related subject would provide orientations for *missio Dei* among people of various cultures and faiths. However, the critical concern would be to not only get the adhesion of each member of teaching staff, but also to ensure that they really possess required academic and spiritual skills for such an involvement. One possibility will be to provide continuing education to all teaching staff in missional theology and in university pedagogy in mission-related subjects.

On the other hand, using the department of missiology as mission catalyst means that such a department, apart from designing its own courses to be offered to the concerned students, could also design mission-related courses to be added to other departments. The academic staff of the department of missiology could develop academic and ministry activities of formal, non-formal, and informal tenures. These activities designed for both students and instructors of the entire faculty of theology should include credited courses, conferences, workshops, mission retreats, mission trips, mission publications, joint mission research, etc. These various activities will be undertaken with the purpose of infusing a mission mindset into the whole life of the faculty of theology in theory and in practice. The department of missiology could then serve as mission lighthouse of the theological curriculum and activities. Nevertheless, one crucial condition for the success of such a proposition would be the extent to which the department of missiology understands its role. For instance, referring to Bosch and Wright who have put their biblical studies in the service of *missio Dei*, keen research would probably demonstrate that they might have been influenced by what the department of missiology achieved within their faculties of theology.

Therefore, those leading and serving within this department should possess either expertise in mission studies or commitment to mission, they should have both a spiritual and moral authority to influence other faculty members, and they should be academically innovative and productive. Without entering into details of their life and experience, missiologists at Fuller Seminary at the time of the School of World Missions have played such a role. Among them, one could think of McGavran, Winter, Glasser and Peter Wagner, just to name a few. Nzash U. Lumeya who pursued his studies in the Old Testament from the same institution was impacted by the School of World Missions, and as Moussa Bongoyok reports, he couldn't hesitate to return to his home continent to share the same impact.[93]

6.4.2.3 *Missiology through a Faculty with Some Specific Departments*

Missiological education can also be provided in the context of a faculty of missiology in which more specific departments operate, or through which other disciplines of theology serve as the basis on which missiological reflection is articulated. According to *Encarta*, a faculty is a group of departments

---

93. Bongoyok, "Influence," 120. It is however important to mention that Nzash finally went back to the United States where he has established a new school for mission. He visits regularly the DR Congo, his home country, to teach at the University Missiological Center he already established in 1990.

dealing with a particular subject in a university or a college. In this case, missiology is the intended subject and any specific department would simply be an arena to approach and discuss this subject.

Some missiological institutions that are structured as faculties of missiology operate through some specific departments or areas of research such as theological perspectives of mission, historical perspectives of mission, cultural perspectives of mission and strategic perspectives of mission. This structure sounds closer to what Winter and Hawthorne promoted through their magnitude work *Perspectives on the World Christian Movement.* Research units are built around these areas and each unit approaches missiology through a specific lens, be it biblical, theological, historical or strategic.

Other institutions create departments that correspond to ministry areas such as Bible translation, leadership development, community development, etc. Therefore, missiological education would be perceived mostly as an applied science preparing students for practical cross-cultural, intercultural and intracultural ministries. Subsequently, courses on theological, historical, cultural and strategic perspectives of mission serve to qualify students for tangible ministries in different contexts. Students benefit from each of these perspectives as to build their capacity and understanding for real ministry.

While the approach of a faculty of missiology sounds simple and attractive, still its implementation requires some prerequisites common to the aforementioned two approaches. One of these requirements could be the existence of qualified academic staff in each teaching and research unit or in each department. Another requirement could be the broadening of the scope of missiological studies instead of narrowing them to some selected departments.

6.4.2.4 Missiology through a Research Center

As discussed earlier in chapter 3 (see section 3.3), one of the current trends in missiological education is the approach of a missiological research center through which candidates to master and doctoral programs undertake their studies. The center prepares students for research in a specific mission-related problem. There is no coursework and the students design their study focus based on their identified problem and within their particular context. If the students lack prerequisites in missiology, it is possible that they graduate with a tremendous gap in theoretical epistemology necessary for any qualified missiologist. Without relevant coursework or systematized orientation in missiology, the graduates would certainly perform poorly when it comes to creativity and knowledge advancement, including thesis supervision of their students.

In the light of the survey of contemporary missiological education conducted in chapter 3, the advantage of providing missiology through a research center includes the fact that the teaching-learning process combines theories and practice, promotes creative and incentive research projects, encourages the spirit of community of learning, and facilitates the coaching and mentorship process through experienced tutors and qualified supervisors. Much of these advantages relates to various factors, including educational philosophy, mission theology, availability of qualified and committed human resources, logistic capacity, etc. More insights on research center will be provided and discussed in a further section (6.5.4).

6.4.2.5 The Essence of a Productive Missiological Higher Education

The above discussion on how missiological education ought to be provided will probably lose its essence if the core features of educational philosophies and principles explored in chapter 3 are ignored. Missiological education can be offered through a department of missiology, through a faculty of missiology, or through a missiological research center without accomplishing the threefold mission of providing quality teaching, promoting incentive research and serving meaningfully the community. The literature survey of chapter 3 has shown that the critical question for such an adult education endeavour (section 3.5.1) is to what extent education at tertiary level aligns with and values of these objectives and how it keeps them in constant tension (section 3.5.2). The same literature survey has also underscored the importance of other educational features such as the transformative purpose of a higher education institution (section 3.5.3), the Bolognization of educational system (section 3.5.4), outcomes-based education (section 3.5.4.1), problem-based education (section 3.5.4.2), content-oriented modules (section 3.5.4.3), learner-centred apprenticeship (section 3.5.4.4), and field education (section 3.5.4.5). These features are determinant for a productive education, be it secular or religion-based.

Therefore, to design, implement and evaluate mission education one not only needs to take into account the interplay of theological studies and social sciences, but also to ensure that a given missiological program passes the test of the following checklist, at least at the theoretical level:

1. To what extent the missiological program keeps in constant and creative tension the purpose of providing quality education, promoting incentive research, and serving meaningfully the community.
2. To what extent its transformative purpose is clearly stated and implemented.
3. To what extent it aligns with the current educational system as to prepare people who will be able to use their education to penetrate the world with competence.
4. To what extent the principles of outcomes-based education are clearly stated and implemented at each level of study (bachelor, master and doctorate).
5. To what extent the principles of the learning theories of adult education are clearly stated and implemented in the teaching-learning process.
6. To what extent the principles of problem-based education are clearly stated and implemented in the teaching-learning process.
7. To what extent the principles of content-oriented education are clearly stated and implemented in the teaching-learning process.
8. To what extent the principles of learner-centered apprenticeship are clearly stated and implemented in the teaching-learning process.
9. To what extent the principles of field education are clearly stated and implemented in the teaching-learning process.

The process of missiological education should not be a mere theoretical exercise. It should rather lead to the practice of God's glocal mission.

6.4.3 Concern for a Transforming Mission Practice

As far as *missio Dei* is concerned, mission theory and mission education would not represent so much if mission practice were missing. The literature survey of this study has surfaced a diversity of theories and a variety of training institutions that, in some contexts, failed to incite students and their churches to actually engage in God's glocal mission. Based on such an experience, some authors (see section 1.3) have contended that mission engagement in the history has been the fruit of revival rather than of formal education. However, the question is, which kind of mission practice would it be without thoughtful mission theories and structured mission education.

The historical accounts of missionary enterprise in some places like in the DRC have revealed that the mere practice of mission caused the church to delay its self-supporting, self-governing, self-propagation and even self-theologizing responsibilities. As Fiedler has demonstrated, there was a zeal for doing mission among Protestant missionaries despite their limited involvement in elaborating sound theories of mission and in providing competitive education for mission.[94] Some of them didn't even undergo formal training in these mission theories and education. Consequently, the practice of mission has become the appanage of Western missionaries.

The mission practice raises many questions including the following: (1) What are the methods and strategies used by a given mission society to accomplish the supreme task of the church? (2) What should be the effective methods and strategies to accomplish the supreme task of the church? To expand these questions, the following adapted from Mashau deserve more attention since mission practice is closely linked to mission theory:[95]

1. What is actually the mission work that needs to be accomplished: To preach and provide salvation or to focus on humanization?
2. Which areas of human life should be addressed by mission work: Physical, spiritual or mental needs?
3. Who are initiators and implementers of mission work: God (*missio Dei*), the church (*missio ecclesiae*), or human beings (*missio humanum*)?
4. Who are objects of mission work? To whom should mission work be done?
5. Where is the mission field? Within the local setting or for the global context?

---

94. Fiedler, *Story of Faith Missions*, 10–14.
95. Mashau, "Hugo Du Plessis' Contribution."

6. How is mission work undertaken?
7. Towards which direction mission work is done: Centrifugal (penetrating) or centripetal (attracting)?

To plan and evaluate mission practice one needs the interplay of theological studies and social sciences.

6.5 A Model of Missiological Higher Education Study Program

After having discussed the theoretical and empirical findings of the precedent chapters, it is noteworthy to propose and sketch a model of a missiological higher education program for the three levels of studies (undergraduate, graduate and postgraduate), taking into account the threefold mandate of providing quality teaching, promoting incentive research and serving the community in a meaningful manner. This proposition of a model of missiological education is an attempt to ensure a transforming missiology (i.e. a missiology that is transformed [different from the existing] and that could lead to transformation [helping stakeholders to become responsive to God's glocal mission]).

6.5.1 Conditions for a Transforming Missiological Education

In order to provide a transforming missiology, the following requirements should be taken into account:

1. The study program should be offered in the context of theological education (through a department, or a faculty, or a research center) following Antioch model as described in section 3.4.1 and re-displayed in table 6.1 below.

Table 6.1 Antioch Model of Missiological Education

Symbol	Antioch
Model	Transforming education
Context	Higher education: Community of learning and serving
Purpose (Goal)	Knowing God for his mission Personal development for God's mission Strengthening the church for God's mission Challenging any mission-mindless tradition
Expected Outcomes	The production of transformed graduates The production of theoretically aware and practically effective graduates The production of missiophiles (with love for God's mission) The production of graduates who know non-denominational God
Learning Ethos	Personal experience Applied reflection Missional theology Denominational identity in the service of God's glocal mission
Theology Is . . .	The process of experiencing God for his glocal mission Thinking about what God's mission purposes and applying theory to the context Missional (that is for the sake of *missio Dei*) Evaluating and orienting tradition in the light of God's mission
Missiological Education Is . . .	The process through which the church and its educational institutions prepare learners for God's glocal and holistic mission through theory, training and practice of mission

2. The study program should be based on clear philosophies of education about teaching-learning process: From pedagogy to heutagogy (section 3.5.1), the threefold mandate of a higher education institution (section 3.5.2), the transformative purpose of higher education (section 3.5.3), following the requirements of the Bologna Process (section 3.5.4) with emphasis on outcomes-based education (section 3.5.4.1), problem-based education (section 3.5.4.2), content-based teaching units (section 3.5.4.3), the learner-centered apprenticeship (section 3.5.4.4) and field education (section 3.4.4.5).

3. The study program requires available and qualified instructors who can ignite the learning community with their personal testimonies, commitment of Christian faith, training and mentoring vocation, intercultural ministries and academic background. They can be of two categories: (1) Missiologists who have gone through formal studies in missiology either through a department of missiology or through a center for mission studies; they are then expected to have studied one or more biblical, theological, historical, cultural or strategic perspectives of mission. (2) Mission-minded scholars who have expertise in other theological disciplines (Old Testament, New Testament, Church History, Practical Theology, Systematic Theology) or in other disciplines of social sciences (Psychology, Sociology, Political Science, etc.); they intentionally resolve to put their academic expertise in the service of God's glocal and holistic mission. Despite the category to which they may belong, instructors should help students move from pedagogical to heutagogical learning continuum, and their contribution to the teaching-learning process should move from close support to synergetic venture.

This process will require that instructors undergo the experience of the cycle of teaching which includes the major steps of qualifying for the task, performing the task and evaluating the task (fig. 6.3). Each of these three steps requires appropriate character, knowledge and skills from the instructor. These three ingredients would undoubtedly determine the efficiency and effectiveness of an instructor whose passion is to positively affect and influence the learning process. Based on Jesus's principle that "A student is not above his teacher, but everyone who is fully trained will be like his teacher" (Luke 6:40), the cycle of the teaching process underscores the transformative purpose of a given missiological education.

Figure 6.3 displays the fact that each of the three steps in the teaching process comprises some specific features or tasks. While the first step is more about the "being" of the instructor (being called and being qualified), the remaining two deal with the "doing" of the instructor (preparing the course, introducing the course, teaching the course, conducting tutorial sessions, evaluating the learning process, evaluating the teaching process, updating and improving the teaching process, updating and upgrading the learning process). Even within each specific task the implication is that the whole personality (character, knowledge and skills) of the instructor is required, both in the "being" and in the "doing." It is important to see the order of intervention, namely first "being" and then "doing." The implication is that in the process of transforming missiology the instructors' being should precede their doing.

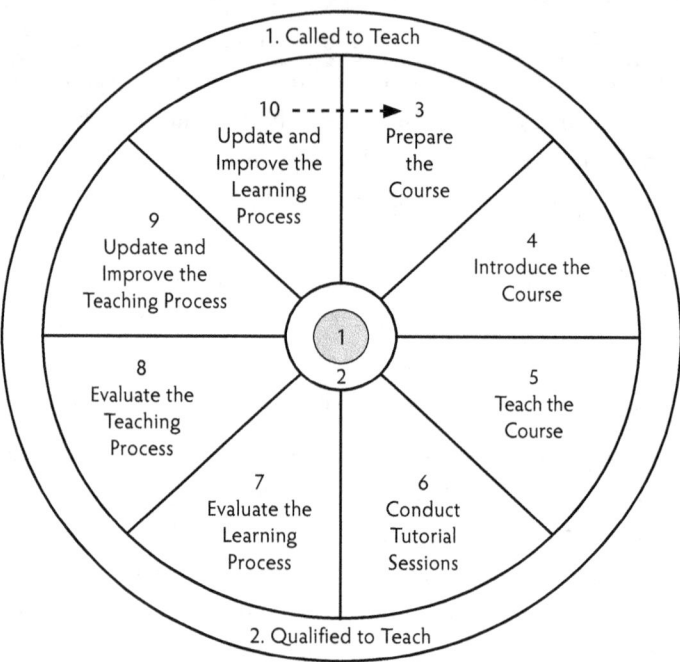

Figure 6.3 The Cycle of Teaching Process

Step 1: The instructors should qualify for the task

1. ***Being called to teach*** (being a master of disciples)
   "A student is not above his teacher, but everyone who is fully trained will be like his teacher" (Jesus in Luke 6:40)
2. ***Being qualified to teach a particular course***
   a. Character: Who the instructors are and who they should be
   b. Knowledge: What the instructors know and what they should know
   c. Skill: What the instructors do and what they should do

Step 2: Performing the task

3. *Preparing the course*
   a. Character: Who the instructors are and who they should be
   b. Knowledge: What the instructors know and what they should know
   c. Skill: What the instructors do and what they should do
4. *Introducing the course*
   a. Character: Who the instructors are and who they should be
   b. Knowledge: What the instructors know and what they should know
   c. Skill: What the instructors do and what they should do
5. *Teaching the course*
   a. Character: Who the instructors are and who they should be
   b. Knowledge: What the instructors know and what they should know
   c. Skill: What the instructors do and what they should do
6. *Conducting tutorial sessions*
   a. Character: Who the instructors are and who they should be
   b. Knowledge: What the instructors know and what they should know
   c. Skill: What the instructors do and what they should do

Step 3: Evaluating the task

7. *Evaluating the learning process*
   a. Character: Who the instructors are and who they should be
   b. Knowledge: What the instructors know and what they should know
   c. Skill: What the instructors do and what they should do
8. *Evaluating the teaching process*
   a. Character: Who the instructors are and who they should be
   b. Knowledge: What the instructors know and what they should know
   c. Skill: What the instructors do and what they should do
9. *Updating and improving the teaching process*
   a. Character: Who the instructors are and who they should be

  b. Knowledge: What the instructors know and what they should know
  c. Skill: What the instructors do and what they should do
10. ***Updating and improving the learning process***
  a. Character: Who the instructors are and who they should be
  b. Knowledge: What the instructors know and what they should know
  c. Skill: What the instructors do and what they should do

4. Students should have a personal testimony of faith commitment, academic prerequisites and thirst for learning activities and personal growth. They can be of two categories: (1) In-service students who may not be students in the ordinary sense of those preparing for a career; they learn on the basis of current ministry experience. (2) Pre-service students are those preparing for a ministry career; they have not yet been in the ministry and have no experience of full-time ministry. Regardless of the category to which one could belong, the principles of adult education will make the philosophy of the study program. Students should be expected to move from pedagogical to heutagogical learning methods; from being receiving learners to synthesizing learners.

5. The study program should be offered in a conducive learning environment comprising a spirit of sharing and interaction, time management, minimal quality logistic, qualified academic facilitators and spiritual mentors and an intentional and multicultural mission-minded community. As Shaw insists, it is about being "a learning community" but not just "a community where learning takes place."[96] A learning community strives for the best, learning from the past experiences and mistakes, through biblical revelation and life in Christ. Ingalls's steps discussed earlier in chapter 3 (section 3.5.1) about managing adult education can be adapted here as to make a conducive learning environment:[97]

---

96. Shaw, *Best Practice Guidelines*, 9.
97. Ingalls, *A Trainer's Guide*.

a. Provide accessible, physically and psychologically comfortable environment.
b. Establish organizational structure at both institutional and instructional levels.
c. Teach skills which allow students to work collaboratively and promoting interaction.
d. Clarify expected values.
e. Commit to something which meets the interest of the students.
f. Promote a problem-solving learning process.
g. Encourage students to learn what is wanted.
h. Provide students with the opportunity of implementing and evaluating their learning activities.

6.5.2 A Three-Level Study Program: Undergraduate, Graduate and Postgraduate

Missiological education should be offered in the context of tertiary education mainly at undergraduate level (bachelor), graduate level (master) and postgraduate level (doctorate). As discussed while surveying the Bologna Process (section 3.5.4), each level of studies has its specific learning outcomes and is complementary to other levels. Missiological education should be a structured and complementary learning process if it is to be coherent, productive and impactful. The bachelor program should prepare students for the master program in order to get them ready for the doctoral program. The master program should prepare students to minister to the bachelor students and to get ready for doctoral studies. The doctoral program should prepare students to minister to both bachelor and master programs and to get ready for building and expanding knowledge. These academic outcomes should also lead the students to professional outcomes of serving the church and its God-given glocal mission.

What Shaw reports on best practice guidelines for doctoral programs should apply to all the three levels of study programs about their "missional impact."[98] Graduate of bachelor, master and doctoral programs should be able to "promote the kingdom of God and advance the mission of the church

---

98. Shaw, *Best Practice Guidelines*, 1.

[both local and global] through Christ-like and transformational service."[99] Table 6.2 summarizes, on the one hand, the relatedness of missiological education to theological corpus, and on the other hand, the progress in the learning process within the field of missiological studies. While the accent for the bachelor program would be of laying the academic foundation for professional involvement, the master program would use such a foundation to help students conduct a critical literature review in order to solve prevailing problems, and the doctoral program will use these prerequisites to build and expand knowledge. Figures 6.4, 6.5 and 6.6 picture how, through the proposed training programs, the graduates would promote the kingdom of God and advance the glocal mission of the church.

Table 6.2 A Model of the Threefold Level of Missiological Higher Education Following the Bologna Process

BTh in Missiology (3 years)	180	MTh in Missiology (2 years)	120	PhD in Missiology (3 years)	180
FIRST YEAR					
9 Foundational Courses	30	8 Foundational Modules	30	7 Foundational Seminars	30
Theories of academic learning	2	Research-based academic writing	4	Issues in thesis writing & supervision	4
Basics of Christian Faith	3	Critical and creative thinking	3	Perspectives in missiology	6
Information Communication Technology	3	Personal leadership development	3	Historical development of*...	4
Research-based academic writing	4	Perspectives on missiology	6	Contemporary issues in*... studies	4
Critical and Creative Thinking	3	OT Missional Exegesis	6	Research methods in*...	4
Greek 1 & 2	6	NT Missional Exegesis	6	*... and mission imperatives	4
Hebrew 1 & 2	6	Field education	2	Educational philosophies & andragogy	4
Personal Leadership Development	3				

---

99. Ibid.

8 Theological Courses	30	8 Mission-Based Modules	30	Doctoral Research Seminar 1	30
Intro. to OT (history and content)	4	Biblical Theology of Mission	6	Research proposal writing	
Intro. to NT (history and content)	4	Contemporary theologies of mission	4	Research proposal registration	
Introduction to World Religions	3	History of world Christianity	4		
Intro. to World Christianity	4	Issues in African mission history	4		
Intro. to Systematic Theology	4	Races, ethnicity & conflict transf.	3		
Intro. to Christian Apologetics	3	Christian ethics for global mission	3		
Intro. to Practical Theology	4	Missiological research design	6		
Intro. to Missiology	4				

SECOND YEAR

8 Theological Courses	30	6 Cross-Cultural Modules	30	Doctoral Research Seminar 2	30
Missional Exegesis of OT	4	Cultural anthropology for Christian mission	4	Literature survey (theoretical framework)	
Missional Exegesis of NT	4	Cross-cultural communication	4		
Missional Theology of OT	4	Gospel advanced in pluralistic context	4		
Missional Theology of NT	4	Apologetic for missions	4		
Biblical & Christian Ethics	4	Church planting, dev. and growth	5		
Research Methods in Theology	4	Research proposal	9		
Elective (Independent studies)	4				
Field Education 1	2				

8 Contextualiza-tion Courses	30	5 Thesis Comple-tion & Defence	30	Doctoral Research Seminar 3	30
Principles of conflict transformation	3	Contemporary issues in missiology	6	Literature survey (theoretical framework)	
World contemporary issues	4	Research literature	4		
History of Miss-Church in DRC	6	Empirical investigation	4		
Leading change for missional church	4	Research findings and discussion	4		
Evangelism: theories & strategies	5	Thesis submission and defence	12		
Interreligious Dialogue	3				
Faith & culture for community transformation	3				
Field Education 2	2				
THIRD YEAR					
8 Ministry-Oriented Courses	30			Doctoral Research Seminar 4	30
Spiritual formation and warfare	3			Empirical investigation	
Homiletics & cross-cultural communication	4			Findings and discussion	
Church planting, dev. & growth	5				
Christian family	4				
Holistic ministries: theories & practice	4				
Strategies of mission	4				
Elective 2	4				
Field education 2	2				

4 Research and Ministries	30		Thesis Completion & Defence	30
Research methodology	5		Implications & recommendations	
Internship (2 months)	10		Thesis submission & defence	
Professional Exit Workshops	3			
Project paper writing & presentation	12			

*Add the concerned PhD research concentration from the list of Table 6.3

Note: 1 credit equals 30h divided as follows: Bachelor (15h of contact, 5h of tutorial, 10h of research) and Master (10h of contact, 20h of research).

To better serve the church for its God-given glocal and holistic mission, each of these levels of study focuses on some features (table 6.3): ministry-based study orientations (bachelor), learning and research orientations (master), and expanding knowledge through research concentrations (doctorate). The proposed study program is done in the context of theological education either within a department or within a research center.

6.5.2.1 Undergraduate Program: Bachelor of Theology in Missiology

Referring to the Bologna Process, the Bachelor of Theology in Missiology will have the main purpose of qualifying students to acquire knowledge and skills in missiology, apply the acquired knowledge and skills, make documented and innovative judgements with reference to these knowledge and skills and communicate gained insights with freedom and competence. While all students will be required to undertake common teaching units and courses, opportunity will be given to each student to choose a specific orientation and to concentrate their field education, independent studies and final project on it. By the end of their studies, bachelor students should have a broad and coherent body of knowledge with some depth in understanding of concepts, theories and principles to be applied in the setting of God's glocal and holistic mission entrusted to the church.

Table 6.3 Purpose-Driven Missiological Higher Education

BTh Missiology Study orientations	MTh Missiology Research orientations	PhD Missiology Research concentrations
Intercultural Holistic Ministries: *to serve God's glocal and holistic mission across cultures in various capacities and ministries*	**Theology of Mission**: *to learn how mission has been biblically, theologically, philosophically and strategically conceptualized*	**Contemporary Theologies of Mission**: *to build or expand applied knowledge on theologies of mission*
Missional Church Leadership: *to serve churches in pastoral ministries which ignites the whole church to God's glocal and holistic mission*	**History of Missions**: *to learn how mission has been practiced throughout various contexts and generations in regard to God's glocal and holistic mission*	**Missional Theology of Old Testament**: *to build or expand applied knowledge on theology of mission from the perspective of Old Testament*
Apologetics for Missions: *to serve in the ministry of proclaiming, teaching and defending the faith within and out of the church*	**Intercultural Holistic Ministries**: *to learn from anthropological insights how God's glocal and holistic mission can serve people*	**Missional Theology of New Testament**: *to build or expand applied knowledge on theology of mission from the perspective of New Testament*
Mission Education: *to serve the church and Christian ministries to mobilize and train for God's glocal and holistic mission*	**Missional Church Leadership**: *to learn from leadership theories and principles for mission-minded pastoral ministry*	**World Christianity**: *to build or expand applied knowledge on the history of Christianity in different contexts and generations*
	Apologetics for Mission: *to learn how the proclamation and the defence of Christian faith can be done in a context of religious pluralism*	**Intercultural Global Ministries**: *to build or expand applied knowledge on anthropological insights to serve God's glocal and holistic mission*

	Mission Education: *to learn theories and principles of education for God's glocal and holistic mission*	**Missional Church Leadership**: *to build or expand applied knowledge on theories and principles of leadership for God's glocal and holistic mission*
		Apologetics for Mission: *to build or expand applied knowledge on theories and principles of apologetics for God's glocal and holistic mission*
		Missiological Higher Education: *to build or expand applied knowledge on philosophies of education for God's glocal and holistic mission*

Orientation courses for bachelor students should prepare students for concrete ministries, and these courses include electives, field education, internship and research projects, designed as independent studies, not only to encourage students to become interdependent with their instructors in the learning process, but also to bridge the gap between academic perspectives and ministerial perspectives. Students take these courses with a particular ministry in mind. Through field education for instance, the study program will strive to help students integrate academic insights with practical issues of ministry. The field education then becomes a process of including professional skills and personal spiritual life. This is a way to address the need expressed by churches that theological education in the DRC gives the impression of having ceased to be in the service of the church and its mission (see the summary of the findings, section 5.5.5).

Table 6.2 contains two electives, two field education sessions, one internship opportunity and a final problem-based research project. Table 6.3 displays four major ministry-oriented concentrations: (1) Intercultural Holistic Ministries (2) Missional Church Leadership (3) Apologetics for

Mission (4) Mission Education. Based on the fact that bachelor programs in the ongoing educational reform aim at equipping students to undertake professional work, these concentrations will help students to be efficient in holistic ministries throughout various cultures, mission-minded church leadership, proclaiming and defending the Christian faith in a pluralistic context and promoting God's glocal mission at local church level. This study has shown that these aspects of training people for church ministries were missing in the prevailing theological corpus.

The Bachelor of Theology in Missiology should also prepare students to acquire knowledge and skills needed to pursue further studies with a high level of autonomy. Therefore, courses relating to languages (biblical and modern), critical thinking and research must be provided to ensure such an autonomy. In addition, courses pertaining to biblical and theological studies in mission, theory and theology of mission, apologetics for Christian mission, world religions and Christianity and mission across culture and strategies should be included. These teaching units form the foundational basis to prepare students for further studies (e.g. Master, PhD). Besides providing knowledge and skills for further studies, these teaching units will also help students to acquire competences for addressing ministerial problems so far as the teaching-learning process will follow outcomes-based and problem-oriented approaches.

Finally, the formation of the students' character represents an important segment in transforming missiology. Transforming students is not only exemplified by the renewal of mind and knowledge, but also by the transformation of their character. Such a process requires a teaching unit on spiritual formation through which the students will consider and reconsider various subjects, including Basics of Christian Faith, Personal Leadership Development, Biblical and Christian Ethics, Spiritual Formation and Warfare and Christian Family.

To sum up the above description, the following six teaching units and their related courses form the essential of the proposed Bachelor of Theology in Missiology for a transforming missiological education:

Teaching Unit 1: Research and Field Education
1. Theories and Principles of Academic Learning
2. Information Communication Technology

3. Research-Based Academic Writing
4. Critical and Creative Thinking
5. Elective 1 and 2
6. Field Education 1 and 2
7. Research Methodology
8. Internship
9. Professional Exit Workshop
10. Project Paper: Writing and Presentation

Teaching Unit 2: Biblical and Theological Studies for Mission
1. Greek 1 and 2
2. Hebrew 1 and 2
3. Introduction to Old Testament (history and content)
4. Introduction to New Testament (history and content)
5. Missional Exegesis of Old Testament
6. Missional Exegesis of New Testament
7. Introduction to Systematic Theology
8. Introduction to Practical Theology
9. Research Methods in Theological Studies

Teaching Unit 3: Theory and Theologies of Mission
1. Introduction to Missiology
2. Missional Theology of Old Testament
3. Missional Theology of New Testament

Teaching Unit 4: Apologetics for Christian Mission
1. Introduction to Christian Apologetics
2. Introduction to World Religions
3. Introduction to World Christianity
4. Evangelization: History, Theories and Strategies
5. Interreligious Dialogue: History, Theories and Strategies

Teaching Unit 5: Mission across Culture and Strategies
1. History of Mission and Church in the DRC
2. Principles of Conflict Transformation
3. World Contemporary Issues
4. Leading Change for Missional Church
5. Faith and Culture for Community Transformation

6. Homiletics and Cross-Cultural Communication
7. Church Planting, Development and Growth
8. Holistic Ministries: Theological Foundation and Contemporary Strategies
9. Strategies of Missions: Historical and Contemporary Issues

Teaching Unit 6: Spiritual Formation
1. Basics of Christian Faith
2. Personal Leadership Development
3. Biblical and Christian Ethics
4. Spiritual Formation and Warfare
5. Christian Family

The crucial question, however, relates to whether the above curriculum would really prepare the students to be in the service of the mission of the church (i.e. to what extent the proposed study program can ensure that graduates will effectively ignite their respective churches for God's glocal mission). The following chart (fig. 6.4) illustrates the answer to such a concern. As one could observe the above description and the study concentrations at bachelor level, missiological education that is done within the context of theological education (e.g. Bachelor *of* Theology *in* Missiology), prepares people who could serve the church for both its local and global ministries.

6.5.2.2 Graduate Program: Master of Theology in Missiology

Master *of* Theology *in* Missiology builds upon the foundational basis laid at the first cycle of Bachelor. At Master level, the students acquire advanced missiological knowledge in the light of recent developments, applied skills for ministerial practice and advanced scholarship for further learning that is mostly self-directed. The Master study program can be done either through coursework (taught Master) or through research (research Master) under the condition that the students passed subjects scheduled for the Bachelor program. Moreover, in the context of the DRC, a research-based Masters will still need more physical contacts during research modules and seminars within the learning community, as discussed earlier in this chapter.

The point is that in a context that values community life and direct interaction, and taking into account the fact that God's mission is to be undertaken by a local community for the global community, a degree pursued and earned in isolation is likely to limit the students. The limitation can relate to learning experience, outcomes and outputs. Instead of enjoying the wealth of community life, isolated students would limit their learning experiences to a reduced core of people, mostly their research supervisors. The outcomes of learning might also have a reduced scope, and the outputs would probably be produced on a limited basis. Isolation in this sense means lack of structured and scheduled contacts and interaction with other scholars including the large learning community.

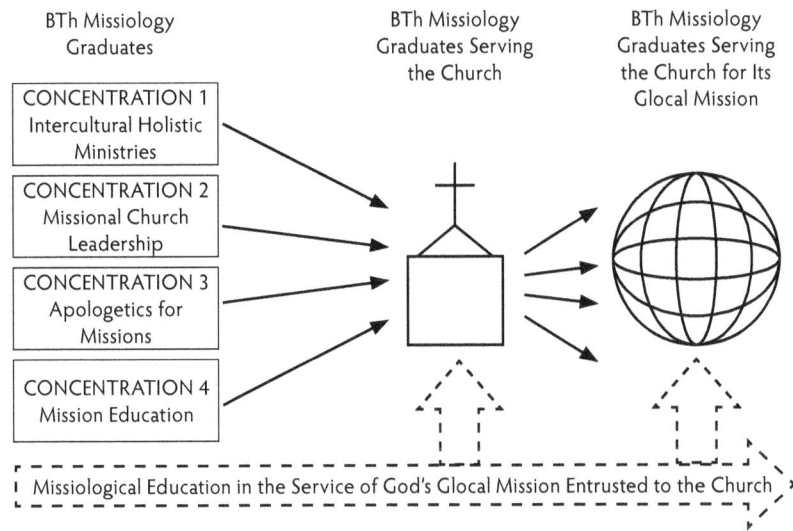

Figure 6.4 How BTh Missiology Graduates Can Serve the Church and Its Glocal Mission

In the process of preparing and equipping master's students for transforming missiology, research concentrations do not function as at bachelor level where the focus is on ministry. The research orientations are rather selected to provide students with the opportunity to acquire cognitive and creative skills for critical review, analysis and synthesis of the existing literature in order to provide solutions with intellectual independence to either abstract or practical problems related to God's glocal mission. Each student could then focus on one of the six research concentrations: (1) Theology of

Mission, to learn how mission has been conceptualized biblically, theologically, philosophically and strategically; (2) History of Missions, to learn how mission has been practiced throughout various contexts and generations with regard to God's glocal and holistic mission; (3) Intercultural Holistic Ministries, to learn from anthropological insights how God's glocal and holistic mission can serve people; (4) Missional Church Leadership, to learn from leadership theories and principles for mission-minded pastoral ministry; (5) Apologetics for Mission, to learn how the proclamation and the defence of Christian faith can be done in a context of religious pluralism; and (6) Mission Education, to learn theories and principles of education for God's glocal and holistic mission.

At master level, a concentration is undertaken through one field education, modules on research proposal and design and the production of an original, relevant, and appropriate problem-based thesis. Unlike the study program for the Bachelor of Theology in Missiology, the program for the Master of Theology in Missiology comprises teaching units through which specific modules are offered in an interdependent delivery method as discussed earlier. The study program for the Master of Theology in Missiology comprises of the following:

Teaching Unit 1: Research and Field Education
1. Research-Based Academic Writing
2. Critical and Creative Thinking
3. Field Education
4. Missiological Research Design
5. Research Proposal
6. Research Literature
7. Empirical Investigation
8. Research Findings and Discussion
9. Thesis (Write-Up, Submission and Defence)

Teaching Unit 2: Biblical and Theological Studies for Mission
1. Old Testament Missional Exegesis
2. New Testament Missional Exegesis

Teaching Unit 3: Theory and Theologies of Mission
1. Perspectives on Missiology
2. Biblical Theology of Mission
3. Contemporary Theologies of Mission
4. Contemporary Issues in Mission and Missiology

Teaching Unit 4: Apologetics for Christian Mission
1. Gospel Advance in Pluralistic Context
2. Apologetics for Missions

Teaching Unit 5: Mission across Culture and Strategies
1. History of World Christianity
2. Issues in African Mission History
3. Races, Ethnicity and Conflict Transformation
4. Cultural Anthropology for Christian Mission
5. Cross-Cultural Communication
6. Church Planting, Development and Growth: Analysis and Evaluation of Trends

Teaching Unit 6: Spiritual Formation
1. Personal Leadership Development
2. Christian Ethics for Global Mission

The same concern raised for the bachelor program applies to the master program. A graduate of Master of Theology in Missiology is expected to render the service to both training institutions and the church. With regard to the relation between theology and missiology, authors have proposed various scenarios, namely integration, independence or dependence.[100] At master level, the proposed study program would concur for both *dependence* on theological education (having a department or a center for missiology within or out of the Faculty of Theology) and *integration* into the theological curriculum (having students of theological institutions get mission insights in each of their courses based on the prevailing fourfold departments of theological institutions). However, while the proposed study program is conceived in the context of dependence, its result can be used in the context of integration where missiology graduates can join the faculty members to

---

100. Bosch, *Transforming Mission*, 480.

facilitate the insertion of mission insights into the theological corpus (fig. 6.5). The crucial question, therefore, relates to whether the above curriculum would really prepare the students to be in the service of both theological institutions and the mission of the church. In other words, to what extent the proposed study program ensures that graduates effectively ignite theological institutions and their respective churches for God's glocal mission. The following chart (fig. 6.5) illustrates the answer to such a concern, because, as already indicated, the proposed study program is done in the context of theological education (e.g. Master *of* Theology *in* Missiology) to prepare candidates who could serve theological institutions (at bachelor level) and church for both local and global ministries.

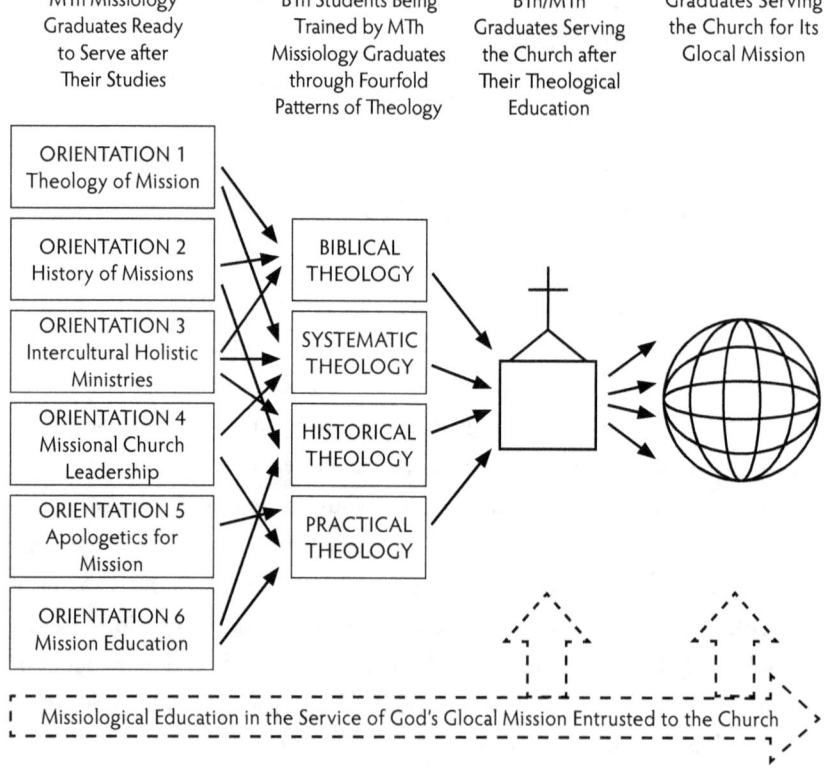

Figure 6.5 How MTh Missiology Graduates Can Serve Theological Institutions and the Church

6.5.2.3 Postgraduate Program: Doctor of Theology (or PhD) in Missiology

The doctoral studies in transforming missiology will strive to help students acquire skills for using the existing body of knowledge in order to research and develop new knowledge relating to God's glocal mission. Though being offered essentially as a research-based study program, doctoral studies should be undertaken in the context of a learning community in which students independently and critically learn theoretical propositions and competently share their own propositions with a spirit of accountability. Accountability has to do with integrity and ethical considerations to ensure the reliability and the validity of the research findings. It also has to do with the character and the commitment of students because missiological education should serve God's glocal mission entrusted to the church in different contexts. Doctoral studies in missiology should prepare for the ministry to teach and do research, but also to serve the church and its mission. As Starcher contends, doctoral studies in the African context should be done according to the task awaiting candidates.[101]

To allow graduates to contribute to both academic scholarship and professional practice at national and international levels, it is a proposition here that the doctoral study program could be undertaken through the following research concentrations: (1) Contemporary Theologies of Mission, to build or expand applied knowledge on theologies of mission; (2) Missional Theology of the Old Testament, to build or expand applied knowledge on the theology of mission from the perspective of the Old Testament; (3) Missional Theology of the New Testament, to build or expand applied knowledge on the theology of mission from the perspective of the New Testament; (4) World Christianity, to build or expand applied knowledge on the history of Christianity in different contexts and generations; (5) Intercultural Global Ministries, to build or expand applied knowledge on anthropological insights to serve God's glocal and holistic mission; (6) Missional Church Leadership, to build or expand applied knowledge on the theories and principles of leadership for God's glocal and holistic mission; (7) Apologetics for Mission, to build or expand applied knowledge on the theories and principles

---

101. Starcher, "Africans in Pursuit," 107–124.

of apologetics for God's glocal and holistic mission; and (8) Missiological Higher Education, to build or expand applied knowledge on the philosophies of education for God's glocal and holistic mission. As one could realize, these research concentrations will help graduates provide a leadership either in the educational setting of scholars or in the practical environment of professionals.

Subsequently, doctoral seminar modules should allow students to focus on their specific research concentrations, which will finally culminate in the production of an original, relevant and appropriate problem-based thesis. For instance, besides other common seminar modules, a doctoral student whose research concentration is "Contemporary theologies of mission" should take the following four specific prerequisite modules on (1) the historical development of contemporary theologies of mission; (2) contemporary issues in the study of theologies of mission; (3) research methods in contemporary theologies of mission; and (4) contemporary theologies of mission and mission imperatives. These prerequisite modules relate to the historical development of a given research concentration, its contemporary issues, its research methods and its relatedness to mission imperatives.

The concern raised for the master program also applies to doctoral program. A graduate of doctoral program in missiology is expected to render the service to both training institutions and the church. At doctoral level, the proposed study program in this study aligns with both *dependence* on theological education (having a department or a center for missiology within or out of the Faculty of Theology) and *integration* into theological curriculum (having students of theological institutions acquire mission insights in each of their courses based on the prevailing fourfold departments of theological institutions). While the proposed doctoral study program is conceived in the context of dependence, its result can be used in the context of integration where missiology graduates can join the faculty members to facilitate the insertion of mission insights into the theological corpus (fig. 6.6). Again, the crucial question would relate to whether the above curriculum could prepare the students to be in the service of both theological institutions and the mission of the church. In other words, to what extent the proposed doctoral study program ensures that graduates will effectively ignite theological institutions and their respective churches for God's glocal mission.

The following chart (fig. 6.6.) illustrates the answer to such a concern, because, as described above, missiological education is intended to be done in the context of theological education (e.g. Doctor *of* Theology [or PhD] *in* Missiology) to prepare candidates who could serve theological institutions and the church for both local and global ministries.

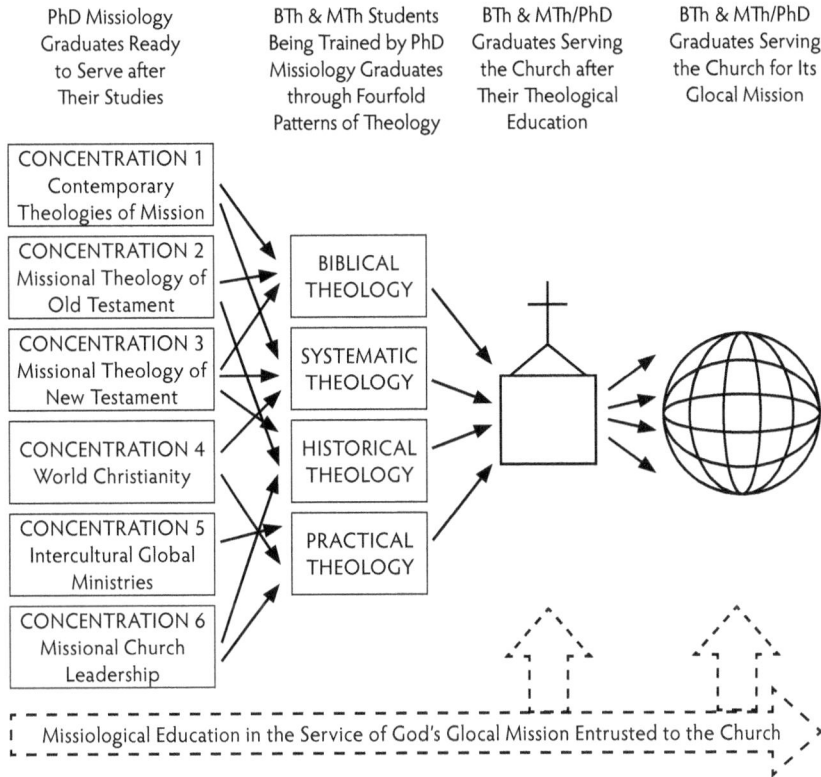

Figure 6.6 How PhD Missiology Graduates Can Serve Theological Institutions and the Church

For instance, if mission insights lack in the prevailing Theology of New Testament in theological institutions, a missiology graduate who joins the Faculty of Theology could compensate such a gap with Missional Theology of New Testament. Similarly, Biblical Theology could be complemented with Biblical Theology of Mission, or Exegesis of New Testament with Missional Exegesis of New Testament, etc. Today, theological institutions can enjoy the company of missiologists who would bring the missing link to the nets that are prepared for God's harvest. As mentioned earlier in chapter 2 (section 2.2.2), authors have shown that missiologists have put their expertise gained through various disciplines of humanities and social sciences in the service of *missio Dei*.[102] Bosch and Wright represent a few samples.[103] *The Theology of the Christian Mission* (edited by Anderson) represents another example. Authors have put their expertise in the service of *missio Dei* and theological education.

6.5.3 Evaluating Missiological Education

When providing educational activities, it is essential to determine whether or not these activities achieve the expected outcomes and how to upgrade and improve these activities. At each level of the study program, evaluation should be done for each course or module session before (pre-session), during (in-session), after (post-session) and for the overall study program. The pre-session evaluation will serve to assess whether or not the students have the required knowledge (or theoretical qualification) to further their learning experience. This evaluation is done to orient and facilitate the teaching-learning process. The instructor will be able to adapt the teaching activities to the level of students, as the latter will be encouraged to fill the gap by adding more time for their independent studies. The in-session evaluation, commonly known as formative or continuous assessments, will help the instructor to measure the progress pace and readjust the teaching activities, and will enable students to realize the existing gap in their own learning process and readjust their learning activities. The post-session evaluation, known as summative assessment, will help the instructors update and upgrade the teaching-learning process.

While session evaluation (pre, in and post) is done for each course or module, the evaluation of the overall study program could be done after five years of implementation. For instance, for a time frame of five years starting in 2018, the evaluation of the overall study program will be done after the graduation of three bachelor promotions, four master promotions, and three doctoral promotions (table 6.4). Such an experience will require

---

102. Priest and DeGeorge, "Doctoral Dissertations."
103. Bosch, *Transforming Mission*; Wright, *Mission of God*.

a 2018–2023 plan or "Vision 2023" by the end of which the outcomes will be measured in terms of the number of graduates, the extent to which their churches are involved in God's glocal and holistic mission, the number of instructors of mission-related studies that have been produced, the concentrations that have been more attractive and for which reasons and the extent to which the research productions have been in the service of *missio Dei*, etc.

Table 6.4 Evaluation Plan for the Overall Study Program

	Academic Years	Bachelor (BTh)	Master (MTh)	Doctorate (PhD)
1	2018–2019			
2	2019–2020		2020 First promotion	
3	2020–2021	2021 First promotion	2021 Second promotion	2021 First promotion
4	2021–2022	2022 Second promotion	2022 Third promotion	2022 Second promotion
5	2022–2023	2023 Third promotion	2023 Fourth promotion	2023 Third promotion
	5	3 promotions	4 promotions	3 promotions

Nevertheless, evaluators of a study program should expect surprise with regard to the performance of master graduates who might not have gone through the bachelor program proposed here. The foundational program of the Bachelor of Theology in Missiology could have provided master candidates with more perspectives in their reflection and actions. The same observation applies to doctoral graduates who might have missed the opportunity of taking master program proposed here. The foundational modules of Master of Theology in Missiology could have enlarged their horizon before being concentrated on their specific area of missiological research. Besides the educational background of the students, variables in the findings of the evaluation of a study program could also be influenced by other conditions listed earlier in section 6.5.1.

6.5.4 Need for Applied Research Projects in Missiology

To achieve its transformational purpose, missiological education would strongly require applied research projects. Applied research purposes the finding of a solution to an immediate problem facing a society or an organization.[104] The goal for a missiological research from such a perspective would be to provide a solution to the observed deficit of the church to responsibly involve in God's glocal and holistic mission. To be productive as far as the vision for transforming missiology is concerned, the missiological research should deal with an applied question: "What should we *understand* before we *know* what to *do* in a given context?" The need is to understand the facts and acquire more theoretical insights about these facts, before proposing contextual plans and strategies to meet the need or to solve the faced problems.

Some biblical references provide a good model of applied research for *missio Dei*. The biblical foundation of applied research can be depicted through the writings of Luke (Luke 1:1–4; Acts 1:1–4), Paul (1 Cor 10:6, 11, 12) and Peter (1 Pet 1:8–13). These writings demonstrate that research can use either written or oral sources. In the three cases, a practical problem was observed and defined, a research question was clearly formulated (either in affirmative or declarative form), a research purpose was stated, methods for data collection were identified and implemented, the result and its implications were reported. A research problem could be an idea, a set of beliefs, an action, a behavior, or a statement, etc. It could also be a positive or negative experience. For each case, the identified practical problem was connected with the life and the mission of God's people. The content of the above passages distil the idea that God's mission was experienced and accomplished by Israel as God's people, by the prophets, by Jesus Christ and his disciples. The outcomes of the research were put in writing to serve as a lesson for readers of all time. It is however interesting to note that not all aspects on the identified problem were discussed in a given research. One could generate some other questions for future research. A good example is the fact that Luke couldn't cover everything in the Gospel of Luke. He needed more research, and the book of Acts of Apostles complemented the Gospel of Luke.

---

104. Kothari, *Research Methodology*, 2.

Towards a Transforming Missiology for a Fruitful Missiological Education 357

These various statements support the need for a formalized, applied and successful missiological research that aims at solving a problem. Otherwise, the interpretation and application of *missio Dei* may not reveal the true will of the initiator of the mission. As discussed in previous chapters, the modern missiologists recognize the triune God to be the initiator of mission and the first missionary.[105] God the Father is the source of the mission, the Son is the message of the mission, and the Holy Spirit is the power of the mission. The church is the visible expression of God's mission, and the world is the target of the mission.[106] God and his creation make the reality of *missio Dei*.

God expects details of his mission to be preserved and passed on from one generation to the next. God's unrevealed things are for him and for his glory; but those he reveals "belong to us and to our children forever, that we may follow all the words of this law" (Deut 29:29). Everything that God reveals in writing, through deeds or words, through the circumstances of Christian or non-Christian life, all must be investigated and analyzed to serve as a lesson to his people. The Apostle Paul emphasized this truth by writing to Timothy: "All Scripture is God-breathed and is useful for teaching, rebuking, correcting and training in rrighteousness, so that the servant of God may be thoroughly equipped for every good work" (2 Tim 3:16, 17). It is important that the details of the mission of God be researched, written and share with other generations: "Write, therefore, what you have seen, what is now and what will take place later" (Rev 1:19). "Blessed is the one who reads aloud the words of this prophecy, and blessed are those who hear it and take to heart what is written in it, because the time is near" (Rev 1:3). Missiological research should be undertaken, reported and shared as to produce concrete effects of a renewed perception and informed actions. Transformation is made possible by the renewal of the mind in order to understand and follow God's will (cf. Rom 12:1, 2).

Such an endeavour will require the following features to be seriously taken into account: the purpose of a missiological research, the prerequisites for a missiological research, the steps for an incentive missiological research, the outcomes of a missiological research project, the development of a community of missiological research, and the application to a given setting.

---

105. Scherer and Bevans, *New Directions*; Tennent, *Introduction*.
106. Van Rheenen, *Missions*, 13–35.

Table 6.5 Biblical Foundation of Missiological Applied Research

Steps in research	LUKE Luke 1:1–4; Acts 1:1–4	PAUL 1 Corinthians 10:6, 11, 12	PETER 1 Peter 1:8–13
Problem	Theophilus had just embraced the Christian faith but was still ignorant of the accuracy of the historical facts and the theological basis of the life and ministry of Jesus	It was amazing that people that received many privileges (1 Cor 10:1–5) were rejected and exterminated by God	It was also surprising to see people love and believe what they have not seen, embracing salvation with great joy
Question	What should Theophilus exactly know?	What is the reason for us?	Why prophets were so concerned?
Purpose	To produce in writing accurate facts	To demonstrate the *raison d'être* of these historical accounts	To understand the time and circumstances of the salvation
Method	Gather verbal and written account and evidence	Collect oral and written history (cf. Deut 6:6–9, 20–25; Acts 7)	Proceed with prayer, and probably with written consultation
Result	The content of the Gospel of Luke and the Acts of Apostles	The content of the Old Testament	The promises were indeed for believers
Implications	Know the certainty of the teachings Theophilus received for him to behave accordingly	Have good conduct and fear of God	Sharpen their intelligence in order to continue in hope
Future research	Future research could deal with the question "Why?"	Future research could deal with the question "What if the accounts were not written?"	Future research could deal with the question "Why these believers were so joyful?"

1. **Purpose of missiological research**: The research projects are not undertaken just to satisfy personal curiosity or for just an academic degree. Instead, students will embark on a research project in order to address an existential problem which relates to God's glocal and holistic mission. A well-articulated research proposal should

include the research background (to state the researcher's personal experience as it relates to the proposed research), the practical problem (to state and substantiate what has been observed by the researcher), the research problem (to state the specific research preoccupation and substantiate it through a preliminary literature review), the research purpose (to state and substantiate what the researcher would like to discover from the proposed research), the research questions (to motivate and state the central question and its related sub-questions for the proposed research), the research methodology (to identify and justify the nature of the research and the techniques for data collection and analysis), concepts clarification (to provide a clear understanding of key words and concepts of the proposed research), and the provisional chapters division (to give an overview of the major parts of the research).

There is no standardized structure of a research proposal. Except the fact that each university suggests its own guidelines with which the students have to comply, the major difference relates to whether the research is quantitative or qualitative. For some authors, while the proposal for quantitative research is highly prestructured and preplanned, that of qualitative research is less structured and preplanned. However, regardless their particularities, universities share important components for any type of research, be it quantitative or qualitative. It is therefore ambitious to join Punch in saying that a qualitative research is not as prestructured and preplanned as a quantitative research. Both research types require an outline which is set before the study is carried out and helps the researcher to stay objective and neutral. The headings and the number of pages of a research proposal depend on the requirements that each university recommends while also attending to the scientific exigencies of each type of research (quantitative or qualitative). In general, 15 to 30 pages are required. Table 6.6 provides a sample of structures of research proposals and their most essential elements:[107]

---

107. Though only four structures are highlighted here, many other outlines exist. See for instance Bui (*How to Write*), Smith (*Academic Writing*), Tichapondwa (*Preparing Your Dissertation*), Kritzinger (*Tutorial Letter*).

Table 6.6 Samples of the Outlines of a Research Proposal

	Denscombe (2012)	STREAM[107] (2010)	NWU Theology (2012)	Transforming Missiology
1	Title	Title page	Proposed title and key words	Title page
2	Keywords	Abstract	Abstract	Title
3	Aims	Working title	Background and problem statement/Rationale	Key words (list only)
4	Background	Background of the research	Preliminary literature study	Abstract
5	Literature review	Problem statement	Research problem, aim and objectives	Background
6	Research questions	Key research questions	Central theoretical argument	Practical and research problem (Literature included)
7	Methods	Detailed literature review	Research design/Methodology	Research purpose (aim)
8	Planning and resources	Importance of the research	Concept clarification (if applicable)	Research questions
9	Ethics	Methodology	Ethical consideration (if applicable)	Central theoretical statement
10	Outcomes	Timescale/Research planning	Provisional classification of chapters	Methodology (Ethics included)
11	-	Hypothesis	References	Clarification of concepts

---

108. STREAM: Strengthen African Higher Education Through Academic Mobility.

	Denscombe (2012)	STREAM (2010)	NWU Theology (2012)	Transforming Missiology
12	-	Source list	Proposed research schedule/ time frame	Provisional chapters division
13	-	-	Schematic presentation	References
14	-	-	-	Proposed research schedule
15	-	-	-	Schematic presentation

2. **Prerequisites for missiological research**: A personal experience in conducting and supervising research projects has taught that without a minimum of prerequisites a researcher is likely predisposed to either give up or produce a poor piece of work. These prerequisites relate to the researcher's own life and include character, knowledge and skill. The missiologist's character and attitude provide a good setting to start and achieve a research project. A character of humility and cooperation is important in the researcher's relationships with supervisors and colleagues; equally important for the needed ingredients of a researcher, is an attitude of endurance and of high morale to achieve what has been started. Students need a conducive spiritual and human environment to build their personalities (character and attitude). Required knowledge constitutes another required ingredient for a successful research project. The experience has shown that without prior epistemological theories in a field of study, the researcher will hardly, poorly and stressfully achieve the aims of a research project. Students need clear and updated academic directions in both scientific research in general and in their specific field of study in particular. Another required ingredient is the skill to craft and develop a research project through critical and creative thinking. This skill can be acquired and developed.

3. **Steps in incentive missiological research**: Incentive research is research that leads to action. As in any scientific inquiry, the process includes the identification of the problem, the evaluation of the existing literature, the definition of the research methodology, the presentation and interpretation of the findings and the analysis and discussion of the findings. As explained in the first chapter (section 1.8), the thesis which generated this book followed these steps. However, the arrangement of these steps can be done based on the nature, scope and size of a given research project. There should be a strong recommendation that students produce original, appropriate, relevant and plagiarism-free research projects according to the requirements of a scientific inquiry. However, the following question is critical while coaching students toward the completion of their thesis or dissertation projects: "How many chapters should a thesis or a dissertation be made of?"

At graduate or postgraduate level in missiological studies, the question becomes even more challenging. The challenge does not result only from the multidisciplinary nature of missiological research, but much more from the necessity of assigning clear function to each chapter. On one side, the researcher will face a diversity of contributions from various disciplines. For instance, in a missiological research, one might find it necessary to acquire biblical, historical, and social science insights in order to fully understand the issue under consideration. Therefore, an unexperienced researcher would wonder how to deal with such a multidisciplinary condition of their research. On the other side, the researcher will struggle with the demanding task of defining the function and content of each chapter. Such an undertaking becomes even more demanding as long as the flow of ideas and the unit of the whole research are highly concerned.

The following chapters division is based on the principle that a research should undergo a cyclical process made of five steps:

problem, literature, methodology, findings, and discussion.[109] The content of an acceptable thesis must contain chapters that accomplish specific functions: (1) Introduction where the missiological problem is amply described and substantiated, (2) Literature review where the researcher explores and evaluates the existing body of literature addressing the similar or related issues, (3) Research design where the researcher selects and describes in details how data were collected and analyzed, (4) Result where the researcher presents and interprets the findings, and (5) Discussion or Conclusion where the researcher discusses the result and proposes recommendations. The researcher could frame the title of each chapter according to the content of the work, but each chapter must achieve its expected function described in the chart below (table 6.7). As far as missiological research is concern, the following chapters division is suggested due to the fact that it provides a clear direction of what the researcher is expected to achieve. Nevertheless, depending on the scope of each research, these steps can bear different names (titles). They can be labelled as "chapters," each having several sections, or as "parts," each having several chapters. Therefore, irrespective of the numbers of chapters or parts, the thesis should undergo a cyclical process of five steps. The suggestion here is that students produce 120–140 pages for MTh and 220–320 pages for PhD exclusive of front and back matters.

---

109. Bui, *How to Write*; Smith, *Academic Writing*; Elliston, *Introduction*; Sampson, "A Guide"; Tichapondwa *Preparing Your Dissertation*.

Table 6.7 Chapters Division of a Dissertation or a Thesis in Missiology

Step	Steps and Task Description	MTh Dissertation	PhD Thesis
1	**Problem** (or Introduction) *Why your research is important and to whom it is important?*	**Chapter 1** (16–18 pages) Problem Substantiation	**Chapter 1** (20–30 pages) Problem Substantiation
2	**Literature** (Theoretical search) *Which concepts, theories and frameworks already exist in the literature on the issue, and what is missing from the existing literature as regards your proposed thesis?*	**Chapter 2** (30–35 pages) Theoretical and Conceptual Frameworks (on key missiological themes of the research)	**Chapter 2** (40–50 pages) Theoretical and Conceptual Frameworks (on key missiological themes of the research)
		Chapter 3 (30–35 pages) Missional exegesis or Scripture-based theological study, or historical perspectives	**Chapter 3** (40–50 pages) Theoretical and Conceptual Frameworks (on key missiological themes of the research)
			Chapter 4 (40–50 pages) Theoretical and Conceptual Frameworks (on missional exegesis/ theology or on historical exploration)
3	**Methodology** (Empirical search) *Which type of research it is and why? Which kind of methods/techniques were used to collect and analyze data? Why?*	**Chapter 4** (16–18 pages) Method design for data collection and analysis, and Findings presentation and interpretation (not analysis yet!)	**Chapter 5** (20–30 pages) Method design for data collection and analysis and Findings presentation and interpretation (not analysis yet!)

Step	Steps and Task Description	MTh Dissertation	PhD Thesis
4	**Findings** (Empirical search) *Now that you have some findings from your empirical research, what are these findings and so what?*	**Chapter 5** **(28–40 pages)** Findings synthesis, analysis and discussion, and practical recommendations (to solve the problem and for future research)	**Chapter 6** **(20–40 pages)** Findings synthesis, analysis and in-depth evaluation of the result based on theoretical research
5	**Discussion** (Recommendations) *Based on some findings from both theoretical and empirical research (see 2, 3, 4 above), what next?*		**Chapter 7** **(40–60 pages)** Theoretical and practical contributions, and recommendations
	Total Pages	**120–140 pages**	**220–320 pages**
	Appendices	Appendices	Appendices
	Bibliography	Bibliography	Bibliography

4. **Outcomes of a missiological research project**: Sometimes it is not easy to go through a research report (thesis, article, and book) and get a clear picture of its outcomes. The outcomes of a given research project are both the findings (the answer to the central and sub-questions) and the recommendations (to solve the specific raised problem and for future research to expand the knowledge). Transforming missiology requires such an approach to research if the service is expected to be rendered to the church and to its God-given glocal and holistic mission.

Moreover, while undertaking a missiological research using a problem-based approach, the researcher is expected to move from mere conceptual or practical questions, privileging instead applied question. As already discussed previously, whereas the conceptual question focuses on "What should we know?" and the practical question wrestles with "What should we do?," the applied question emphasizes, "What should we understand before we know what to do?" Good questions lead to insightful and constructive elements of the answers, the latter being actually based on a clearly stated problem. Such a concern demonstrates the importance of a problem-based approach in doing a postgraduate research in missiology. According to W. G. Cunningham and P. A. Cordeiro, a problem-based learning is "an instructional approach that uses typical problems of practice as the context for an in-depth investigation of core content."[110] It is about a practical problem which leads to either learning experience or research activities.

5. **Developing a community of missiological research:** Applied research cannot be done in isolation. Instead, it requires a community of sharing and interaction. Such a community is both a learning and an academic community and an apprenticeship and life community. These two aspects cannot be found in a closed setting of the academic institution, or in the pragmatic setting of the church ministry. There should be a continuing oscillation between the two communities. The missiologist should move from the academic community to observe and learn from the ministry community, and *vice versa*. A one-sided research is likely to become irrelevant and unfruitful. While some community members live out the problems without spending time in reflection, other members have the opportunity of building theories to address these problems. Therefore, in the research process the missiologist will learn from both educated and uneducated community members; from theorists and practitioners; from realistic life of daily experience and from idealistic world of knowledge and assumptions.

---

110. Cunningham and Cordeiro, *Educational Leadership*, 354.

Figure 6.7 Missiological Study Areas and Application Settings

6. **Settings of application:** Applied research should have a clear and delimited setting of application. A research is then carried out "with special reference to" a given setting (fig. 6.7). Based on the context of African Christianity, the following settings could be considered for a fruitful and meaningful applied research in missiology: (1) Mainline-related churches, (2) African Initiated Churches, (3) African immigrant (diaspora) churches, (4) Contemporary religions and society, (5) Global and intercultural ministries, (6) Community holistic transformation, (7) Higher Christian education. For instance, a master research project done in History of Missions can be applied (or be carried out with special reference) to one of the above settings. Similarly, a doctoral research project undertaken in the area of contemporary theologies of mission can be applied to one of the above settings. There is one thing to choose a study area,

but there is another thing to apply the study to a given setting. Eight doctoral students can work on contemporary theologies of mission while having seven different settings of application. Even within one given setting, e.g. Mainline-related churches, there are various sub-settings. For instance, Baptist Church, Methodist Church, Presbyterian Church, Lutheran Church, Anglican church, etc. Even within a sub-setting, e.g. Baptist Church, several sub-sub-settings can be identified: American, British, Norwegian, Swedish Baptist churches, etc. Applied research should have a clear and delimited setting of application. A research is then carried out "with special reference to" a given setting.

More details are provided through charts (table 6.8 to 6.14) as they display how to correlate the study areas with the application settings.

Table 6.8 Missiological Studies Applied to Mainline-Related Churches

Perspectives on Missiology Study Areas	
1	**Contemporary Theologies of Mission**: At Master level to learn how mission has been biblically, theologically, philosophically and strategically conceptualized by evangelicals, ecumenicals, Pentecostal and other bodies; At doctoral level to build or expand applied knowledge on theologies of mission.
2	**Missional Theology of Old Testament**: At Master level to learn how the Old Testament makes a basis for God's mission through the experience of God's people and community; At doctoral level to build or expand applied knowledge on theology of mission from the perspective of Old Testament.
3	**Missional Theology of New Testament**: At Master level to learn how the New Testament makes a basis for God's mission through the experience of God's people and community; At doctoral level to build or expand applied knowledge on theology of mission from the perspective of New Testament.
4	**World Christianity**: At Master level to learn how mission has been practiced throughout various contexts and generations in regard to God's glocal and holistic mission; At doctoral level to build or expand applied knowledge on the history of Christianity in different contexts and generations.

5	**Intercultural Global Ministries**: At Master level to learn from anthropological insights how God's glocal and holistic mission can serve people of various contexts and cultures; At doctoral level to build or expand applied knowledge on anthropological insights to serve God's glocal and holistic mission.
6	**Missional Church Leadership**: At Master level to learn from leadership theories and principles for mission-minded pastoral ministry; At doctoral level to build or expand applied knowledge on theories and principles of leadership for God's glocal and holistic mission.
7	**Apologetics for Mission**: At Master level to learn how the proclamation and the defence of Christian faith can be done in a context of religious pluralism; At doctoral level to build or expand applied knowledge on theories and principles of apologetics for God's glocal and holistic mission.
8	**Missiological Higher Education**: At Master level to learn theories and principles of education for God's glocal and holistic mission; At doctoral level to build or expand applied knowledge on philosophies of education for God's glocal and holistic mission.
Explanation of the Application Settings	
Mainline-related churches are historical churches initiated through Western missionary movements of the 19th and the 20th centuries. Examples: Baptist, Methodist, Presbyterian, Mennonite, Lutheran, Anglican, Reformed churches. In this case, missionaries were *carriers* of these churches or denominations from their home countries. Some of these churches generated other "new mainline churches" through split and division on the mission field. There are related Baptist, Methodist, Presbyterian, Mennonite, Lutheran, Anglican, Reformed churches initiated on the mission field. In this case, missionaries were *founder*s of these neo-churches or neo-denominations from the mission field.	

Table 6.9 Missiological Studies Applied to African Initiated Churches

Perspectives on Missiology Study Areas	
1	**Contemporary Theologies of Mission**: At Master level to learn how mission has been biblically, theologically, philosophically and strategically conceptualized by evangelicals, ecumenicals, Pentecostal and other bodies; At doctoral level to build or expand applied knowledge on theologies of mission.
2	**Missional Theology of Old Testament**: At Master level to learn how the Old Testament makes a basis for God's mission through the experience of God's people and community; At doctoral level to build or expand applied knowledge on theology of mission from the perspective of Old Testament.
3	**Missional Theology of New Testament**: At Master level to learn how the New Testament makes a basis for God's mission through the experience of God's people and community; At doctoral level to build or expand applied knowledge on theology of mission from the perspective of New Testament.
4	**World Christianity**: At Master level to learn how mission has been practiced throughout various contexts and generations in regard to God's glocal and holistic mission; At doctoral level to build or expand applied knowledge on the history of Christianity in different contexts and generations.
5	**Intercultural Global Ministries**: At Master level to learn from anthropological insights how God's glocal and holistic mission can serve people of various contexts and cultures; At doctoral level to build or expand applied knowledge on anthropological insights to serve God's glocal and holistic mission.
6	**Missional Church Leadership**: At Master level to learn from leadership theories and principles for mission-minded pastoral ministry; At doctoral level to build or expand applied knowledge on theories and principles of leadership for God's glocal and holistic mission.
7	**Apologetics for Mission**: At Master level to learn how the proclamation and the defence of Christian faith can be done in a context of religious pluralism; At doctoral level to build or expand applied knowledge on theories and principles of apologetics for God's glocal and holistic mission.

8	**Missiological Higher Education**: At Master level to learn theories and principles of education for God's glocal and holistic mission; At doctoral level to build or expand applied knowledge on philosophies of education for God's glocal and holistic mission.
Explanation of the Application Settings	
African initiated churches are local congregations and denominations initiated by African without being the emanation of the mainline-related churches. Some of these churches may even bear names such as Baptist, Methodists, etc. or not. Most of these churches have a strong Pentecostal or charismatic orientation. They bear names that reflect biblical conviction of the founders. Examples: Deeper Life Church, Lighthouse Church, Restoration Church, Bethany Holy Church, Winners Chapel, New Hope Church, etc.	

Table 6.10 Missiological Studies Applied to African Immigrant (Diaspora) Churches

	Perspectives on Missiology Study Areas
1	**Contemporary Theologies of Mission**: At Master level to learn how mission has been biblically, theologically, philosophically and strategically conceptualized by evangelicals, ecumenicals, Pentecostal and other bodies; At doctoral level to build or expand applied knowledge on theologies of mission.
2	**Missional Theology of Old Testament**: At Master level to learn how the Old Testament makes a basis for God's mission through the experience of God's people and community; At doctoral level to build or expand applied knowledge on theology of mission from the perspective of Old Testament.
3	**Missional Theology of New Testament**: At Master level to learn how the New Testament makes a basis for God's mission through the experience of God's people and community; At doctoral level to build or expand applied knowledge on theology of mission from the perspective of New Testament.
4	**World Christianity**: At Master level to learn how mission has been practiced throughout various contexts and generations in regard to God's glocal and holistic mission; At doctoral level to build or expand applied knowledge on the history of Christianity in different contexts and generations.

5	**Intercultural Global Ministries**: At Master level to learn from anthropological insights how God's glocal and holistic mission can serve people of various contexts and cultures; At doctoral level to build or expand applied knowledge on anthropological insights to serve God's glocal and holistic mission.
6	**Missional Church Leadership**: At Master level to learn from leadership theories and principles for mission-minded pastoral ministry; At doctoral level to build or expand applied knowledge on theories and principles of leadership for God's glocal and holistic mission.
7	**Apologetics for Mission**: At Master level to learn how the proclamation and the defence of Christian faith can be done in a context of religious pluralism; At doctoral level to build or expand applied knowledge on theories and principles of apologetics for God's glocal and holistic mission.
8	**Missiological Higher Education**: At Master level to learn theories and principles of education for God's glocal and holistic mission; At doctoral level to build or expand applied knowledge on philosophies of education for God's glocal and holistic mission.

Explanation of the Application Settings

African immigrant (diaspora) churches are initiated by Africans out of their own countries either on the continent or outside the continent. These churches usually started either as the continuation of the work that originated from the home country or a new initiative that emerges from the hosting country. They can be considered as evidence of engagement to *missio Dei*.

These churches could also be considered as African initiated churches in the diaspora context. Most of them have a strong Pentecostal or charismatic orientation. They bear names that reflect biblical conviction of the founders. Examples: Deeper Life Church, Lighthouse Church, Restoration Church, Bethany Holy Church, Winners Chapel, New Hope Church, etc.

Table 6.11 Missiological Studies Applied to Contemporary Religions and Society

Perspectives on Missiology Study Areas	
1	**Contemporary Theologies of Mission**: At Master level to learn how mission has been biblically, theologically, philosophically and strategically conceptualized by evangelicals, ecumenicals, Pentecostal and other bodies; At doctoral level to build or expand applied knowledge on theologies of mission.
2	**Missional Theology of Old Testament**: At Master level to learn how the Old Testament makes a basis for God's mission through the experience of God's people and community; At doctoral level to build or expand applied knowledge on theology of mission from the perspective of Old Testament.
3	**Missional Theology of New Testament**: At Master level to learn how the New Testament makes a basis for God's mission through the experience of God's people and community; At doctoral level to build or expand applied knowledge on theology of mission from the perspective of New Testament.
4	**World Christianity**: At Master level to learn how mission has been practiced throughout various contexts and generations in regard to God's glocal and holistic mission; At doctoral level to build or expand applied knowledge on the history of Christianity in different contexts and generations.
5	**Intercultural Global Ministries**: At Master level to learn from anthropological insights how God's glocal and holistic mission can serve people of various contexts and cultures; At doctoral level to build or expand applied knowledge on anthropological insights to serve God's glocal and holistic mission.
6	**Missional Church Leadership**: At Master level to learn from leadership theories and principles for mission-minded pastoral ministry; At doctoral level to build or expand applied knowledge on theories and principles of leadership for God's glocal and holistic mission.
7	**Apologetics for Mission**: At Master level to learn how the proclamation and the defence of Christian faith can be done in a context of religious pluralism; At doctoral level to build or expand applied knowledge on theories and principles of apologetics for God's glocal and holistic mission.
8	**Missiological Higher Education**: At Master level to learn theories and principles of education for God's glocal and holistic mission; At doctoral level to build or expand applied knowledge on philosophies of education for God's glocal and holistic mission.

Explanation of the Application Settings
Contemporary Religions have to do with Christianity and non-Christian faiths (African Traditional Religions, Islam, Buddhism, Hinduism, etc.) as regard to their relationship with the society in which they are established or exported. How their teachings and practices relate to and affect other religion and the society in the light of *missio Dei*. Aspects of contemporary religions and society will include the study of social and spiritual integration while taking into account the issues pertaining to poverty, development, security, peaceful cohabitation, ecumenism, interreligious dialogue, etc.

Table 6.12 Missiological Studies Applied to Glocal and Intercultural Ministries

Perspectives on Missiology Study Areas	
1	**Contemporary Theologies of Mission**: At Master level to learn how mission has been biblically, theologically, philosophically and strategically conceptualized by evangelicals, ecumenicals, Pentecostal and other bodies; At doctoral level to build or expand applied knowledge on theologies of mission.
2	**Missional Theology of Old Testament**: At Master level to learn how the Old Testament makes a basis for God's mission through the experience of God's people and community; At doctoral level to build or expand applied knowledge on theology of mission from the perspective of Old Testament.
3	**Missional Theology of New Testament**: At Master level to learn how the New Testament makes a basis for God's mission through the experience of God's people and community; At doctoral level to build or expand applied knowledge on theology of mission from the perspective of New Testament.

4	**World Christianity**: At Master level to learn how mission has been practiced throughout various contexts and generations in regard to God's glocal and holistic mission; At doctoral level to build or expand applied knowledge on the history of Christianity in different contexts and generations.	
5	**Intercultural Global Ministries**: At Master level to learn from anthropological insights how God's glocal and holistic mission can serve people of various contexts and cultures; At doctoral level to build or expand applied knowledge on anthropological insights to serve God's glocal and holistic mission.	
6	**Missional Church Leadership**: At Master level to learn from leadership theories and principles for mission-minded pastoral ministry; At doctoral level to build or expand applied knowledge on theories and principles of leadership for God's glocal and holistic mission.	
7	**Apologetics for Mission**: At Master level to learn how the proclamation and the defence of Christian faith can be done in a context of religious pluralism; At doctoral level to build or expand applied knowledge on theories and principles of apologetics for God's glocal and holistic mission.	
8	**Missiological Higher Education**: At Master level to learn theories and principles of education for God's glocal and holistic mission; At doctoral level to build or expand applied knowledge on philosophies of education for God's glocal and holistic mission.	
Explanation of the Application Settings		
It is about various kinds of Christian ministries carried out at either local or global contexts as they also relate to intercultural, intracultural, cross-cultural, or multicultural engagements to *missio Dei*. These Christian ministries may include education, business as mission, urban ministries, medical service, literacy and Bible translation, peace-making activities, evangelism and church planting, etc.		

Table 6.13 Missiological Studies Applied to Community Holistic Transformation

	Perspectives on Missiology Study Areas
1	**Contemporary Theologies of Mission**: At Master level to learn how mission has been biblically, theologically, philosophically and strategically conceptualized by evangelicals, ecumenicals, Pentecostal and other bodies; At doctoral level to build or expand applied knowledge on theologies of mission.
2	**Missional Theology of Old Testament**: At Master level to learn how the Old Testament makes a basis for God's mission through the experience of God's people and community; At doctoral level to build or expand applied knowledge on theology of mission from the perspective of Old Testament.
3	**Missional Theology of New Testament**: At Master level to learn how the New Testament makes a basis for God's mission through the experience of God's people and community; At doctoral level to build or expand applied knowledge on theology of mission from the perspective of New Testament.
4	**World Christianity**: At Master level to learn how mission has been practiced throughout various contexts and generations in regard to God's glocal and holistic mission; At doctoral level to build or expand applied knowledge on the history of Christianity in different contexts and generations.
5	**Intercultural Global Ministries**: At Master level to learn from anthropological insights how God's glocal and holistic mission can serve people of various contexts and cultures; At doctoral level to build or expand applied knowledge on anthropological insights to serve God's glocal and holistic mission.
6	**Missional Church Leadership**: At Master level to learn from leadership theories and principles for mission-minded pastoral ministry; At doctoral level to build or expand applied knowledge on theories and principles of leadership for God's glocal and holistic mission.
7	**Apologetics for Mission**: At Master level to learn how the proclamation and the defence of Christian faith can be done in a context of religious pluralism; At doctoral level to build or expand applied knowledge on theories and principles of apologetics for God's glocal and holistic mission.
8	**Missiological Higher Education**: At Master level to learn theories and principles of education for God's glocal and holistic mission; At doctoral level to build or expand applied knowledge on philosophies of education for God's glocal and holistic mission.

Explanation of the Application Settings
It is about activities related to the holistic transformation of a given community, be it at local, national or regional levels. These activities can be of social, economic, or political engagements within the community as a demonstration of church engagement to *missio Dei*.
Aspects of holistic transformation will deal with body, soul and spirit. Integrated development is the major concern of this application setting and it has to do with the philanthropic concern of an individual or a group of people.

Table 6.14 Missiological Studies Applied to Higher Christian Education

	Perspectives on Missiology Study Areas
1	**Contemporary Theologies of Mission**: At Master level to learn how mission has been biblically, theologically, philosophically and strategically conceptualized by evangelicals, ecumenicals, Pentecostal and other bodies; At doctoral level to build or expand applied knowledge on theologies of mission.
2	**Missional Theology of Old Testament**: At Master level to learn how the Old Testament makes a basis for God's mission through the experience of God's people and community; At doctoral level to build or expand applied knowledge on theology of mission from the perspective of Old Testament.
3	**Missional Theology of New Testament**: At Master level to learn how the New Testament makes a basis for God's mission through the experience of God's people and community; At doctoral level to build or expand applied knowledge on theology of mission from the perspective of New Testament.
4	**World Christianity**: At Master level to learn how mission has been practiced throughout various contexts and generations in regard to God's glocal and holistic mission; At doctoral level to build or expand applied knowledge on the history of Christianity in different contexts and generations.
5	**Intercultural Global Ministries**: At Master level to learn from anthropological insights how God's glocal and holistic mission can serve people of various contexts and cultures; At doctoral level to build or expand applied knowledge on anthropological insights to serve God's glocal and holistic mission.

6	**Missional Church Leadership**: At Master level to learn from leadership theories and principles for mission-minded pastoral ministry; At doctoral level to build or expand applied knowledge on theories and principles of leadership for God's glocal and holistic mission.
7	**Apologetics for Mission**: At Master level to learn how the proclamation and the defence of Christian faith can be done in a context of religious pluralism; At doctoral level to build or expand applied knowledge on theories and principles of apologetics for God's glocal and holistic mission.
8	**Missiological Higher Education**: At Master level to learn theories and principles of education for God's glocal and holistic mission; At doctoral level to build or expand applied knowledge on philosophies of education for God's glocal and holistic mission.
Explanation of the Application Settings	
Focus on Higher Education has to do with tertiary education (college or university) carried out by churches based on Christian values. It comprises theological and non-theological study programs as church engagement to *missio Dei* in order to "transform by the renewal of the mind."	

6.5.5 Serving Meaningfully the Community

To ensure that missiological education is provided for *missio Dei*, both local and global communities should be served by the training institution.

1. To the local community (within the city and the country where the training institution is established), the following activities could be thought of: mission mobilization and training by students and instructors including their guests; partnerships with church and Christian ministries, including other philanthropic organizations; conferences and seminars to share insightful and practical theories and strategies for God's glocal and holistic mission; research and publication to address felt needs and to disseminate the findings; university pedagogy workshops to assist emerging instructors to acquire the necessary knowledge and skills in leading the learning process successfully.

2. To the global community (outside of the country in which the training institution is established), the following activities

could be undertaken: a professional association which provides a platform for sharing, discussion and action; partnerships and networks to create synergy for meaningful reflection and fruitful actions; research, conferences and publications to address felt needs and to disseminate the outcomes and proceedings of these fora.

6.6 Summary

This chapter is intended to be a theoretical reflection through which some practical strategies related to mission theory, mission education and mission practice can be drawn and implemented. Based on the literature and empirical findings of the preceding chapters, the purpose was to brainstorm major trends of the current state of missiology and missiological education in the context of the theological education in the DRC. Therefore, if one plans to address the issue on the current state of missiology and missiological education in the DRC, the root causes identified in chapters 4 and 5, along with the meaning of transforming missiology developed in the present chapter, would be good starting points. This chapter strived to make it clear that the intended "transforming missiology" implies the transformation of (1) the understanding of missiology, (2) the curriculum and its learning outcomes, (3) the structure of theological education, (4) the pedagogical methods, (5) the research procedures and outcomes, and (6) the mindset of expected stakeholders (i.e. students, instructors and their respective churches). The next chapter summarizes the implications and recommendations derived from these findings.

CHAPTER 7

Conclusions, Implications and Recommendations

7.1 Introduction

This study emerged from an observation that the DRC, despite of being a well-Christianized nation and housing several tertiary theological institutions and churches, tends to be a less "missionary-sending country" at the global level. The assumption was that a revisit of missiology in theological education could undoubtedly lead to some discoveries susceptible to build significant theories about missiology and missiological education. The purpose of the study was then to better understand how the prevailing missiological training programs in the DRC align with the preoccupation of providing missiological education for God's glocal mission. The guiding question was, "How does the prevailing missiological education in the DRC align with the purpose of *missio Dei*?"

The first chapter substantiated the research problem and provided a plan for the study. The results of the literature survey were reported from chapter 2 to chapter 4. These chapters focused on how arising key concepts were discussed by scholars and authors. The findings of the empirical investigation were presented, interpreted and analyzed in chapter 5. Based on these findings, a proposition for transforming missiology was submitted and substantiated in chapter 6. The present chapter is a place for conclusions, implications and recommendations.

7.2 Conclusions

In the beginning of this study, mention was made of the recent global survey on theological education whereby the findings showed that missiology was among the four areas which have been either ignored or side-lined in the prevailing theological curricula. The reality is not different in the DRC. This research has revealed that missiology is ignored, marginalized and unfruitful. In many Protestant universities in the DRC, missiology is simply ignored; it does not exist and students, even instructors, do not know it as an academic discipline in its own right. In other cases, missiology is marginalized, becoming a non-attractive field of study; it is perceived as a study area which does not ensure a professional scholarship in the academe. In a few institutions where missiology exists, the discipline is just unfruitful; there is no visible sign of outcomes susceptible to display a clear difference between missiology or missiological education and other disciplines of the theological corpus. In general, missiology is still misunderstood. I faced two peculiar reactions to be mentioned here. In one place, missiology was confused with either criminology or musicology. In another place, missiology was simply treated as a "theological fraud" for not being a scientific discipline, or a discipline in the service of Western imperialism. These realities convey the message that there is a need for well-structured missiological education in the DRC.

To address the triggering problem for this study and to correct some of the above misunderstandings, the proposition of transforming missiology was identified, substantiated and exemplified. The implications of such a submission and the recommendation for further research are presented below.

7.3 Implications

The assumption at the end of this study is that if some of the above suggestions were implemented, the discipline of missiology, the courses on missiology, the instructors of missiology, the students of missiology, the research in missiology and the Protestant churches in the DRC would be transformed and would lead to transformation as far as God's glocal mission is concerned. These expected outcomes emerge from the research and are displayed in table 7.1.

Table 7.1 Implications and Recommendations for a Transforming Missiology

	Missiological features	Recommendations
Missiology	That the discipline of missiology...	-become mandatory and be valued in all theological education -become a department in each faculty of theology -have consistent content (but not an instable content) -lead to academic publications on the subject -lead to regular academic and professional conferences
Provide Quality Teaching	That courses on missiology...	-be well-designed and scheduled -be taken into account in theological institutions -be allocated more credit hours -be specific enough (but not confused with other study areas) -be dynamic (but not static, without improvement) -be more practical (rather than too speculative) -be well-designed (well-articulated and well-elaborated) -be more contextualized -be taught by various missiologists (not the same people)
Provide Quality Teaching	That instructors of missiology...	-be all missiologists (who are qualified in this field of study) -be mission-minded theologians (using their areas of expertise for mission; e.g. NT in the service of mission like David Bosch) -be scholars of this field of study (missiology or related disciplines) -be given opportunities of professional development -be fully committed to the promotion of this discipline -be members of professional associations of mission studies -help churches for their mission engagement -publish books and articles in missiology for local & global context

Provide Quality Teaching	That students of missiology...	-be men and women with a clear vision of the future -be sent out for mission work of their respective churches -be active on the ground to transform the community -be cared for by their churches -influence their churches towards mission engagement
Promote Incentive Research	That research in missiology...	-be deepened (well-undertaken with in-depth reflections) and promoted -lead to scientific interaction between scholars (instructors and students) -lead to publications (valuable books and articles) -be well-oriented according to missiological various areas of research -help theological institutions acquire well-equipped, appropriate and updated library in missiology -lead to easy access to the electronic library in missiology
Serve Meaningfully the Community	That Protestant churches in the DRC...	-become mission-minded churches and committed to *missio Dei* -become laboratories for mission and for missiology -become active in mission and missionary churches -be well-informed and trained about mission -have an impact both inside and outside the country -facilitate intercultural interaction in order to minimize the prevailing climate of tribalism, obstacle to mission

7.4 Recommendations for Future Research

The empirical investigation conducted in this study did not intend to be an experimental inquiry, which could prove or disapprove a given hypothesis. The assumption raised through this study was mostly theory-based, or the discovery of theory. It contemplated the elaboration of theory, which could be tested in further experimental studies to determine to what extent missiological education can cause students and their churches to engage in God's glocal and holistic mission. The empirical investigation conducted in this study, however, had the main expectation of surfacing the current situation in the understanding and the practice of missiology and missiological education in the DRC, and based on the literature explored in the precedent chapters, drawing some inferences.

This research was mostly a theoretical (theory-based) and prominently qualitative study using concurrent mixed method. In general, there are theoretical research and experimental research. The former was chosen for the present research due to the fact that an experimental research (that bridges theory and practice) would not only necessitate available universities willing to participate in ministry intervention to test the theory suggested in this study, but it would also require an extended period of implementation (three years for bachelor, two years for master, and three years for doctorate). Such a study could be done through quantitative inquiry with statistical and probability data to state the extent to which theological institutions would have prepared graduates for mission involvement.

Another aspect of future research could include the comparison of performance of master and doctoral students who would have taken their bachelor programs based on the model proposed in this study (section 6.6.3) and those with a bachelor degree of another model. If students graduate during the academic year 2020–2021 with a bachelor's degree and join a master's program during the academic year 2021–2022, they will graduate with a master's degree during the academic year 2022–2023. A research project could be conducted to compare their performance with students who join a master's program of the proposed model but with a bachelor's degree from another model. One could certainly predict the difference between the two groups of students. The same research could be done for students of a doctoral program. The performance to be measured would concern both theoretical insights in missiology and practical experience about mission engagement of the graduates and their respective churches. The result of such a research project could tell the extent to which the theory of transforming missiology developed in this study is relevant and productive for God's glocal and holistic mission in a given context.

A final proposition for research relates to an expected outcome of this study. It has been stated that theological typologies (section 3.4) could help evaluate the prevailing theological education activities to infer whether God's glocal mission is promoted or not. A proposition of a typology of Antioch was made. Adapted from Edgar's survey, a research questionnaire can be designed for professors in the faculty of theology in order to surface the prevailing landscape of theological education in a given institution (table 7.2).

Table 7.2 Perception of Professors of Theology on Typologies of Theological Education

Symbol, *Context* and Model	N (...)
Athens *Academy* Classical model	
Berlin *University* Vocational model	
Jerusalem *Community* Missional model	
Geneva *Seminary* Confessional model	
Antioch *Academy, University, Community* Transforming missiological education model	

The conviction here is that the way missiology is provided, either in the general context of theological corpus or in a strict setting of missiological education, will determine the extent to which graduates and their respective churches get involved in God's glocal and holistic mission. More research projects are needed to build upon or to expand such a conclusion because *missio Dei* matters in each generation and in every context. However, from a personal experience, the project of transforming missiology is justified by the fact that my previous publication entitled *Missiologie: identité, formation et recherche dans le context africain* and the initiative of establishing the department of missiology at the International Leadership University in Burundi in 2011 are challenged by this study. The last chapter of the aforementioned publication dealt with a proposed curriculum, which was partially implemented in Burundi. Based on the findings of this study, both publication and training programs need serious revision and readjustment to further God's glocal and holistic mission. One could then realize how a missiological research project undoubtedly leads to a transformation of reflection and actions.

Instead of being kept ignored or side-lined, missiology and missiological education need to be either strengthened where they are still weak, or rediscovered and promoted where they are not yet known. Through a project of transforming missiology, this study has proposed some steps toward such an undertaking.

Bibliography

Academy of Mission at University of Hamburg, The. http://www.missionsakademie.de/en/. Accessed 2 January 2016.

Aina, T. A. "Beyond Reforms: The Politics of Higher Education Transformation in Africa." *African Studies Review* 53, no. 1 (April 2010): 21–40.

Allier, R. "Review of the Book L'âme des peuples à évangéliser: compte-rendu de la Sixième Semaine de Missiologie de Louvain (1928)." *International Review of Missions* 18 (1929): 282–284.

Almquist, A. *Missionary, Come Back!* Cleveland, OH: World Publishing, 1970.

Altbach, P. G. "The United States: Present Realities and Future Trends." In *Doctoral Studies and Qualifications in Europe and the United States: Status and Prospects,* edited by J. Sadlak, 259–277. Bucharest: UNESCO, 2004.

Altbach, P. G., L. Reisberg, and L. E. Rumbley. *Trends in Global Higher Education: Tracking An Academic Revolution.* Paris: UNESCO, 2009.

Amanze, J. N. "Paradigm Shift in Theological Education in Southern and Central Africa and Its Relevance to Ministerial Formation." *International Review of Mission* 98, no. 1 (2009): 120–131.

———. "History and Major Goals of Regional Associations of Theological Schools in Africa." In *Handbook of Theological Education in World Christianity: Theological Perspectives, Regional Surveys, Ecumenical Trends,* edited by D. Werner, D. Esterline, N. Kang, and J. Raja, 346–367. Eugene, OR: Wipf & Stock, 2010.

Anderson, G. H., ed. *Biographical Dictionary of Christian Missions.* Grand Rapids: Eerdmans, 1998.

———. "Professional Academic Associations for Mission Studies." *International Bulletin for Missionary Research* 37, no. 1 (January 2013): 13–16.

———. *The Theology of the Christian Mission.* New York: McGraw-Hill, 1961.

Anet, H. "Congo Native and Belgian Administration." *International Review of Missions* 10 (1921): 196–206.

———. "Protestant Missions in Belgian Congo." *International Review of Missions* 28 (1939): 415–424.

Apindia, R. A. "La réforme de l'enseignement supérieur et Universitaire en République Démocratique du Congo." *Revue Congolaise de Théologie Protestante* 19, no. 21 (2009): 101–110.

Association of Professors of Mission. "Meeting Announcement and Call for Papers, 2014." http://www.asmweb.org/assets/APM_2014_callforpapersfinal.pdf.

Attard, A., ed. *Student Centered Learning: An Insight into Theory and Practice.* Bucharest: European Students' Union, 2010.

Authority of Faith, The. Volume 1 of the Tambaran Madras Series published for the International Missionary Council. London: Oxford University Press, 1939.

Bachmann, E. T. "North American Doctoral Dissertations on Mission: 1945–1981." *International Bulletin of Missionary Research* 7, no. 3 (July 1983): 98–134.

Bahigwa, N. "Approche biblique pour une œuvre missionnaire en milieu pygmée. Cas des Mbuti de la forêt de l'Ituri au Zaïre" [Biblical approach to missionary work among Pygmies. Case of Mbuti of the Ituri Forest in Zaire]. Mémoire de Maîtrise en théologie, FATEB, Bangui, Centrafrique, 1992.

Bailey, Laurie D. "From the Editor." *Common Ground Journal* 3, no. 1 (Fall 2005): 8–9.

Bakengela, P., C. Mabi, and C. Tagou. *Le rôle des universités face aux défis du développement en Afrique* [The role of universities in regard to development challenges in Africa]. Kinshasa: EDUPC, 2014.

Baker, A. G. *Christian Missions and a New World Culture.* Chicago: Willett, Clark & Co., 1934.

Baker, D. P. "Missiology as an Interested Discipline – and Where Is It Happening?" *International Bulletin of Missionary Research* 38, 1 (2014): 17–20.

Balia, D., and K. Kim., eds. *Edinburgh 2010: Witnessing to Christ Today.* Oxford: Regnum Books, 2010.

Banks, R. *Reenvisioning Theological Education.* Grand Rapids: Eerdmans, 1999.

Barr, R. B., and J. Tagg. "From Teaching to Learning: A New Paradigm for Undergraduate Education." *Change* 27, no. 6 (1995): 12–25. Available at http://critical.tamucc.edu/~blalock/readings/tch2learn.htm.

Barrett, D., and T. Johnson. "Global Top Ten Lists on 145 Major Missiometric Categories." *World Christian Trends.* Pasadena: William Carey, 2001.

Bassham, Rodger C. *Mission Theology: 1948–1975 Years of Worldwide Creative Tension Ecumenical, Evangelical, and Roman Catholic.* Pasadena, CA: William Carey, 1979.

Bates, S. M., C. Baeta, F. Michaeli, and B. Sundkler. *Survey of the Training of the Ministry in Africa: Part II.* London: International Missionary Council, 1954.

Beaver, R. P. "The American Protestant Theological Seminary and Missions: An Historical Survey." In *Missions and Theological Education in World Perspective,* edited by Harvie M. Conn and Samuel F. Rowen, 65–80. Farmington, MI: Associates of Urbanus, 1984.

———. *Ecumenical Beginnings in Protestant World Mission: A History of Comity.* New York: Nelson & Sons, 1962.

Beisswenger, D. F. "Field Education and the Theological Education Debates." *Theological Education* 33, no. 1 (1996): 49–58.

Bell, S. "Research Priorities in the Seminary Professorate: Scholarly Research and Academic Writing As Criterion for Rank Advancement in Graduate Theological Education." *Journal of Research on Christian Education* 14, no. 2 (2005): 129–157.

Berlach, R. G. "Outcomes-based Education and the Death of Knowledge." Paper presented at The Australian Association for Research in Education Conference, The University of Melbourne, Victoria, Australia, 28 Nov–2 Dec 2004.

Berquist, J. A. "The TEF and the Uncertain Future of Third World Theological Education." *Theological Education* 9, no. 4 (1973): 244–253.

Bernhardt, R. "Bolognization of Theological Education in Germany and Switzerland." In *Handbook of Theological Education in World Christianity: Theological Perspectives, Regional Surveys, Ecumenical Trends,* edited by D. Werner, D. Esterline, N. Kang, and J. Raja, 584–593. Eugene, OR: Wipf & Stock, 2010.

Bevans, S. "From Edinburgh to Edinburgh." In *Mission after Christendom: Emergent Themes in Contemporary Mission,* edited by O. U. Kalu, P. Vethanyagamony, and E. K. F. Chia. Louisville, KY: Westminster John Knox, 2009.

Beyerhaus, P. *Shaken Foundations: Theological Foundations for Mission.* Grand Rapids, MI: Zondervan, 1972.

Blair, C. E. "Understanding Adult Learners: Challenges for Theological Education." *Theological Education as Teaching and Learning* 34, no. 1 (1997): 11–24.

Blaschke, L. M. "Heutagogy and Lifelong Learning: Review of Heutagogical Practice and Self-Determined Learning." *The International Review of Research in Open and Distributed Learning* 13, no. 1 (January 2012): 56–71. Also available at http://www.irrodl.org/index.php/irrodl/article/view/1076/2087.

Bonk, J. et al. "Missiological Journals: A Checklist." *International Bulletin of Missionary Research* 37, no. 1 (2013): 42–49.

Bokeleale, J. B. "From Missions to Mission: The Church in Zaire and New Relationships." *International Review of Mission* 62 (1973): 433–436.

Bongoyok, M. "The Influence of Unreached Peoples Thinking on Francophone African Theological Education and Mission." In *Evangelical and Frontier Mission Perspectives on the Global Progress of the Gospel*, edited by B. Snodderly and A. S. Moreau, 119–125. Edinburgh: Regnum, 2011.

Booth, N. S. "Mission Priorities in Africa." *International Review of Missions* 37 (1948): 93–98.

Bosch, D. J. "Hermeneutical Principles in the Biblical Foundation for Mission." *Evangelical Review of Theology* 17 (1993): 437–451.

———. "Mission in Theological Education." In *Missions and Theological Education in World Perspective*, edited by Harvie M. Conn and Samuel F. Rowen, xiv-xli. Farmington, MI: Associates of Urbanus, 1984.

———. *The Scope of Mission*. London: Church Missionary Society, 1982.

———. *Transforming Mission: Paradigm Shifts in Theology of Mission*. Maryknoll, NY: Orbis, 1991.

———. *Witness to the World: The Christian Mission in Theological Perspective*. Atlanta: John Knox Press, 1980

Botha, N. "Transforming Missiology: A Dialogue with Some Reviewer of David's Bosch's Transforming Mission." *Missionalia* 39, no. 1/2 (2011): 18–31.

Bowers, Paul. *Evangelical Theological Education Today: Agenda for Renewal*. Nairobi: Evangel Publishing, 1982.

Braekman, E. M. *Histoire du protestantisme au Congo*. Bruxelles: Libraries des Eclaireurs Unionistes, 1961.

Braun, W. *Winning Zaïre*. Wilmore, KY: Evangelism Resources, 1996.

Brenner, N. "Global Cities, Glocal States: Global City Formation and State Territorial Restructuring in Contemporary Europe." *Review of International Political Economy* 5, no. 1 (Spring 1998): 1–37.

Brown, H. D. "The Church and Its Missionary Task in Congo." *International Review of Missions* 41 (1952): 301–309.

Brunner, E. *The Word and the World*. New York: Charles Scribner's Sons, 1931.

Bui, Y. N. *How to Write a Master's Thesis*. Los Angeles: SAGE, 2009.

Bujo, B., and J. I. Muya., eds. *Théologie africaine au 21è siècle*. [African theology in 21st century]. Vol. 1. Kinshasa: Paulines, 2002.

Camp, Bruce K. "A Survey of the Local Church's Involvement in Global/Local Church." In *Between Past and Future: Evangelical Mission Entering the Twenty-First Century*, edited by Jonathan J. Bonk, 203–248. Pasadena: William Carey Library, 2003.

"Cape Town Commitment 2010: The Third Lausanne Congress on World Evangelization." https://www.lausanne.org/gatherings/congress/cape-town-2010-3.

Carpenter, G. W. "Co-operation in Christian Literature Production in Belgian Congo." *International Review of Missions* 43 (1954): 414–420.

———. "Whose Congo?" *International Review of Missions* 50 (1961): 171–285.

Chilisa, B., and J. Preece,. *Research Methods for Adult Education in Africa*. Gaborone: Pearson, 2005.

Clair, R. St. "Andragogy Revisited: Theory for the 21st Century? Myths or Realities." *ERIC Clearinghouse on Adult, Career, and Vocational Education* 19 (2002): 1–4.

Cole, V. B. "Landscape of Theological Education in Africa." Unpublished paper presented at the Forum of the Faculty of Theology, Nairobi Evangelical School of Theology, 15 February 2006.

Coleman, R. *The Heart of the Gospel: The Theology behind the Master Plan of Evangelism*. Grand Rapids: Baker, 2011.

Conn, H. M. "The Missionary Task of Theology: A Love/Hate Relationship?" *Westminster Theological Seminary Journal* 45, no. 1 (1983): 2–21.

Conn, H. M, and S. F. Rowen., eds. *Mission and Theological Education in World Perspective*. Farmington: Associates of Urbanus, 1984.

Conseil Protestant du Congo. *Procès-Verbal de la 42è session*. Stanleyville, Léopoldville: LECO, 24 Feb – 3 Mar 1963.

Corrie, John., ed. *Dictionary of Mission Theology: Evangelical Foundations*. Downers Grove, IL: InterVarsity Press, 2007.

Courtenay, B., and R. Stevenson, R. "Avoiding the Threat of Gogymania." *Lifelong Learning: An Omnibus of Practice and Research* 6, no. 7 (1983), 10–11.

Coxill, H. W. "Protestants in the Belgian Congo." *International Review of Missions* 24 (1945): 273–279.

Crawford, J. R. "Protestant Missions in Congo 1960–1969." *International Review of Missions* 55 (1966): 86–95.

———. *Protestant Missions in Congo 1878–1969*. Kinshasa & USA: LECO Press, 1969, 1981.

———. "Protestant Missions in Congo 1878–1969." Unpublished (n.d.).

Creswell, J. "Controversies in Mixed Methods Research." In *Strategies of Qualitative Inquiry* edited by N. K. Denzin, and Y. S. Lincoln, 101–133. Los Angeles: SAGE, 2013.

———. *Research Design: Qualitative, Quantitative and Mixed Methods Approaches*. 2nd ed. Thousand Oaks, CA: SAGE, 2003.

———. *Research Design: Qualitative, Quantitative and Mixed Methods Approaches*. 3rd ed. Thousand Oaks, CA: SAGE, 2009.

Cunningham, W. G., and P. A. Cordeiro. *Educational Leadership: A Problem-Based Approach*. 3rd ed. Boston: Pearson, 2006.

Cyr, A. V. "Overview of Theories and Principles Relating to Characteristics of Adult Learners 1970s-1999." 30 September 1999. Available from *Educational Resources Information Center (ERIC)*, http://files.eric.ed.gov/fulltext/ED435817.pdf.

Dallas Theological Seminary, *Catalog* 2003.

Davis, O. J. "Educational Development in the Belgian Congo." *International Review of Missions* 43 (1954): 421–428.

De Gruchy, S. "Theological Education and the Mission of the Church." In *Global Survey on Theological Education 2011–2013: Summary of Main Findings*, edited by D. Esterline, D. Werner, T. Johnson, and T. Crossing. Prepared for the WCC 10th Assembly, Busan, 30 October – 8 November 2013.

Dehn, U., and D. Werner. "Protestant Theological Education in Germany and the Role of Religious Studies, Missiology and Ecumenics." In *Handbook of Theological Education in World Christianity: Theological Perspectives, Regional Surveys, Ecumenical Trends*, edited by D. Werner, D. Esterline, N. Kang, and j. Raja, 577–583. Eugene, OR: Wipf & Stock, 2010.

De Lange, M. C., Paul J de Bruyn, and Fika J van Rensburg. "Guide for M & D Students to Writing: A Research Proposal." Potchefstroom, South Africa: NWU, Faculty of Theology, 2012.

Denscombe, M. *Research Proposals: A Practical Guide*. Berkshire, England: Open University Press, 2012.

Dietch, B. M. *Reasoning and Writing Well: A Research Guide, Reader, and Handbook*. 5th ed. Boston: McGraw-Hill, 2009.

Dolmans, D. H. J. M, W. De Grave, I. H. A. P. Wolfhagen, and Cees P. Van der Vleuten. "Problem-Based Learning: Future Challenges for Educational Practice and Research." *Medical Education* 39 (2005): 732–741.

Dossou, S. "Un tour d'horizons des facultés de théologie de l'Afrique Francophone." [A survey of faculties of theology in the Francophone Africa]. In *Handbook of Theological Education in Africa*, edited by Isabel A. Phiri, and D. Werner, 193–217. Oxford: Regnum, 2013.

Douglas, J. D., ed. *Let the Earth Hear His Voice; Official Reference Volume: Papers and Responses*. Minneapolis: World Wide Publications, 1975.

Du Preez, K. P., H. J. Hendriks, and A. E. Carl. "Missional Theological Curricula and Institutions." *Verbum et Ecclesia* 35, no. 1 (August 2014). http://dx.doi.org/10.4102/ve.v35i1.1326.

Edgar, B. "The Theology of Theological Education." *Evangelical Review of Theology* 29, no. 3 (2005): 208–217.

Editorial. *International Review of Mission* 58, no. 230 (April 1969): 141.

Eglise du Christ au Congo. *Constitution*, 2è & 3è eds. Kinshasa: CEDI, 1970, 2004, 2014.

———. *Procès verbal du Comité Exécutif National*, Lubumbashi 25–29 Mars, 1994.
———. *Procès verbal du Comité Exécutif National*, Kinshasa 13–29 Juillet, 1996.
———. *Procès verbal du Comité Exécutif National*, Kinshasa 22–28 Février, 1997a.
———. *Procès verbal du Comité Exécutif National*, Kinshasa 29 Juillet – 1 Août, 1997b.
———. *Procès verbal du Comité Exécutif National*, Kinshasa 13–15 Juillet, 1999.
———. *Procès verbal du Comité Exécutif National*, Kinshasa 24 Septembre – 8 Octobre, 2000.
Eisner, E. W. *The Educational Imagination: On Design and Evaluation of School Programs*. 3rd ed. New York: Macmillan, 1994.
Elliston, E. J. *Introduction to Missiological Research Design*. Pasadena: William Carey, 2011.
Encarta, Microsoft. *Encyclopedia*. 2007.
Engel, J. E., and W. A. Dyrness. *Changing the Mind of Missions*. Downers Grove, IL: InterVarsity Press, 2000.
Engelsviken, T. "The Church as Both Local and Global: A Missiological Perspective." In *The Church Going Glocal: Mission and Globalisation*, edited by Tormod Engelsviken, Erling Lundeby, and Dagfinn Solheim, 51–69. Oxford: Regnum, 2011.
———. "*Missio Dei*: The Understanding and Misunderstanding of a Theological Concept in European Churches and Missiology." *International Review of Mission* 92, no. 367 (2003): 481–497.
Engelsviken, T., E. Lundeby, and D. Solheim. *The Church Going Glocal: Mission and Globalisation*. Oxford: Regnum, 2011.
Enns, P. *The Moody Handbook of Theology*. Rev. edition. Chicago: Moody, 2014.
Escobar, S. "Evangelical Missiology: Peering into the Future at the Turn of the Century." In *Global Missiology for the 21st Century: The Iguassu Dialogue*, edited by William D. Taylor. Grand Rapids: Baker Academic, 2000.
———. *The New Global Mission: The Gospel from Everywhere to Everyone*. Downers Grove, IL: InterVarsity Press, 2003.
Esterline, D., D. Werner, T. Johnson, and T. Crossing. *Global Survey on Theological Education 2011–2013: A Summary of Main Findings*. Prepared for the WCC 10th Assembly, Busan, 30 October–8 November 2013. Accessible at: http://www.globethics.net/web/gtl/research/global-survey.
European Association for Quality Assurance in Higher Education. *Standards and Guidelines for Quality Assurance in the European Higher Education Area*. Helsinki, Finland: EAQAHE, 2005.
European Communities. *ECTS Users' Guide*. Brussels: Office for Official Publications of the European Communities, 2009. DOI: 10.2766/88064.

Falk, P. *The Growth of the Church in Africa*. Grand Rapids: Zondervan, 1979.

Ferguson, S. B., and D. F. Wright. *New Dictionary of Theology*. Leicester, UK: Inter-Varsity Press, 1998.

Feshman, C., ed. "Group Discussion Conclusions on the Future of the Discipline of Missiology: Annual Meeting of the American Society of Missiology." *Missiology: An International Review* 42, no. 1 (2013): 80–86.

Fey, H. C., ed. *A History of the Ecumenical Movement, Volume 2: 1948–1968*. Eugene, OR: Wipf & Stock, 2004.

Fiedler, K. *The Story of Faith Missions: From Hudson Taylor to Present Day Africa*. Oxford: Regnum, 1994.

Flyvbejerg, B. "Case Study." In *Strategies of Qualitative Inquiry*, edited by N. K. Denzin, and Y. S. Lincoln, 169–203. Los Angeles: SAGE, 2013.

Forman, Charles W. "A History of Foreign Mission Theory in America." In *American Missions in Bicentennial Perspective*, edited by R. Pierce Beaver. Pasadena, CA: William Carey, 1977.

Fuller School of Intercultural Studies. Accessible from: http//www.fuller.edu.

Gairdner, W. H. T. *Edinburgh 1910: An Account and Interpretation of the World Missionary Conference*. Edinburgh: Oliphant, Anderson & Ferrier, 1910.

Gall, M. D., J. P. Gall, and W. R. Borg. *Applying Educational Research: How to Read, Do, and Use Research to Solve Problems of Practice*. 6th ed. Boston: Pearson, 2010.

Gangel, K. O. "Delivering Theological Education That Works." *Theological Education as Teaching and Learning* 34, no. 1 (1997): 1–9.

Garrard, D. J. "The Protestant Church in Congo: The Mobutu Years and Their Impact." *Journal of Religion in Africa* 43 (2013): 131–166.

Gatwa, T. "A Survey of Theological Education in Francophone Africa." In *Handbook of Theological Education in Africa*, edited by Isabel A. Phiri and D. Werner, 174–192. Oxford: Regnum, 2013.

Gerber, V. *Missions in Creative Tension: The Green Lake '71 Compendium*. Pasadena: William Carey Library, 1971.

Gibaldi, J. *MLA, Handbook for Writers of Research Papers*. 6th ed. New York: The Modern Language Association of America, 2003.

Gibungola, P. B. "Vivre l'évangile de paix parmi les musulmans à l'est de la Républiqu Démocratique du Congo: Une lecture missionale du sermon sur la montagne." [Living the gospel of peace among Muslims in the East of the Democratic Republic of Congo: A missional reading of the sermon on the mount]. DTh in Missiology. Pretoria: UNISA, South Africa, 2010.

Gichimu, John. "Theological Education in African Instituted Churches (AICs)." In *Handbook of Theological Education in World Christianity: Theological Perspectives, Regional Surveys, Ecumenical Trends*, edited by D. Werner,

D. Esterline, N. Kang, and J. Raja, 368–374. Eugene, OR: Wipf & Stock, 2010.

Glasser, A. F. *Announcing the Kingdom: The Story of God's Mission in the Bible.* Grand Rapids: Baker Academic. 2003.

———. "Conciliar Perspectives: The Road to Reconceptualization." In *Contemporary Theologies of Mission,* edited by Arthur F. Glasser, and Donald A. McGavran, 82–99. Grand Rapids: Baker, 1983.

———. "Missiology." In *Evangelical Dictionary of Theology*, edited by Walter A. Elwell. Grand Rapids: Baker, 1984.

Glasser, A. F., and D. A. McGavran. *Contemporary Theologies of Mission.* Grand Rapids: Baker, 1983.

Gleeson, J. "The European Credit Transfer System and Curriculum Design: Product Before Process?" *Studies in Higher Education* (Sep. 2011): 921–938. Available from: http://www.tandfonline.com/doi/abs/10.1080/03075079.2011.610101.

Goheen, M. C. *A Light to the Nations: The Missional Church and the Bible Story.* Grand Rapids: Baker Academic, 2011.

Gration, J. "Willowbank to Zaire: The Doing of Theology." *Missiology: An International Review* 12, no. 3 (July 1984): 297–309.

Grimes, D. A., and K. F. Schultz. "Descriptive Studies: What They Can and Cannot Do." *The Lancet* 359 (January 2002): 145–149.

Guder, D., ed. *Missional Church: A Vision for the Sending of the Church in North America.* Grand Rapids: Eerdmans, 1998.

Gunther, W. "The History and Significance of World Mission Conferences in the 20th Century." *International Review of Mission* 92, no. 367 (2003): 521–537.

Gutek, G. L. *Historical and Philosophical Foundations of Education: A Biographical Introduction.* 4th ed. Upper Saddle River, NJ: Pearson Education, 2005.

Harden, R. M., J. R. Crosby, and M. H. Davis. "An Introduction to Outcome-Based Education." *Medical Teacher* 21, no. 1 (1999): 7–14.

Harkness, A. G. "De-Schooling the Theological Seminary: An Appropriate Paradigm for Effective Ministerial Formation." *Teaching Theology and Religion* 4, no. 4 (2001): 141–154.

Hase, S., and C. Kenyon. "Heutagogy and Developing Capable People and Capable Workplaces: Strategies for Dealing with Complexity." *Proceedings of The Changing Face of Work and Learning Conference*, Alberta, Canada, 25–27 Sept 2003. Available from: http://epubs.scu.edu.au/cgi/viewcontent.cgi?article=1123&context=gcm_pubs.

———. "Moving from Andragogy to Heutagogy in Vocational Education." Paper presented at the Australian Vocational Education and Training Research Association (AVETRA) Conference, Adelaide, Australia, 28–30 March 2001. Available from: http://files.eric.ed.gov/fulltext/ED456279.pdf.

Hastings, A. *The Church in Africa 1450–1950.* Oxford: Clarendon, 1994.
Hay, I. M. "The Emergence of a Missionary-Minded Church in Nigeria." In *Church-Mission Tensions Today,* edited by C. Peter Wagner, 193–213. Chicago: Moody Press, 1972.
Henry, C. F. H., and W. S. Mooneyham. *One Race, One Gospel, One Task; Official Reference Volume: Papers and Reports.* Minneapolis: World Wide Publications, 1967.
Hesselgrave, D. J. *Today's Choices for Tomorrow's Mission.* Grand Rapids: Academic Books, 1988.
———. "Will We Correct the Edinburgh Error? Future Mission in Historical Perspective." *Southern Journal of Theology* 48, no. 2 (2007): 121–149.
Hill, B. N. "Rethinking Comity: Conflict or Confluence along the Ubangi-Mongala Border?" *Missiology: An International Review* 13, no. 2 (1985): 175–182.
Hinchey, P. H. *Becoming a Critical Educator: Defining a Classroom Identity, Designing a Critical Pedagogy.* Lang, Oxford, 2004.
Hobgood, B. C. "History of Protestant Higher Education in the Democratic Republic of the Congo." *Lexington Theological Quarterly* (1998): 23–38. A paper originally presented to the National Conference on Protestant Higher Education in the Congo, held under the auspices of the National Church of Christ (ecumenical) of Congo.
Hocking, W. E., ed. *Rethinking Missions: A Laymen's Inquiry after One Hundred Years.* New York: Harper & Brothers, 1932.
Hoekendijk, J. C. *The Church Inside Out.* Philadelphia: Westerner Press, 1966.
Hogg, W. "The Teaching of Missiology: Some Reflections on the Historical and Current Scene." *Missiology: An International Review* 15, no. 4 (1987): 487–506.
Hollander, Jet den. "Some European Notes." *International Review of Mission* 94, no. 373 (2005): 216–227. Available from: http://onlinelibrary.wiley.com/doi/10.1111/j.1758-6631.2005.tb00497.x/full.
Hyslop, R. D. "Missions and the Missionary." *International Review of Mission* 53, no. 212 (1964): 459–466.
Ingalls, J. D. *A Trainer's Guide to Andragogy.* Rev. edition. Washington, DC: US Dept. of Health, Education and Welfare, 1972.
Inter-University Council for East Africa (IUCEA). *East African Qualifications Framework for Higher Education (EAQFHE).* Kampala: IUCEA, 2015.
Irvine, C. *The Church of Christ in Zaire: A Handbook of Protestant Churches, Missions and Communities, 1878–1978.* Indianapolis, IN: Christian Church Services, 1978.
Isichei, E. *A History of Christianity in Africa.* London: SPCK, 1995.

Johnson, A. "A Model for Understanding the Missionary Task." *International Journal of Frontier Mission* 18, no. 3 (Fall 2001): 133–140.

Johnson, C. N. "Toward a Marketplace Missiology." *Missiology: An International Review* 31, no. 1 (January 2003): 87–97.

Johnson, R. B., and A. J. Onwuegbuzie. "Mixed Methods Research: A Research Paradigm Whose Time Has Come." *Educational Researcher* 33, no. 7 (October 2004): 14–26. Available from: http://www.jstor.org/stable/3700093.

Johnston, A. P. *The Battle for World Evangelism*. Wheaton: Tyndale, 1978.

Johnstone, P. *The Future of the Global Church: History, Trends and Possibilities*. Colorado Springs, CO: Biblica, 2011.

Joint Quality Initiative. "Shared Dublin Descriptors for Short Cycle, First Cycle, Second Cycle and Third Cycle Awards." A report from Joint Quality Initiative Informal Group Meeting, Dublin, Ireland, 18 October 2004.

Jones, D. L. "The Teaching and Learning Cycle: Integrating Curriculum, Instruction, and Assessment." *Christian Perspectives in Education* 2, no. 1 (Fall 2008): 1–22. Available from: http://digitalcommons.liberty.edu/cpe/vol2/iss1/.

Jongeneel, J. A. B. *Philosophy, Science and Theology of Mission in the Nineteenth and Twentieth Centuries*. Vol. 1. Frankfurt: Peter Lang, 1995.

———. *Philosophy, Science and Theology of Mission in the Nineteenth and Twentieth Centuries*. Vol. 3. Frankfurt: Peter Lang, 1997.

———. "Philosophy, Science, and Theology of Mission in the 19th and 20th Centuries: A Missiological Encyclopedia." *Missiology: An International Review* 27, no. 1 (January 1999): 27–30.

Journal Officiel de la République Démocratique du Congo. Loi-Cadre no 14/004 du 11 Février 2014 de l'Enseignement National. Kinshasa, 19 Février 2014.

Kane, J. H. *Understanding Christian Missions*. Grand Rapids: Baker, 1974.

Kasdorf, H. "Current State of Missiology: Reflections on Twenty-Five Years 1968–1993." *Direction Journal* 23, no. 1 (Spring 1994): 64–81. Available from: http://www.directionjournal.org/issues/gen/art_823_.html.

Kelsey, D. H. *Between Athens and Berlin: The Theological Debate*. Grand Rapids: Eerdmans, 1992.

Kickbusch, I. "Global + Local = Glocal Public Health." *Epidemial Community Health* 53, no. 8 (1999): 451–452.

Kirk, A. *What Is Mission? Theological Explorations*. Minneapolis: Fortress Press, 2000.

Kirkpatrick, D. J., and J. Kirkpatrick. *Evaluating Training Programs: The Four Levels*. 3rd ed. San Francisco: Berrett-Kohler, 2005.

Klapan, A. "Andragogy between Theory and Practice." Paper presented at the International Scientific Colloquium "Relationship of Pedagogical Theory and Pedagogical Practice," Crikvenica, Croatia, 18–20 April 2002. Available from: http://files.eric.ed.gov/fulltext/ED471249.pdf.

Knowles, M. S. *The Modern Practice of Adult Education: Andragogy versus Pedagogy*. Rev. edition. Englewood Cliffs, NJ: Cambridge Adult Education, 1980.

———. *The Modern Practice of Adult Education: From Pedagogy to Andragogy*. New York: Associated Press, 1970.

Kostenberger, A. J., and P. T. O'Brien. *Salvation to the Ends of the Earth: A Biblical Theology of Mission*. Downers Grove, IL: InterVarsity Press, 2001.

Kothari, C. R. *Research Methodology: Methods and Techniques*. New Delhi, India: New Age International Publishers, 2004.

Kraemer, H. *The Christian Message in a Non-Christian World*. London: Edinburgh House, 1938.

Kritzinger, J. N. J. "'Mission as . . .' Must We Choose? A Dialogue with Bosch, Bevans & Schroeder and Schreiter in the South African Context." *Missionalia* 39, no. 1/2 (2011): 32–59.

———. *Tutorial Letter: Research Proposal Module for the DTh in Missiology*. Johannesburg: UNISA, 2014.

Kritzinger, J. N. J., P. G. J. Meiring, and W. A. Saayman. *On Being Witnesses*. Johannesburg: Orion, 1994.

Laing, M. "*Missio Dei*: Some Implication for the Church." *Missiology: International Review* 37, no. 1 (July 2009): 89–99.

Langmead, R. "What Is Missiology?" *Missiology: An International Review* 42, no. 1 (2013): 67–79.

Laton, D., J. Reynolds, T. Davis, and D. Stringer. "From Pedagogy to Heutagogy: A Teaching and Learning Continuum." (n.d.). Retrived from: https://www.google.bi/?gws_rd=cr,ssl&ei=KUasV976GOHU6ATsjKbIAg#q=From+pedagogy+to+heutagogy:+A+teaching+and+learning+continuum.

Latourette, K. S. *A History of Christianity*. New York: Harper & Brothers, 1953.

Leedy, P. D. *Practical Research: Planning and Design*. Boston: Macmillan, 1993.

Leedy, P. D., and J. E. Ormrod. *Practical Research: Planning and Design*. 11th ed. Boston: Pearson, 2015.

Lerrigo, P. H. J. "Protestant Missions in Relation to the Future of Congo." *International Review of Missions* 25 (1936): 227–234.

Leyden, S. G. "Unity and Mission in the Consultation on Church Union." PhD Thesis. Temple University, USA, 1976.

Lindsell, H., ed. *The Church's Worldwide Mission: An Aanalysis of the Current State of Evangelical Missions, and a Strategy for Future Activity*. Waco, TX: Word Books, 1966.

Lodico, Marguerite G., Dean T. Spaulding, and Katherine H. Voegtle. *Methods Educational Research: From Theory to Practice*. San Francisco: Jossey-Bass, 2006.

Lund University. Centre for Theology and Religious Studies. http://www.teol.lu.se/.

Lygunda li-M, F. "Missiologie comme une discipline de et en transformation: défi aux institutions théologiques Protestantes de l'Afrique francophone avec référence à la République Démocratique du Congo." *Revue Congolaise de Théologie Protestante* 23–24 (2014): 257–271.

———. *Missiologie: identité, formation et recherche dans le contexte africain*. [Missiology: Identity, training and research in African context]. Kinshasa: Mabiki. 2011.

———. "Toward A Reconstructionist Philosophy of Missiological Education in Francophone Africa: Case of DR Congo." Undergraduate research paper. Munich: GRIN Verlag, 2012. Available from: http://www.grin.com/en/e-book/215395/toward-a-reconstructionist-philosophy-of-missiological-education-in-francophone

———. "Understanding and Evaluating the Participation of Francophone Africans in World Mission: Congolese Working in Burundi." *Evangelical Review of Theology* 39, no. 3 (2015): 255–270.

Lyons, P. "Cooperative Learning Methods and the Adult Learner." *Educational Resources Information Center (ERIC)*, 1988. Available from: http://files.eric.ed.gov/fulltext/ED304962.pdf.

———. "Cooperative and Workplace Learning Approaches." *Educational Resources Information Center (ERIC)*, 1989.

Mahaniah, K. *L'impact du christianisme sur le Manianga 1880-1980*. [The impact of Christianity on the Manianga District 1880–1980]. Kinshasa: Centre de Vulgarisation Agricole, 1981.

Mandryk, J. *Operation World: The Definitive Prayer Guide to Every Nation*. 7th edition. Colorado Springs: Biblica, 2010.

Markham, I. S. "Theological Education in the 21st Century." *Anglican Theological Review* 92, no. 1 (2010): 157–165.

Martin, A. *The Means of World Evangelization: Missiological Education*. Pasadena: William Carey, 1974.

Mashau, T. D. "Hugo Du Plessis' Contribution to the Reformed Church's Struggle for a relevant mission and missiology." PhD Thesis, Potchefstroom Campus: North-West University. 2004.

———. "A Reformed Perspective on Taking Mission and Missiology to the Heart of Theological Training." *In Luce Verbi* 46, no. 2 (2012): 8 pages. Available from: http://www.indieskriflig.org.za/index.php/skriflig/article/viewFile/64/779

Matthey, J. "God's Mission Today: Summary and Conclusions." *International Review of Mission* 92, no. 367 (October 2003): 579–587.

———. "Missiology in the World Council of Churches: Update. Presentation, History, Theological Background and Emphases of the Most Recent Mission Statement of the World Council of Churches." *International Review of Mission* 90, no. 358 (2001): 427–443.

Maynard, Michael L. "From Global to Glocal: How Gillette's Sensor Excel Accommodates to Japan." *Keio Communication Review* 25 (2003): 57–75.

McClung, G. "Missiology in the Middle: The Pentecostal Journey Toward A Balanced, Biblical Mission Agenda for World Evangelization." Unpublished paper, 2010.

McGavran, D. A., and N. Riddle. *Zaire: Midday in Missions.* Valley Forge, PA: Judson Press, 1979.

McKim, D. K. *Westminster Dictionary of Theological Terms.* Louisville, KY: Westminster John Knox, 1996.

McMahon, F. "The Impact of the Bologna Process on the Design of Higher Education Programmes in Europe." In *Education and Leadership,* edited by T. Claes, F. McMahon, and S. Preston, 209–226. Amsterdam: Rodopi, 2008.

Mehra, B., and D. Papajohn. "'Glocal' Patterns of Communication-Information Convergences in Internet Use: Cross-Cultural Behavior of International Teaching Assistants in a Culturally Alien Information Environment." *The International Information and Library Review* 39 (2007): 12–30.

Messes, D. E. *Calling Church and Seminary into the 21st Century.* Nashville: Abingdon, 1995.

Mohring, P. M. *Andragogy and Pedagogy: A Comment on Their Erroneous Usage.* St. Paul: University of Minnesota, Training and Development Research Center, 1989.

Molo, K. "Quest for Ecclesiastical Self-Understanding of the Church of Christ in Zaire: Towards the Retrieval of Contextual Models of the Church in an African Setting." DTh dissertation. Chicago: Lutheran School of Theology, 1987.

Molyneux, K. G. "Book Review: Between Athens and Berlin – the Theological Education Debate." *Africa Journal of Evangelical Theology* 13, no. 2 (1994): 127–129.

Moreau, A. S. "Comprehensive Contextualization." In *Discovering the Mission of God,* edited by Mike Burnett. Grand Rapids: IVP Academic, 2012.

———., ed. *Evangelical Dictionary of World Missions.* Grand Rapids: Baker Academic, 2000.

Moreau, A. S., G. R. Corwin, and G. B. McGee. *Introducing World Missions: A Biblical, Historical, and Practical Survey.* 2nd edition. Grand Rapids: Baker Academic, 2015.

Mouton, J. *Understanding Social Science Research.* Pretoria: Van Schaik Publisher, 2002.

Moulton, J. S., and R. R. Bake. *Synergogy: A New Strategy for Education, Training and Development.* San Francisco, CA: Jossey-Bass, 1984.

Mpinga, A. C. "Towards Mission Spirituality in the Presbyterian Community of Kinshasa." MTh dissertation. Pretoria: UNISA, South Africa, 2007.

MRL 12: Ecumenical Conference on Foreign Missions, Box 1, Folder 1, The Burke Library Archives at Union Theological Seminary, Columbia University, New York, 1900. Available from: http://library.columbia.edu/content/dam/libraryweb/locations/burke/fa/mrl/ldpd_4492656.pdf.

Muck, T., and F. S. Adeney. *Christianity Encountering World Religions: The Practice of Mission in the Twenty-First Century.* Grand Rapids: Baker Academic, 2009.

Mugabi, H. "Institutional Commitment to Community Engagement: A Case Study of Makerere University." *International Journal of Higher Education* 4, no.1 (2015): 187–199.

Mugenda, O. M, and A. G. Mugenda. *Research Methods: Quantitative and Qualitative Approaches.* Nairobi: ACTS Press, 2003.

Muller, K. "Missiology: An Introduction." In *Following Christ in Mission: A Foundational Course in Missiology,* edited by S. Karotempel. Boston: Pauline Books & Media, 1996.

Munayi, M. M. "Enseignement universitaire protestant versus enseignement universitaire étatique: approche historique et comparative." In *Le rôle des universités face aux défis du développement en Afrique,* edited by P. Bakengela, C. Mabi, and C. Tagou. Kinshasa: EDUPC, 2014.

———. *Les vingt-cinq ans de la Faculté de Théologie Protestante au Zaïre, 1959–1984.* [The twenty-five years of the faculty of Protestant Theology in Zaire 1959–1984]. Kinshasa: CEDI, 1984.

Musolo W'Isuka, P. K. "Encountering the Mbuti Pygmies: A Challenge to Christian Mission in the Democratic Republic of Congo." DTh Thesis, Pretoria: UNISA, South Africa, 2013.

———. *Towards a Mission Cycle: Shift from Maintenance Christianity to a Holistic Comprehensive Understanding of Mission.* Saarbrucken: Lambert Academic, 2013.

Musuvaho, P. D. *Quelle Eglise du Christ au Congo pour le Nord-Kivu?* [Which kind of the Christ Church in Congo is needed for the North-Kivu?]. Geneva: COTMEP, 1998.

Myklebust, O. G. "Missiology in Contemporary Theological Education: A Factual Survey." *Mission Studies* 18 (1989): 87–107.

———. *The Study of Missions in Theological Education to 1910*. Vol. 1. Oslo: Egede Instituttet, 1955.

———. *The Study of Missions in Theological Education from 1910 to 1950*. Vol. 2. Oslo: Egede Instituttet, 1957.

Naidoo, M., ed. *Between the Real and the Ideal: Ministerial Formation in South African Churches*. Pretoria: UNISA Press, 2012.

Nel, R. "Mixing African Colours into the Paradigm Shifts in Theology of Mission." *Missionalia* 39, no. 1/2 (2011):114–129.

Neuman, W. L. *Social Research Methods: Qualitative and Quantitative Approaches*. 5th ed. Boston: Allyn & Bacon, 2000.

Newbigin, L. "The Missionary Dimension of the Ecumenical Movement." *International Review of Mission* 70, no. 280 (1981): 240–255.

———. *The Open Secret: An Introduction to the Theology of Mission*. Grand Rapids: Eerdmans, 1995.

North-West University. Faculty of Theology. http://www.nwu.ac.za/missiological-perspective.

Nussbaum, S. "A Future for Missiology as the Queen of Theology?" *Missiology: An International Review* 42, no. 1 (2013): 57–66.

———. *A Reader's Guide to Transforming Mission: A Concise, Accessible Companion to David Bosch's Classic Book*. Maryknoll, NY: Orbis Books, 2005.

Nyama, L. "L'université Congolaise et ses problèmes." *Revue Congolaise de Théologie Protestante* 19, no. 21 (2009): 71–78.

Oldham, J. H. "The Editor's Notes." *International Review of Mission* 1, no. 1 (1912): 1.

Ott, C., S. J. Strauss, and T. C. Tennent. *Encountering Theology of Mission: Biblical Foundations, Historical Developments, and Contemporary Issues*. Grand Rapids: Baker Academic, 2010.

Oxford Centre for Mission Studies. http://www.ocms.ac.uk. Accessed 2 January 2016.

Oxley, S. "Review of the Handbook of Theological Education in World Christianity: Theological Perspectives, Ecumenical Trends, Regional Surveys." *The Ecumenical Review* 62, no. 4 (2010): 428–432.

Padilla, R. C., ed. *New Alternatives in Theological Education*. Oxford: Regnum, 1988.

Parsons, G. "History and Impact of the Fuller School of World Mission." In *Evangelical and Frontier Mission Perspectives on the Global Progress of the Gospel,* edited by Beth Snodderly, and A. Scott Moreau, 55–67. Oxford: Regnum, 2011.

Pentecost, E. C. *Issues in Missiology: An Introduction*. Grand Rapids: Baker, 1982.

Peterson, C. N., and C. M. Ray. "Andragogy and Metagogy: The Evolution of Neologisms." *Journal of Adult Education* 42, no. 2 (2013): 80–85.

Phillips, J. P., and R. T. Coote, R. T., eds. *Toward the 21st Century in Christian Mission*. Grand Rapids: Eerdmans, 1993.

Pierard, R. V. "Gustav Adolf Warneck." In *Evangelical Dictionary of Theology*, edited by Walter A. Elwell. Grand Rapids: Baker, 1984.

Plueddemann, J. E. "Towards a Theology of Theological Education." In *Evangelical Theological Education: An International Agenda,* edited by Paul Bowers. Springwood, Australia: ICAA, 1994.

Pobee, John S. "Stretch Forth Thy Wings and Fly: Theological Education in the African Context." In *Handbook of Theological Education in World Christianity: Theological Perspectives, Regional Surveys, Ecumenical Trends,* edited by D. Werner, D. Esterline N. Kang, and J. Raja, 337–344. Eugene, OR: Wipf & Stock, 2010.

Pocock, M., G. Van Rheenen, and D. McConnell. *The Changing Face of World Missions: Engaging Contemporary Issues and Trends*. Grand Rapids: Baker Academic, 2005.

Pratt, Z., M. D. Sills, and J. K. Walters. *Introduction to Global Missions*. Nashville, TN: B & H, 2014.

Pretorius, H. L, A. A. Odendaal, P. J. Robinson, and G. Van der Merwe, eds. *Reflecting on Mission in the African Context*. Bloemfontein: Pro Christo, 1982.

Priest, R. J., and R. DeGeorge. "Doctoral Dissertations on Mission: Ten-Year Update, 2002–2011." *International Bulletin of Missionary Research* 37, no. 4 (October 2013): 195–202.

Proceedings of General Conference on Foreign Missions, London, October 1878. London: John F. Shaw & Co. Paternoster Row, 1879.

Programmes des cours: Réforme de la table ronde des universités du Congo. [Programme handbook: the roundtable reform of universities in Congo]. Kinshasa: CPE, 2010.

Pruitt, H. E. "Ecumenism and Theological Convergence: A Comparative Analysis of Edinburgh 1910 and the Lausanne Movement." DTh Thesis, Johannesburg: University of South Africa, 2009.

Puett, T. "On Transforming Our World: Critical Pedagogy for Interfaith Education." *Cross Current* 55, no. 2 (Summer 2005). 264–273.

Raja, I. S. "Review of Pastoral Leadership Training: Case Study of HBI Model." Unpublished paper. India (n.d.).

Reardon, B. A. "Human Rights and the Global Campaign for Peace Education." *International Review of Education* 48, no. 3–4 (July 2002): 283–284.

Reese, R. "John Gatu and the Moratorium on Missionaries." *Missiology: An International Review* 142, no. 3 (2014): 245–256.

Reynolds, D. L. J., and T. D. D. Stringer. "From Pedagogy to Heutagogy: A Teaching and Learning Continuum." Online PDF, n.d.

Robert, D. "Forty Years of the American Society of Missiology: Retrospect and Prospect." *Missiology: An International Review* 42, no. 1 (2013): 6–25.

———. "Mission Study at the University-Related Seminary: The Boston University School of Theology as a Case Study." *Missiology: International Review* 17, no. 2 (1989): 193–202.

Ross, K., and T. Johnson. *Atlas of Global Christianity.* Edinburgh: Edinburgh University, 2009.

Rowdon, H. H. "Edinburgh 1910, Evangelicals and the Ecumenical Movement." *Vox Evangelica* 5 (1967): 49–71.

Roxborogh, A. J "Missiology after Missions." An unpublished paper presented at ANZAMS Symposium: Laidlaw College, 30–31 October 2009.

———. "The Missional Church." Theology Matters: A Publication of Presbyterians for Faith, Family and Ministry 10, no. 4 (Sept/Oct 2004).

Saayman, W., and K. Kritzinger, eds. *Mission in Bold Humility: David Bosch's Work Considered.* Maryknoll, NY: Orbis Books, 1996.

Sakenfeld, K. D., ed. *The New Interpreter's Dictionary of the Bible.* Vol. 4. Nashville: Abingdon, 2009.

Sampson, J. P. Jr. "A Guide to Quantitative and Qualitative Dissertation Research." In *Educational Psychology and Learning Systems*, The Florida State University, Faculty Publication, Paper 1 (2012): 1–92. http://diginole.lib.fsu.edu/edpsy_faculty_publications/1.

Samuel, V., and C. Sugden. *Mission as Transformation: A Theology of the Whole Gospel.* Oxford: Regnum, 1999.

Sanderson, C. "Shaping the Academic Enterprise." In *Shaping a Christian World View: The Foundation of Christian Higher Education,* edited by D. S. Dockery, and G. A. Thornbury, 377–389. Nashville, TN: B & H, 2002.

Sanz, N., and S. Bergan, eds. *The Heritage of European Universities.* 2nd edition. Higher Education Series No. 7. Strasbourg: Council of Europe, 2006.

Savery, J. R. "Overview of Problem-Based Learning: Definitions and Distinctions." *Interdisciplinary Journal of Problem-Based Learning* 1, no. 1 (2006). Available from: http://dx.doi.org/10.7771/1541-5015.1002

Scherer, J. *Missionary. Go Home!* Englewood Cliffs, NJ: Prentice Hall, 1964.

———. "Mission in Theological Education." In *The Future of the Christian World Mission,* edited by W. J. Kang. Grand Rapids: Eerdmans, 1971.

———. "Missiology as a Discipline and What It Includes." *Missiology: An International Review* 15, no. 4 (October 1987): 507–522.

Scherer, J. A., and B. S. Bevans, eds. *New Directions in Mission and Evangelization: Basic Statements 1974–1991,* vol. 1. Maryknoll, NY: Orbis, 1992.

———. *New Directions in Mission and Evangelization: Basic Statements 1974–1991*. Vol 2. Maryknol, NY: Orbis, 1994.
Schnabel, E. J. *Early Christian Mission: Jesus and the Twelve*. Vol. 1. Downers Grove, IL: InterVarsity, 2004.
———. *Early Christian Mission: Paul and the Early Church*. Vol. 2. Downers Grove, IL: InterVarsity, 2004.
Schreiter, R. J. *Constructing Local Theologies*. 4th ed. Maryknoll, NY: Orbis, 1994.
Shaw, I. J., ed. *Best Practice Guidelines for Doctoral Programs*. Carlisle, UK: Langham Global Library, 2015.
Shaw, P. *Transforming Theological Education: A Practical Handbook for Integrative Learning*. Carlisle, UK: Langham Global Library, 2014.
Shenk, W. R., ed. *The Challenge of Church Growth: A Symposium*. Scottdale, PA: Herald, 1973.
———. *Changing the Frontiers of Mission*. Maryknoll, NY: Orbis, 1999.
Shepherd, J. F. "Is the Church Really Necessary?" In *Church-Mission Tensions Today*, edited by C. Peter Wagner, 17–38. Chicago: Moody, 1972.
Sidorkin, A. M. "On the Essence of Education." *Studies in Philosophy & Education* 30, no. 5 (June 2011): 521–527. DOI 10.1007/s11217-011-9258-3.
Skreslet, S. H. *Comprehending Mission: The Questions, Methods, Themes, Problems, and Prospects of Missiology*. Maryknoll, NY: Orbis, 2012.
———. "Doctoral Dissertations on Mission: Ten-Year Update, 1992–2001." *International Bulletin of Missionary Research* 27, no. 3 (July 2003): 98–133.
———. "Missiology and the International Review of Mission over a Century." *International Review of Mission* 100, no. 2 (2011):160–180.
Slade, R. M. *English-Speaking Missions in the Congo Independent State 1878–1908*. Bruxelles: Academie Royale des Sciences Colonials, 1959.
Smalley, W. A. "Doctoral Dissertations on Mission: Ten-Year Update, 1982–1991." *International Bulletin of Missionary Research* 17, no. 3 (July 1993): 97–125.
Smith, H. *Fifty Years in Congo: Disciples of Christ at the Equator 1879–1949*. Indianapolis: United Christian Missionary Society, 1949.
Smith, K. G. *Academic Writing and Theological Research: A Guide for Students*. Johannesburg: SATS, 2008.
Smither, E. L. "The Impact of Evangelical Revivals on Global Mission: The Case of North American Evangelicals in Brazil in the Nineteenth and Twentieth Centuries." *Verbum et Ecclesia* 31, no. 1 (2010), Art. #340, 8 pages. DOI:10.4102/ve.v31i1.340
Snyder, H. A. "MI 750 Theories and Models of Mission." *Syllabi* Book 2336 (2002). Available from: http://place.asburyseminary.edu/syllabi/2336.

Spady, W. O. *Outcome-Based Education: Critical Issues and Answers.* Arlington, VA: American Association of School Administrators, 1994.

Stanley, B. "Edinburgh 1910 and the Genesis of the *IRM.*" *International Review of Mission* 100, no. 2 (2011): 149–159.

Starcher, R. L. "Africans in Pursuit of a Theological Doctorate: A Grounded Theory Study of Theological Doctoral Program Design in a Non-Western Context." PhD Thesis, Lincoln, NE: University of Nebraska, 2003.

Steffen, T. A. "Missiology's Journey for Acceptance in the Educational World." *Missiology: An International Review* 31, no. 2 (April 2003): 131–153.

Stenstrom, Gosta. *The Brussels Archives 1922–1968.* Uppsala: Swedish Institute of Mission Research, 2009.

Stonelake, A. R. *Congo Past and Present.* London: World Dominion Press, 1937.

———. "The Missionary Situation in Congo." *International Review of Missions* 8 (1919): 314–330.

Stott, J. R. W. *Christian Mission in the Modern World.* London: Falcon, 1975.

Sundquist, S. W. *Understanding Christian Mission: Participation in Suffering and Glory.* Grand Rapids: Baker Academic, 2013.

Teddlie, C., and A. Tashakkori. "Mixed Methods Research: Contemporary Issues in an Emerging Field." In *Strategies of Qualitative Inquiry,* edited by N. K. Denzin, and Y. S. Lincoln, 135-167. Los Angeles: SAGE, 2013.

Tennent, T. C. *Introduction to World Missions: A Trinitarian Missiology for the Twenty-First Century.* Grand Rapids: Kregel, 2010.

Terry, J. M. ed. *Missiology: An Introduction to the Foundations, History, and Strategies of World Missions.* Kansas City: B & H, 1998.

Theological Education Fund. Ministry in Context: The Third Mandate of the Theological Education Fund (1970–1977). Bromley, UK: Theological Education Fund, 1972.

Thomas, N. E. *Classic Texts in Mission and World Christianity: A Reader's Companion to David Bosch's "Transforming Mission."* Maryknoll: Orbis, 1995.

———. "Globalization and the Teaching of Mission." *Missiology: An International Review* 18, no. 1 (July 1990): 13–23.

Tichapondwa, S. M., ed. *Preparing Your Dissertation at a Distance: A Research Guide.* Vancouver: Virtual University for Small States of the Commonwealth, 2013.

Tippett, A. R. *Introduction to Missiology.* Pasadena: William Carey Library, 1987.

———. "Probing Missionary Inadequacies at the Popular Level." *International Review of Missions* 49 (1960): 411–419.

Torp, L., and S. Sage. *Problems as Possibilities: Problem-Based Learning for K–16 Education.* 2nd edition. Alexandria, VA: Association for Supervision and Curriculum Development, 2002.

Tshibangu, T. *Théologie positive et théologie speculative*. Louvain: Publications Un. de Louvain, 1965.
Tuckman, B. W., and B. E. Harper. *Conducting Educational Research*. 6th edition. New York: Rowman & Littlefield, 2012.
Turabian, K. L. *A Manual for Writers of Term Papers, Theses, and Dissertations*. 7th edition. Chicago: University of Chicago Press, 2007.
University of Edinburgh, The. http//www.ed.ac.uk/divinity/studying/graduate-school/postgraduate-research.
University of Hamburg, http://www.uni-hamburg.academica.edu. Accessed January 2, 2016.
University of South Africa. http://www.unisa.ca.za/Default.asp?Cmd=ViewContent&ContentID=16863.
Uppsala University. Accessed 7 January 2016. http://www.uu.se/en/admissions/master/selma/amne/?aKod=KYI&lasar=15%2F16.
Utuk, Efiong S. "From Wheaton to Lausanne: The Road to Modification of Contemporary Evangelical Mission Theology." In *New Directions in Mission and Evangelization: Basic Statements 1974–1991. Vol 2.*, edited by James A. Scherer, and Stephen B. Bevans, 99–112. Maryknoll, NY: Orbis, 1992.
Van der Walt, B. J. *Transformed by the Renewing of Your Mind: Shaping a Biblical Worldview and a Christian Perspective on Scholarship*. Potchefstroom: ICCA, 2001.
Van Engen, C. E. "The Glocal Church: Locality and Catholicity in a Globalizing World." In *Globalizing Theology: Belief and Practice in an Era of World Christianity*, edited by Craig Ott, and Harold A. Netland. Grand Rapids, MI: Baker Academic, 2006.
———. *God's Missionary People: Rethinking the Purpose of the Local Church*. Grand Rapids: Baker, 1991.
———. *Mission on the Way: Issues in Mission Theology*. Grand Rapids: Baker, 1996.
———. "The Relation of Bible and Mission in Mission Theology." In *The Good News of the Kingdom,* edited by C. E. Van Engen, Dean S. Gilliland, and Paul Pierson. Maryknoll, NY: Orbis, 1993.
Van Gelder, C. "The Future of the Discipline of Missiology: Framing Current Realities and Future Possibilities." *Missiology: An International Review* 42, no. 1 (2013): 1–18.
———. *The Ministry of the Missional Church: A Community Led by the Spirit*. Grand Rapids, MI: Baker Academic, 2007.
———. ed. "Missiology and the Missional Church in Context." In *The Missional Church in Context: Helping Congregations Develop Contextual Ministry,* edited by C. Van Gelder, 12–27. Grand Rapids, MI: Eerdmans, 2007.

Van Gelder, C., and D. J. Zscheile, eds. *The Missional Church in Perspective: Mapping Trends and Shaping the Conversation*. Grand Rapids, MI: Baker Academic, 2011.

Van Rheenen, G. *Missions: Biblical Foundations and Contemporary Strategies*. Grand Rapids: Zondervan, 1992.

Verkuyl, J. *Contemporary Missiology: An Introduction*. Grand Rapids: Eerdmans, 1978.

Vyhmeister, N. J. *Quality Research Papers: for Students of Religion and Theology*. Grand Rapids, MI: Zondervan, 2009.

Walls, A. F. "Missiology." In *Dictionary of the Ecumenical Movement*, 2nd edition. Edited by N. Lossky, and J. M. Bonino, 781–783. Geneva: World Council of Churches, 2002.

———. "Missions or Mission? The *IRM* after 75 Years." *International Review of Mission* 100, no. 2 (2011): 181–188.

Ward, A. M. "The Theological Education Fund of the International Missionary Council." *International Review of Missions* 49 (1960): 137–141.

Warren, M. "The Fusion of IMC and WCC at New Delhi: Retrospective Thoughts after a Decade and a Half." *Occasional Bulletin of Missionary Research* (July 1979): 104–108.

Werner, D. "Theological Education in the Changing Context of World Christianity: An Unfinished Agenda." *International Bulletin of Missionary Research* 35, no. 2 (2011): 92–100.

Werner, D., and Kang, N. "Theological Education and Formation." In *Edinburgh 2010: Mission Today and Tomorrow*, edited by Kirsteen Kim, and Andrew Anderson, 158–165. Oxford: Regnum, 2011.

Werner, D., D. Esterline, N. Kang, and J. Raja. *Handbook of Theological Education in World Christianity: Theological Perspectives, Regional Surveys, Ecumenical Trends*. Eugene, OR: Wipf & Stock, 2010.

White, H. V. *A Theology for Christian Missions*. Chicago: Willett, Clark & Co., 1937.

Whitworth, D. M. "*Missio Dei* and the Means of Grace." PhD Thesis. Calver: University of Manchester, Cliff College, 2012.

Winter, R. "Missiological Education for Lay People." In *Missiological Education for the 21st Century*, edited by J. Dudley Woodberry et al., 169–185. Maryknoll: Orbis, 1997.

Winter, R. D., and S. C. Hawthorne, eds. *Perspectives On the World Christian Movement*. Pasadena: William Carey, 1999.

Wittenbach, H. A. "The Training of A Missionary." *International Review of Missions* 49 (1960): 405–410.

World Education Services. *Understanding and Evaluating the Bologna Bachelor's Degrees*. New York: WES, 2007. Available from: http://www.wes.org.

Wright, C. *The Mission of God's People: A Biblical Theology of the Church's Mission*. Grand Rapids: Zondervan, 2010.

———. *The Mission of God: Unlocking the Bible's Grant Narrative*. Downers Grove, IL: IVP Academics, 2006.

Yates, T. *Christian Mission in the Twentieth Century*. Cambridge: Cambridge University Press, 1996.

Yoder, J. H. *Theology of Mission: A Believers Church Perspective*. Downers Grove, IL: IVP Academic, 2014.

APPENDIX

Research Questionnaire / Theology Students

(English translation of the original French questionnaire.)

This questionnaire is designed for a research on the status of missiology within Protestant universities in the DRC. Your identity will not be revealed (except if you want your name to appear in the text due to the relevance of your contribution).

1. Your university: _____
   _____

   Your cycle of studies: ___ Graduate; _____ Licence; _____ DEA/ Master; _____ Doctorate

   Your department within the Faculty of Theology: _____
   _____

   Your names: _____
   Email: _____

2. As for today (2015), and according to you, what is the current status of missiology within your Faculty of Theology? *[Kindly tick all that apply and provide any comment if possible]*:
   a. Missiology doesn't have any special status within our Faculty of Theology;
   b. Missiology is not perceived as one of essential disciplines within our Faculty of Theology;

c. Missiology is a full department as others (Biblical theology – OT & NT, Systematic theology, Church history, Practical theology);
d. Missiology is important but not mandatory; it is an elective;
e. We don't think that missiology should be part of our curriculum which aims at training church ministers as far as the philosophy of our institution is concerned;
f. Our problem is that missiology is not yet clearly defined to be demarcated from other prevailing disciplines of theological corpus indicated in item **c** above;
g. Missiology is instead part of the department of _____ because _____ .
h. Our Faculty of Theology offers a department of missiology at *graduate* (3 years) level;
i. Our Faculty of Theology offers a department of missiology at *licence* (3 + 2 years) level;
j. Our Faculty of Theology offers a department of missiology at *DEA/master* (2 years) level;
k. Our Faculty of Theology offers a department of missiology at doctorate level;
l. One of our problems is that the curriculum on missiology is not well-designed;
m. We have a program handbook on missiological education.

3. In regard to courses taught within your Faculty of Theology, the following delivery method is used by instructors in their teaching process *[Please, tick only that applies most often and kindly comment if possible]*:
a. Students depend on what instructors propose in their course notes (course outline and notes) in addition to explanation and some assignments along with the final exam; _____

b. Students make their own course notes based on the course outline that the instructors provide followed by their explanation, assignments and final exam; _____

c. Instructors and students discuss the course outline and students conduct research in order to compose course notes before producing their personal reflections and taking a final exam to validate the course; _____

_____

4. When you consider how courses are designed, developed, and delivered within your Faculty of Theology in general, your impression is that the prevailing teaching method makes students:
   a. *Too dependent* on what instructors design and provide;
   b. *Somehow independent* because they also have possibility to choose among subjects that instructors propose for students to deepen before validating the course through an assignment or a final exam;
   c. *Plus or minus interdependent* because students are involved in the design of the course outline and content while taking into account students' learning needs and interest.
5. Please suggest some special courses (important/essential/mandatory) which could have made the missiological program but which are absent in your study program:

	Courses
1	
2	
3	
4	
5	
6	
7	
Etc.	

6. From your point of view, mission departments within various *communautés* of the Church of Christ in Congo should undertake the following activities *[Please, tick all that better match with your understanding]*:
   a. ___ Evangelization in other provinces of the DRC
   b. ___ Evangelization in urban centers (cities) of the DRC
   c. ___ Evangelization in rural areas (villages) of the DRC
   d. ___ Evangelization outside of the DRC
   e. ___ Planting new churches in other provinces of the DRC
   f. ___ Planting new churches in urban centers (cities) of the DRC
   g. ___ Planting new churches in rural areas (villages) of the DRC
   h. ___ Planting new churches outside of the DRC
   i. ___ Social actions (education, medical service, development, etc.) in other provinces of the DRC
   j. ___ Social actions (education, medical service, development, etc.) in urban centers (cities) of the DRC
   k. ___ Social actions (education, medical service, development, etc.) in rural areas (viallages) of the DRC
   l. ___ Social actions (education, medical service, development, etc.) outside of the DRC

7. Besides activities that you just ticked above, are there any additional acitivities you would suggest to be done by the department of mission within the *communautés* of the Church of Christ in Congo? *[Please name them and the location]*:
   a. _____
   b. _____
   c. _____
   d. _____
   e. _____

8. Indicate one or two biblical references which, according to you, better explain the mission of the church and the *raison d'être* of divers *communautés* of the Church of Christ in Congo:
   a. _____
   b. _____

9. When you consider all *communautés* of the Church of Christ in Congo, which obstacles hinder their mission engagement outside the country? *[Please, answer by inserting a number against each obstacle according to their importance (1, 2, 3, 4, 5, 6, 7) according to you]*:
   ____ Lack of finances
   ____ Lack of strategies within the *Commununté* about mission
   ____ Lack of qualified people to lead the department of mission
   ____ Lack of qualified people to go for mission
   ____ Lack of unity among pastors in regard to mission involvement
   ____ Materialism in many church members
   ____ Ignorance about mission involvement of the church in the life of church members

10. Any other comment about the mission involvement of the *communautés* of the Church of Christ in Congo?

Done in _____, **on** _____/_____/ **2015**
Signature: _____

For questions [tick] ___2, ___3, ___4, ___5, ___6, ___7, ___8 **(above), I would like to be named in your thesis due to the relevance of my reflection.**

NB: Contact flygunda50@gmail.com

Person Index

A

Adeney, F. S. 58
Aina, T. A. 26
Allen, R. 63, 66
Allier, Raoul 42
Almquist, Arden 197
Altbach, P. G. 150, 156
Amanze, J. N. 6, 112, 114, 136, 137, 138, 139
Anderson, G. H. xxiv, 40, 62, 91, 317
Anderson, R. 63, 66
Anet, H. 187, 193, 205, 209, 216, 217
Apindia, R. A. 158
Arias, M. 91
Attard, A. 168

B

Bachmann, E. T. 50, 52
Bahigwa, N. 11
Bailey, L. D. 21
Bake 30
Bakengela, P. 10
Baker, A. G. 80
Baker, Dwight P. 49
Balia, D. 113, 116
Bangura 144
Banks, R. 129, 132, 133
Baraka, Assani 233
Barrett, David 7
Barr, R. B. 168, 169
Barth, Karl 12, 13, 85
Bassham, R. C. 18
Bates, S. M. 135, 226, 240
Baxton, T. F. 70
Beaver, R. P. 20, 64, 72, 73, 82, 184, 209
Bediako, Kwame 16, 113, 126
Beisswenger, D. F. 170, 171
Bell, S. 150, 151, 152
Bergan, S. 149
Berlach, R. G. 161
Bernhardt, R. 157, 168
Berquist, J. A. 135
Bevans, S. B. 40, 139, 357
Beyerhaus, P. 81, 83, 91
Blair, C. E. 30, 31
Blake 143
Blaschke, L. M. 146
Bokeleale, I. B. 5, 84, 196, 203, 204, 230, 233, 240, 279, 313
Bongoyok, Moussa 113, 326
Bonk, Jonathan i, xxiv, 56
Booth, N. S. 218, 219
Bosch, David J. xix, xxi, 12, 13, 15, 16, 19, 40, 55, 57, 58, 59, 60, 64, 81, 90, 91, 92, 101, 108, 109, 111, 113, 126, 287, 319, 323, 324, 326, 349, 354, 383
Botha, Nico xxi, 15, 16, 19, 90
Braun, W. 9

Breckenridge, C. 66, 72
Brenner, N. 6
Brown, H. D. 11, 12, 206, 207, 210, 219, 220, 221, 222, 225, 226, 239, 245
Brunner, Emil 13, 17, 202
Bui, Y. N. 33, 34, 359, 363
Bujo, B. 16
Buys, Flip xviii, xxiii

C
Camp, Bruce K. 86
Carey, William 65, 67, 68, 185
Carpenter, G. W. 187, 204, 207, 208, 213, 221, 222, 225
Carr, B. 91
Clair, R. St. 141, 142
Coleman, Robert 58
Cole, Victor B. 31
Comber 186
Conn, H. M. 72, 86, 87, 111, 178, 179
Coote, R. T. 40
Cordeiro 165, 366
Cornelius 194
Corrie, John 58
Costas, O. 81
Courtenay, B. 143
Coxill, H. W. 187, 196, 199, 201, 205, 206, 207, 210, 217, 218, 219, 224, 225
Craven, H. 186
Crawford, J. R. 7, 9, 184, 191, 208, 221, 222, 223, 226, 227, 229, 230, 245
Creswell, John 250, 251, 252, 258, 259, 261, 264, 265, 271, 273
Cunningham, W. G. 165, 366
Cyr, A. V. 145, 146

D
Davies, J. D. 91
Davis, O. J. 187, 208
DeGeorge, R. 50, 51, 53, 354
De Gruchy, S. 113
Dehn, U. 128
Dikoufiona, Philippe 113
doctorate 159
Dolmans, D. H. J. M. 165, 166, 167
Dossou 12
Douglas, J. D. 88
Duff, A. 66
Du Plessis, J. 198, 199
Du Preez, K. P. 20
Dyrness, W. A. 58

E
Edgar, B. 106, 109, 114, 128, 129, 131, 133, 386
Eisner 3
Elliston, Edgar J. 23, 34, 111, 112, 250, 251, 253, 254, 255, 263, 363
Engel, James E. 58
Engelsviken, T. 5, 6, 31, 82, 85, 97, 203
Enns, P. 309
Escobar, Samuel 45, 46, 47, 58, 81
Esterline, D. 3
Evers 143

F
Falk, Peter 192, 196
Ferguson, S. B. 118
Feshman, C. 5, 27, 30, 45, 304
Fey, H. C. 83
Fiedler, K. 20, 55, 184, 185, 186, 187, 330
Flyvbejerg, B. 256, 257, 258
Forman, C. W. 20, 87
Fuller, Charles 122

G

Gairdner, W. H. T. 115, 116
Gall, M. D. 263
Gangel, K. O. 30
Garrard, D. J. 185
Gatu, John 83
Gatwa, T. 12
Genischen, H. W. 91
Gerber, V. 86
Gibungola, P. B. 11
Glasser, A. F. 18, 33, 56, 58, 91, 203, 306, 318, 326
Gleeson, J. 156, 160, 162
Goheen, M. C. 320, 321
Graham, Billy 81
Gration, J. 195
Grenfell 186
Grimes, D. A. 255
Grow 144
Guder, D. 94
Gunther, W. 203, 206, 207, 208
Gutek, G. L. 140

H

Harden, R. M. 161, 162
Harkness, A. G. 115
Harper, B. E. 250, 251, 253, 263, 264, 266
Hartenstein, Karl 82
Hase, S. 143, 146, 147
Hastings, A. 7
Hay, I. M. 82
Henry, C. F. H. 86
Hesselgrave, David J. 41, 43, 75, 76, 83, 136
Hill, B. N. iii, xxv, 183
Hinchey, P. H. 144
Hobgood, B. C. 227
Hocking, W. E. 63, 79
Hoekendijk, J. C. 64, 83, 85, 91
Hogg, W. 203

Hollander, J. den 14, 20
Holt 161
Hyslop, R. D. 196

I

Ingalls, J. D. 147, 148, 336
Inkomo, Boyaka 233
Irvine, C. 198

J

Johnson, A. 91, 183, 185
Johnson, A. P. 81
Johnson, C. N. 94
Johnson, R. B. 251
Johnson, Todd xxiv, 7, 26
Johnstone, P. 7, 26
Jones, D. L. 140
Jongeneel, J. A. B. i, xxiv, 13, 21, 42, 57, 58, 66, 74

K

Kalombo, S. 10, 281
Kane, J. H. 70, 73, 91, 101, 183, 187, 211
Kang, N. 116
Kasdorf, H. 6, 112
Kato, Byang 83, 91
Kelsey, D. H. 129, 133
Kennedy, John F. 82
Kenyon, C. 143, 146, 147
Kim, Kirsteen 113, 116
Kirk, A. 31, 55, 58
Kirkpatrick, D. J. 31
Kivengere, Festo 81
Klapan, A. 141
Knowles, M. S. 141, 142, 143, 146
Knudson 143
Kostenberger, A. J. 58
Kothari, C. R. 356
Kraemer, Hendrick 63, 80, 202

Kritzinger, J. N. J. xxv, 19, 57, 62, 65, 90, 317, 359
Kuyper, A. 13

L

Laing, M. 73, 85
Langmead, R. xx, 27, 304
Laton, D. 144, 145
Latourette, Kenneth S. 65, 202
Lavoie 144
Leedy, P. D. 34, 254
Leopold II, King 66, 67, 190, 192
Lerrigo, P. H. J. 187, 193, 194, 205, 217, 218
Leyden, S. G. 87
Lindsell, H. 86
Livingstone, David 66, 192, 196
Lodico, M. G. 33
Lumeya, Nzash U. 237, 324, 326
Lundeby, E. 5
Luther King Jr., Martin 82
Lygunda, LM. F. i, ii, iii, xix, xxv, 6, 7, 25, 91, 286, 296, 303, 308, 312, 324
Lyons, P. 30

M

Mahaniah, K. 214, 229, 233
Malcolm X 82
Mandryk, J. 8
Markham, I. S. 113, 115
Martin, A. 43, 111
Mashau, T. D. 43, 317, 330
Matthey, J. 64, 81, 85
Maynard, M. L. 6
Mbiti, John 91
McClung, G. 40
McConnell, D. 58, 60
McGavran, D. A. 7, 58, 83, 89, 91, 98, 182, 183, 184, 186, 187, 188, 192, 200, 204, 206, 229, 326

McKim, D. K. 118, 122
McMahon, F. 155, 156, 157, 158
Mehra, B. 6
Messes, D. E. 115
Mohring, P. M. 141, 143
Molo, Kakule 77, 91, 214, 232, 243, 279
Molyneux, K. G. 131
Moreau, A. Scott 28, 56, 58, 135, 304
Mott, John, R. 63, 75, 77, 79, 83, 199, 210, 228, 231, 240
Moulton, J. S. 30
Mouton, J. 143
Mpinga, A. C. 11
Muck, T. 58
Mugabi, H. 149, 150
Mugenda, O. M. 265, 267
Muller, Karl 47
Munayi, M. M. 9, 227, 228, 290
Mushila, N. 92, 120, 281, 324
Musolo, W. P. K. xxiv, 10, 11, 12
Muya, J. I. 16
Myklebust, O. G. 13, 57, 66, 73, 91, 107, 112, 178, 179, 209, 269

N

Naidoo, M. 115
Neill, S. 91
Nel, Reggie xxi, 15
Neuman, W. L. 261
Nevius, J. 63, 66, 197
Newbigin, Lesslie 64, 76, 82, 91, 94, 96, 97
Njerareou, Abel 113
Nussbaum, S. 90, 92, 108
Nyama, L. 158

O

O'Brien, P. T. 58
Oduyoye, Amba 16

Oldham, J. H. 76, 201
Onwuegbuzie, A. J. 251
Ormrod, J. E. 34
Ott, C. 33, 56, 58, 60, 65, 74, 81
Oxley, S. 114, 115

P
Padilla, R. C. 81, 115
Papajohn, D. 6
Parsons, G. 89, 122
Pentecost, E. C. 111
Peterson, C. N. 141, 142, 143
Phillips, J. P. 40, 55
Pierard, R. V. 118
Plueddmann, J. E. 152
Pobee, John S. 136, 137
Pocock, M. 58, 60
Potter, P. 202
Pratt, Z. 43, 110
Pretorius, H. L. 101
Priest, Robert J. 50, 51, 53, 354
Pruitt, H. E. 91
Puett, T. 153

R
Ray, C. M. 141, 142, 143
Reardon, B. A. 152
Reese, R. 83
Reynolds, D. I. J. 143, 144
Riddle, N. 7, 182, 183, 184, 186, 187, 188, 192, 200, 204, 206, 229
Robert, Dana iii, xxiv, 27, 125
Rockefeller, J. D. 79
Rosenkranz, G. 91
Ross, K. xxiv, 7, 26
Rowdon, H. H. 75, 76
Rowen, S. F. 178, 179
Roxborogh, A. J. 43, 44, 304
Roxborogh, J. 43
Rutti, L. 91

S
Saayman, W. 90
Sage, S. 165
Sakenfeld, K. D. 315
Sampson, J. P. Jr. 33, 34, 363
Samuel, V. 25, 58
Sanderson, C. 141, 150, 154
Sanguma, Mossai 113
Sanz, N. 149
Savery, J. R. 165, 166
Schaeffer, F. A. 64
Scherer, J. A. 27, 40, 55, 64, 113, 197, 357
Schlafly 161
Schleiermacher, F. 63, 66, 73, 149, 294
Schreiter, R. J. 16
Schultz, K. F. 255
Sharpe, E. 91
Shaull, R. 91
Shaw, I. J. 336, 337
Shaw, P. ii, 3, 152
Shenk, W. R. 89, 196, 197
Shepherd, J. A. 86
Shepherd, J. F. 86
Sidorkin, A. M. 152
Sills, M. D. 43, 110
Skreslet, S. H. 4, 18, 27, 30, 31, 33, 44, 45, 50, 51, 53, 56, 58, 61, 201
Slade, R. M. 187
Smalley, W. A. 50, 53
Smither, E. L. 20
Smith, H. 77
Smith, K. G. 250, 254, 255, 359, 363
Snyder, H. A. 61
Solheim, D. 5
Spady, W. O. 160, 161
Stanley, B. 126, 201, 202
Stanley, Henry Morton 66, 192, 196
Starcher, R. L. iv, xx, xxiv, 17, 18, 351

Steffen, T. A. 5, 28, 30, 45
Stenstrom, G. 91
Stevenson, R. 143
Stonelake, A. 7, 77, 83, 184, 186, 187, 192, 193, 196, 198, 199, 200, 201, 204, 210, 215, 216, 218, 223, 224
Stott, John R. W. 19, 58, 64, 81, 83, 87, 102
Strauss, S. J. 58, 60, 65, 74, 81
Stringer, T. D. D. 143, 144
Sugden, C. 25, 58
Sundkler, B. 91
Sundquist, Scott W. 13, 27, 58, 67, 68, 70, 74, 75, 76, 79, 82, 88

T
Tagg, J. 168, 169
Tanaka 143
Taylor, Hydson 65, 185, 186
Teddlie, C. 258, 259
Tempels, Placide 16, 213
Tennent, Timothy C. 31, 58, 60, 65, 74, 81, 312, 357
Terry, J. M. 13, 42, 118
Thomas, M. M. 91
Thomas, Nelson, E. 14, 20, 90
Tippett, A. R. 45, 46, 47, 104, 111, 211, 212, 213, 214, 306
Torp, L. 165
Tshibangu, Tharcisse 16
Tuckman, B. W. 250, 251, 253, 263, 264, 266
Turabian, K. L. 306

U
Utuk, E. S. 18

V
van der Walt, B. 17, 29, 153, 154
van Engen, C. E. 97, 309, 319, 320
Vaneste 16
van Gelder, C. 5, 32, 59, 60, 61, 62, 64, 65, 66, 67, 76, 78, 81, 84, 85, 88, 89, 91, 92, 94, 95, 96, 97
van Rensburg, Fika J. i, xxiii
van Rheenen, G. 58, 60, 357
van Rijckevorsel, L. J. 42
Venn, Henry 63, 66
Verkuyl, Johannes 12, 13, 20, 46, 47, 64, 83, 91, 98, 99, 100, 118, 306
Vicedom, G. F. 64
Von Humboldt, W. 149
Vyhmeister, N. J. 251

W
Wagner, P. 89, 326
Walls, Andrew xxiv, 28, 43, 202
Walters, J. K. 43, 110
Ward, A. M. 134, 135
Warneck, Gustave 13, 57, 63, 66, 99, 118
Warren, M. 76
Weanzana, Nupanga 113
Werner, D. xxiv, 115, 116, 128
White, H. V. 80
Whitworth, D. M. 32
Wieser, T. 91
Winter, Ralph 64, 83, 91, 122, 197, 326, 327
Wittenbach, H. A. 211, 212, 213
Wright, Christopher xxiv, 43, 56, 58, 64, 96, 101, 102, 318, 319, 320, 323, 324, 326, 354
Wright, D. F. 118

Y
Yates, Timothy 61
Yeo 143
Yoder, John H. 33, 56

Z
Zscheile, D. 32, 61, 85

Subject Index

A
academia 82, 109, 110
African ethnography 209
African Immigrant (diaspora)
    churches 371
African initiated churches 7, 370
African Inland Mission 195, 238
All African Churches Council 90
alma mater 111, 274, 277
American Baptist Foreign Missionary
    Society 187, 205, 207, 208,
    213, 227
American Society of Missiology 4,
    40, 45, 89
Analysts 14
aner 141
Apologetic for missions 339
applied research
    biblical foundation 356, 358
    steps 356
Asbury Theological Seminary xxv,
    124
Association of Evangelicals in Africa
    91
Association of Professors of Mission
    (APM) 4, 40, 61
Association of Theological Seminaries
    124, 150
Atlas of Global Christianity 7, 26, 27
atonement 87

Authority of Faith, the 80
autonomy 164, 180, 185, 229, 243

B
backward races 215, 216
Bantu linguistics 209
Bantu philosophy 16, 213
Baptist Missionary Society 66, 70,
    77, 185, 187, 192, 204
Bates's report 240
Belgian
    church 205, 216
    government 187, 193
Belgian government 190
Belgian
    missionaries 16, 209
Bible Translation Society 188
Biola University iv, xx, 124
Bolenge 77, 227
Bologna
    ECTS 155
Bologna Process
    Bologna I 155
    Bologna II 155
    Bologna III 155
    Bolognization 140, 155, 157, 168,
        174, 328
    ECTS 16, 155, 157, 159
    history of 149
    requirements 159

425

Boston Theological Institute 124
Boston University iii, xxv, 124, 125, 126, 199
bouclier humain 236

C
Campus Crusade for Christ 188
Cape Town Commitment xvii, 117
catalysts 14
Centenary Conference on Protestant Missions of the World, the 70
Center for Missiological Research (Fuller) 124
Central African Republic ii, iii, xix, 6, 17, 113, 194
Centre Universitaire de Missiologie xxiv, 237, 269, 282, 283, 324
child psychology 212
Christ-centered mission 85
Christian education 4, 45, 52, 113, 141
Christology 85
church growth xviii, 11, 98, 122
Church Growth Movement 64, 83, 89
Church of Christ in Congo
 constitution of 79, 91, 185, 241
 history of 7
 history of 228, 231
 meetings and minutes 8, 244
 mission era 234
 post-missionary era 234
clericalism 14
Cold War 82
comity 70, 183, 186, 230
Communauté Evangélique de l'Ubangi-Mongala 188, 238
Communauté Evangélique du Christ en Ubangi 188, 238
community holistic transformation 376

comparative religion 212
Congo Balolo Mission 227
Congo Mission News 199, 237
Congo Protestant Council 5, 79, 84, 91, 181, 183, 184, 187, 190, 200, 201, 202, 203, 204, 205, 206, 207, 209, 218, 224, 225, 227, 228, 229, 230, 241, 243, 307, 313
contemporary religions and society 373, 374
contemporary theologies of mission 339, 342, 351, 352, 368, 370, 371, 373, 374, 376, 377
contextualization 11, 53, 94, 165, 195, 311, 340
criminology 3, 382
Culte Protestant au Congo 185

D
dark land 215, 216
DEA (Diplome d'Etudes Approfondies) 29, 159, 269, 270, 274, 280, 281, 282, 283, 286, 293, 310
Democratic Republic of Congo xix, xxii, 6, 14, 39, 58, 65, 66, 77, 120, 158, 247, 249, 259, 296
DESS (Diplome d'Etudes Supérieures Spécialisées) 159
DEUG (Diplome d'Etudes Universitaires Générales) 159
diakonia 320
dichotomist perspective 17
didactics xxii, 14
disciples xviii, 9, 67, 83, 124, 132, 232, 246, 318, 334, 356
Disciples of Christ Congo Mission 227, 228
doctorate xxi, 17, 18, 29, 36, 121, 158, 159, 162, 163, 205, 269,

270, 280, 281, 283, 322, 323, 324, 329, 337, 341, 355, 385

E
East African Community 157
ecclesiocentric 98
ecclesiocentrism 99
Ecumenical and evangelical differences 101
ecumenical evangelicals 81, 91
Ecumenical Institute at Bossey 121
ecumenical meeting
London 1878 69
ecumenical Protestant 40
ecumenism iii, 11, 64, 79, 117, 120, 280, 281, 293, 311, 374
Edinburgh Conference
in 1910 77, 134, 135, 193, 195
Edinburgh Series 89
educational and conceptual frameworks in DRC xxii, 11, 24, 39, 105, 260, 274, 283, 299
educational evangelization 223
emic 309
English Baptist Missionary 68
etic 309
European Credit Transfer System 155
European Higher Education Area 155
Evangelical Covenant Church xxv, 188, 238
evangelical ecumenical 91
Evangelical Free Church 188, 227, 238
evangelicalism 83, 88, 101, 241
evangelical Protestant 40
evangelism 8, 9, 11, 70, 73, 86, 87, 117, 122, 123, 125, 126, 136, 181, 211, 220, 221, 225, 244, 295, 312, 340, 375
exclusivism 64, 93

F
Faculté de Théologie des Assemblées de Dieu 6
Faculté de Théologie Évangélique de Bangui ii, iii, 6, 113
Faculté de Théologie Évangélique du Cameroun 6
Faith and Order 76, 78
freedom 93, 149, 155, 193, 222, 279, 293
Fuller Theological Seminary 89, 111, 122, 123, 313, 324

G
Garanganze Evangelical Mission 192
General Conference of Foreign Missions
Liverpool 1860 68
Gentiles 92
globalization 14, 120, 123
glocal
definition 5
gogymania 143, 144
Gordon Conwell Seminary xxv
graduate xxii, 9, 29, 36, 125, 128, 150, 156, 158, 159, 173, 269, 280, 281, 282, 293, 327, 331, 337, 352, 362, 385
Great Commission ii, 85, 122, 154

H
Harvard University 199
heathen 72, 73, 185, 192
hermeneutics 101, 125, 308, 317, 319
Higher Christian education 377
higher education
for combined training 133, 154
for professional training 154
for scientific apprenticeship 154
quality assurance 157

transformative purpose 16, 18, 26, 140, 173
HIV and AIDS 138
holistic mission xxii, 9, 11, 14, 22, 24, 25, 47, 48, 106, 118, 119, 127, 133, 134, 135, 173, 260, 276, 280, 283, 304, 314, 316, 323, 332, 341, 342, 343, 351, 352, 355, 356, 358, 368, 369, 370, 371, 372, 373, 375, 376, 377, 378, 384, 385, 386, 387
Humboldtian University 149

I
identity theology 5
imago Dei 320
IMC conference 78
imperialism 59, 242, 295, 323
Imperialism 382
incarnation 87
inclusivism 64, 93
Intercultural Global Ministries 342, 351, 369, 370, 372, 373, 375, 376, 377
interdependent learning 143, 283, 284, 285
interfaith dialogue 5
International Association for Mission Studies 40, 41, 89, 116
International Bulletin of Missionary Research 41, 49, 56, 89
International Leadership University xxiv, xxv, 3, 158, 386
International Missionary Council 76, 83, 89, 134, 199, 226, 239
International Review of Mission(s) 41, 56, 76, 84, 89, 198, 200, 202, 203, 204, 206, 214, 230, 241, 312, 313
interreligious dialogue 11, 120, 124, 128, 295, 340, 374

Inter-University Council for East Africa 158
Islam 11, 216, 374
Israel 91, 92, 356
(IUCEA) Inter-University Council for East African Community 157
Ivory Coast 6

J
Judea 95, 315
justice 99, 100, 120, 279

K
Karawa 238
kerygma 320
Kikongo 235
Kimpese 223, 224, 226, 227, 239
kingdom of God 43, 44, 46, 64, 96, 99, 219, 222, 337, 338
koinonia 320

L
Lausanne Movement
    and missiological education 241
    Cape Town 2010 xvii, 117
    history of 207
Léopoldville 193, 199, 210
liberation 15, 16, 101, 126, 222, 277, 279, 319
licence 29, 158, 159, 269, 270, 274, 280, 281, 282, 283, 286, 291, 293, 310
Life and Work 76, 78
Lingala 235, 270
*lingua franc*a 215
literature review 35, 172, 195, 247, 259, 304, 317, 338, 359, 360, 363
Livingstone Inland Mission 66, 67, 186, 192, 195

Subject Index

local church ii, 44, 86, 103, 124, 135, 225, 315, 320
Luba 16
Lund University 121

M

mainline-related churches 182, 368, 369
maîtrise 159
martyria 320
Medieval university 109, 149
missio Dei
   debate 85, 320
   within theological education 325, 326
missio ecclesiae 107, 203, 318, 330
missio humanum 318, 330
missiological education and research in DRC 260, 274, 299
Missiological Encyclopedia i
missiological graduates
   serving theological institutions 350, 352, 353
missiological higher education xx, 300, 331, 338, 342, 343, 352, 369, 371, 372, 373, 375, 376, 378
missiological research methods
   mixed 249, 251, 258, 271, 272, 273, 385
   qualitative 23, 151, 250, 251, 252, 253, 258, 259, 271, 272
missiology
   BTh in 338, 342
   DTh in 322
   ecumenical 308
   evangelical 308
   in Francophone Africa i, iv, xx, xxii, 6, 14, 18, 35, 39, 89, 113, 296
   MTh in 126, 338, 342, 364, 365

Orthodox 40, 308
Pentecostal 308
PhD in 12, 61, 125, 126, 322, 323, 338, 342, 351, 353, 364, 365
Queen of theology 108, 109
Roman Catholic 40, 308
scholarly journals 41
scientific discipline xx, 3, 43, 47, 49, 50, 306, 382
Missional Church Leadership 342, 343, 351, 369, 370, 372, 373, 375, 376, 378
missional exegesis
   of New Testament 339
   of Old Testament 339
Missionalia xxi, 15, 41, 56, 89
missional theology
   of New Testament 339, 342, 351, 368, 370, 371, 373, 374, 376, 377
   of Old Testament 339, 342, 351, 368, 370, 371, 373, 374, 376, 377
Missionary, Come Back! 197
Missionary, Go Home! 197
missionary-minded church 82
missionary-receiving country 7, 8, 12, 26
missionary-sending country xxii, 8, 12, 25, 26, 249, 381
Missionary Society, the 68, 313
mission
   centrifugal 92, 318, 331
   centripetal 92, 318, 331
Mission Évangélique en Ubangi 180, 238
mission library
   Merensky 199
   SACat 199
   Waternweiler 199

WorldCat 199
mission-mindless 9, 15, 133, 221, 225, 332
Missions-Church relations 190
missions
   denominational 64, 68, 185, 186, 187, 188, 196
   interdenominational 185, 186, 187, 188, 196
   non-denominational 186, 188, 192, 196, 211
Missions-State relations 190
missiophile
   definition of 13
monasteries 109
moratorium 64, 83, 92
musicology 3, 382

N
Netherlands Missionary Society 68
Network of Protestant Universities in Africa (RUPA) 10
North-West University i, xxi, xxiv, 11, 49, 126, 127, 274
null curriculum 3

O
oikoumene 315
Operation World 8
orthodoxy 48
orthopraxis 48
outcomes-based education 153, 160, 161, 162, 328, 329
Oxford Centre for Mission Studies 41, 118

P
paideia 142
Palabala 186
panta ta ethne 315
paradigm iii, 14, 60, 95, 161, 168, 169, 183
paradigms of theology of mission in DRC 39, 260, 275
particularism 91, 92
pedagogics xxii, 9, 14
philosophies of education 165
   accepting learners 145
   andragogy 140, 141, 142, 143, 144, 145, 146, 151
   anthrogogy 143
   Antioch typology 132, 171, 385
   Athens typology 129, 171
   Berlin typology 129, 171
   Bologna Process 16, 152, 155, 156, 157, 159, 160, 161, 270, 337, 338
   content-oriented modules 157, 167, 328, 337
   coursework 173, 327, 328
   dependent learners 144
   Dublin Descriptors 162, 163
   ergonagy 143
   field education 170, 171, 328, 329, 338, 339, 340
   Geneva typology 129, 171
   gerogogy 143
   heutagogy 143, 145, 146, 151
   humanagogy 143
   input-based education 161
   involved learners 146
   learner-centered apprenticeship 328, 329
   mesagogy 144, 145, 151
   metagogy 143, 144
   problem-based education 153, 157, 165, 310, 328, 329
   receiving learners 144, 145, 336
   results-orientated thinking 160
   self-determined learning 146
   subject-oriented courses 157

summative assessment 354
synergogy 143
teacher-centered learning 146, 168
ubuntugogy 144
plantatio ecclesiae 98
pluralism 64, 93, 188, 342, 369, 370, 372, 373, 375, 376, 378
practical skills 3, 288
Princeton Seminary 66, 72, 73
problem-based learning 165, 166, 167
professional training 17, 149, 153, 165
prophets 315, 356, 358
proselytism 80, 295
Protestant missions 205, 220, 223, 224, 225, 226, 227, 228, 230, 232, 234, 239, 240, 241, 242, 243, 313
Protestant University in Congo 9, 10

R
radicalization 86, 241
reconceptualization 64
reconciliation 11
reconstructionist philosophy 10
Redcliff College 126
Réseau de Missiologie Evangélique pour l'Afrique Francophone 113
Réseau des Universités Protestantes en Afrique 10

S
sacerdotal ministry 14
salvation 44, 46, 69, 72, 80, 87, 93, 101, 193, 276, 318, 330, 358
Samaria 95, 132, 315
School of Intercultural Studies 123, 313

School of World Missions 88, 118, 122, 123, 124, 326
scientific training 17, 153
Scripture Union 188
secular 85, 87, 101, 103, 104, 112, 154, 172, 236, 328
secularization 74, 81
self-control 222
self-dependent learning 283, 284, 285
self-theologizing 135, 330
Seventh-Day Adventist 185
shalom 64, 85
social gospel 99
Southern African Missiological Society xxi, 89
spiritual formation 3, 130, 340
Student Volunteer Movement 75
Swahili 235, 270

T
Tambaran 193, 205, 206, 212
Tandala 238
teacher-dependent learning 283, 284, 285
The Gospel and Our Culture Network 94
theological corpus 73, 106, 107, 109, 110, 113, 116, 127, 168, 172, 324, 338, 352, 382, 386, 414
theological curriculum 3, 21, 66, 73, 107, 108, 116, 121, 138, 168, 234, 280, 291, 303, 322, 323, 324, 325, 326, 352
theological education
    Antioch model 129, 132, 133, 173, 331, 332
Theological education Fund 83, 134
Théologie positive 16
théologie speculative 16
theology
    anti-cultural 138

biblical 87, 101, 106, 108, 270, 294, 325
historical 106, 294, 323, 325
of liberation 5, 138
male-dominated 138
practical 12, 66, 73, 106, 108, 125, 168, 250, 255, 270, 281, 291, 292, 293, 294, 303, 311, 322, 323, 325, 339
systematic xix, 106, 108, 128, 168, 270, 281, 291, 293, 294, 311, 322, 323, 325, 339
Western-oriented 138
three-self 66, 98, 135
Togo 6
Topoke 270

U
universalism 91
Université Chrétienne de Kinshasa xxiv, 269
Université Evangélique de l'Alliance de Boma 269
Université Evangélique en Afrique 269
Université Libre des Pays de Grands Lacs xxiv, 269, 283
Université Méthodiste du Katanga xxiv, 269, 282, 283
Université Protestante au Coeur du Congo 269
Université Protestante au Congo xxiv, 269, 283
Université Protestante de l'Equateur 269
Université Shalom de Bunia xxiv, xxv, 269, 282, 283
University of Berlin 66
University of Edinburgh 125
University of Geneva 121
University of Halle 66
University of Hamburg 120, 324
University of Kinshasa 16

University of South Africa xxi, xxv
Uppsala University 119
urban mission 11
US Center for World Mission 122

V
Vietnam War 82

W
Whitby 63, 78
Willingen 64, 82, 84, 85, 86, 191, 193, 203, 206, 207, 208, 212, 222
women and mission 11
World Christianity iii, 27, 42, 44, 49, 90, 114, 118, 125, 126, 128, 152, 313, 339, 342, 351, 368, 370, 371, 373, 375, 376, 377
World Christian Trends 7
World Council of Churches 41, 91, 121, 203, 207, 219
World Education Services 156
World Evangelical Alliance 86, 87, 91
World Missionary Conference 77, 115, 193, 200, 203, 204
world religions 64, 79, 181, 212, 339
World War I 63, 76, 190, 205, 238
World War II 43, 63, 64, 81, 84, 88, 190, 205, 206

Y
Yale University 199

Z
Zaire xix, 5, 6, 9, 84, 186, 195, 203, 204, 230, 279, 313

Scripture Reference Index

Old Testament

Genesis
1:30, 31 320
11:1–10 315
12:1–3 315

Deuteronomy
6:6–9 358

6:20–25 358
29:29 357

Psalm
8:4 320
96 315

Isaiah
53 315
61:1 .... 276, 277

Hosea
4:6a 102
4:6b 102

New Testament

Matthew
5:14–16 92
9:35 .... 276, 316
10:1–3 276
10:5–6 92
13:4–8 184
13:47–50 277
15:24–26 92
16:18 320
19:16–20 276
19:21 276
24:14 92
26:13 92
28:16–20 .... 276, 277
28:16ff 277
28:18–20 .... 63, 67, 92, 277
28:18ff 277
28:19 .... 276, 315
28:19–20 .... 276, 277
28:19ff 277

Mark
1:17 277
1:35–39 .... 276, 277
6:15 67
8:37 319
16:15–20 277
28:1 277

John
3:16 315
4:34 276
4:35 246
7:23 316
17:18 276
17:21 276
20:21 277

Luke
1:1–4 .... 356, 358
4:17–21 .... 277, 316
6:40 334

6:49–50 277
10 277
24 277
24:27–47 318

Acts
1:1–4 358
1:8 .... 276, 277, 278, 294, 315
1:12 232
7 358
8 132
8:1–4 132
10:34, 35 194
11 132
13:1–3 27
13:1–4 132

Romans
5:8 315

433

12:1, 2 .... 307, 312, 357

1 Corinthians
10:1–5 358
10: 6, 11, 12 .... 356, 358
12:4–11 .... 276, 277

2 Corinthians
5:10–21 315
5:20 276

Galatians
2:1–10 277

Ephesians
3:10 .... 102, 320

1 Timothy
1:3 276

2 Timothy
3:16, 17 357
4:1–5 276
4:1–6 276

Hebrews
8:6 315
9:15 315
12:24 315

1 Peter
1:1–13 358
1:8–13 356

Revelation
7:9–17 315
1:3 357
1:19 357

Langham Literature and its imprints are a ministry of Langham Partnership.

Langham Partnership is a global fellowship working in pursuit of the vision God entrusted to its founder John Stott –

to facilitate the growth of the church in maturity and Christ-likeness through raising the standards of biblical preaching and teaching.

Our vision is to see churches in the majority world equipped for mission and growing to maturity in Christ through the ministry of pastors and leaders who believe, teach and live by the Word of God.

Our mission is to strengthen the ministry of the Word of God through:
- nurturing national movements for biblical preaching
- fostering the creation and distribution of evangelical literature
- enhancing evangelical theological education

especially in countries where churches are under-resourced.

Our ministry

Langham Preaching partners with national leaders to nurture indigenous biblical preaching movements for pastors and lay preachers all around the world. With the support of a team of trainers from many countries, a multi-level programme of seminars provides practical training, and is followed by a programme for training local facilitators. Local preachers' groups and national and regional networks ensure continuity and ongoing development, seeking to build vigorous movements committed to Bible exposition.

Langham Literature provides majority world preachers, scholars and seminary libraries with evangelical books and electronic resources through publishing and distribution, grants and discounts. The programme also fosters the creation of indigenous evangelical books in many languages, through writer's grants, strengthening local evangelical publishing houses, and investment in major regional literature projects, such as one volume Bible commentaries like *The Africa Bible Commentary* and *The South Asia Bible Commentary*.

Langham Scholars provides financial support for evangelical doctoral students from the majority world so that, when they return home, they may train pastors and other Christian leaders with sound, biblical and theological teaching. This programme equips those who equip others. Langham Scholars also works in partnership with majority world seminaries in strengthening evangelical theological education. A growing number of Langham Scholars study in high quality doctoral programmes in the majority world itself. As well as teaching the next generation of pastors, graduated Langham Scholars exercise significant influence through their writing and leadership.

To learn more about Langham Partnership and the work we do visit **langham.org**

www.ingramcontent.com/pod-product-compliance
Lightning Source LLC
Chambersburg PA
CBHW050524300426
44113CB00012B/1950